THE ARCTIC INSTITUTE
OF NORTH AMERICA

Founded in 1945, the Arctic Institute of North America is a membership, nonprofit, tax-exempt research and educational organization. Its purposes are to assist and cooperate towards the orderly development of the Arctic and Middle North and towards a steady improvement of man's knowledge of the North and his ability to apply that knowledge. Its activities embrace the earth and life sciences and the social sciences. Although concerned with the North, its interests also extend to Antarctica and to alpine regions. The Institute awards research grants, carries out nonprofit contract research, and initiates its own research projects. In addition to publishing scientific papers and other contributions in the quarterly journal *Arctic*, the Institute compiles *Arctic Bibliography*, publishes a series of translations of Russian works entitled "Anthropology of the North," and issues other publications from time to time. The only criterion for membership in the Institute is an interest in the North. Members receive the Institute's journal *Arctic*, the Annual Report, and other publications. The Institute has its headquarters in Montreal, Quebec, and offices in Ottawa, Ontario, and Washington, D.C. The library, located in the Montreal office of the Institute, contains the largest Arctic collection on the North American continent, and its resources are available everywhere throughout North America on interlibrary loan.

BOARD OF GOVERNORS

ARCTIC INSTITUTE OF NORTH AMERICA

ANTHROPOLOGY OF THE NORTH: TRANSLATIONS FROM RUSSIAN SOURCES

Editor: HENRY N. MICHAEL

Information Programs Committee

W. P. ADAMS (*Chairman*)
Trent University, Peterborough, Ontario

JOHN MARTIN CAMPBELL
University of New Mexico, Albuquerque, New Mexico

M. F. COFFEY
Canadian Forces Northern Region, Yellowknife, N.W.T.

ANDREW COWAN
Canadian Broadcasting Corporation, Ottawa, Ontario

YVES FORTIER
Geological Survey of Canada, Ottawa, Ontario

NORMAN J. WILIMOVSKY
University of British Columbia, Vancouver, British Columbia

ARCTIC INSTITUTE OF NORTH AMERICA
ANTHROPOLOGY OF THE NORTH:
TRANSLATIONS FROM RUSSIAN SOURCES

NUMBER 9

ARCTIC INSTITUTE
OF NORTH AMERICA

Anthropology of the North:
Translations from Russian Sources
Edited by HENRY N. MICHAEL

1. *The Ancient Culture of the Bering Sea and the Eskimo Problem.* By S. I. RUDENKO. 1961. Reprint, $9.50.

2. *Studies in Siberian Ethnogenesis.* Edited by H. N. MICHAEL. 1962. $6.50.

3. *Ethnic Origins of the Peoples of Northeastern Asia.* By M. G. LEVIN. 1963. Reprint, $12.50.

4. *Studies in Siberian Shamanism.* Edited by H. N. MICHAEL. 1963. Reprint, $7.50.

5. *The Archaeology and Geomorphology of Northern Asia: Selected Works.* Edited by HENRY N. MICHAEL. 1964. $8.50.

6. *The Soviet Far East in Antiquity.* By ALEKSEI PAVLOVICH OKLADNIKOV. 1965. $8.50.

7. *Lieutenant Zagoskin's Travels in Russian America.* By L. A. ZAGOSKIN. 1967. $12.50.

8. *Yakutia before Its Incorporation into the Russian State.* By A. P. OKLADNIKOV. 1970. $20.

Other Publications
Arctic Laboratory. By JOHN C. REED and ANDREAS G. RONHOVDE. 1971. $5.

Arctic Bibliography, volumes 13 and 14. Editor, MARIE TREMAINE. 1967 and 1969, respectively. $12.50 and $20, respectively.

Arctic Bibliography, volume 15. Editor, MARET MARTNA. 1971. Students, $15; AINA members, $20; others, $25.

Arctic Environment and Resources. By J. E. SATER, A. G. RONHOVDE, and L. C. VAN ALLEN. 1971. $10.

Man in the North. Technical Paper. Communications Study Parts I and II. 1971. $1 each.

Proceedings of the Arctic Basin Symposium. October 1962. $5.

Arctic and Middle North Transportation. Edited by BEVERLY F. SATER. 1969. $9.50.

The Periglacial Environment. Edited by TROY L. PÉWÉ. 1969. $25.

Position paper prepared by the Institute for the United Nations Conference on the Human Environment, Stockholm, 1972. $2.

The Arctic Institute of North America *Information North* newsletter. Written and produced at the Institute's Montreal office.

Prehistory of Western Siberia

V. N. Chernetsov
and
W. Moszyńska

Edited by Henry N. Michael

Arctic Institute of North America

McGill-Queen's University Press

MONTREAL AND LONDON

1974

© Arctic Institute of North America 1974

Printed in Great Britain by
William Clowes & Sons, Limited,
London, Beccles and Colchester

International Standard Book Number 0–7735–9074–9

Library of Congress Catalog Card No. 73–79092

Legal Deposit third quarter 1974

ANTHROPOLOGY OF THE NORTH:
TRANSLATIONS FROM RUSSIAN SOURCES
*is supported by National Science Foundation
grants GN–362 and GN–537*

Editor's Foreword

Valeriy Nikolayevich Chernetsov (1905–70) and his wife Wanda Moszyńska are archaeologists-ethnographers who have specialized in the problems of the origins of the Ugrian peoples who at present inhabit extensive areas of the north of western Siberia. In developing and tracing their principal themes, they have employed all available data of archaeology, linguistics, ethnography, folklore, and physical anthropology.

The selections published here may be regarded in many ways as a summary of a life's work of a dedicated husband-wife team. Chernetsov's field training began early, for in 1925 we find him playing an important role in ethnographic investigations in the Ostyak-Vogul national district. In 1927, at age 22, he published his first ethnographic article. After serving with the Committee of the North, he became, in 1930, a member of the Institute of Northern Peoples, and in 1935 a senior scientist in the Siberian Division of the Institute of Ethnography. His final appointment, to the Institute of Archaeology of the Academy of Sciences of the U.S.S.R., came in 1940.

Chernetsov's works are characterized by the extensiveness of the materials he employed. This allowed him to view phenomena against a broad historical background in his attempts to resolve the problems of Siberian, and particularly Ugrian, ethnogenesis. In one of his early works, "An Essay on the Origins of the Ob Ugrians," published in 1941, he analyzed materials ranging from the Late Neolithic to medieval times and came to general conclusions which were confirmed in subsequent investigations.

In the remains of Iron Age cultures in western Siberia, Chernetsov discerned and clarified the combination of two major elements: the northern (arctic) and the southern (steppe). This enabled him to point rather accurately to the origins of the Mansi (Ostyaks) and the Khanty (Voguls) and to their mutual ties with the Samoyeds. The preciseness of his archaeological investigations played no small role in the development of Ugrian studies in this century. Chernetsov's "Principal Stages in the History of the Ob Basin" reflects such a development to a high degree, being based on the rich materials which he gathered during his many archaeological and ethnographic expeditions as well as on museum collections which he painstakingly analyzed over the years.

Among Chernetsov's major interests were the ancient cliff paintings and carvings in the Urals. Prior to his thorough investigations, their periodization was hotly debated and unsettled. His critical analysis of the various points of view and his dating system, based on comparisons of the ornamental motifs of the cliff representations with patterns on the ceramics from various archaeological sites, proved to be the only valid criteria for correct periodization. Further, an analysis of the representational arts of the Mansi and the Khanty enabled him to assign the Uralian cliff paintings and carvings specifically to the ancient Ugrian element of the population.

The scope of Chernetsov's interests had broadened during his late years. He became interested in the ethnic substratum of circumpolar peoples, and in several articles he developed an hypothesis of possible genetic ties of the Aleut-Eskimo groups with the Uralian family.

The present work is much more than a direct translation of major articles written between 1953 and 1961. The authors carefully examined the translations and during 1968 and 1969 annotated them, and in some cases they rewrote paragraphs to express their conceptual changes. The latter are footnoted by the editor. Some of these changes are also expressed in Chernetsov's preface to the English edition and in the notes and references.

Although the articles contained in this ninth volume of the series Anthropology of the North: Translations from Russian Sources deal in large part with the archaeology of the periods they describe, there is also a considerable amount of ethnography rarely mentioned elsewhere in Russian publications and unknown in Western ones.

As in previous volumes of this series, transliterations of most names, titles, and place names have been rendered according to the system recommended by the United States Board on Geographic Names, with the exception that the Russian "soft sign" has not been transliterated as an apostrophe. Names of non-Russian authors who have published or have been published in Russian are transliterated directly—for example, Shrenk, not Schrenk. In cases where ambiguity could result, the name is spelled in the author's mother tongue in parentheses.

General names for the various types of administrative divisions have been retained in their transliterated forms, since no ordered or accepted translations of them exist. A *kray* is a very large administrative unit. There are nine krays in the Soviet Union at the present: six of them in the R.S.F.S.R. and three recently established ones in the agriculturally "pioneer" areas in the north of Kazakhstan. Each kray, except the Primorskiy (Maritime) in the Soviet Far East, contains subdivisions called *oblasts*. These may be *autonomous* oblasts assigned to an ethnic group (as they are in the six krays of the R.S.F.S.R.) or simply administrative oblasts (as in the case of the recently established Kazakhstan krays). Additionally, krays or oblasts may contain *national okrugs*—very large areas sparsely inhabited by small ethnic groups with limited autonomy. The archaeological and ethnographic scene depicted in this work takes place largely in the western half of western Siberia, that is, in Tyumen oblast and its two national okrugs, the Khanty-Mansi and the Yamal-Nenets, which together occupy almost 90 percent of the oblast's

1,435,000 km². In turn, oblasts are subdivided into *rayons* and rayons into the smallest administrative units, the *soviets*. In addition to this fairly complicated scheme (which seems to be a compromise between ethnic and central administrative aspirations), some of the pre-Soviet and early Soviet works, particularly ethnographic and geographic ones, contain names of administrative divisions no longer in existence, such as *guberniya*, *uyezd*, *uprava*, *ulus*, and *sloboda*. Whenever it is necessary to mention them, they are also transliterated rather than translated.

The two peoples most often mentioned in the ethnographic passages of this work are the Khanty and the Mansi. In 1970 they numbered 21,000 and 7,700, respectively. They are viable groups, having increased slightly since the 1959 census. By preference, 69 percent of the Khanty and 53 percent of the Mansi use their native tongues, although half of the former and two-thirds of the latter are bilingual and some are trilingual.

Four experienced translators, David Kraus, Penelope Rainey, and Ethel and Stephen Dunn, have lent their talents to this work. Chernetsov's preface to the English edition was translated by the editor. The site and regional maps have been redrawn by Edward Schumacher of the Smithsonian Institution. The regional maps were based in major part on those published by I. A. Talitskaya, as was the majority of the place names in the list of those of major importance.*

June 1973   HENRY N. MICHAEL

---

* I. A. Talitskaya, Materialy k arkheologicheskoy karte nizhnego i srednego Priobya (Explanatory notes to the archaeological map of the middle and lower Ob basin), *MIA*, no. 35, 1953, pp. 242–339.

Contents

Illustrations

FIGURES

PLATES

MAPS   *following Index*

Author's Preface to the English Edition

Sixteen years have elapsed since the original publication of the first three of the articles appearing here in translation and twelve since the fourth, "The Region of the Lower Ob in the First Millennium A.D.," was published. This is time enough to allow the authors to take a long view of their works and discover the major blunders and deficiencies in them. This is the more necessary because the territory with which these works deal had been little investigated at the time and had not been archaeologically elucidated in the literature. In the elapsed period of time, field investigations have been broadened (although only in parts of the territory) and young scholars who have applied themselves with new energy to the tasks of studying the early remains of the northern Trans-Ural and western Siberia have appeared on the scene.

Elizabet M. Bers, from the Uralian University of Sverdlovsk, has indefatigably conducted field work over a period of more than twenty years and has collected extensive materials on the Uralian Neolithic. Her works take on added importance because they make it possible to re-evaluate many of the collections which had been accumulated in Uralian museums as early as the end of the last century and to tie chance finds or badly documented ones to specific sites or cultures.

In the mid-1950s, Amaliya I. Rassadovich began field investigations in the Tagil River basin, becoming interested in the excavation of a large group of predominantly Neolithic and Bronze Age sites at Yurino Lake. The archaeologist Vadim Starkov then joined her and already has carried out a number of fruitful excavations. Also in the 1950s, Vera M. Raushenbakh with the now-deceased Aleksandr Ya. Bryusov continued the works begun in the 1920s by D. Eding in the Gorbunovo peat bog. Their work at the Strelka site has enabled us to obtain the first radiocarbon date for the Uralian Neolithic.

For the past ten years Valentina D. Viktorova, from Sverdlovsk, has conducted field excavations. Although the principal theme of her investigations is the Iron Age, she has contributed much toward the understanding of the Uralian Neolithic with her excavation of the clearly stratified site on Sosnovyy Ostrov [Pine Island] in the Tavda River, which contains sequential layers from the Middle Neolithic to the Early Bronze Ages.

Finally, there are our own works [that is, of W. Moszyńska and

V. Chernetsov], which we have continued principally in the region of Andreyevskoye Lake—a locality unusually rich in archaeological remains.

At present, it becomes evident that in the article "The Early History of the Lower Ob Region"* I have succeeded, more or less, in distinctly characterizing only one phase (and it proves to be the last one) of the Neolithic of the Trans-Ural and the lower Ob regions. Earlier phases, identified only on the basis of isolated finds, were treated summarily. At that, the dating of the last, *comb-impressed* phase of the Neolithic within the 3rd millennium B.C. proved to be a good enough analysis, now being confirmed by radiocarbon dates. At this time, I am concluding a study on the Neolithic of the Trans-Ural and, in part, of western Siberia, with which I hope to fill the principal gaps in the early history of this territory. Nowadays, it is possible to trace the principal periods of the Neolithic. As was mentioned in part in my recent articles, the Neolithic may be divided into three major sequential phases, each characterized by a distinct complex of artifacts and specific ways of life.[1] The phases are as follows:

1. Kozlov, comprising the Early Neolithic of the Trans-Ural, with the tentative chronological framework of 4000–3300 B.C. To this phase belongs the majority of the flint artifacts illustrated in Plate VII (p. 23) and the ceramics numbered items 4 and 6 in Plate VIII (p. 26).

2. The Yurino-Gorbunovo phase, dating 3300–2700 B.C. To it belong points illustrated as item 6 in Plate VII and ceramics of the type illustrated as items 1–3 and 5 in Plate VIII and item 2 in Plate VI.

3. The phase of comb-impressed ceramics, or the Ches-tyy-yag phase, 2700–2200 B.C., to which, as already mentioned, belongs the major part of the material illustrated in Plates II–VI of the article which follows this preface.

Additionally, I have just finished the second, and principal, part of the work *Naskalnye Izobrazheniya Urala* [Cliff pictographs of the Urals], and it is hoped that it will be published in the near future.†

In the eastern part of the extensive territory occupied by the Urals and western Siberia, along the Yenisey River from the Minusinsk basin downstream to the north, and including the lower reaches of the Angara, Podkamenaya ["Stony"] Tunguska, and Lower Tunguska, there have been found in recent years Neolithic sites whose materials (both stone materials and pottery) are genetically tied with those of the Trans-Ural. At the same time they differ strongly from the materials of the Cis-Baykal and the Trans-Baykal. At present, these sites are being investigated by Harald Andreyev and Leonid Zyablin.

Lately, much has been done in studying the Bronze Age of the Trans-Ural and the forested zone of western Siberia. Besides the Suzgun (or

---

* Drevnyaya istoriya nizhnego Priobya, *MIA*, no. 35, 1953, pp. 7–71.

† In the intervening months since this preface was written, the above-mentioned work has been published in *Arkheologiya SSSR, Svod arkheologicheskikh istochnikov*, V 4–12, Moscow, 1970.

lower Ob) culture, which had been earlier described by W. Moszyńska,[2] the late K. V. Salnikov described the forested Trans-Ural, the Cherkaskul and the local Koptyakovo cultures which seem to occupy an intermediate position between the Fedorovo and Alakul steppe cultures and the Suzgun culture of the wooded zone.[3] In the eastern part of this territory, the Samuski culture has been established and studied in detail by the young investigators M. F. Kosarev[4] and V. Matyushchenko.[5] In this connection, the archaeologists G. A. Maksimenko and E. Vadetskaya discovered the Okunevo culture, which is synchronous and apparently close in origin to the Samuski culture and which occupied the middle, and in part the upper, reaches of the Yenisey valley and, to all appearances, the upper reaches of the Irtysh. All of these more or less related cultures are assignable to the Trans-Ural–western Siberia region and represent further developments of the Neolithic within it. For the middle part of the Trans-Ural, where the excavated materials are more numerous, Moszyńska established post-Neolithic and early Bronze Age phases: the Lipchinka phases, with the tentative dating of 2200–1800 B.C., and the Ayat phase (1800–1500 B.C.), which then are displaced with the developed Bronze Age cultures of the Cherkaskul-Koptyakovo and Suzgun types.

Concerning the Early Iron Age, we refer to the further investigations of the Ust-Poluy culture by Moszyńska. In our articles published in *MIA* 35, aside from a general description of the culture, we have concentrated on its southern, Ugrian component, which played such an important role in the formation of the Ust-Poluy culture proper, as well as on the later Ugrian settlement of the lower Ob region, represented mainly by the present-day Khanty (Ostyaks). The aboriginal arctic component had been studied to a much lesser degree. In filling this gap, Moszyńska in her last work concerned with this problem, aside from describing the newly discovered remains of the Ust-Poluy culture, concentrated on artifacts of aboriginal character which were used in land hunting, sea-mammal hunting, dog sledding, and other activities, as well as on the very distinctive and splendid carvings of elk antler and mammoth and walrus ivory.[6] These materials are considered in their relations to other circumpolar cultures.

The dating of the Ust-Poluy culture also must be somewhat modified. The acquisition of new material, both that from the lower Ob region and comparative materials from other regions, compels us to date the formative phase of this culture before 500 B.C. and its termination at 200 B.C., at which time the hollow-pedestaled vessels, bronze celts, three-vaned bronze arrowheads, and other artifacts so specific to the Ust-Poluy culture disappear. The young archaeologist Vladislav Mogilnikov, who has recently concluded a detailed investigation of 1st millennium A.D. cultures on the middle Irtysh and, in part, the middle Ob, came to the same conclusion. Mogilnikov suggested a new chronological span for the Yarsalino (post-Ust-Poluy) stage, which he fixed at 200 B.C.–A.D. 200.* This correction should be accepted. May I point out that I had given the

* See *MIA*, no. 58, 1957, p. 133. Author.

beginning date for the Yarsalino as a conditional one, allowing for a potential extension of it.* The end of this period may be established with satisfactory reliability by stratigraphy. Ceramics of the Yarsalino type were found in the fill of a burial in the Ust-Tartas mound on the Om River, dated after A.D. 200 and consequently preceding the latter. Furthermore, these ceramics are never found in complexes synchronous with this burial. In conformity with these corrections, the Karym phase should be dated A.D. 200–500.

In accounting for materials datable to the 1st millennium A.D., some more precise definitions should be introduced. Setting aside individual artifacts which do not affect the whole construct importantly, I will dwell on a group of artifacts from the Lenk-Ponk burial mound and from the Kintusovo yurts on the Salym River.† As was noted at the time, the Lenk-Ponk burial mound may have contained interments of a much later Orontur stage. The collections of Vtorushin from the Kintusovo yurts also do not present a single complex. It can now be pointed out with satisfactory reliability that the flat-cast bracelets should be separated from the complex. They are datable to a later time, most likely between A.D. 900 and 1200, conforming to the age of the Molchanova cache.‡ Also, it should be noted that the schematic representations of bears on the bracelets are stylistically quite different from representations of animals during the Orontur period.

The results of the investigations of V. Mogilnikov into the developed Iron Age on the middle Irtysh have not been published yet, but he has published a number of articles in which the principal problems were posed.[7] Among these is his assumption that cultures found to the east of the Irtysh apparently should be connected with the ancestors of the Samoyeds. It is interesting that at the same time M. Kosarev independently reached the same conclusion in regard to the Bronze Age cultures on the Chulym River, east of the middle Ob. This considerably enhances the value of both assumptions. Additionally, the latter's are confirmed by the works of the linguist and archaeologist Andrey P. Dulzon, who carried out excavations in a number of late burial mounds in the same territory. These allowed him to correlate quite successfully archaeological and ethnographic data.[8]

Of considerable importance for the late history of the population along the Irtysh and Ob are the findings of Mogilnikov concerning the first appearance on that territory of Tyurks [Turkic-speaking peoples] and the subsequent Turkization of the southernmost groups of Samoyeds and Ugrians, which resulted in the formation of a number of present-day Turkic-speaking peoples, such as the Chulym Tatars, Shors, Barabinsk Tatars, and Kamasins.

No less interesting and fruitful is the continuation of studies concerned with the Iron Age of the central Trans-Urals (begun by Bers and Salnikov).

* See *MIA*, no. 58, 1957, p. 155. Author.
† See p. 209 of this work; also Plates L and LI and Fig. 19.
‡ See p. 228 of this work.

It is represented by the results obtained by Valentina D. Viktorova, who has just completed a major investigation into the early and developed phases of the Trans-Uralian Iron Age based on field work over a number of years. She succeeded in expanding the southern extent of the Ust-Poluy type of cultures to the Tavda River. South of this limit there begins territory containing a fairly large number of locally varying cultures which had their bases in Late Bronze and Early Iron Age cultures of the Gamayun-Kamennogrosk type and which had been influenced, at that time, by the increasing movements of separate groups which had left the western Siberian plain for the piedmont of the Trans-Urals. As Dulzon did in the east of the area under discussion, Viktorova succeeded in correlating archaeological and ethnographic materials to the point of time of the historically documented Mansi (Voguls). In recent years, A. I. Rassadovich has also taken up the study of the late phases of the Iron Age.

Equally fruitful works are being carried out (mostly by a group of archaeologists from Sverdlovsk) in the southern Trans-Uralian piedmont as well as on the plain to the east of the Tobol River. However, this territory is outside the framework of the issues being surveyed here, so I will mention only those finds of recent years which throw light on the history of more northerly regions.

Several years ago Salnikov discovered a culture to the south of Sverdlovsk which he named the Boborykino culture and dated to the 3rd–2nd millennia B.C. Together with typical Uralian materials, there were also distinctive traits of the Late Kelteminar culture of Central Asia. During the same period, or at the beginning of the 2nd millennium B.C., there appear in the central Trans-Ural the signs of a new economy— sheep breeding. In all probability these two facts should be viewed as forming a tie. In recent years the young Sverdlovsk archaeologist V. Stoyanov also found distinctive Central Asiatic traits, particularly those of the Late Bronze Age Amirabad culture, in ceramics and house construction in a number of sites in the southern reaches of the middle Trans-Ural. To all appearance, the ties between the population of the Trans-Caspian part of Central Asia with that of the Trans-Ural and western Siberia, which had begun already in the Mesolithic as a result of northerly migrations, persisted to the Early Iron Age and played a definite role in the development of the culture of the peoples in the Trans-Ural and western Siberia.

One hopes that further field investigations along the lower Ob and Irtysh will lead to more corrections and additions in the early history of this region which played such an important role in the composition of cultures, not only of the taiga zone of western Siberia, but also of a considerable part of the Eurasian arctic littoral. Even now it is possible to point to a number of characteristic forms of Trans-Uralian Neolithic cultures which have spread westward to Karelia, Finland, and northern Norway, and eastward, although only with separate traits, to the mouth of the Lena, and even to the Kolyma, where they very likely affected the progenitors of the present-day Yukagirs. In this connection, recent researches carried out by L. Kholbytsin on the Taymyr Peninsula and by N. Dikov on the arctic coast near Chaun Bay and at the mouth of the Amguena River should be mentioned.

It is to be hoped that more detailed explanations of these interesting issues will be forthcoming in the near future.

In conclusion, it should be mentioned that a number of minor corrections, and also some substantive ones, were made in preparing the present English edition.

Finally, both of us, Wanda Moszyńska and the writer of these lines, should like to express our gratitude to Dr. Henry N. Michael, who gave so much of his energy in arranging for the translation of our works and in editing this volume.

Moscow, March 1969   V. N. CHERNETSOV

REFERENCES

(For list of abbreviations of the names of journals, see p. 327)

1. V. N. Chernetsov, K voprosu o meste i vremeni formirovaniya Uralskoy (finno-ugro-samoyedskoy) obshchnosti (On the issue of place and time in the formation of the Uralian [Finno-Ugro-Samoyedic] community), *Congressus Internationalis Fenno-Ugristarum*, Budapesti Habitus, 20–24 IX, 1960, Budapest, 1963; idem, K voprosu ob etnicheskom substrate v tsirkumpolyarnoy zone (To the question of the ethnic substratum in the circumpolar zone), presented at the 7th International Congress of Anthropology and Ethnography, Moscow, 1964; idem, K voprosu o slozhenii neolita Urala (To the question of the composition of the Uralian Neolithic), *Istoriya, Arkheologiya i Etnografiya Sredney Azii*, Institut etnografii, Moscow, 1968.

2. W. I. Moszyńska, Suzgun II—pamyatnik epokhi bronzy lesnoy zapadnoy Sibiri (Suzgun II—a Bronze Age site in the forested zone of western Siberia), *MIA*, no. 58, Moscow, 1957, pp. 114–35.

3. K. V. Salnikov, Nekotorye voprosy istorii lesnogo Zauralya v epokhu bronzy (Some issues pertaining to the history of the forested Trans-Ural during the Bronze Age), *Voprosy Arkheologii Uralya*, no. 6, Sverdlovsk, 1964.

4. M. F. Kosarev, Khronologiya i kulturnaya prinadlezhnost rannikh Nizhnetomskikh pamyatnikov (The chronology and cultural affiliation of early sites on the lower Tom River), *Pamyatniki Kamennogo i Bronzovogo Veka Yevrazii, Sbornik,* Institut Arkheologii AN SSSR, Moscow, 1963; idem, O proiskhozhdenii Irmenskoy kultury (On the origin of the Irmen culture), ibid.; idem, Sredneobskiy tsentr Turbinsko-Seyminskoy metallurgii (A Turbino-Seyma metallurgical center on the middle Ob), *SA*, no. 4, 1963.

5. V. I. Matyushchenko, K voprosu o bronzovom veke v nizovyakh Tomi (On questions pertaining to the Bronze Age of the lower Tom), *SA*, no. 4, 1959.

6. W. I. Moszyńska, Arkheologicheskiye pamyatniki Severa Zapadnoy Sibiri (Archaeological antiquities of the northern part of western Siberia), *Svod Arkheologicheskikh Istochnikov,* no. DZ-8, Institut Arkheologii AN SSSR, Moscow, 1965.

7. V. A. Mogilnikov, Ananevskoye gorodishche i vopros o vremeni tyurkizatsii v rayone Srednego Irtysha i v Barabe (The fortified hillsite of Ananevo and the timing of the Turkization of the population along the middle Irtysh and in the Barabinsk steppe), *SA*, no. 1, 1965.

8. A. P. Dulzon, Pozdniye arkheologicheskiye pamyatniki Chulyma i problema proiskhozhdeniya chulymskikh tatar (Late archaeological sites on the Chulym River

and problems pertaining to the origin of the Chulym Tatars), *Uchenye Zapiski Tomskogo Gosudarstvennogo Pedagogicheskogo Instituta*, v. X, Tomsk, 1953; idem, Ostyatskiye mogilniki XVI–XVIII vv. u sela Molchanova na Obi (Ostyak 16th–18th century burial grounds near Molchanova on the Ob River), ibid., v. XIII, Tomsk, 1955; idem, Dorusskoye naseleniye Zapadnoy Sibiri (The pre-Russian population of western Siberia), in *Voprosy istorii Sibiri i Dalnego Vostoka*, Novosibirsk, 1961.

PART I

THE EARLY HISTORY OF
THE LOWER OB REGION

V. N. CHERNETSOV

Introduction

The Ob region includes eastern Trans-Uralia, broad expanses of western Siberia bordering on northern Kazakhstan and the Altay foothills, the taiga area of the Khanty-Mansi National *okrug*, and the littoral tundra of the Yamal-Nenets [National] *okrug*. Thus it crosses several geographic zones, but despite its size and the diversity of its landscapes and climatic conditions, it has been an historically unified region and the arena for the evolution of the East Uralian, that is, the Ugrian and Samoyedic, peoples, because of the Ob-Irtysh river system with its mighty mainstreams and their tributaries which cross the region from east to west.

Before the October revolution, archaeologists did not pay sufficient attention to this region, despite the systematic predatory excursions that had been made to the burial mounds of southern Tobolsk *guberniya* since the late 17th and early 18th centuries. The mound robbers, or as they are still called, the Ishimtsy,* fearing encounters with hostile nomads, organized into armed bands of several dozen men and set out on summer-long expeditions to excavate the mounds. It was a lucrative business; some mounds are known to have yielded as many as forty or fifty pounds of gold, mostly in art objects. As a consequence, undisturbed burial mounds with abundant grave goods are a rarity today in western Siberia. Only a very small fraction of the robbers' booty found its way into museum collections, notably the Hermitage collection; in most cases the finds were melted down and many valuable objects were lost to art and science.

Often individual objects and whole complexes have been found by chance, for example, the famous Istyak hoard discovered by a peasant while digging a roadside ditch on the Vagay highway. From time to time museum collections have been enriched by amateur students of local lore, for example, the peasant Usov and his son from Serebryanka on the Ishim River, and Yushkov, a statistician on the Statistics Committee of Tobolsk *guberniya*. The Usov collections are in the Tobolsk and Omsk museums; these, with the materials from the Tyukalinsk and

Translated by David Kraus from *MIA*, no. 35, 1953, pp. 7–71.

* [After the city of Ishim and region surrounding it, where most of the robbed grave mounds were located. Editor, A.I.N.A.]

Tara *rayons* (now in the State Historical Museum*) nearly exhaust the finds donated by the Usovs. Yushkov, through his indefatigable collecting of archaeological, ethnographic, and natural-history objects, played an important role in forming the museum of the Tobolsk Provincial Statistics Committee, which subsequently became the Museum of the Tobolsk Guberniya and is now the [Tobolsk] Regional Museum, famed for its extensive collections. However, not everyone was as unselfish as the Usovs and Yushkov. M. S. Znamenskiy, an artist of some repute, undertook archaeological excavations in Tobolsk in the 1870s. Without any training in the field and without taking sufficient pains to record the material he collected, he excavated many mounds in the vicinity of Tobolsk and completely ruined a highly interesting fortified hill site on Cape Potchevash (Cape Chuvashskiy) dating to the last centuries B.C. He assembled his materials into a collection, but without appropriate scientific documentation, and sold it to the merchant Mameyev for 3,000 rubles, an enormous sum for that time. Mameyev in turn donated it to Tomsk University. Another of Znamenskiy's collections was eventually sold to the Finnish National Museum in Helsinki. Only negligible bits of Znamenskiy's collections found their way into the Tobolsk Museum.

A. I. Dmitriyev-Mamonov, who also excavated burial mounds on Cape Potchevash, did more systematic and noteworthy work. His collection of materials was sent to Tomsk, where, unfortunately, some of the labels got mixed up, making subsequent processing of the collection difficult. However, his records contain a complete description of the excavation of Mound 15, which has made it possible to establish the manner of the burial and to separate the grave goods from the objects belonging to the fortified hill site. Of the Tobolsk citizens who worked in archaeology, V. N. Pignatti, once curator of the Tobolsk Museum, deserves mention. He made a careful survey of the fortified hill site Isker, where he gathered an abundance of materials and excavated an Early Iron Age mound near the village of Tyukova. The materials from the mound and the hill site are preserved in the Tobolsk Museum, but unfortunately all its documentation has been lost.

In 1891, F. Martin excavated a burial ground in the Surgut region, near the fortified hill site Barsov. A description of the material found there was published in 1935 by T. Arne.[1] In 1893, A. Heikel visited the Siberian museums, particularly the Tobolsk Museum, and published a brief description of the collections. The publication contains sketches by the author, which give only a very approximate idea of the objects. In 1890, N. A. Lytkin, a teacher in Tobolsk High School and the first scientifically trained curator of the Tobolsk Museum, published a catalogue of the archaeological collections of the museum containing descriptions of 957 objects. The photographs in the catalogue are quite good.

Among the collectors of archaeological materials, one should mention the museum's librarian, S. N. Mameyev, and V. K. Imsen, member of

* [Gosudarstvennyy Istoricheskiy Muzey, Moscow. Translator.]

the Museum Council, who explored the vicinity of Tobolsk: Suzgun, Potchevash, Isker, and other sites. There was also M. Novitskiy, who worked in the Ob delta region and who published in 1916.* K. D. Nosilov and the geologist D. Ilovayskiy collected archaeological materials in the Konda and Severnaya Sosva river basins at about this time, and their collections may be found in the Museum of Physical Anthropology at Moscow State University.

In the postrevolutionary period, D. N. Redrikov and M. Stekkelis worked on the lower Ob in the Salekhard and Kushevat regions, where they collected material from the campsites Salekhard I and II, from the fortified hill site Vozh-Pay near Kushevat, and from several other archaeological sites. They gathered abundant materials, and although they did not go into the stratigraphy of the objects, their position can be established to some extent from the field notes. I began my work in 1926, chiefly in the Severnaya Sosva basin and later on the Konda. R. E. Kols made his finds in the Taz delta (Khalmer-sede, Mameyev's winter camp, and others) in 1927, and I excavated the dune campsite and settlement on Cape Morzhovoy (Tiutey-sale) on the western coast of the Yamal Peninsula and the pit house settlement on [Cape] Khaen-sale on Malygin Strait in 1929. During this same period (1929, 1930, 1935), the geologist S. G. Boch surveyed the Severnaya Sosva and Konda basins and in the process gathered information on the archaeological remains in these regions. He investigated twenty-nine campsites and fortified hill sites and published valuable data on them.[2] In the 1930s, A. Trapeznikov, a local amateur, collected materials from the fortified hill site and the campsite at Nyaksimvol (upper Severnaya Sosva) and donated them to the Sverdlovsk Regional Museum.

In 1935–36, V. S. Adrianov, on assignment from the Museum of Physical Anthropology and Ethnography [in Leningrad], made excavations at the Ust-Poluy fortified hill site and found particularly abundant material, which is now preserved in the Archaeology Department of that museum.

In 1937, A. F. Palashenkov, director of the Omsk Regional Museum, made surveys along the Severnaya Sosva and in part on the Ob, conducting a detailed investigation of a number of sites. His detailed site maps, well supported by the materials he brought back, are highly interesting.

In 1946, the historical-archaeological expedition of the Institute of the History of Material Culture and the Arctic Institute of the U.S.S.R. made excavations at the campsite Salekhard I as well as the campsite and large village site at Cape Zelenaya Gorka [Green Hill] on the right bank of the Poluy River, 1.5 km from the Ust-Poluy fortified hill site. The expedition investigated the Ust-Poluy site in passing to get more exact information on the stratigraphy of Adrianov's materials. In 1945–49, the Ob-Irtysh expedition of the Institute of the History of Material

---

* [V. M. Novitskiy, Dyunnye stoyanki v delte Obi (Dune sites in the delta of the Ob), *Trudy Obshchestva yestestvoispytateley pri Kazanskom Universitete*, vol. 10, no. 1, Kazan, 1916. Editor, A.I.N.A.]

Culture conducted surveys and excavations on the Irtysh near Tobolsk (Suzgun, the Ivanovskaya burial mounds, and others) and at a number of archaeological sites on the Ob in Mikoyan *rayon*.

The southern part of the Ob region, along the middle Irtysh and its tributaries, attracted less attention from the archaeologists than did the northern part. In prerevolutionary times, the only systematic study of the archaeological sites on the Iset and Tura rivers and in the vicinity of Tyumen was made by the principal of the Tyumen Technical High School, I. Ya. Slovtsov. After the revolution, his work was continued by P. A. Dmitriyev and by P. A. Rossomakhin, director of the Tyumen Museum. These men added much new information to the study of local history. Before the revolution, the only excavations of burial mounds made in the present Omsk *oblast*, besides those of the Usovs, were by S. M. Chugunov in 1894 and by A. P. Plakhov in 1897.

For the postrevolutionary period, one should mention the local amateur, Dr. S. A. Kovler, who discovered the Bronze Age campsite at Omsk and its particularly interesting material. He also discovered a Bronze Age burial ground near the former Yurgenson factory and other sites, with abundant finds which are now in the Omsk Museum. In 1925–1928, V. P. Levasheva,[3] a staff member of the Omsk Museum, assisted by local amateurs, undertook surveys and studies of the archaeological remains and the highly interesting excavations of the Sargatskoye and Kokonovka burial mounds.

The late P. L. Dravert, who conducted systematic surveys of Omsk *oblast* in 1923–45, contributed a great deal to its archaeology. In particular, he was the first to investigate the Bronze Age campsite near the village of Yekaterininskoye in Tara *rayon*. A. V. Vaganov, director of the Tara Regional Museum, was instrumental in discovering the archaeological remains of that region and in attracting many young amateurs to help with his productive work.

In recent years, the archaeological activity of the Omsk Museum has been noticeably enlivened by the activity of the director of the museum, A. F. Palashenkov, who has collected abundant data for an archaeological map of the district.

Thanks to all these efforts, made over a period of many decades, extensive archaeological materials have been assembled in the museums of Tobolsk, Tyumen, Omsk, Tomsk, and to some extent Sverdlovsk, and at the Museum of Physical Anthropology and Ethnography [in Leningrad], the State Historical Museum [in Moscow], and the Museum of Physical Anthropology at Moscow State University. However, systematic work was begun only recently and the material is rather fragmentary, in many cases without any sort of documentation. No one has attempted to generalize this material even to the extent of a preliminary periodization, to say nothing of using it to recreate the history of the peoples who inhabit the Cis-Ob region and particularly to establish the ethnogenesis of the Ugrian peoples of the Ob basin.

These themes, when touched on at all in the literature, have been treated exclusively from the standpoint of linguistic research and, moreover, as isolated problems. Of the older works there are S. Patkanov's articles *O proiskhozhdenii slova "Sibir"* [The origin of the word "Siberia"] and *Über das Volk der Sabiren*, B. Munkácsi's *A magyar lovasélet ösisége* [The antiquity of Hungarian horse breeding], V. N. Chernetsov's *Terminy sredst v peredvizheniya v mansiyskom yazyke* [Transportation terms in the Mansi language], and in particular, the works of G. N. Prokofyev.[4]

Although specific problems may have been correctly posed or solved in these works, the authors did not draw on archaeological material, thus they could not localize pertinent historical processes in space and time, and consequently, they could not deal with the general problem of Obian history. What is more, the data cannot be understood nor brought to life to a sufficient degree without recourse to ethnography and folklore, which often can acquaint us, albeit in vestigial form, with phenomena that appeared and developed in the remote past.

I have attempted to pose and solve this problem by taking into account, as far as possible, all available data of archaeology, linguistics, ethnography, folklore, and physical anthropology. My first attempt along these lines was an article *Ocherk etnogeneza obskikh yugrov* [An outline of the ethnogenesis of the Ob Ugrians], in which I noted, in a most general way, the historical processes involved in the past of the Ob region. Now that I have more complete archaeological information on the region, I can develop the theme much more fully and substantiate what I had offered merely as hypotheses before, some of which I have changed substantially, especially with regard to dating.

Chapter 1

The Neolithic of the Lower Ob Region

The Neolithic period in the northern Trans-Ural and Ob regions is represented by archaeological sites and numerous random finds, among which are some noteworthy stone implements of quite unique form. One such implement was found by an inhabitant of Nyaksimvol village in 1930 on the Man-ya River, near its mouth.[5] It is a transverse adze of superb workmanship (Plate I, item 1), made of diorite and retouched by point flaking. It is 19.8 cm long and 7.3 cm wide at its widest point. Its lower edge is almost completely flat with a slight groove extending along the long axis of the implement. The upper edge is equally convex in axial and cross sections. The working edge was made oval and sharpened by additional polishing, but the rough surface of the implement was not completely smoothed. In the main, only the lower surface of the cutting edge was sharpened. The tapered butt of the adze has the form of an irregular triangle with its base angles projecting laterally. In general, the shape and workmanship of the implement suggest a comparison with the so-called lug, or trunnion, adzes, widely known in eastern Siberia and dated to the Serovo period.[6]

The Man-ya find is not an isolated case. Two other adzes, quite similar with regard to the material used, the shape, and the working, were found in "Perm *guberniya* on the eastern side of the Urals" (Plate I, items 2 and 7)[7] and one of this type "in a Chud* grave in the Urals" (Plate I, item 6).[8] Four implements were found during the digging of the Ob-Yenisey canal. Two of them were polished, of diorite and flint, similar to the preceding type (Plate I, item 4);[9] however, the other two (Plate I, items 3 and 5), which were of "dark-gray granite" and "flinty stone" [respectively], may be compared to the Angara type of trunnion adzes in that they are triangular in cross section and elongated.[10]

There are also several similar implements in the Tomsk University Museum labelled "From Yekaterinburg and Shadrinsk *okrugs*."

Recently, thanks to the work of O. N. Bader at the Neolithic campsite Poludenka I (near Tagil), another trunnion adze was found which can be associated stratigraphically with the complex of this campsite and, consequently, with other Neolithic campsites of the north.

---

* [*Chud*, a semimythical people, likely of Finnic origin, inhabiting the northern reaches of European Russia. Editor, A.I.N.A.]

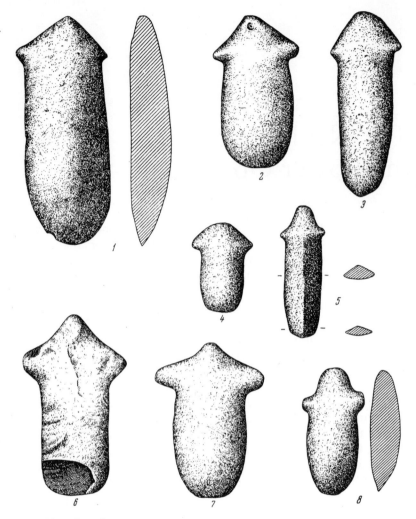

Plate I. Trunnion adzes.

1–from the Man-ya River; 2, 7–from the former Perm *guberniya*; 3 to 5–from the Ob-Yenisey canal; 6–from a Chud grave in the Urals; 8–from the former Olonets *guberniya*.

I would like to mention one more find of such a tool which constitutes a very important indication of the direction and the area of diffusion of the ancient cultural and ethnic relationships. This adze (Plate I, item 8), which is in the Butenev collection (Museum of Physical Anthropology and Ethnography, Archaeology Department), was found in the former Olonets *guberniya* and is a splendid specimen, approaching the best of the Baykal type.

Perhaps the earliest of the known campsites of the Lower Cis-Ob is the Neolithic site on Cape Ches-tyy-yag, discovered in 1934 by the geologist S. G. Boch, who made a small-scale excavation there.[11] In 1935, I too made a brief study of this site.

The campsite (Fig. 1) is situated on a cape on a small island called, in

Fig. 1. Sketch map of the Ches-tyy-yag campsite.

Zyryan, Ches-tyy-yag (Trap Forest*), located in the swampy floodplain terrace on the left bank of the Lyapin River, 3.4 km from Saranpaul village and 2.5 km from the present-day stream bed. The island, consisting of stone-free sand,[12] rises 5.5 m above swamp level and is the remnant of a terrace [once] situated above the floodplain. The campsite, consisting of the remains of more than seventeen very closely spaced pit houses, is in the southwestern part of the island. These houses are represented by rectangular, more or less square depressions ranging from 9 × 9 to 20 × 20 m on an average. Two of the houses are exceptionally large: no. V is 22 × 27 m and no. VI is 25 × 26 m. The depth of the pits reaches 3 to 4 m.

Each pit is surrounded by a smooth embankment, evidently the remains of roof fill. In the center of one of the walls, the pits show traces of entrances in the form of filled-in trenchlike depressions that intersect the wall and descend into the houses. In house no. VI, one can distinguish traces of two entrances situated opposite each other halfway along the longer sides of the house. No specific orientation of the entrances is indicated, but we do note that the entrances of the houses at the edge of the island (nos. II and III) are on the downslope. The culture-bearing layer, "which is from 0.3 to 1.5 m thick, is reddish and gray and contains streaks of charcoal; it lines the bottom of the house pits and wedges out toward their edges, increasing in thickness. Undoubtedly, this is due to the gradual slipping of the pit walls."[13] The culture-bearing stratum is covered with a layer of sandy soil formed since the collapse of the roof

---

* [*Sloptsovyy bor* in the original.]

by aggradation in the pits. The stratum contained splintered bones of mammals and birds, fish scales, pieces of charcoal, ashes, fragments of a clay vessel, and stone implements and articles. Hearthstones with traces of charring were found.

The following artifacts were discovered in the extreme southwestern pit, into which S. G. Boch excavated a test trench in 1934, which I cleared and lengthened in 1935:

1. A polished adze of greenish rock (Plate II, item 2). It is 9.3 cm long, forming an elongated triangle that widens toward the working edge. The cutting edge, which is almost straight, is carefully sharpened on one side and is 3.5 cm wide. In cross section, it forms an isosceles triangle near the butt, becoming an irregular trapezoid toward the cutting edge.

2. A miniature grooved chisel (Plate II, item 11), also of greenish rock. It is 5.3 cm long and 1.2 cm wide along the forward edge. One of its sides is sharpened and forms a knifelike cutting edge.

3. Two knives of similar material and of identical shape and size (Plate II, items 12, 13). The backs of the knives were made thick and were polished for convenient holding. A third knife, a fragment, is of a completely different type: it is thinner, has a sharp point, and apparently was shaped somewhat like our present metal knives (Plate II, item 9). Another knife, of which we have a fragment with both ends broken off, probably is of this type.

The following slate arrowheads were found: one unfinished, [partly] polished, a fragment of a similar one, and a sawed-off blade, evidently a blank for an arrowhead (Plate II, items 6, 7). Of the other artifacts, the following are noteworthy: a slate blade, 6.0 × 2.3 cm, also sawed off, with a groove along one edge; a stone stamp with seven teeth, used for applying comb ornamentation to clay vessels, and a small grinding stone with a notch on its surface (Plate II, item 1). Small scrapers (Plate II, item 4) and a small chisel made from a flint core (Plate II, item 10) were found in addition to the polished implements.

Pottery is fairly abundant, but only as small fragments, rarely as large as 7 cm. About one hundred pieces of eighteen to twenty vessels were collected. Insofar as can be determined, the vessels varied greatly in size. The largest were 40 to 50 cm in diameter, but there were also miniature pots about 10 cm wide at the upper edge. The vessels were either paraboloid or, more often, ovoid (Plate II, item 5). The upper part of the walls of the ovoid vessels tilted slightly inward, and the pots were widest about one-third of the way from the top. It is quite difficult to establish the height of the vessels, but it may be estimated that some were as much as 50 cm high.

The composition of the clay is uniform. There are no obvious artificial admixtures. On fracture, most sherds prove brittle; many readily crumble. The outer surface, and in some cases the inner surface as well, is light in color, from sandy to reddish, while the middle of the fracture is usually dark, running to gray or grayish brown. The surface of the

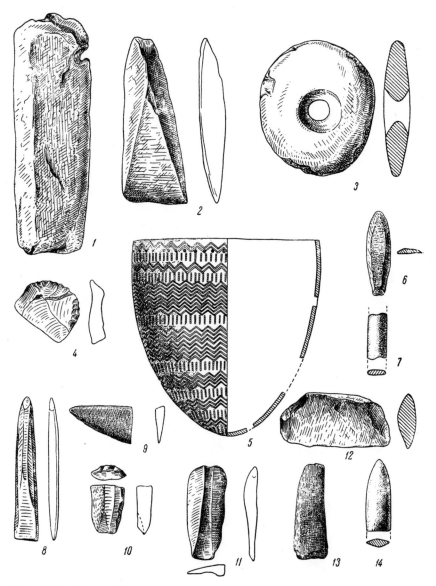

Plate II. Implements from Neolithic campsites in the Severnaya Sosva basin and a
vessel from Ches-tyy-yag.

1–polished flat stone; 2–adze; 3–discoidal implement; 4–scraper; 5–reconstruction of
a vessel from Ches-tyy-yag; 6, 7, 14–fragments and blanks of slate arrowheads; 8–
slate blade; 9, 12, 13–fragments of knives; 10–small flint chisel; 11–miniature grooved
chisel. (Items 1, 2, 4 to 7, and 9 to 13 are from Ches-tyy-yag; 3 is from Khulyum-sunt;
8 and 14 are from Nyaksimvol.)

vessels usually had numerous fine cracks and peeled off in many places.
The firing was extremely uneven.

The vessels were made by [spirally] adding coils [of clay]; weak lines
formed at the point of contact of the coils. The outer surface is very well
smoothed and sometimes even looks burnished; the inner surface is
quite uneven, with traces of smoothing by means of a comb. Perhaps

some of the vessels were painted or rubbed with ochre, which would explain the orange and reddish color of the surface.

The entire surface of the vessels was decorated. In some cases the decoration was incised, and one vessel was ornamented even on the inside of its oblique, somewhat beveled, rim. In nearly all cases, the decoration was applied with comb stamps, having from four to fifteen or even twenty teeth. As a rule, the short stamps were broad and the longer ones narrow.

On the basis of composition, the ornamentation may be divided in two groups. The first group, with zonal patterns in the form of bands made by a comb oriented vertically (Plate III, item 1), at an angle (Plate III, items 2, 3), or with a herringbone pattern, forming zigzag bands, or two to four lines made with a comb oriented horizontally.

This group is characterized by a row of depressions [pits] at the edge

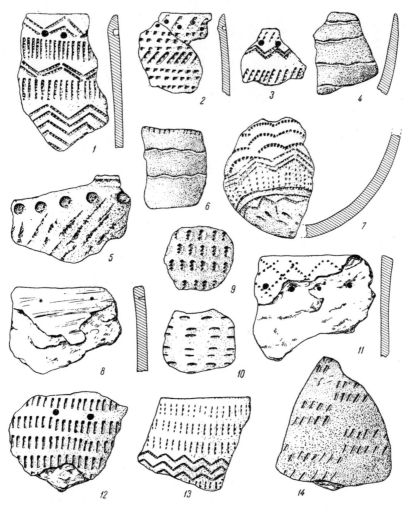

Plate III. Pottery from Neolithic campsites of the Severnaya Sosva basin.
1 to 6, 8, 10–from Ches-tyy-yag; 7, 9, 11 to 14–from Sortynya I.

of the vessel applied with either a sharp or a blunt stick. As a rule, the mode of ornamentation of an individual vessel is uniform. Usually one motif is basic and the other (for example, horizontal lines) is added merely to separate the zones (Plate II, item 5).

The ornamentation of the second group is quite difficult to trace on the small fragments. Most likely, it consists of irregular triangles, rhombs, and trapezia filled with comb impressions. Perhaps in individual cases these figures were also arranged in broad zonal bands.

Besides the comb impressions, three of the vessels were stamped with very shallow depressions made, apparently, with the edge of a small flat pebble. In two cases, these depressions form a band that combines with comb stamping, while in a third case the surface of the small vessel was completely covered with them.

The ornamentation of two or three of the vessels was applied with a thin stick, sometimes in double lines; these lines are parallel to each other or at an angle, perhaps forming triangular figures (Plate III, item 4). On one vessel, these lines were combined with small single and paired depressions made on the lines, evidently with the same stick.

Three of the fragments, belonging to different vessels, have conical perforations that were drilled after firing. They could have served either for suspending the vessel or for reinforcing a cracked vessel.

Material similar to that found at the Ches-tyy-yag campsite has been found at other places on the Severnaya Sosva as well, that is, at the campsite in Nyaksimvol village, the eroded peat bog campsite at Khulyum-sunt-paul, the campsite at Petkash village, and the campsite on the left bank of the Sosva, 1 km upstream from the village of Sortynya. None of these sites has been excavated, and only two have been explored—Sortynya and Khulyum-sunt.

The Sortynya campsite is situated on an elevated terrace (about 10 m above river level), the upper part of which consists of rubbly sand, becoming very compact conglomerate farther down. On the surface of the terrace there is an Early Iron Age fortified hill site surrounded by an embankment, within which one may clearly distinguish the remains of many pit houses (Sortynya I; see Fig. 4 [on p. 66]). Beneath the culture-bearing stratum of this hill site, and separated from it by a sterile layer 0.1 to 0.3 m thick, is the campsite stratum (Fig. 2), which extends for 40 to 50 m along the river bluff. In this 40 to 50 m stretch, it fills three lenticular depressions up to 0.6 m thick. The upper horizon of the stratum consists of sand with streaks of charcoal; in the lower horizon the sand is interrupted by layers and lenses of red (burnt?) earth and tightly

Fig. 2. Cross section of the Sortynya I campsite.
1–layer of fortified hill site; 2–sterile layer; 3–sand, the upper horizon which contains the campsite layer; 4–compact, cemented sand; 5–floors of pit houses.

packed charcoal and contains an abundance of potsherds. The accumulations of charcoal and red earth are especially thick in the middle of the lenticular depressions, which leads us to believe they were the sunken floors of the dwellings. The pits are about 13 to 15 m in diameter, which would give the houses, if they were square, an area of more than 200 m².

Most of the material found, the pottery and the implements, was in these house pits. A nearly complete vessel was found in the middle one; it had merely been crushed by the mass of earth resting on it. Exploration of the fortified hill site has shown that the campsite, which has been partially destroyed by the river, also occupied space back from the bank, but at the present we do not know its total area. Beyond the fortified hill site there are large square holes, quite similar in size and depth to those discovered at Ches-tyy-yag. It is quite possible that they were part of the campsite, particularly since some of them seem to have been damaged by the construction of the rampart.

A considerable quantity of ceramics and several stone implements were extracted from the campsite layer:

1. An adze of greenish rock, 9 to 9.2 cm long, 4.8 cm wide along the cutting edge, 3.7 cm wide at the butt, and plano-oval in cross section. The implement was carefully polished, even the butt (Plate IV, item 1).

2. A knife made from a blade of the same kind of stone (Plate IV, item 4). Its cutting edge is 10.5 cm long and it is 4.6 cm across the middle. The cutting edge is bilaterally polished, but the polishing is quite crude. The rest of the surface is unworked, except for the spine. The knife is quite blunt.

3. A small wedgelike implement, perhaps unfinished, since only its working end is polished. It could scarcely have been intended for woodworking, since the planes that form the working edge converge at too blunt an angle. Most likely it was a pick used for loosening earth in the construction work on the dwellings (Plate IV, item 3).

4. An adzelike implement of the trunnion type, made from crystalline schist, unfinished. Evidently the butt was split off in the making and therefore the work was discontinued (Plate IV, item 2).

5. A semicircular knife of crystalline schist, unfinished (Plate IV; item 5).

In addition to these objects, a fragment of a polished implement, several chips, and one very small scraper of atypical shape (Plate IV, item 6) were found.

The composition of the clay, the quality of the firing, and the ornamentation of the Sortynya pottery is very much like that of Ches-tyy-yag. It is represented by fragments of ovoid vessels, one of which has been completely restored (Plate IV, item 8). The ornamentation in nearly all cases is comb-impressed (Plate IV, items 7, 10; Plate III, items 7, 13), but the character of the stamping and the composition of the ornamentation is more diverse than that of Ches-tyy-yag. In addition to the familiar ornamentation elements, we find incisions made by a small paddle (Plate IV, item 9; Plate III, items 12, 14) and by the *stab-and-drag* method

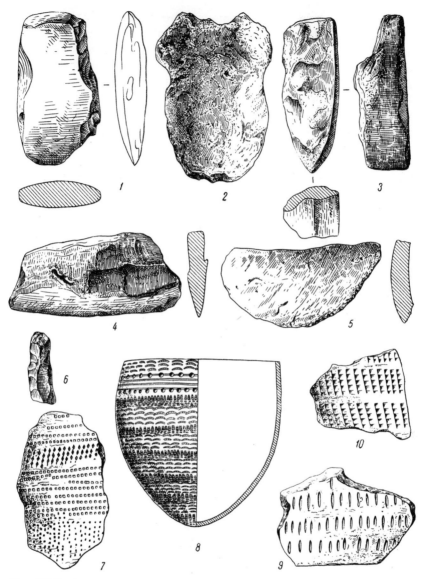

Plate IV. Implements and pottery from the Sortynya I campsite.

1–adze; 2–adzelike implement; 3–wedgelike implement; 4–knife; 5–knife of crystalline schist; 6–asymmetric scraper; 7, 9, 10–potsherds; 8–reconstructed vessel.

with a three-toothed comb (Plate III, item 9), a semicircular comb (Plate III, item 7), and a comb with rhombic [in cross section] teeth (Plate IV, item 7). The ornamentation is also zonal over the entire surface, but the combination of patterns is somewhat more complex. New types of patterns are also found—for example, a network or grid of comb impressions (Plate III, item 11).

The Khulyum-sunt campsite is on the right bank of the Severnaya Sosva, 1 km below the Khulyum-ya [river] (Fig. 3). The Sosva is eroding the floodplain terrace here, and in the exposed terrace bank there is a layer of peat, about 1 m thick, containing tree trunks. This peat layer is being carried away by river drift. Below the peat on the pebble bed is a layer of silty clay, sapropel. Insofar as we can judge by the stratigraphy of the site and the relief of the foreshore, the campsite was once situated on a stony-pebbly riverbank that was lower than the present one. When the riverbed changed course and the hydrologic cycle of the river changed, the campsite became a marshy floodplain and was subsequently covered with a layer of peat and river drift. Recently, within the memory of the inhabitants, the river approached its original right bank and, having washed away the floodplain deposits, bared the campsite and partially destroyed it. However, one may assume that the campsite area extends into the uneroded part of the bank to the foot of the terrace above the floodplain, and it would be quite expedient to conduct excavations there. About sixty years ago the floodplain terrace was broader, and there was a small lake between the present shore and the rocky spit which now extends to the middle of the river.

The finds were made in part on the rocky spit, which is exposed only at low water, and in part on the surface of the greenish-gray clay horizon, where the potsherds and stone implements had lain among thin interlayers of [char]coal.

The following implements are of note:

1. An adzelike polished implement about 22 cm [long], made of hard greenish rock. The working is quite crude; the butt was left unpolished. The implement widens toward the working edge and is squarish in the middle part and toward the butt. The cutting edge is very dull and worn.

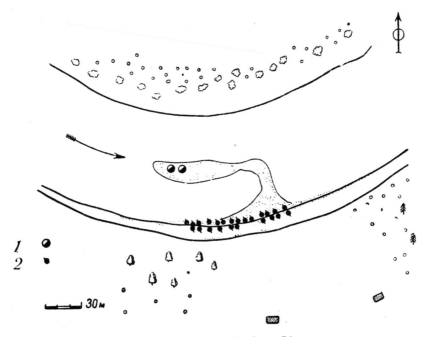

Fig. 3. Plan of the Khulyum-sunt campsite on the Sosva River.
  1–stone implements; 2–potsherds.

Judging by the crude workmanship, the blunt angle of the working edge, and evidence of heavy use, one may assume that it was used to loosen earth (Plate V, item 1).

2. A wedge-shaped adze 9 cm long, made of greenish rock, quadrangular in cross section. It is quite carefully polished (Plate V, item 2).

3. A polished disk 8 cm in diameter, made of the same type of stone and tapering toward the edges. In its center there is a perforation 1.2 cm in diameter that was drilled through from both sides with conical drills. The implement was carefully made, but shows signs of heavy wear along the edges (Plate II, item 3).

4. A mallet made of a flat, oval boulder of crystalline rock. It is girdled by a groove, probably used for fastening. It is quite worn at the ends (Plate V, item 6).

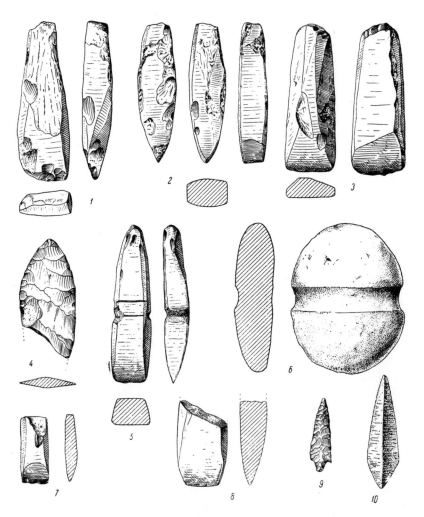

Plate V. Stone implements from Neolithic campsites of the Severnaya Sosva basin. 1, 2, 6–from Khulyum-sunt; 3, 5–from Nyaksimvol; 4–from Tyukalinsk *okrug*; 7, 8–from Khorsem-paul; 9, 10–from Petkash.

The pottery from Khulyum-sunt consists of small fragments, often rounded by the action of the water. The sherds are dark gray and black, which may be the result of the condition of their deposition. Grains of quartz and mica are visible in the clay. Insofar as we can judge from the rim fragments and one bottom fragment, the Khulyum-sunt vessels differed little from those of the previously described campsites.

The ornamentation is appreciably more complex than that of Chestyy-yag and even more complex than that of Sortynya. Although the basic element continues to be the comb stamp, it shows much more variety (Plate VI). Besides the forms already known, the following were employed: a very delicate fine-toothed comb (Plate VI, item 1); a broad slant-toothed comb, resulting in a pseudocorded appearance of the ornament (Plate VI, items 8, 9); a short oval comb (Plate VI, item 15), and the so-called rocking comb ("walking comb"), not found in the previous campsites (Plate VI, item 11). Pitted ornamentation is more frequent, and one finds semicircular as well as circular impressions (Plate VI, items 10, 14). The greater complexity of the patterns is evident even in the small fragments. Often one finds a rhombic network (Plate VI, items 6, 16), triangular compositions, and a unique wavy pattern made with a comb (Plate VI, item 2).

The Nyaksimvol campsite is in the actual settlement of Nyaksimvol, on the terrace above the floodplain on the left bank of the upper Severnaya Sosva River. Only random finds are available from the campsite, and their stratigraphy is not known.

The following objects were found:

1. An adze of hard greenish slate, 20.6 cm long, 5.2 cm wide, and 3.6 cm thick. It is trapezoidal in cross section; the butt narrows to form a wedge. The entire surface is carefully polished. A small band is chipped out of the thickest part of the implement; the workmanship here is much cruder than that of the rest of the adze and probably was done at another time and by a different craftsman (Plate V, item 5).

2. A polished adze of hard greenish slate, of superb workmanship. It is rounded-trapezoidal in cross section (Plate V, item 3).

3. A small, polished chisel-like implement of similar material. It is 8.5 cm long. Its purpose is vague, since its working edge is blunt; perhaps it simply was never sharpened (Plate II, item 8).

4. Fragment of a polished arrowhead of diorite (?). It is planorhombic in cross section, with rounded blunt facets. The fragment seems to indicate that the arrowhead was elongated, with parallel sides. It has a rounded-triangular point (Plate II, item 14).

Finds near the village of Petkash on the Severnaya Sosva included two polished adzes, now kept in the Helsinki Museum, found on the right bank of the river opposite Petkash, at the locality called Petkaspaul.[14] The Tobolsk Museum has two arrowheads also from this area. One of them is polished, of hard slate, elongated-rhombic in shape (7.5 cm long and 2.1 cm wide) and plano-rhombic in cross section (Plate V, item 10). The other is of flint, elongated-triangular, with barbs

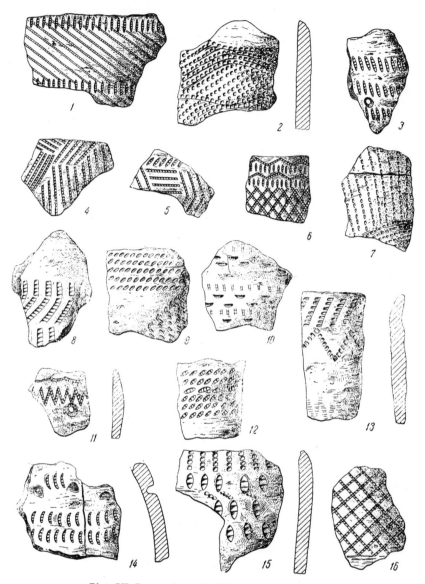

Plate VI. Pottery from the Khulyum-sunt campsite.

and a short tang (Plate V, item 9). Both points were made very meticulously. Boch found a fragment of clay vessel here with ornamentation very much like that described for Khulyum-sunt (Plate VI, item 13).

Perhaps the flint core 8 cm long, whose facets show a superb stone-working technique, also belongs to this group of finds. It was discovered at the base of a sandy terrace above the floodplain, near the summer fishing camp of Khorsem-paul on the left bank of the Severnaya Sosva somewhat above the site of the Petkash finds. A polished chisel (Plate V, item 7) and a fragment of a large diorite adze (Plate V, item 8) were also found at Khorsem-paul.

As we shall see later, these Neolithic sites are not isolated cases but are related to archaeological sites in the Urals and the more southerly parts of western Siberia. In the pottery, in addition to the general indications such as the paraboloid and ovoid shape of the vessels, the straight or slightly inverted lip, the continuous ornamentation, the very weak ornamental separation of the rim [from the rest of the vessel], and so on, one may certainly see a definite similarity of ornamentation, greater or lesser for the individual sites, which probably indicates the degree of their chronological similarity. One is struck by the similarity of the Khulyum-sunt and Strelka pottery and the early layer of Section 6 of the Gorbunovo peat bog site,[15] and in part from the Levshino camp-site.[16] The pottery also reveals the similarity of the material from Sortynya I and Poludenka I.[17]

Of the elements common to the pottery of these sites, one should note the toothed rocker,* the large, slant-toothed cordlike comb (Plate VI, item 8),[18] the undulating ripple patterns made with a comb, and the patterns that imitate, as it were, the interlacing of broad ribbons.[19] Perhaps the site most like Ches-tyy-yag, besides Strelka, is Borovoye Ozero I, discovered and investigated by O. N. Bader in 1947–48.[20] The pottery of Borovoye Ozero I, like that of Ches-tyy-yag, has a uniform ornamentation, with a prevalence of comb stamping, along with which one finds irregular depressions and incised [with a stick or comb] linear ornamentation. Rocker ornamentation, which apparently was not used at all at Ches-tyy-yag, is found only in isolated cases at Borovoye Ozero I. The similarity of the two sites is also pointed up by Bader's rule that the toothed stamp was never used in combination with drawn lines at the Borovoye Ozero I site: "They were mutually exclusive, being equivalent." This is fully applicable to the pottery of Ches-tyy-yag.

The sites regarded here as being analogous—Section 6 of the Gorbunovo peat bog, Poludenka I, Strelka, Borovoye Ozero I, and the Levshino campsite—lie chronologically within the 3rd millennium B.C. Although A. V. Shmidt determined the age of the Levshino site as about the turn of the 2nd millennium B.C., the copper knife and the awl upon which he based his dating of the site were regarded by Shmidt himself as belonging to the middle of the third quarter of the 3rd millennium B.C. (between the middle of that quarter and 2300 B.C.).[21] Bader dates Borovoye Ozero I to the middle of the 3rd millennium and Poludenka I to the second half of the 3rd millennium,[22] while A. Ya. Bryusov considers Strelka to be earlier—the end of the 4th or the beginning of the 3rd millennium B.C.[23]

Thus, the absolute chronology of the Neolithic remains on the Severnaya Sosva places them in the second half of the 3rd millennium B.C. It is very difficult to discuss the sequence of these sites owing to the fragmentary nature of the material, but the material from Ches-tyy-yag and Khulyum-sunt (the stratigraphic data from this site, too) indicates that they are earlier, toward the middle of the 3rd millennium.

As we have already pointed out, the ornamentation of the pottery of

---

* [A curved stamp rocked from side to side while being advanced over the surface of a pot to apply ornamentation. Translator.]

these sites is striking for the small number of elements (simple comb stamping, shallow oval depressions made with a pebble, and lines incised with a round stick) and for the monotony of the patterns and compositions. We scarcely ever find even the rocker stamping, which is characteristic of the pottery of most of the known Developed and Late Neolithic sites of the Urals and western Siberia.

The campsite discovered in 1950 by G. A. Chernov on the Shchuchya River (a left tributary of the Ob that joins it below Salekhard) is probably Neolithic; that is, it probably belongs to the middle or the end of the 3rd millennium B.C. The site is on the middle Shchuchya, considerably north of the polar circle, and is the northernmost known Neolithic site in the Ob region. The material collected by Chernov is scanty and consists only of some pottery, but it is unmistakably similar to the pottery of the Neolithic sites of the Severnaya Sosva.[24]

The similarity of the Uralian and western Siberian sites, established on the basis of the shapes and ornamentation of the vessels, is confirmed by the similarity of the stone implements as well. Indeed, the shape of the knives is the most common and widely known analogy. These knives are similar to the *ulo*, for example, the Sortynya knives (Plate IV, item 4), the splendidly polished knife from Ches-tyy-yag (Plate II, item 12), and the polished and in part flint knives from Poludenka I,[25] Gremyachiy Ruchey,[26] Lake Gryaznoye,[27] and from more remote regions. The universality of this type of knife and its persistence through time make it less interesting as a criterion for distinguishing between the Ural and the western Siberian complexes and as a means of dating them.

The discoidal implements of the Khulyum-sunt type (Plate II, item 3), which were most likely cudgel heads, are found quite widely among the Neolithic sites of the Urals, Siberia, and the northwestern U.S.S.R. In the Urals, finds of this kind have been made at the Levshino campsite[28] and at Gremyachiy Ruchey.[29]

Both the area of diffusion and the time of existence of the discoidal implements are somewhat narrower than those of the knives, apparently not later than the 3rd millennium B.C., which agrees in general with the stated chronological framework based on the analysis of pottery forms.

The adzelike implements of rectangular and, in some cases, squarish cross section (Khulyum-sunt, Plate V, items 1, 2; Sortynya I, Plate IV, item 3; Petkash,[30] and others) are undoubtedly typical of the polished stone implements of the Neolithic campsites of the Urals and western Siberia; some of them (with a steeply retouched, usually well-worn, cutting edge) evidently were used as picks for loosening earth. Implements of trapezoidal cross section are also typical (Nyaksimvol, Plate V, items 3, 5; Khulyum-sunt, Poludenka I); sometimes they taper toward the butt—for example, the adze from Ches-tyy-yag—and they are similar in shape to the Russo-Karelian axes.

Small, usually carefully polished artifacts in the form of chisels, sometimes with a semicircular cutting edge, are fairly abundant (Ches-tyy-yag, Nyaksimvol). The uniquely shaped lug, or trunnion, axes, or adzes, are particularly interesting. At present, in addition to the chance finds described at the beginning of this chapter, we have the highly typical adze from Poludenka and the obviously unfinished adze (butt fractured [during manufacture]) from Sortynya I, which allow us to associate the entire group of these implements with a specific cultural complex. A. P. Okladnikov's data, based on eastern Siberian materials, indicate that the trunnion adzes can be dated to the second half of the 3rd millennium, which again coincides with the datings mentioned above.

Some of the campsites of Andreyevskoye Lake near Tyumen may be classified as western Siberian Neolithic sites, although they are at the southern edge of the taiga. These are Andreyevskoye Ozero [Lake] I, Kozlova Pereyma [Narrows], Point VIII, and so on. The Andreyevskoye Ozero I campsite was discovered and investigated along with other sites as early as 1883 by I. Ya. Slovtsov, who collected an abundance of flint artifacts from it. These are now preserved in the Tyumen Regional Museum.[31] Slovtsov classified his find as Neolithic, but subsequently P. A. Dmitriyev, who worked at Andreyevskoye Lake in the 1920s, found Slovtsov's conclusion to be erroneous.[32] Although the portion of the shoreline investigated by Slovtsov, namely, the section between the second and third narrows, contains a large number of sites of quite different age, Dmitriyev called the place where Slovtsov worked the Pervaya [First] Andreyevskaya site and, using as his basis the iron-smelting forge discovered by Slovtsov, dated this "campsite" to "the Neometal Age, that is, about the beginning of the 1st millennium B.C."[33] One cannot agree with him in any respect. Even if we allow that Slovtsov's description of the material and the conditions under which it was found are very vague, Slovtsov's collections of material from various layers (stored in the Tyumen Museum) are mounted on different boards and are numbered differently. Even the most cursory on-the-spot examination will show unequivocally that Slovtsov's material cannot belong to a single site. It is also quite obvious that the foundry, which Slovtsov states lay in the upper horizons (about 30 cm from the surface), should be associated with the fortified hill site complex and not the Neolithic flints. These upper horizons also yielded the 1st century B.C. pottery in the collection, pottery which is identical to that from the Andryushin fortified hill site.

Inasmuch as the excavation sites were not described adequately in Slovtsov's work, I shall dwell briefly on the sites on the south shore of Andreyevskoye Lake in the vicinity of the second and third narrows. Although the investigation of these sites is far from completed and the collected materials have not yet been completely analyzed, one can already distinguish the different campsites and get a rough idea of the Neolithic cultures represented by them.

The earliest of the known material at Andreyevskoye Lake was discovered in one of Slovtsov's excavations, for which we still use the name Pervaya Andreyevskaya stoyanka [Andreyevskaya I].* From Slovtsov's description and on-the-spot investigation, one may establish that this site, which apparently was completely excavated by Slovtsov, was situated between the second and third narrows on the south shore

---

* [First Andreyevskaya site. Translator.]

of the lake, where it lay at a depth of about 2 m, that is, beneath the layers of dune sand, in the upper horizons of a coarse-grained sand permeated with ferrous salts and lying somewhat below the present mean level of the lake. Slovtsov collected numerous highly interesting flint artifacts at this site. Regarding these, one should note first of all the gross preponderance of lamellar blades.

Slovtsov's material preserved in the Tyumen Museum contains 186 lamellar blades and implements made from lamellar blades, among which there are only sixteen to eighteen flakes. One must keep in mind that the inhabitants of the site did not have a sufficient supply of good fabricating material. Often they used rock more difficult to work than flint, namely, flinty slate, jasperlike rocks, and even quartzite. This is even more indicative of the advanced stone working technique and the distinctive shapes of the products. The principal types of implements were also made from lamellar blades: knives (Plate VII, items 13, 14, 15), end scrapers (Plate VII, items 22, 25, 26), a drill (Plate VII, item 20), and practically all the arrowheads (eight of nine) were made from lamellar blades (Plate VII, items 1–7). These are usually elongated triangles or

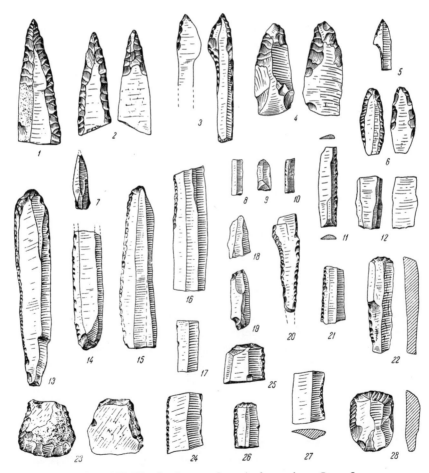

Plate VII. Flint implements from Andreyevskoye Ozero I.

ovals, retouched, but for the most part only on the dorsum. On the ventral side, the retouching is limited to shaping the point itself. Usually the base of this type of arrowhead was made by breaking the blade, without further retouching (Plate VII, items 1–7). Two of the arrowheads are asymmetrical; one has a long stem made by the burin type of flaking. This point was also made from a lamellar blade and is only slightly retouched at the very tip (Plate VII, item 3). The other asymmetric arrowhead differs from the first in that it has a shorter stem. Further, many of the flint side blades in the collection were made from retouched lamellar blades (Plate VII, items 8–11, 17, 21, 24, 27). There are also two scrapers made from flakes (Plate VII, items 23, 28).

As a whole, the flint material from Andreyevskoye Ozero I is certainly very archaic in appearance. Nothing like it has yet been found in any of the Ural or western Siberian campsites. Moreover, this material cannot be associated with any of the known types of pottery from Andreyevskoye Lake. Neolithic pottery has been found at the campsites Point VIII, less than 100 m from Andreyevskaya I, and at Kozlova Pereyma, 2 km away (excavations of 1952), but the flint artifacts from these sites, as we shall see, differ sharply from those just described. Arrowheads made from lamellar blades were found both at these sites and in the lower horizons of the Omsk campsite, but these are isolated cases and differ sharply in shape from the Andreyevskaya specimens, with retouching along the base as well, sometimes forming a notch. The only analogue of Andreyevskaya I is perhaps the Nizhneye Adishchevo campsite at the mouth of the Chusovaya River, investigated by Bader.[34] The ratio of lamellar blades to flakes is similar at these sites.

Campsite	Lamellar Blades (%)	Flakes (%)
Nizhneye Adishchevo	82	18
Andreyevskaya I	90	10
Borovoye Ozero I	15	85

Thus, the ratio of the materials at the Nizhneye Adishchevo and Andreyevskaya I sites is similar, but it differs sharply from that of Borovoye Ozero I, where it is very much like that of Point VIII. The arrowheads found in the remains of the Khin period in the Cis-Baykal are similar in shape to those of Andreyevskaya I.[35] Asymmetric arrowheads with a lateral notch also appear in the Kelteminar culture of the Cis-Aral region, but there they are found with pottery indicative of an earlier period. The Kozlova Pereyma and Point VIII sites on Andreyevskoye Lake belong to the Developed Neolithic. We discovered these sites in 1951–52. The material obtained from them has not yet been analyzed, and for now we can speak of it only in the most general terms. Stratigraphically these sites lie somewhat above Andreyevskaya I— specifically, below the lower horizon of dark-colored silty dune sand and on the coarse-grained sands that contain the culture-yielding layer of Andreyevskaya I. But this horizon, too, is just slightly above the present low-water level of the lake. Not only in spring, but also in summer when the lake is at average level, half of the houses of Point VIII are at water level or slightly below it. Therefore, the position of the Developed Neolithic campsites and, even more, the position of the earlier site bear evidence that the hydrologic regime was quite different when these sites were inhabited.

Andreyevskoye Lake, or more accurately, a chain of lakes, swamps, and channels, is apparently a remainder of a river which once flowed through the area. The mainstream, insofar as it can be discerned, after passing through the narrows which separated the various lakes in the chain, formed broad loops over the areas between the narrows, areas now covered with shallow waters. These areas, or pools, have been given various names: Great Andreyevskoye, or First Lake; Little Andreyev-skoye, or Second Lake; Pesyanka Lake; Zhulkino Lake, and others. Aside from the mainstream, the pools are very shallow, and if their summer level dropped one or two meters, there would be no pools, but only a small stream meandering over the swampy floodplains. In such a case, the places most suitable for settlement would be the sandy promontories within the narrows.

The cursory survey made in 1952 and excavations carried out in following years revealed that indeed such was the landscape during the Early and Middle Neolithic. On Kozlov Cape, on the southern side of the narrows of the same name, the oldest archaeological materials were found in the lowest stratum, which lay just above water level, below an accumulation of yellowish and dark brown sands. The site Andreyev-skaya I is located in the vicinity of the Second Narrows, and its materials were also in the damp coarse sand under an accumulation of dark and yellowish dune sands. Another Neolithic site was found on the right bank of the narrows that connects lakes Pesyanka and Batarlyga. Here lamellar blades were found on a sand bar and at the bottom of a slope of a sandy cape, near the landing dock of a hunting pavilion. The conditions of bedding in the Early and Middle Neolithic sites reflect a period of relative aridity. This would also explain the absence of sinkers, which later, during the Late Neolithic and Early Bronze Ages, become abundant. Thus, the conditions described for these sites are similar to those underlying peat bogs, as, for instance, at Khulyum-sunt on the Sever-naya Sosva and Strelka in the Gorbunovo bog.[36] As we shall see later, the materials found at these sites are also similar.

We are not yet certain how close in time Kozlova Pereyma [Narrows] and Point VIII are, but perhaps the first site is somewhat older, inasmuch as its pottery has largely the undulating patterns that gradually dis-appeared in the Late Neolithic and Early Bronze Ages. Before finishing our study of these sites, and keeping in mind what has been said, let us examine their material jointly, particularly since both sites undoubtedly belong to the Developed Neolithic and, perhaps, to its earlier stages at that.

The stone articles at both sites include quite a large number of lamellar blades, among which are small forms, sometimes with one blunted side, probably intended for side-bladed implements. Scrapers made of lamel-lar blades and flakes are common. There is quite a variety of arrowhead shapes. Arrowheads made from lamellar blades persist, but are retouched more painstakingly, not only at the point but along the sides and base as well. Elongated leaflike forms are most common. Fragments of polished implements and polishing stones were found. One of them was discovered in a pit house at Point VIII, on a small "table," a rectangular sandy elevation. The regular outlines of this table indicate that at one time it must have been reinforced with a wooden frame.

The pottery consists of ovoid and paraboloid vessels (Plate VIII). The thickening on the inside of the rim is highly characteristic of this pottery, and it is quite apparent in profile. The base is rounded or pointed.

Plate VIII. Neolithic pottery from the Andreyevskoye Lake campsites.

The ornamentation is simple and uniform. The comb stamp plays the major role; occasionally a rocker was used. In other cases, the decoration was applied with a comb on the stab-and-drag principle, or the comb was used to apply slightly undulating, ripplelike lines by varying the pressure. Wavy or, less often, straight-line patterns pressed in or drawn with a comb or stick were widely employed. Sticks of different width and thickness were used, sometimes with a split end. Pit ornamentation is rare. The ornamentation of the vessels is continuous, covering the entire surface, even the bottom; sometimes it even continues to the inside of the rim. Not rarely, the ornamentation is zonal, but often one finds the ornamental field broken up into triangular areas (or other polygonal forms), hatched in various manners and directions.

In the shape of the vessels (including the characteristic thickening, or "excrescence," of the inner rim), their ornamentation, and the composition of the ornamentation, the pottery of the Andreyevskoye Lake campsites, Kozlova Pereyma, and Point VIII are strikingly similar to the pottery of Strelka[37] and almost equally so to that of Borovoye Ozero I.[38] We find the same wavelike motifs, made with comb or stick, the same breaking up of the ornamental field into triangles. The relatively rare use of toothed rockers (also called "walking combs") and the apparent complete absence of round pit ornamentation are the common features.

Proceeding from the similarity of form and ornamentation of the pottery, we cannot agree with A. Ya. Bryusov's opinion that the central Ural Neolithic culture is isolated and unique. "However little we may know of the Neolithic of neighboring regions," he wrote, "there can be no doubt that the material from the excavations in Tyumen *rayon*, on the lower Chusovaya and the Kama . . . have little in common with the materials of the ancient tribes of the central Urals, except for rare individual items and some elements of the ornamentation of the clay vessels."[39] It is easy to convince oneself that the similarity is by no means limited to "some elements," but is specified by the common shape of the vessels, right down to the characteristic details, and by the unity of the ornamental system, the unity of the elements, and the technique of applying the ornamentation. Undoubtedly, Bryusov's error can be attributed to the poor knowledge of the Neolithic of the neighboring regions; new material on these regions had not yet been published when he wrote his paper.

Analogous elements of similarity with the pottery of the Developed Neolithic sites at Andreyevskoye Lake may be noted for the Khulyum-sunt campsite as well. This similarity is particularly interesting in that it provides a basis for determining how much in common the cultures of the lower Ob had. Unfortunately, the pottery material from Khulyum-sunt is quite desultory, and consequently a complete comparison cannot be made. We may note that almost identical ornamentation appears on individual fragments (Plate VI, item 2 of this article and Fig. 18, item 1 of Raushenbakh's work [see reference 37]). However, the Khulyum-sunt pottery also has pit ornamentation characteristic of later times. Perhaps Khulyum-sunt is somewhat younger than the Andreyevskoye Lake sites and Strelka and should be compared rather with Poludenka I.

Another, territorially more remote, analogue is still more interesting. Earlier, when mentioning the asymmetric arrowheads from Andreyevskaya I, we compared them with the arrowheads of the campsite Dzhanbas-kala No. 4, which belongs to the Kelteminar culture. The relation between these two regions is demonstrated incomparably more clearly and fully by the pottery.

As early as 1941, S. P. Tolstov pointed out the similarity of the pottery of the Kelteminar culture, which he discovered at that time, to the Neolithic pottery of the lower Ob, in particular that of Ches-tyy-yag.[40] Here one may note a great similarity in the distinct, drawn patterns, to say nothing of the comb ornamentations and herringbone compositions.[41] A. V. Zbruyeva noted the similarity of the Dzhanbas-kala material to that of the Levshino campsite on the western slopes of the Urals.[42] In subsequent works, Tolstov published fuller data on the Kelteminar culture that confirmed his earlier opinion.[43] The results of the investigations of Neolithic sites in the Urals and western Siberia have pointed out an even greater similarity to the material of the Kelteminar culture. This similarity emerges particularly clearly in the material from Point VIII, and even more so in that of Kozlova Pereyma. Here, besides the comb, herringbone, and wavy patterns, we find a highly specific and characteristic compositional feature of the ornamentation. Along the edge of vessels from both Dzhanbas-kala No. 4 and Andreyevskoye Lake, most often following the band made by a comb or a stick, there are special "ladders" descending vertically and made with the same instrument as the basic ornamentation, that is, with a comb or a stick. An oblique hatching or hatched triangles in straight or wavy lines run along both sides of the ladder. Such, for example, are the fragments shown in Plate VIII (items 4, 6), which are completely analogous to those in Plates 14 and 15 of Tolstov's work.[44]

For the time being, we can assign only a tentative date to the Developed Neolithic sites of the lower Ob. As we have already seen, they have a uniform stratigraphy: they lie either beneath peat or in layers covered with lacustrine deposits. The Dzhanbas-kala No. 4 site is of the latter type. Using pollen analysis and the stratigraphy of the peat and sapropelic deposits of the Gorbunovo peat bog, which has been best studied in this respect, Bryusov referred the Strelka site to the late phases of the Atlantic period, in absolute chronology to the end of the 4th or the first half of the 3rd millennium B.C.[45] This dating seems sufficiently well founded, and we do not consider it possible or necessary to refine or change it at present. Tolstov assigns a similar date to Dzhanbas-kala No. 4.[46]

Several sites on the taiga-covered right bank of the middle Irtysh, some 500–600 km to the east, should be classified among the cultures of the western Siberian forest Neolithic, but probably in its later phases. These include the campsite near the large village of Yekaterininskoye in the Tara *rayon* of Omsk *oblast*[47] and the burial ground in Ust-Kurenga village (upper Shish River, a right tributary of the Irtysh) in the same *rayon*. Unfortunately, both these interesting sites are known only very superficially. The Omsk Museum has collections of material from the

Yekaterininskoye site, made chiefly by the late P. L. Dravert, who discovered it. In 1945, I had the occasion to study Yekaterininskoye and to establish that it comprised a single layer and that the pottery found there was completely uniform, that is, it consisted of quite large ovoid and paraboloid vessels with round or pointed bottoms. The entire surface of the vessels was ornamented. Sometimes the ornamentation appears on the inner surface of the bottom as well. Comb ornamentation with zonal arrangement of the bands predominates. The bands consist of herringbone and vertically or obliquely set combs, sometimes combined with rows of pits of various shapes that divide the ornamental field into zones. There are also bands made by a stab-and-drag or a toothed rocker. In several instances there is a coarse rhombic pattern of lines drawn in or applied with a comb (Plates IX, X).

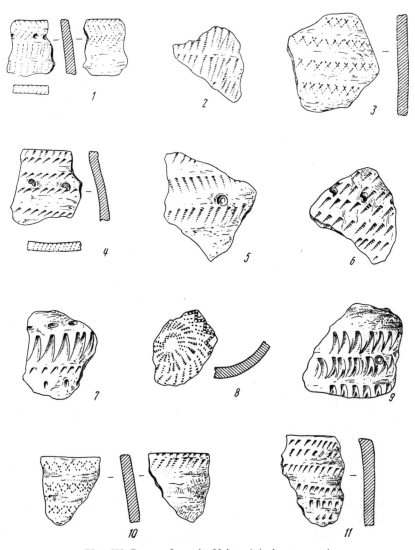

Plate IX. Pottery from the Yekaterininskoye campsite.

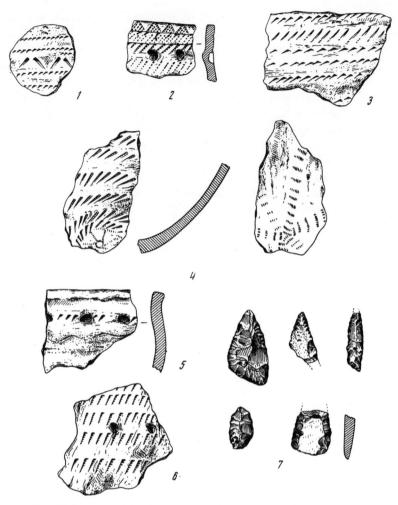

Plate X. Pottery and implements from the Yekaterininskoye campsite.

The stone implements of the Yekaterininskoye campsite consist of numerous flint arrowheads with rounded bases, chiefly of almond or willow-leaf shape (Plate X, item 7), a small elongated-triangular flint chisel, and scrapers, primarily round ones. The polished implements include adzes of oval and circular cross section, three broad chisels, or more likely, knives with a slightly concave cutting edge, and one meticulously made small beak-shaped knife or graver.

The general nature of the stone implements and objects, the shape of the arrowheads, and the type of pottery (if we take into account regional differences) place Yekaterininskoye closest to Poludenka, but not to its latest phases, and to the Sosva sites Khulyum-sunt, Sortynya, and Nyaksimvol. There is also some similarity to the earlier material of such sites as Lipchinskaya and Andreyevskaya II.[48] In absolute chronology, the Yekaterininskoye campsite may be assigned approximately the same date as the Poludenka site, that is, the end of the 3rd millennium B.C.

The Ust-Kurenga burial ground is on the upper Shish river, a right tributary of the Irtysh, at the boundary of the Vasyuganye [swamps]. Here only one burial is known, probably an incomplete one. What remained of the grave goods was sent to the Tara Museum by the collective-farm workers of Ust-Kurenga village and constitutes the following objects:

1. A polished adze of hard greenish slate, 12.5 cm long and 5.4 cm wide at its widest point. It is trapezoidal in cross section. It narrows and flattens slightly toward the butt (Plate XI, item 2). Only the cutting end is polished; the rest of the implement is flaked.

2. Two oval polished blades, one of red slate, the other of greenish-gray slate, with the edges sharpened by grinding. One of the blades has sawlike indentations along the entire edge; the other has only a few notches on one side. Transverse bands in fine lines are drawn on the flat sides of the implements. The purpose of the object is not clear; perhaps it was used as a pendant, as the two opposing notches on the long

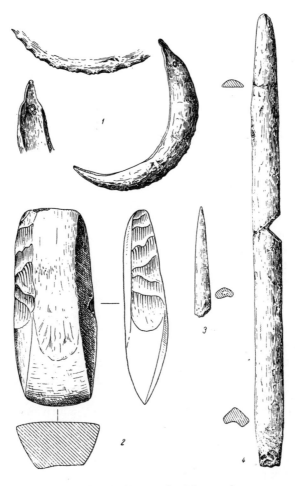

Plate XI. Grave goods from the Ust-Kurenga burial ground.
1–boar-tusk ornaments; 2–polished adze; 3–fragment of a spear; 4–spearhead.

blade seem to indicate. These notches could have been used for suspension. Both ends of the other blade are broken off.

3. Two polished representations of animal heads, made of gray slate. It is difficult to establish the species of animal represented; perhaps they are beasts of prey, but they may be dogs, since one of the heads has a "collar" depicted by deeply incised line and lines that look like some sort of harness. Judging by the perforations, these representations were sewn to clothing.

4. A spearhead made from a tubular bone, most likely that of an elk. The end of the spearhead is broken off. The remnant is 28.5 cm long. It is carefully polished and is trihedral in cross section (Plate XI, item 4).

5. A fragment of a bone spearhead or dart point, 7.0 cm long (Plate XI, item 3).

6. Several boar tusks, apparently [originally] comprising a necklace. Only one tusk is intact; the rest are fragments. The tusks are decorated along the edges with painstakingly incised scalloping, and the upper ends have small perforations drilled through with some sort of point (Plate XI, item 1).

Most likely there was no pottery in this burial, this being typical of Neolithic burials in western Siberia and the Trans-Ural. Without pottery, the site can be dated only approximately. The only fairly reliable indication is the trapezoidal adze, which is quite characteristic of the Neolithic of western Siberia and the Urals. Evidently this type of adze disappeared by the Bronze Age, when it was replaced by hexahedral adzes.

One interesting find from the Neolithic sites of the forest region of the middle Irtysh should be mentioned, namely, the large flint spearhead designated by Usov as being from "Tyukalinsk *okrug*" and preserved at the State Historical Museum [in Moscow]. This spearhead is flat (1.1 cm thick) and leaf-shaped. It is a fragment about 15 cm long; when intact it must have been 17 to 18 cm long. Its maximum width is 7.6 cm (Plate V, item 4). The item is interesting in that it points up the possibility of finding Neolithic remains in the middle Irtysh region, a locale with no stone whatsoever. Only imported stone materials could have been worked here, and as Dravert indicates, "The flint, together with some other minerals and rocks used for the implements found in the campsites of the former Omsk, Tyukalinsk, and Tara *uyezds*, was foreign, imported chiefly from the Kirgiz steppe."[49] These finds compelled me to change my earlier viewpoint that Omsk *oblast* was settled late. Undoubtedly man existed there prior to the Bronze Age. One should note the definite similarity of the spearhead described above to the flat, leaf-shaped spearheads from the Kuznetsovaya burial ground (on the right bank of the Tom River, near Starokuznetsk), which in turn may be associated with those of the eastern Siberian Neolithic.

In concluding this chapter devoted to the Neolithic of the lower Ob, it is expedient to summarize the data. Two facts stood out as we plotted the archaeological sites on our map: the inadequate state of knowledge of the region and the abundance of archaeological sites in areas which had been explored but slightly. For example, the cluster of sites in the

Severnaya Sosva basin is the result of better investigation of this territory (1927–35) than of others. Sites in Tara and Tyukalinsk *rayons* were discovered through the activities of a local amateur, A. V. Vaganov. Whenever any kind of archaeological or geological investigations have been made, invariably Neolithic sites have been discovered or individual finds have been made that indicate the presence of an archaeological site. There can be no doubt that sites exist in other regions of the northern part of the Ob basin as well, and that they are at least as abundant as those on the Severnaya Sosva or near Tagil. There is some basis for stating that the banks of the lower Irtysh and Ob have been relatively thickly settled since the Early Neolithic, even though the sites described above embrace a period of only about 1,500 years.

The approximate chronological sequence of the archaeological sites is as follows:

Period	Name of Site	Analogues
End of 4th, beginning of 3rd millennium B.C.	Andreyevskoye Ozero I	Nizhneye Adishchevo Shigir finds
	Kozlova Pereyma Point VIII	Dzhanbas-kala No. 4 Strelka (Gorbunovo) Borovoye Ozero I
First half of 3rd millennium B.C.	Ches-tyy-yag	Lower horizon of Section 6 (Gorbunovo)
Middle to second half of 3rd millennium B.C.	Sortynya I Nyaksimvol Khulyum-sunt Ust-Kurenga Yekaterininskoye Shchuchya(?) Trunnion adzes	Poludenka Levshino

Chapter 2

The Eneolithic
and Bronze Ages
on the Lower Ob

The epoch transitional to the Metal Age in the history of the forest tribes of the Ob-Irtysh basin is well represented by only the Lipchinskaya and, in part, the Andreyevskaya II campsites. The Lipchinskaya site is on the left bank of the Tura, 55 km upstream from Tyumen.[50] Its area, according to P. A. Dmitriyev, is about 3,000 m². The thickness of the culture-yielding layer (0.4 to 0.9 m) is indicative of its duration. Dmitriyev, together with Rossomakhin, excavated about 90 m² of the site. They did not gather a great deal of material, but it gives a satisfactory idea of the site. Dmitriyev, in publishing the results of the excavations, for some reason did not provide any sketches of the pottery, nor did he describe it adequately. Plate XII shows the most typical examples of the pottery according to the material at the Tyumen Museum. A general comment should be made about the site. Dmitriyev dated the Lipchinskaya site to the Iron Age on the basis of finds of iron slag and pieces of bog ore. However, on examining the pottery, we discovered potsherds that are completely different from the main mass of material and that Dmitriyev for some reason does not mention in his paper.

This type of pottery is familiar to us, particularly for the Bogandinskoye fortified hill site on the Pyshma River, approximately 30 km from Tyumen, as well as for other sites datable to the end of the 1st millennium B.C. A characteristic feature of these late fortified hill sites is the abundance of slag, scale, and ore in the cultural layer. There can be no doubt that the chunk of slag from the Lipchinskaya campsite is associated with the later layer, certainly not with the early one. The early culture-yielding layer has vessels that are primarily paraboloid and mitre-shaped. However, flat-bottomed vessels are also found, and in somewhat larger numbers than indicated by Dmitriyev. As a rule, the profile of the edge is even, but there are cases of a thickening or excrescence on the inside, a vestigial trait of the Neolithic. The decoration is continuous, covering the entire surface of the vessels.

The various comb stampings were most widely used (Plate XII), but shallow, most often triangular, and oval depressions are very common, and stab-and-drag paddles and combs were used to make the bands and to fill the field. The dentated rocker is very common. Incised ornamentation is less common, and the wavy pattern that was so characteristic of Neolithic pottery is not represented here. Deep round pits, as

Plate XII. Eneolithic pottery from the Lipchinskaya campsite.

a rule, were made only along the rim, or they were used to set off the ornamental zones. Continuous filling of the field with pits, which is characteristic of somewhat later sites, is very rare here.

The stone inventory from the Lipchinskaya campsite is interesting. The arrowheads, which are in part similar to those from Poludenka, are leaf-shaped, elongated, and have a small tang.[51] There is also an arrowhead of quite archaic aspect, made from a lamellar blade with a tapered base; in addition, there are arrowheads of broad leaf and triangular shapes with continuous retouching. Yet another type may be pointed out. It is elongated-triangular in shape with a notched base and

a marked constriction, shapes undoubtedly later than those of Poludenka.[52] The later origin is also indicated by a polished elongated-oval
slate arrowhead with longitudinal grooves ending in barbs at the base.
Arrowheads of very similar shape were found at the Beregovaya [bank]
campsites of the Gorbunovo peat bog, in the consequence of which
Bryusov dated them as Uralian of the middle and second half of the 2nd
millennium B.C.[53] Recently such arrowheads have been found in many
Neolithic sites and burials; radiocarbon dating places them within the
period 2500–2000 B.C.*

One should note, among the other stone implements from Lipchinskaya, the polished slate knives reminiscent of the Yekaterininskoye
and Poludenka sites. Thus, the Lipchinskaya site, in addition to the
early forms relating to the 3rd millennium B.C. (thickening of the inside
of the lip in vessels, shallow straight lines, and relatively rarely, wavy
lines, and small oval pits), has shapes, albeit few in number, that were
most widespread in the Bronze Age. Of these, one should note especially
the flat-bottomed pottery and the overall pit ornamentation typical of a
good part of the pottery of Andreyevskaya II.

Thus, the Lipchinskaya site should be placed in the transitional
period, which we may call arbitrarily Eneolithic. Evidently this period
is not characterized by any specific and unique forms, but only by a
relation between the disappearing archaic features and the newly forming ones. These new features of the pottery, a flat bottom and overall
pit ornamentation,[54] are similar to those of the early Andronovo sites.

There is every reason to assume that during this transitional period,
metal, which was known at the Levshino campsite, began to spread to
the Urals and western Siberia, as it had on the Yenisey during the
Afanasevo period. A knife was found at Levshino that can be dated
2300 B.C.,[55] and the pottery has many features in common with that of
Lipchinskaya.

As we have already mentioned, some of the finds from Lipchinskaya
are similar to those of Andreyevskaya II, which was also excavated by
Dmitriyev and Rossomakhin. The Andreyevskaya II campsite is situated
on a small sand ridge, only slightly above water level, on the shore of
Kozlova Pereyma. The campsite was defined by Dmitriyev as a one-
layer site datable to the beginning of the 1st millennium B.C.[56] However,
in this case too, study of the material in the Tyumen Museum and the
stratigraphic data published by Dmitriyev inevitably leads me to another
conclusion. The culture-yielding layer of the Andreyevskaya II campsite,
according to Dmitriyev's data, is as much as 1.3 m thick in places, which
indicates a settlement of very long duration on Kozlova Pereyma.
Furthermore, the houses themselves lie even deeper—25 cm (first house),
50 cm (second house), and 35–71 cm (third house) below the culture-
yielding layer[57]—and, of course, can in no way be synchronized with all
its strata. Either these houses should be assigned to the earliest period
of the campsite or, what is more likely, to the latest stage (on the assumption that while they were being built they were dug into the earlier

* [This sentence has been added by the author in 1968. Editor, A.I.N.A.]

cultural strata). Dmitriyev did not trace this assumption stratigraphically, but it is confirmed by the presence of cylindrical sinkers of the same age as the houses in the campfire area 25 cm below the present surface.[58]

Our observations, made during the surveys and excavations in 1952, show that a layer containing just a small amount of pottery of the Andreyevskaya II type is found almost everywhere on Kozlova Pereyma, also at a depth of 25–30 cm. On Kozlova Pereyma, but only at the base of the cape which faces Vtoroye Pleso [Second Lake], and at a depth of 1 m and more, we discovered a layer of the Andreyevskaya II Neolithic campsite. We know from the material of this campsite, including the fragments Dmitriyev did not publish, that there is a certain amount of Neolithic pottery on the cape itself, on the shore of Kozlova Pereyma where the Andreyevskaya II site was excavated. Quite clearly, several stone arrowheads in Dmitriyev's collection also belong to this underlying Neolithic layer.[59] One of the heads is asymmetric, quite similar in form to the head from Andreyevskaya I; another, with a half-moon- or poleaxe-shaped transverse cutting edge, does not appear to have a counterpart either in the Urals or in western Siberia.

Thus, until we have better stratigraphic data, we should approach an evaluation of Andreyevskaya II with some caution. In any event, we should exclude from the examination the few fragments that are either archaic or late. We may regard the fragments which must belong to the beginning of the 1st millennium B.C. (judging by the "collar") as late types.[60] These are isolated cases in the general mass of material and, of course, should be disregarded.

The vessels of the Andreyevskaya campsite are predominantly mitre-shaped and flat-bottomed. The paraboloid form, evidently vestigial, is in the definite minority. According to Dmitriyev's count, the flat-bottomed vessels comprise 41 percent of the total. The development of profiling is obvious; even on mitre-shaped vessels it is separated from the shoulders by a very sharp bend.[61] However, pottery similar to that of the Andronovo sites, with angular ribbon patterns and hatched triangles, is almost never found at Andreyevskaya II. This type is well represented, not only in the late pottery from the Beregovaya campsites, in the upper layer of the 6th section of the Gorbunovo peat bog, and at the campsite Suzgun II, but also in the archaeological sites beyond the polar circle, which are synchronous with the Developed Bronze Age, for example, Mameyev's winter camp on the Taz River. There is no reason to assume that at Andreyevskoye Lake, which is 50 km from the Yalutorovsk burial mounds in which we find typical Andronovo pottery, there should be some departure from the phenomenon quite typical of the lower Ob, that is, the proliferation of Andronovo features in the pottery of the forest belt. Dmitriyev published only two fragments with such ornamental elements.[62] A few more can be found in the remainder of the material. At the same time it should be kept in mind that some of these fragments may have come from the surface layer.

These concepts also give us a basis for setting the upper limit for the campsite as not later than the middle of the 2nd millennium B.C. Thus, the early stage of the Andreyevskaya II campsite undoubtedly coincides with the last human habitation of the Lipchinskaya campsite. In turn, nearly all of the latter site is younger than Poludenka. I propose that it would not be too much of an error if the beginning of Andreyevskaya II is dated to the end of the 3rd or the very beginning of the 2nd millennium B.C.

In concluding our characterization of Andreyevskaya II, I must again stress one feature of pottery ornamentation. We find pit ornamentation widely developed there, in contrast to the Lipchinskaya pottery and also the pottery of all known campsites dated to a later period than Andreyevskaya II. The pits (less frequently round, more frequently of irregular shapes) appear in horizontal rows and form broad ribbons bordered by small bands of comb impressions or a completely filled field, which includes the flat bottom of the vessels. The question arises as to whether this characteristic and distinct feature of the ornamentation is typical only of archaeological sites on the lower Tura River or is a more general phenomenon. There is not one case of overall pit ornamentation in the pottery of the Middle Ural campsites published in V. M. Raushenbakh's article.[63] One gets the impression that it does not exist. However, Raushenbakh does not report the material of the synchronous Andreyevskaya II site. She assumes somewhat later dates for a number of early Uralian sites, in particular Strelka and Poludenka, than do Bryusov and Bader.[64] Raushenbakh dates the lower layer of Section 6 to the beginning of the 2nd millennium B.C. and Poludenka II as the first half of that millennium. It is difficult to agree with her, especially because typologically the pottery of Poludenka II differs only very slightly from that of the sites that immediately precede it—Poludenka I and the lower layer of Section 6.

Using Raushenbakh's work as his basis, Bryusov synchronized the lower layer of Section 6 with "the more ancient horizon I of the Poludenka campsite."[65] All evidence indicates that Poludenka II existed only slightly later than Poludenka I and that it can scarcely be placed beyond the 3rd millennium. Raushenbakh's data indicate that the Poludenka II site yielded only one example of pottery with a flattened bottom, which places the site even a little earlier than the final period of the Lipchinskaya site, whose pottery includes a large number of vessels with flattened and even flat bottoms.

Thus there do not appear to be any Middle Uralian sites which can be placed in the first third of the 2nd millennium B.C., and we cannot make the relevant comparisons.* However, let us note that a very cursory examination of the pottery which is in the Sverdlovsk Museum and was collected at various points shows that pit ornamentation does appear now and then. Evidently it is not completely foreign to the Middle Uralian region.

We find a certain analogy to this type of ornamentation in the pottery of Suzgun II, a Bronze Age site near Tobolsk. However, the analogy is

---

* [Such was the case in the early 1950s. Today many such excavated sites are a matter of the archaeological record. (Information from the author.) Editor, A.I.N.A.]

only partial and quite remote, since one finds only deep elongated depressions much farther apart than in the pit ornamentation of the Andreyevskaya pottery. Furthermore, the ornamentation of the Suzgun vessels was applied only in the area near the bottom of the vessel and never occupies the whole surface of the vessel. We find an incomparably better analogy to the Andreyevskaya ornamentation in the pottery of early Andronovo sites, where overall pit ornamentation covers the surface and occurs in flat-bottomed vessels.[66]

Unfortunately, very little is known of the early Andronovo sites, and only for the Yenisey at that, a territory quite remote from the middle Irtysh, even by Siberian standards. No early Andronovo sites have yet been discovered either in Kazakhastan or in the Trans-Ural. The material from the Tomsk burial ground is therefore of great interest for solving the stated problem. This material remained practically unknown for a long time, but now, thanks to the work of M. N. Komarova, it has been made available.[67] Pottery with overall pit ornamentation and flattened bottoms was discovered in burial sites nos. 1–8 on Malyy mys [Small Cape].[68] It differs somewhat from the Andreyevskaya pottery in that the pits are not rounded, but probably this difference merely reflects a local feature and does not affect the obvious similarity.

Komarova classifies the graves as Neolithic, chiefly on the basis of the lack of metal in them, but this dating is not very convincing, particularly because Komarova, not finding analogues among the pottery of the Neolithic sites of eastern and western Siberia, took the position that the "pottery of the Tomsk burial ground occupies a special place among the pottery of the Neolithic sites."[69] She seeks an analogy to the ornamentation of the vessels from these graves in the ornamentation on a vessel from the Yekaterininskoye campsite, referring to my short article.[70] However, as I pointed out in my previous article and in this one, the typical Yekaterininskoye pottery has shallow stab-and-drag ornamentation, while pitting is rare and does not have independent significance. The stone items play a substantial role in dating the graves on Bolshoy mys [Large Cape]. Here, most of the adzes discovered have a distinct hexagonal cross section. This shape is absent in the Neolithic sites of western Siberia and the Urals, but it is highly characteristic of the Bronze Age. Pit ornamentation is also found on vessels from the graves of Malyy Cape, which Komarova classifies as belonging to Group I. They have a more clearly defined [flattish] bottom than do the vessels found at Bolshoy Cape, and Komarova with justification compares this group with the vessels of the "Early Andronovo culture of Okunevo *ulus*."[71] The grave goods of Malyy Cape also include superbly polished hexagonal adzes. To all appearances, the graves of Bolshoy Cape are somewhat earlier and belong to the very beginning of the Bronze Age.

Despite the incompleteness and the fragmentary nature of the examples, they do indicate that the overall pit ornamentation was widespread during the initial period of development of flat-bottomed pottery, which, according to the chronology of the Andronovo culture, occurred during the first half of the 2nd millennium B.C. Thus, we must reject the proposal that this phenomenon is of a local nature, restricted to cultures of the Andreyevskaya II type—in other words, to the lower Tura basin. The reasons why an ornamentation of the same type found in the Early Andronovo should appear on the Tura is quite another matter. Unfortunately, we must leave that question unanswered for the time being until we have answered the basic question: What is the origin of the Andronovo culture?

The beginning of the Bronze Age in the Ob region is also marked by the appearance of new forms of polished stone implements. These include the collection of stone implements sent to the State Historical Museum [in Moscow] with the label "Samarovo near Tobolsk."[72] One more implement that is definitely from this unknown site (similar to item 2 of Plate XIII) is in the collections of the Tyumen Regional Museum, also with the remark "from Samarovo." No further information is available on this find.

All the Samarovo implements are polished, meticulously finished; one of them is of diorite (Plate XIII, item 2), the rest are of hard greenish-gray slate. Two are elongated rectangles, the remaining ones taper toward the butt. In profile, all are somewhat asymmetric, and in cross section five are hexagonal, one is oval (Plate XIII, item 7), and one is

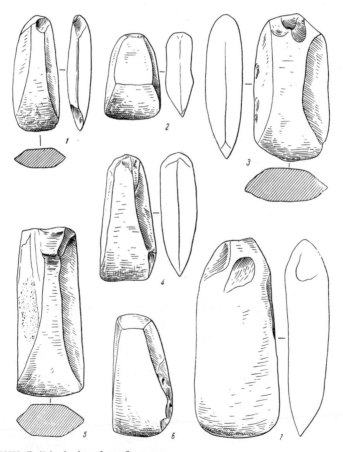

Plate XIII. Polished adzes from Samarovo.
1, 3, 5—with a rectangular middle facet; 2, 4, 6—elongated subtriangular; 7—oval.

asymmetric with two facets polished on one side (as in the case of the hexagonal implements), while the other side is flat (Plate XIII, item 6). Depending on the outlines of the implements, the middle facet either is rectangular or broadens only toward the cutting edge itself (Plate XIII, items 1, 3, 5), or it is elongated-subtriangular (Plate XIII, items 2, 4, 6).

No hexagonal adzes of the Samarovo types, as we have seen, were found among the previously described materials from the Neolithic and Eneolithic sites. However, we have a complete analogue in the find near the village of Krasnogorskoye on the Iset River (about 50 km south of Tyumen). The material was collected by I. Ya. Slovtsov from a blowout dune on which the campsite or burial ground was situated. The collection consists of implements only; there is no pottery. It contains the following objects:

1. Two polished adzes of greenish slate, 12.3 cm and 7.3 cm long, respectively. Both are hexagonal in cross section. One of them is rectangular with also a rectangular middle facet, the other tapers toward the butt and its middle facet is of the same shape (Plate XIV, items 3, 9).

2. Two adzes of the same material. They are elongated, taper somewhat, and are rectangular in cross section (Plate XIV, items 1 and 6).

3. Two gouge adzes of the same material, superbly polished, round in cross section (Plate XIV, items 2, 5).

4. Several small polished slate adzes or knives, trapezoidal and hexagonal in cross section (Plate XIV, items 7, 8). They are very similar in form to the Yekaterininskoye implements.[73]

5. A leaf-shaped bronze knife with a short flat tang and a distinct spine (Plate XIV, item 4). The end of the knife is broken off. The remainder is 15 cm long.

The leaf-shaped bronze knife allows us to date the implements from Krasnogorskoye as approximately the middle of the 2nd millennium, whereby, considering the similarity of the small adzes to those of Yekaterininskoye, we can consider this date to be the maximum. In general, the Samarovo implements should be assigned a similar date.

At present, there are four sites on the lower Irtysh and Ob (not counting the finds of individual objects) that can be classified as Bronze Age: the campsite Salekhard I; Mameyev's winter camp; Sortynya II; and the sacrificial place, Suzgun II.

Salekhard I was discovered in 1925–26 by Redrikov, who sent his finds to the Museum of Physical Anthropology and Ethnography. In 1946, during the Mangazeya expedition, we were able to visit this campsite and conduct excavations. The material has been processed by W. Moszyńska and is published in this volume [that is, *MIA* 35].

The pottery of Salekhard I differs sharply from that known to us from the earlier sites. Along with the paraboloid vessels that still occur, there are small jar-shaped vessels with very straight sides and a flattened bottom, shallow cups or basins with a ridge at the widest diameter,[74] and cuvettelike rectangular vessels with straight sides.[75] The pottery was decorated with compositions of large triangles, rhombs, and

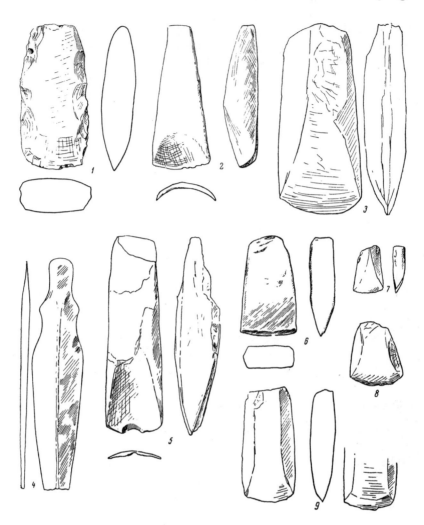

Plate XIV. Implements from the Krasnogorskoye campsite on the Iset River.
1 to 3, 5 to 9–slate adzes; 4–bronze knife.

stepped figures.[76] Some vessels have small modeled handles in the form of animals, and heads of animals (sables?) on the edges of the vessels, counterparts of which were found at the Beregovaya site of the Gorbunovo peat bog.[77] Bryusov dates the latter to the 14th or 13th centuries B.C.

Many features of the ornamentation of the Salekhard pottery are unexpectedly reminiscent of the Andronovo pottery. This similarity is further emphasized by the presence of a unique vessel of the "rectangular saucer" (cuvette) type. According to K. V. Salnikov, this form is characteristic of the graves of the Early Andronovo period. For want of more accurate dating material, we must assign Salekhard I to this period, that is, to the middle or the second third of the 2nd millennium B.C. The Sortynya II campsite is close to the Salekhard I campsite in its pottery and, evidently, chronology.

The fortified hill site and the campsite Sortynya II, which I discovered during my survey of 1931 and investigated in more detail in 1935, are situated on the left, high bank of the Severnaya Sosva River, 2 km upstream from the village of Sortynya. The upper layers belong to a fortified hill site of the Ust-Poluy period. The embankments and houses greatly damaged the lower layers. Therefore, the early pottery, which for the most part occurred together with stone implements in the lowest horizon, appears in the embankment of the houses as well; however, it does not occur at all in the layer beneath the turf in places undisturbed by construction of dwellings. A considerable amount of pottery and implements was discovered in the sides of a house excavated at the fortified hill site. The following were found there:

1. A small adzelike implement of squarish cross section tapering toward the butt. Total length 11.7 cm. It is of greenish rock similar to serpentine, coarsely flaked; only the working edge is polished; it has indentations made at a later date, indicating that it had been used (Plate XV, item 11). From the coarseness of the working, the shape, and the signs of wear, one may assume that the implement, like others mentioned earlier, was used to loosen earth.

2. A piece of crystalline rock with a semicircular notch on one side; the edge of the notch was sharp. In all probability the implement was never finished (Plate XV, item 12).

3. An arrowhead or a dart point struck from the same kind of rock; also unfinished (Plate XV, item 13).

The shape of the vessels, the composition of the paste, the working of the surface, and the ornamentation of the pottery from the Sortynya campsite are almost identical to those of the Salekhard campsite. It also includes paraboloid vessels reaching quite large dimensions (30 to 40 cm in diameter), small beaker-shaped vessels with completely straight walls and a flattened bottom, and shallow basins with the lip bent inward (Plate XV, item 4). The decoration consists not only of the horizontal herringbone pattern (Plate XV, items 1, 6, 7) and rocker-made (Plate XV, item 5) and other archaic motifs, but the widely distributed rhombic (Plate XV, items 3, 8), hexagonal "honeycomb" (Plate XV, items 2, 4), and stepped composition, which indicate the closeness of the Sortynya pottery to that of Salekhard. However, there is also a difference between them: in Salekhard the overwhelming majority of the patterns on the vessels were made with a paddle, while the paddle was not used at Sortynya II. Instead the comb was used, which brings the Sortynya pottery somewhat closer to the earlier local forms on the one hand and to the Ural forms on the other.

In 1927, R. E. Kols, leader of the Taz expedition of the Russian Geographical Society, collected archaeological material from the left bank of the Taz River between the village of Khalmer-sede and Mameyev's winter camp, at 67°20′ N. In one place (Point IV), he discovered fragments of ornamented, clay, flat-bottomed vessels very similar in type to the pottery of the Bronze Age Suzgun culture of the Tobolsk region.

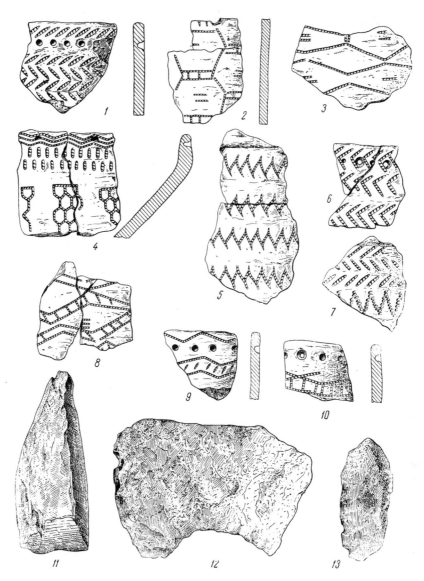

Plate XV. Pottery and implements from the lower horizon of the culture-yielding layer of the Sortynya II fortified hill site.
1 to 10—potsherds; 11 to 13—stone implements.

Until recently, both Salekhard I and Sortynya II were very difficult to explain. The presence of distinct Andronovo-like features in the vessel shapes (cuvette-shaped rectangular saucers, flat-bottomed cups ridged at their widest diameter) and in the ornamentation (triangular, rhombic, hexagonal, and honeycomb,[78] stepped and ribbon compositions) in areas remote from the regions of dissemination of Andronovo culture and, what is more, in the northern part of the taiga zone was difficult to understand. A general solution to the problem was not found until 1948.

During the activities of the Ob-Irtysh expedition, we discovered a unique and interesting site about 8 km from Tobolsk, near the *yurts* [nomad tents] of Suzgun. Although the site was not fully uncovered in the two summer excavation seasons of 1948 and 1950, its stratigraphy was established quite clearly, and the abundant material taken from it (more than a ton and a half of pottery) gives us a basis for stating its characteristic forms. The complete publication, being prepared by W. Moszyńska, will not appear in print for another two or three years, but some idea of it can be presented even now.

This site, which has been called Suzgun II, lies in a small ravine that separates the high, steep-sloped conical hill Suzge-tura from the elevated right bank of the Irtysh. The excavation showed that the culture-yielding layer occupies the entire ravine from one side to the other, gradually wedging out at its high point, which opens onto the scarp of the flood-plain, toward the ancient channel of the Irtysh. The culture-yielding layer was traced practically through the entire lower part of the ravine to its exit into a deep gorge opening onto a small river valley. A firepit was discovered in the middle part of the ravine, on both sides of which, at the base of the slopes of the hill and the spur, a large quantity of fragments from crushed vessels as well as separate fragments were found. It was determined that the vessels had originally been placed in straight rows at the foot of once-steep slopes which had collapsed several times, covering the rows of pots with sand. However, new rows of vessels were invariably placed atop the sandfalls, until the place was deserted by its inhabitants for some reason. There were a few objects besides vessels, chiefly spindle whorls, small pebbles with trimmed edges, a clay horse head; all these objects were found inside large vessels, sometimes together with miniature pots. The total number of vessels uncovered has not yet been established, but it should amount to many tens or even hundreds. For a number of reasons, which I will not go into here, it would appear that Suzgun II is an ancient sacrificial site, most probably associated with some burial rite.

The pottery of Suzgun II is particularly interesting and must be treated in more detail. Even now we may think in terms of several types. Among the finds, we may single out large vessels more than 30 cm high and with a maximum diameter of about 30 cm at the upper third of the vessel. All the vessels are flat-bottomed, well profiled, with a low, somewhat expanding neck that works smoothly into the shoulder and body of the vessel. In general outline, they are similar to the Andronovo ones, but have bottoms of much smaller relative diameter. The second type consists of small, comparatively low, flat-bottomed pots, which are a variant of several Andronovo forms. There are quite close analogies in the pottery of the Alekseyevka settlement on the Tobol River.[79] The third type consists of shallow basins with a flat or plano-circular bottom; in the profiling of their upper part, they are similar to the pots of the second type. With a good measure of caution, one may say that the basins with the round bottom are found more often in the upper horizons of the cultural layer. Finally, we should mention the rare finds of miniature vessels, sometimes with emphasized ridging at the widest diameter. They usually are not ornamented and were made quite carelessly.

Almost without exception they were found inside large pots and, probably, had some religious significance.

Except for the miniature vessels, all the pottery of Suzgun II was made with exceptional care. Often the vessels were polished both outside and inside. The ornamentation is especially rich and varied and to some extent is similar to that of Andronovo. The vessels of the first and second types are especially well ornamented. As a rule they are decorated over the entire surface, often including the bottom, and the ornamentation is divided into several sharply defined zones. There are four such zones on the large pots. The upper zone, which occupies the neck and shoulders, consists of two well-balanced ornamental bands separated by a smooth, usually polished strip. The bands of the upper zone consist of impressions of a fine-toothed comb, less often of other stamps. Each of these bands is set off by at least one row of rounded pits. The next zone, occupying the middle of the vessel, below the line of greatest diameter, consists of a broad (up to one-third of the height of the pot) meandering ribbon pattern, with triangular and rhombic fill-ins. As a rule, this is the most effective part of the ornamentation. The third zone is formed of large, incised, hatched inverted triangles, sometimes reaching the very bottom. In some cases, the triangles are replaced by herringbone and other types of comb ornamentation. The fourth zone, the bottom one, is usually filled with rows of pits, that is, impressions with a short, large-toothed comb or smooth paddle, an incised rhombic network, or some such ornamentation. When the bottom was also ornamented, the ornamentation was usually the same as that of the fourth zone.

Vessels of the second type were ornamented approximately on the same principle, but the third zone is sometimes missing, which brings them close to the Andronovo. However, sometimes they are covered with a continuous, more or less uniform, pattern, such as herringbone comb impressions or those made with a paddle and combined with pit ornamentation.

The vessels of the third type are deep bowls incomparably less ornamented. Zonal separation is also apparent here, but no regularity could be discovered in the filling of the zones. Usually the bowls are ornamented over the entire surface; sometimes (chiefly in the case of round-bottomed vessels) only the upper part is ornamented. As a rule, the pattern is uniform and stands out only on the upper part of the neck and rim. Despite the simplicity of their ornamentation, burnishing gives these bowls the appearance of being beautiful, carefully made vessels.

The lower and upper horizons of the culture-yielding layer show some variety of forms and ornamentation of the pottery. For the time being, the age and chronological frame of reference of Suzgun II can be given only approximately. Despite its variety, the Suzgun pottery is undoubtedly similar to the Andronovo and, in particular, the pottery from the sites on the Tobol and its tributaries (the Alekseyevka settlement on the Upper Tobol, the Yalutorovsk burial mounds, and other places). Some elements of the ornamentation of the vessels from the upper horizons of Suzgun II—for example, the row of large pinch marks along the neck—are familiar from the material of a site near Ivanovskaya (16 km from Suzgun), which is dated on the basis of a celt to the 9th–8th centuries B.C.[80] However, we did not find any other elements at Ivanovskaya that are characteristic of Suzgun, or any forms at Suzgun that are typical of Ivanovskaya. Accordingly, we may conclude that the late layer of Suzgun II antedates the Ivanovskaya settlement, and consequently, the limit of existence of Suzgun II should be set not later than 1100–1000 B.C. This date is also confirmed by the striking similarity between the pottery of Suzgun II and the materials of the Lugovskaya campsite, a late Bronze Age site on the Kama, excavated by A. V. Zbruyeva. Unfortunately, these two sites cannot be compared in detail at present, because the materials from them have not yet been fully processed. However, even now we may say that the ornamentation and the form of the pottery from the Suzgun and Lugovskaya campsites are identical in some cases, which indicates not only that the sites are partially synchronous, but that they are probably ethnically related.

The thickness of the culture-yielding layer of Suzgun II, which reaches a meter and a half in the northern parts of the site (near the foot of the hill), with the pottery saturation reaching 40 to 50 kg/m³ in places, leaves little doubt that the site existed for a very long period of time. We still do not have any objective indications for determining the lifetime of the site. The continuous ornamentation found on some of the Suzgun vessels does not provide a sufficient basis for stating that the culture-yielding layer of the archaeological sites of the forest belt is of very great age. The only answer to the thickness and saturation of the layer is that Suzgun II was not a settlement, but a place for religious rites, for which reason the culture-yielding layer would have grown much more slowly. We can hardly be far wrong in stating that Suzgun II existed for several centuries and that it originated in the middle of the 2nd millennium B.C.

Pottery identical to that of Suzgun II was discovered not only in the ravine but also on the summit of the hill (Suzgun I). However, the layer there was disrupted by the later fortified hill site, with which the local inhabitants (Tartars) associate the legend of Suzge, the wife of Kuchum, whence the name of the hill and the fortified hill site, Suzge-tura. At the same time, no traces of an ancient settlement were discovered in the excavations on the summit of the hill, and it is quite possible that Suzgun I, like Suzgun II, was a ritual site. This is supported by the fact that Suzge-tura is an isolated, high hill dominating the boundless floodplain of the Irtysh and affords a view (as at Glyadenovo) for tens of kilometers. It is highly probable that there had been a foundry here, inasmuch as we found a fragment of a celt-casting mould in the material that was washed down from the summit and contained pottery of the Suzgun type. In this connection, it is interesting to mention one more find, made by A. G. Shananin.[81] While still a student, he discovered a bronze sword 40 to 50 cm long in a rill at the foot of the hill, on the floodplain side. He stated that the sword was similar to the one found at Andreyevskoye Lake near Tyumen. Unfortunately, this sword has not been preserved, but the very fact that it was found is highly interesting.

Suzgun I and Suzgun II are not isolated instances of this culture. In

1948, V. V. Khramova, a member of the Institute of Ethnography of the Academy of Sciences of the U.S.S.R. and of the West Siberian expedition, discovered a settlement with pottery of the Suzgun type in Zabolotye, a nearly inaccessible swampy region on the left bank of the Irtysh near the village of Laytamak on the Layma River. One may assume that further work and search will help reveal the character of the Suzgun culture more completely and comprehensively, and this would be especially interesting and important for understanding the historical processes.

Besides the Bronze Age sites described in the present chapter, one should also keep in mind the individual finds made along the middle and lower Irtysh and held mostly by local museums. They include the bronze sword extracted, according to Rossomakhin, from the bottom of Andreyevskoye Lake in 1940 in the vicinity of Kozlova Pereyma opposite the site of Andreyevskaya II. Unfortunately the sword has been lost, and one can form opinions about it only from a small photograph. It is very similar to the Vilyuy sword, but not to the extent indicated by A. P. Okladnikov, who called them "twins."[82] The Andreyevskaya sword is somewhat longer than the Vilyuy; further, its blade is narrower, its handle rounder, and its crossguard more protruding. The pommel of this sword, like that of the Vilyuy sword, is shaped like a nailhead, and the hilt itself is decorated with cross ridges or ribs (Plate XVI, item 1).* The blade was forged, evidently cold-hammered to give the bronze rigidity and hardness. The Andreyevskaya sword is equal if not superior to the Vilyuy sword as an example of the craftsmanship of the ancient casters, and it illustrates the advanced stage of development of Late Bronze Age metallurgy in the forested-steppe region of western Siberia. Evidently, the Suzgun sword was very much like the Andreyevskaya sword, but somewhat shorter.

The celts of the Seyma type belong to an earlier period, the second half of the 2nd millennium B.C. One of them, highly typical, is preserved in the Tobolsk Museum and comes "from Samarovo," according to the inscription in the accessions book (Plate XVI, item 2).[83] It was cast from superb yellowish bronze and is 13.5 cm long and 6.9 cm wide at the widest point of the cutting edge. The socket is oval, but the middle profile hexagonal; the middle, broad facet is separated from the lateral ones by sharply defined ridges. The socket is decorated with a "trestle," characteristic of such celts. Hatched triangles descend from the trestle, three on the broad facets and one on the lateral. On one of the broad faces, two hatched rhombs hang from the middle triangle. The cutting edge of the celt was meticulously forged.

A mould for casting celts similar to the one just described was found by V. N. Pignatti,[84] together with a stone hammer for crushing ore, approximately 15 km from Tobolsk, near the village of Tyukova on the Rogalikha River. This mould was designed for a rectangular celt of hexagonal cross section. The broad facet, separated from the lateral

---

* [For a detailed account of the Vilyuy sword in English see *Anthropology of the North: Translations from Russian Sources*, no. 8, pp. 173–78 *passim*. Editor, A.I.N.A.]

ones by sharp triangular ridges, is decorated with triangles and rhombs. This ornamentation brings it close to the Seyma-Andronovo type of celt. However, the Tyukova celt mould differs somewhat in its outlines (hexagonal socket, no broadening along the cutting edge) and in its ornamentation (no trestle). It is still difficult to say definitely whether these differences are local or chronological. It is more likely that they are chronological, since the Tyukova mould may be associated to a certain extent with the western Siberian celts of Group I.[85] However, its ornamentation is probably older and should be dated to the last quarter of the 2nd millennium B.C., thus falling within the chronological span of the Suzgun culture.

Celts of the Seyma-Andronovo type have also been found in the forest regions of the lower Ishim River, at the southern boundary of this territory. Two of the celts are from "Kargalinsk *volost* of Tara *okrug*"[86] (Plate XVI, item 3) and a third "from the lower Ishim river." This latter was listed in the Tobolsk Museum as item No. 55, but apparently has been lost. The Tyumen Museum also has a celt of this characteristic type (Plate XVI, item 4). It is a large, superbly made implement, 13 cm long, 5.3 cm wide at the socket, and 7.5 cm at the blade edge. The blade is well forged, thus it is quite broad. In cross section the socket is oval, becoming

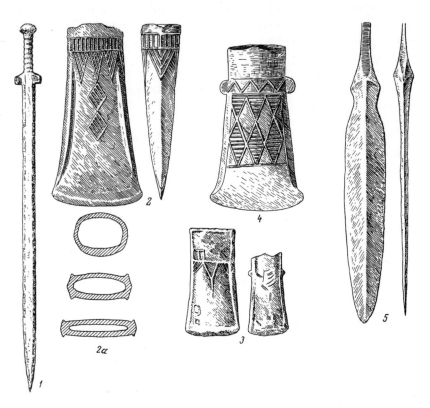

Plate XVI. Bronze Age weapons and implements.
1–sword from Andreyevskoye Lake; 2, 2a–celt from Samarovo; 3–celt from Tara *okrug*; 4–a Tyumen celt; 5–a dagger from Lake Kunchur.

hexagonal in its middle part. The ornamental band of the celt terminates in lobes, one to a side, which, in M. P. Gryaznov's opinion, is characteristic of the Siberian variant of the Seyma and Turbino celts.[87] The ornamentation of the Tyumen celt is unusual. Its ornamental band, in contrast to more typical specimens, has a zigzag, not a trestle, pattern; on the broad facet, below a row of [hanging] triangles, is a row of rhombs instead of the usual pendant rhombs. In general appearance and abundance of ornamentation, the Tyumen celt is most reminiscent of the celt "from Vyatka *guberniya*" preserved in the Museum of Physical Anthropology in Moscow.[88] According to the card file of the Tyumen Museum, where it is listed as item No. 49 (896), this celt, together with two others (items 897 and 898), "was found in a burial mound in the vicinity of the village of Voynova-Gileva, near Tyumen" (between Tyumen and Andreyevskoye Lake). The celt listed as item No. 898 actually is an asymmetric adze. This type is as widespread as the Seyma-Turbino, and Gryaznov scarcely has grounds for calling it "Karasuk,"[89] inasmuch as adzes of similar form have been found on the Kama and the Volga.[90] The Tyumen adze found near Voynova-Gileva is 8.4 cm long and 3.3 × 4.3 cm along the asymmetrical hexagonal socket.

Although the card catalog lists them as having been found in a burial mound, it is evident that they are not from a single complex and, evidently, are of different age. While the celt should more likely be dated to the 2nd millennium and apparently not even the very end of the millennium, the adze is probably not older than the turn of the 1st millennium B.C. The third item, a celt (Tyumen Museum, item No. 49/897), is younger than the adze, and in shape it belongs to the second type of western Siberian celt.[91] A. Heikel had expressed doubt as to the accuracy of the cataloging and was inclined to regard these implements as coming from sites in the region of the Varvarinka *yurts* on the Tobol River, below the mouth of the Tura.[92] Perhaps this assumption of Heikel's is correct, but it is just as likely that there were burial mounds of different age or some other type of site near Voynova-Gileva (surveys have not yet been made there), whence came the finds. Finally, this is not an essential point, since in the present stage of archaeological investigation of the Ob-Irtysh we are interested most in establishing the types and forms of implements that existed in a given territory during a particular epoch.

Among separate finds of bronze objects, a dagger of superb workmanship found in 1949 by A. D. Bukleyev, a collective-farm worker of Kunchur village, is worthy of mention. He found it while plowing a field not far from the broad Lake Kunchur, which lies amidst the forest marshes between the Tura and the Iska rivers about 60 km from Tyumen. The dagger was cast from yellowish bronze covered with a lustrous dark patina. Its overall length is 22.5 cm, 17 cm of which is the willow-leaf-shaped blade. There is a slight constriction near the base of the blade, following which is a well-modeled bulge that gradually becomes a flat tang of rectangular cross section (Plate XVI, item 5). The end of the tang is broken off. There is a well-defined spine along the entire blade, which gives greater strength to the dagger. The spine and the long rectangular tang indicate that this is a Late Bronze Age dagger, but still datable within the limits of the 2nd millennium B.C.

The discovery of Suzgun II, the pottery of which shows definite Andronovo traits, the finds of celts in the forested region of the Irtysh, and what is even more important, the mold for celts of the Seyma-Andronovo type are clear evidences that close ties existed among the forest tribes, on the one hand, and the steppe and forested-steppe tribes, on the other. The tribes of the Suzgun culture, inhabiting the southern belt of the taiga zone on the banks of the mighty river system stretching from Kazakhstan and western China to the Arctic coast, were the link between the tribes of the Bronze Age steppe culture and the people of the taiga and its northern reaches next to the tundra, and they were responsible for the appearance of the surprising Andronovo features in the shape and ornamentation of the pottery of Salekhard I and Mameyev's winter camp, both sites beyond the Arctic Circle.

Although the Neolithic, Eneolithic, and Bronze Age materials from the northern Ob-Irtysh region are incomplete and fragmentary, some attempt at systematizing them can and must be made. First, one must attempt to explain the typology and development of the forms of the individual objects of the material culture. Of course, such an effort can give reliable results only if there is a mass of material, which we do not have as yet. At present, we can only establish the basic tendencies of this development, which will be of use in classifying the material for future work.

I have attempted in Plate XVII to indicate a chronological account of the individual categories of objects of the material culture and ornamentation of the pottery and to compare them with similar categories of adjacent regions. This comparison, although it does not bring us particularly close to revealing the absolute chronology of the archaeological sites of western Siberia, does help disclose and eliminate errors in their relative dating. In the process, we have clearly demonstrated those common forms of material culture which may be regarded as traces of the ancient ties that existed in various epochs between the individual regions.

The earliest of these associations may be the finds of implements of microlithic aspect in the lower horizons of the sands on the southern shore of Andreyevskoye Lake near Vtoraya Pereyma [Second Narrows]. Similar objects—in particular, asymmetric arrowheads—have been found in the Urals at the campsites near the village of Palkino, but no indications were given of the conditions under which they were found.[93] Much more interesting analogues have been found in eastern Siberia, where a microlithic inventory identical to that of Andreyevskoye Lake has been located in complexes of the Khin period.[94] Finally, similar objects have been found far to the south as well, in the Neolithic campsite Dzhanbas-kala No. 4.[95] Moreover, the proportions of the asymmetric arrowhead with a side notch from Andreyevskaya I and one of the arrowheads from Palkino (with a long side notch) are closest to the Kelteminar points. It should be added that although we have not yet been able to associate the Andreyevskoye Lake finds with any of the

KEY:

1 to 3–campsite at Palkino village (P. A. Dmitriyev, *MIA*, no. 21, fig. 1, items 18, 19); 4 to 7–Shigir (A. Ya. Bryusov, *Ocherki po istorii plemen . . .* , figs. 32, 36); 8 to 11–Andreyevskaya I campsite; 12 to 19–Dzhanbas-kala No. 4 (S. P. Tolstov, *Drevniy Khorezm*); 20 to 24–Cis-Baykal (A. P. Okladnikov, *MIA*, no. 18, fig. 6, items 15, 16); 25 to 29–Gorbunovo (D. N. Eding, Gorbunovskiy torfyanik; *Reznaya skulptura Urala*); 30 to 37–the Chestyy-yag campsite and the Severnaya Sosva basin; 38 to 42–Cis-Baykalia (A. P. Okladnikov, *MIA*, no. 18, and *VDI*, no. 1, 1938, fig. 4); 43 to 52–Poludenka (O. N. Bader, *KSIIMK*, no. 16, fig. 50, and *SE*, no. 2, 1949, fig. 2); 53–Man-ya River (Sev. Sosva); 55, Ob-Yenisey canal; 54, 56 to 60, 62, 63–the campsites Sortynya I, Khulyum-sunt, Nyaksimvol (Severnaya Sosva); 61–Tara *rayon*; 64 to 66–campsites belonging to the Kelteminar culture in Kazakhstan (A. A. Formozov, *KSIIMK*, no. 39, fig. 2, items 12, 13, and fig. 3, item 1); 94–same locality (ibid., fig. 3, item 5); 91, 92–same locality (*KSIIMK*, no. 25, fig. 16, items 10 and 13); 95–same locality (ibid., fig. 17, item 1); 67 to 74–Cis-Baykal (A. P. Okladnikov, *MIA*, no. 18); 75 to 78–Gorbunovo (D. N. Eding, Reznaya skulptura Urala, fig. 10, items 5 and 7, and fig. 11, item 7; A. Ya. Bryusov, *Ocherki po istorii plemen . . .* , fig. 37); 79–Tavda River; 80 to 83–Krasnogorskoye campsite, Iset River; 84 to 90–Andreyevskaya II and Lipchinskaya campsites; 93, 96, 97, 100, 101–Dzhal Ambet (according to S. S. Chernikov's data); 98, 99–Kazakhstan (A. A. Formozov, *KSIIMK*, no. 39, fig. 9); 102 to 108–Cis-Baykal (A. P. Okladnikov, *MIA*, no. 18); 109 to 114–Gorbunovo (D. N. Eding, Reznaya skulptura Urala, fig. 10, item 2, and fig. 5) and Shigir peat bog (P. A. Dmitriyev, *MIA*, no. 21, fig. 1, items 11, 13); 115 and 116–same locality (Ye. M. Bers, *MIA*, no. 21, fig. 1, items 17 and 23, and fig. 3, items 8, 2); 117 and 125–Sortynya II (lower layer); 126–Salekhard I; 118 and 119 Khara-Patka; 120–Konda; 121–Lake Kunchur; 122–Tara *rayon*; 123–lower Irtysh; 124–Tyumen; 127 and 128–Suzgun II; 130 and 135–Issyk-Kul (National Museum of History); 129, 131 to 133, and 136–Omsk (State Museum of History and Omsk Museum); 134–Mynchunkur (S. S. Chernikov, *Drevnyaya metallurgiya i gornoye delo zapadnogo Altaya*, Alma-Ata, 1949, Plate VII, fig. 3); 137–burial ground near Isakovo village (K. V. Salnikov, *MIA*, no. 21, 1951, pp. 94–151, fig. 3, item 4); 138 and 139–Alekseyevka settlement (O. A. Krivtsova-Grakova, *TGIM*, no. 17); 140 to 145–Cis-Baykal (A. P. Okladnikov, *MIA*, no. 18, fig. 9, bottom row).

(The illustrations not referenced appear in the present volume. Illustrations 88 and 89 are not quite true representations; actually the vessels have rounded bottoms.)

types of pottery as yet found there, the pottery of the later campsites, classified as Neolithic and Eneolithic, is very similar in ornamentation and some vessel shapes to the pottery of Dzhanbas-kala No. 4.

The indicated similarity of the material could have been considered a chance coincidence, if the similarity of the Ob-Irtysh and eastern Siberian and Kazakhstan materials had not been observed for the subsequent epochs as well.

The similarity to the Cis-Baykal appears in the diffusion of the paddling technique of manufacturing clay vessels in the Ob region and in the arrangement of the ornamentation (comb, ripply band, and other types) in interlocking bands,[96] reminiscent of the broad plaiting of the Cis-Baykal vessels of the Isakovo type,[97] in the ornamentation applied by a stab-and-drag paddle. In western Siberia we also find large, broad "laurel-leaf" daggers or spearheads identical to the Serovo ones. Finally, among the numerous chance finds as well as in the individual sites (the lower layer of Sortynya I, and Poludenka) there are axes and adzes with trunnions identical to the Serovo adzes from the Angara and Cis-Baykal

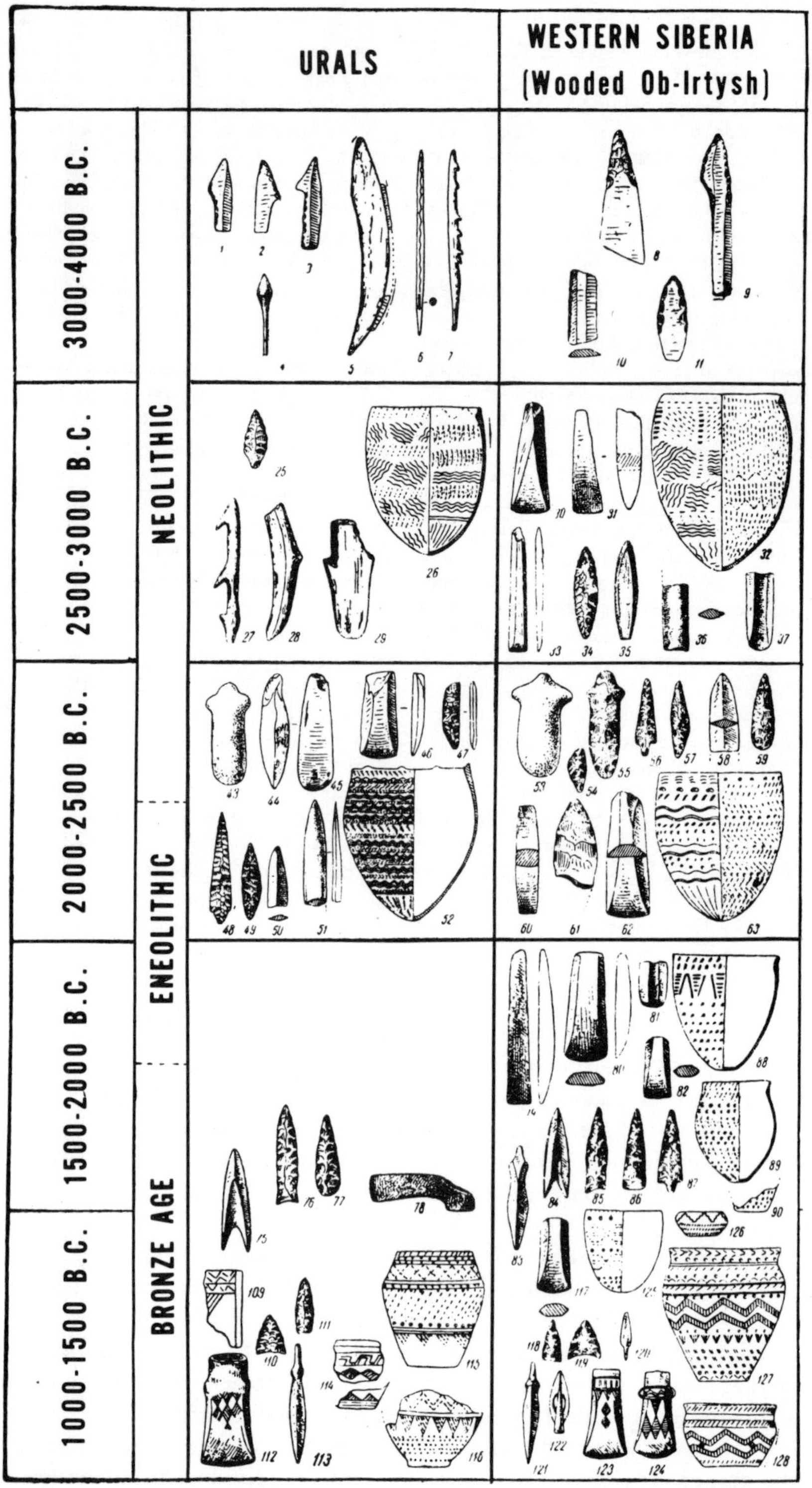

Plate XVII. Typological table of the epochs of the Neolithic era and of the Bronze Age in the lower Ob region. (See p. 53 for key to epochs.)

		KAZAKHSTAN and CENTRAL ASIA	EASTERN SIBERIA (Cis-Baykal)
3000-4000 B.C.	NEOLITHIC		
2500-3000 B.C.			
2000-2500 B.C.	ENEOLITHIC		
1500-2000 B.C.			
1000-1500 B.C.	BRONZE AGE		

regions. The shape of these adzes is so unique and their distribution so localized that one must dismiss any thought that they appeared independently under similar conditions.

However, it appears that there were no ties with eastern Siberia in the Neolithic and Early Bronze Age beyond the Serovo period. No forms specific to the Angara and the Cis-Baykal have been discovered in the Ob region beyond the end of the 3rd millennium B.C., at least not in the forest zone. Evidently the ethnic movement from the east had ceased by that time. However, the occurrence of ovoid vessels with comb ornamentation in Cis-Baykalia during the Kitoy period may indicate some sort of influence from the west, perhaps from the Ob.

A. P. Okladnikov has already expressed this viewpoint. "In the east, the last traces of it (that is, the eastern Ural Neolithic and Early Bronze Age culture—Author) were found unexpectedly in the Yenisey valley at Krasnoyarsk. In this region, the most ancient Neolithic finds evidence a profound Cis-Baykalian influence (pottery of the Serovo type, stone figures of fish, et cetera). Later, the eastern Ural culture spread along the Yenisey; at Krasnoyarsk it is represented, in particular, by the lower layers of the remarkable settlement on the Sobakina river."[98]

The development of ties with the steppe and the forested steppe to the south presents quite a different picture. The extremely fragmentary and random nature of the Kazakhstan materials, which may be dated to the 3rd millennium B.C., prevents us from forming a continuous picture of these relations. Nonetheless, the basic time elements can be noted. We have already mentioned the similarity of the Kelteminar pottery to that of the Neolithic sites on the lower Ob and of the Urals and western Siberia. These sites are, primarily, Borovoye Ozero I, discovered and investigated by O. N. Bader;[99] Poludenka I, on the eastern slope of the Urals, investigated by Bader;[100] and the Neolithic and Eneolithic campsites on Andreyevskoye Lake, near Tyumen in western Siberia, described earlier. The Omsk campsite, especially its lower horizons, shows great similarity not so much to Dzhanbas-kala No. 4 as to the somewhat later Eneolithic campsites on the Aral, both in the pottery and in the flint items.

Recently, A. A. Formozov published articles on the cultures of Kazakhstan, Central Asia, and the southern Trans-Ural that existed from the 3rd to the beginning of the 2nd millennium B.C.[101] However, for the most part Formozov's materials are surface finds from disturbed campsites and, in a number of cases, from mixed layers. Formozov quite incorrectly attempted to distinguish between the Aralian (Kelteminar), southern Uralian, and Semipalatinsk cultures, characterizing on the basis of materials that were of different age and, what is more, incomplete and random. Having compared indicators that cannot actually be compared because of their different age and random nature, he naturally came to completely incorrect conclusions—for example, that the Kelteminar culture had a specific technique for making flint implements from lamellar blades,[102] that the short, wide arrowheads with a notched base were characteristic only of the Semipalatinsk culture,[103] and that the ornamentation of the southern Uralian pottery (with comb and pit depressions) contrasts with that of the "Kelteminar" pottery (with incised and drawn lines). It will become apparent that this is not a proper contrast if we note that the pit ornamentation is highly typical of the Trans-Ural sites and, evidently, of Kazakhstan in the first half of the 2nd millennium B.C.; that drawn lines—in particular, wavy lines—are typical of the Neolithic and the Eneolithic, that is, of the 3rd millennium B.C.; and that incised ornamentation dominated in this very region during the Late Bronze Age and in the transitional period, that is, at the turn of the 1st millennium B.C. The comb ornamentation is characteristic of almost all epochs.

In opposition to Formozov's deductions, we must insist that all the materials known to us, including that in Formozov's articles, indicate that cultures very similar to each other existed in the extensive forested-steppe and steppe areas of Kazakhstan and the Trans-Ural and, in part, the Cis-Ural during the Neolithic and the Eneolithic, that is, at the end of the 4th, during the 3rd, and at the beginning of the 2nd millennia B.C. These were genetically allied local variants of a single cultural-ethnic area. These cultures had a primarily ovoid pottery, which gradually became paraboloid toward the end of the period. At the same time, there were vessels with a distinct neck, and apparently, the flattened-bottom type became more widespread toward the beginning of the 2nd millennium.

There also appears to be a quite definite regularity in the development of the ornamentation. In the early stages of the period—at the end of the 4th and for most of the 3rd millennia—the ornamentation of the vessels consisted primarily of impressions of a comb stamp and both straight and wavy lines, the latter being especially characteristic. Pit ornamentation is entirely secondary. The rocker ornamentation appeared during the 3rd millennium; it was chiefly of the comb type and, less often, smooth. This characteristic pattern gradually became widespread and existed right up to the Bronze Age, during the early stages of which it disappeared. In the northeastern and eastern parts of the region (the Irtysh basin, the south of the Omsk *oblast*, and the Semipalatinsk *oblast*), at least during the Eneolithic, the stab-and-drag and stamped pseudo-textile ornamentation was employed in addition to the above-mentioned and apparently penetrated from the southeast. We do not yet know how far to the southwest these elements spread.

At the present, it is impossible to trace the development of the stone-working technique over this entire area, owing to the scarcity and fragmentary nature of the material. One may only note that for the earlier stages, in both the southern and the northern parts of it, the microlithic technique in connection with lamellar blades is characteristic. The arrowheads are worked primarily on one side only, although bilaterally retouched heads were found at Dzhanbas-kala No. 4. Undoubtedly the asymmetric forms with the lateral notch are typical; later they seem to have disappeared completely. The microlithic aspect of the flintworking technique persisted relatively longer in the steppe and forested steppe sites. At any rate, objects of that type, for example, the small subtriangular arrowheads made from lamellar blades with unilateral retouch (but already with the notch in the base) were found at the Omsk camp-site, the early layers of which do not date back any further than the turn of the 2nd millennium B.C.[104]

It seems that in the first half of the 2nd millennium B.C., vessels with flattened bottoms and primarily pit ornamentation were characteristic of the entire territory, and in the east as well, in the region of the Minu-sinsk basin. Later this pottery was replaced by typical Andronovo pottery, whose general features were more or less uniform over the entire territory. We will not discuss the origin of the Andronovo culture here, since that would take us far afield, and what is more, we do not have sufficient material as yet to solve the problem.[105] The solution to the problem lies in the future, but perhaps the near future. Here it is important to note merely that the Andronovo culture, which was characteristic of the steppes and the forested steppes, had a profound influence beyond its territorial limits. During the Andronovo period, throughout the southern and middle Trans-Ural region and, farther to the east, in the Tobolsk region and along the right bank of the Irtysh, cultures appeared that are represented by such sites as Suzgun II, the Krasnoye Ozero campsite,[106] the Tyumen campsites and burial mounds, and the Ural sites—Gorbunovo peat bog (uppermost layer of Section 6, and Beregovaya, among others), Koptyaki III and V,[107] and others—with undoubted Andronovo-like features in the form and ornamentation of the pottery and typically Andronovo forms of bronze implements.

Thus, for the entire period examined here (the Neolithic period and the Bronze Age), the forest regions of the Trans-Ural and Ob areas show an indubitable cultural and, insofar as can be judged by the pottery ornamentation, ethnic community with the more southerly forested-steppe and steppe regions, the influence of which is increasingly evident, especially during the Bronze Age. These ties with the south emerge particularly clearly in the southern and southwestern parts of the taiga zone. They are much weaker in the north and northeast, where the pottery continued to preserve local, more archaic, features, including traces of a strong influence of the eastern Siberian ripple pattern, even though the flat-bottomed vessels with ornamentation elements that are very similar to Andronovo (for example, at Salekhard I and Mameyev's winter camp) appeared at that time as far as the Arctic Circle.

Having acquainted ourselves with the material and areal associations presented in Plate XVII, we shall attempt an historical interpretation of the data now available to us.

We still do not know at what time the lower Ob region was settled or the conditions of settlement. We do not know of a single reliable Paleolithic site or even a chance find in the central parts of this territory. True, M. P. Gryaznov published a note on a tusk fragment of a young mammoth.[108] This item is now in the State Historical Museum and was donated by the peasant S. Usov together with other finds to the Archaeo-logical Commission. Gryaznov perceived on the tusk traces of workings assignable to the Paleolithic. However, his deductions are not too con-vincing. "Both the state of preservation and the working technique indicate it is Upper Paleolithic." A few lines later we find, "The main

mass of the tusk is particularly well preserved and gives the impression
of an ordinary 'elephant's tusk' found in permafrost and suitable for
making implements. . . . Only the periphery, the very surface of the tusk,
had undergone any noticeable change. . . . The surface of the tusk did
not retain its original micro-structure. It is uniformly rough everywhere,
covered with a multitude of fine grooves, apparently effects of corrosion
by plant roots. Therefore, it is impossible to establish accurately the
method by which the object was worked" (pp. 165–66). As we see,
Gryaznov's conclusion contradicts his own description. Moreover he
points out, "The object is not of special interest in itself. What is interesting is the locality at which it was found. . . . Unfortunately, we do not
know the conditions under which it was found and the exact location of
the place where it was found" (p. 166).

In my opinion, the traces of working on the tusk, which Gryaznov
mentions, can scarcely be Paleolithic. The good state of preservation of
the inner part of the bone "suitable for making implements" indicates
that it was found in permafrost, and the poor state of preservation of
the surface with traces of plant-root corrosion indicates that the object
was not found at its original site. Most likely the tusk (whose original
size is not known) was found after having been washed out [of the
permafrost], as "mammoth bones" are found even now, and was used
for some purpose requiring application of the ring-shaped notching.
Ultimately, the tusk remained in the cultural layer of the settlement in
which it was used and suffered surface deterioration while it was in the
soil. However, this deterioration was shallow, indicating that the period
between the time the object got into the soil and the time it was found
was relatively short.

Finally, one should hardly ascribe this object to even the early phases
of the Neolithic, much less the Paleolithic.

That the lower Ob could have been inhabited in the Paleolithic period
is implied by sites of that period having been found to the west and east.
For the east, I refer to the temporary mammoth-hunters' camp found in
the area of Lagernyy Sad [Garden] in Tomsk and reported by N. F.
Kashchenko.[109] For the west, one may cite the Paleolithic traces dis-
covered by O. N. Bader on the eastern side of the Urals in the Medved-
Kamen [Bear Stone] grotto on the Tagil River, and in the Tokareva
Log [Ravine] on the Tura River near the Nizhne-Turinskiy *zavod* [fac-
tory].[110] Finally, further indications are provided by the ample finds of
Quaternary fauna at different places in the Ob-Irtysh region.

We do not have good data on the extent of settlement of the territory
in the Mesolithic period. The nearest sites of Mesolithic aspect have
become known through the work of O. N. Bader on the Kama, near the
mouth of the Chusovaya River.[111] A. Ya. Bryusov is also inclined to
classify the finds at the Shigir peat bog as Epipaleolithic.[112] However,
in this case he is speaking of chance finds of needlelike arrowheads,
whose stratigraphy is very vague, and we must regard the question of
the post-Paleolithic sites in the Urals as an open one until relevant field
studies have been made.

Our knowledge of the archaeology of the lower Ob begins only with the Early Neolithic. Nonetheless, by the end of the 4th and the beginning of the 3rd millennia B.C., we find well-developed local cultures in the taiga with firmly established forms of material production, indicating a considerable period of habitation of the territory.

The recent finds in the Urals, western Siberia, and Kazakhstan have defined more precisely the extent of the Kelteminar culture and have also revealed very closely allied forms even in the North, in the forest zone. These finds have considerably extended the territorial range specified for it by S. P. Tolstov, and we may say with confidence that in the Neolithic and Early Bronze Ages there existed over this broad territory a distinctly manifested cultural and ethnic community. Later, within that community, features close to the Andronovo type began to appear in the ornamentation and shape of the vessels, and later, in the Bronze Age, we see the blossoming of the Andronovo culture almost everywhere in this territory. Individual features of the Andronovo culture penetrated very rapidly far to the north in western Siberia, as far as the polar circle at the mouths of the Ob and Taz rivers.

The region over which the Aral Neolithic culture spread reflects, to varying degrees, the paths of settlement of its specific carriers.

The Kelteminar culture and cultures similar to it evidently were one of the foundations of the Neolithic cultures of the Ob region. In all probability, the ancient Europoid physical type, which anthropologists trace in the modern Mansi and Khanty, is associated with this ethnic current, as are the few finds of early skulls, in particular in the Trans-Ural region. Of these, the skull found in the lower layers of the Shigir peat bog and reconstructed by M. M. Gerasimov is very interesting. This reconstruction showed a Europoid type Gerasimov classified as Suburalian.

As mentioned above, the forms of the material culture indicate that two components, a southern and an eastern, played a role in the founding of this culture; thus, it is quite legitimate to connect the spread of these forms with the migration of specific ethnic groups. The trunnion axes found in numbers along the Angara and in the Cis-Baykal and (we can now consider this as established) in considerable quantities as far as the Urals are an element that reflects the movement of the eastern component. Only one find has been made farther to the west, the afore-mentioned Karelian axe. The stamping technique of the pottery and the stab-and-drag ornamentation may also be considered eastern features in the material culture of the ancient Obians. In the earlier cultures, these elements apparently are found more often in the northern and eastern parts of the Ob region. For example, the stamping and stab-and-drag techniques are clearly expressed in the Bronze Age pottery of Salekhard I and appear to be completely absent in the synchronous pottery of Sorty-nya II. Later, these differences were completely obliterated.

The ethnic ties stretching from east to west over the northern fringe of the Eurasian continent can be traced in material other than the archaeological. G. N. Prokofyev also noted these ties in the linguistic evidence—the lexical similarity of the languages of the peoples of the lower Ob to those of northeastern Asia. These observations have been confirmed by other linguists and ethnographers, who have established Yukagir elements in the languages and ethnic composition of the present population of the lower Ob and Yenisey rivers.[113]

Some specific features that the Khanty and Mansi languages have in common and that the Saami language has in common with those two are worthy of attention. Without going into the details of the phenomenon, let me mention one fact that is important because it can in no way be explained as a feature common to the lexicon and morphology of the Finno-Ugric languages—namely, that among the Finno-Ugric languages, only the Khanty, Mansi, and Saami languages have the dual number. It is highly developed in Khanty and Mansi, while in Saami traces of it are found in the pronominal endings.

Archaeological, linguistic, and ethnographic data[114] indicate that the ancient population of the Far North was ethnically unified and perhaps that this ethos spread from east to west. It is highly probable that it should be associated with the Mongoloid element which, according to the latest data of physical anthropology,[115] was widely distributed in the Cis-Baykal region and to the west of it in the taiga zone across the Urals to the White Sea.

As we have seen, during the Bronze Age the ties between the population of the taiga and tundra on the one hand and the middle Irtysh on the other not only continued but even strengthened. In the material from the archaeological sites of that era, one may find a combination of local elements which had their roots in the Neolithic of the taiga and in the Andronovo motifs of the steppes. It is likely that the tribes that settled the middle Irtysh region where it flows westward in a broad stream and forms the boundary between two cultural-geographic zones (the forests and the steppes) played a large part in this process. On its banks, the cattle breeders encountered the hunters and fishermen of the Trans-Irtysh taiga. The latter had adopted their new technical skills and disseminated them northward along the mainstream. This may have been a locale of more profound intertribal associations through marriages and the adoption of the settled way of life by groups of nomads, perhaps in connection with the development of agriculture. In any case, only deep ethnic ties could explain the penetration of the Andronovo-like ornamentation amidst the taiga tribes.[116] This ornamentation formed the basis for the development of the present ornamentation of the Mansi and the Khanty. The ornamentation common to these peoples could hardly be explained without assuming similar semantics and, consequently, extensive contacts, perhaps even a kinship of the tribes of the lower Ob-Irtysh and northern part of the forested steppe.

These ancient ties between the north and the south are also expressed in the penetration of the physical type of the European steppes into the taiga zone of northwestern Siberia. In the opinion of physical anthropologists, this process could have continued "over many centuries."[117] The slow northward movement of peoples of the forested steppe, bringing about some similarity in the forms of the material culture and probably a linguistic affinity as well, prepared the ground for the events of the 1st millennium B.C., which played an important role in the ethnogenesis of the present population of the lower Ob region. Naturally, the penetration of the Europoid population was reflected more strongly in the southern part of the territory. Even among the present Mansi and Khanty, the Mongoloid features are more noticeable in the north and northeast. Further, remnants of the ancient population continued to exist along the Arctic coast even during the Iron Age, finally disappearing only after the Nentsy entered the northern tundras. But more about this later. The ancient taiga people who left the archaeological sites described previously were hunters and fishermen. Judging by the remains of animal bones found in the floor layer of the Ches-tyy-yag semisubterranean house, one may assume that the elk was especially important to the hunt.

The villages of these taiga hunters were directly at the water, on dry, sandy, and pebbly beaches. At present, the cultural layers of some of these villages lie in damp horizons and sometimes even below the mean water level (Andreyevskoye Lake, and Ches-tyy-yag, if we consider the great depth of some of the houses); in other cases they are covered with a layer of peat (Khulyum-sunt), which indicates that the climate was different at that time. The habitations of the Neolithic settlers, at least in winter, were earth-covered semisubterranean houses sometimes 600 m² or more in area. The size of the dwellings suggests the level of social development of their inhabitants, in that such houses could have been built only by the efforts of a large community, if we consider the relatively low level of Neolithic technology. Judging by the area of the Ches-tyy-yag dwellings, one may infer that at least 150 to 200 persons lived in each of them, perhaps even 250 persons. We may assume that in sites such as Ches-tyy-yag, we are dealing with clan communities similar to the one that had constructed the settlement Dzhanbas-kala No. 4, representing the Kelteminar culture. Ches-tyy-yag is similar to Dzhanbas-kala No. 4 not only in the size of the dwellings, but in the forms of the material culture. However, Dzhanbas-kala No. 4 consists of only one house, while Ches-tyy-yag has two houses of 600 m² each, and three from 300 to 400 m² each, not to mention the smaller ones.

What was the settlement in the Ches-tyy-yag forest like? Was it the habitation of a tribe or of a large clan? We find some data for answering that question in the ethnography of the modern Ob region. On examining a map of the settlement patterns of the present Ugrian clans of the Ob basin, we see that the clans are grouped by phratrial affiliation, whereby the clans belonging to one phratry often occupy a considerable territory. For example, the upper Lyapin River basin is settled by clans of the *mos* phratry; clans of the *por* phratry occupy the lower Lyapin basin, beginning with the village of Khoryng-paul. The upper Lozva and Sosva rivers belong to clans of the *por* phratry, who claim descent from a common ancestor, the elk. The Kazym River basin is settled entirely by clans of the *mos* phratry, who claim a common ancestor, the heath hen, called *Kasum-Nay-Ekva* (Great Woman of the Kazym River).

Often the concept remains, in vestigial form, that the ancestors of the clans who settled this territory were brothers and sisters or sons and daughters of the ancestor. In the folklore, these latter are depicted as brothers and sisters, children of the phratrial progenitors Numi and Kaltashch, and are none other than a mythological representation of the primary clans.[118] One may assume that settlements of the Ches-tyy-yag type were the habitation of an exogamous community of this type, a primary clan.[119] The low level of development of productive forces determined the size of the community. Only a large commune could have carried out battue hunting and built pens and fishweirs that could assure a large catch. During the Late Neolithic, when the level of technology had risen, smaller settlements became possible, the prerequisites for which we can see in the obviously fully populated Ches-tyy-yag, where the inhabitants could no longer be housed in the two main lodges. When the large exogamous communities such as Ches-tyy-yag broke up, the filial clans gradually settled the surrounding territory, forming consanguineous territorial groups phratrially affiliated under the same name and considering themselves to be "descendants" of the basic, primary clan.

In territories populated by two groups, such as the Lyapin basin, or by even one group, such as the upper Lozva and Sosva, which as a rule were delimited by natural boundaries and quite remote from each other, special local features developed in the material culture and language.

Strict adherence to exogamy called for marriages outside the exogamous territories, which often led to the establishment of relations with populations of distant regions, even those inhabited by ethnic groups speaking a different language (for example, from the Lyapin River to the Synya, beyond the Urals to the Pechora River; from the Lozva across the Urals to the Vishera River; from the Kazym to the middle Ob and the upper Taz). This latter also led to different linguistic associations for these groups, which caused the establishment and strengthening of dialectal features in the language. For each such territory, along with the dialect, one may note an ornamentation specific to it, as a rule reflecting the zoomorphism of the mythical ancestor of the clans inhabiting it. Examples of such specific ornamentation are the heath hen on the Kazym, the pike jaw on the Lyapin, the sable on the Tapsuy, the frog on the middle Sosva, the antlers on the Lozva, and the gull wings on the Ob above Berezov.

Later (probably in the Early Iron Age), such groups of related clans formed the bases for what were now nonexogamous territorial-tribal formations with overtones of a defensive-offensive military organization, vestiges of which remained until the appearance of the Russians in the north.

Chapter 3

The Early Iron Age

In the late 1880s, a bronze celt found near the Ivanovskiy Convent was presented to the Tobolsk Museum. It is a very large one, 9.4 cm long, with its greatest width (along the cutting edge) being 6.0 cm and its least width 5.8 cm (in the first quarter of the implement, figuring from the cutting edge). The cross section of the haft is irregularly oval, approaching a hexagon in its middle part. The middle facet expands abruptly toward the cutting edge and is separated from the lateral ones by raised ridges. The celt has subrectangular perforations which expand inward. In writing my paper on the typology of celts,[120] I could not be completely certain about placing the Ivanovskiy find in the first group, because I did not have enough information at the time.[121] Now, however, I can add that it, like the others, has a well-developed inner partition 3.1 cm high, 0.5 cm thick at the base, and 0.3 cm in the upper part. Chronologically, the Ivanovskiy celt can scarcely be assigned to the late stage of the first group. On the basis of its nearly complete analogy to a celt from Derbeden, it can be dated not later than 900 B.C.

In 1948, a reconnaissance was made near the former Ivanovskiy Convent. We discovered a fortified hill site and many burial mounds on the high bank of the Irtysh on both sides of its junction with the Ivanovskaya River.[122] They yielded material of the same kind and appeared to belong to the same complex. The pottery showed features similar to the Suzgun pottery and a certain likeness to the pottery of the burial mounds of the middle Irtysh, which are associated with the Late Scythian and Sarmatian periods. Thus, the dating of the celt, based on typology, coincides with the dating of the pottery, which allows us to date the deep layers of the site to the beginning of the 1st millennium B.C. and the upper horizons of the fortified hill site to the middle of the 1st millennium B.C. Pottery of the Ivanovskaya type has never been found farther north. Perhaps the northern boundary of this culture ran somewhat south of Tobolsk and did not enter the taiga zone. On the lower Irtysh and Ob we encounter pottery of an entirely different aspect. There the sites include the fortified hill sites Sortynya I on the Severnaya Sosva and Evi-Vozh near Kushevat on the Ob, sites whose character has not yet been established, namely, Khara-Patka near Kushevat and Salekhard II, campsites on the Shaytanka (a tributary to the Poluy), at Zelenaya Gorka near

Salekhard, and the dune campsite on the western coast of the Yamal Peninsula near Cape Tiutey-sale.

I discovered the fortified hill site Sortynya I (Fig. 4) in 1931 on the left, precipitous bank of the Sosva River, approximately 1 km upstream from the village of Sortynya. The upstream boundary of the fortified hill site is formed by a small ravine; the land side is marked off by a double row of ramparts and ditches. They are well preserved, except for the outer ditch, which has been filled almost completely. The preserved embankment is 1 to 1.5 m high and up to 2 m wide. The ditch is 1 to 1.5 m deep and about 1 m wide. At the northwest corner, the

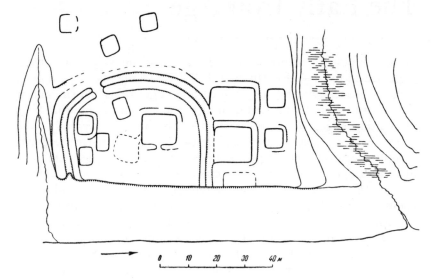

Fig. 4. Plan of the Sortynya I fortified hill site on the Sosva River.

embankments and ditches are intersected by a narrow passageway. The fortified hill site[123] is about 45 m long along the river side and has an area of about 1,500 m².

The surface of the site is pitted with depressions of a more or less square shape; these are the remains of semisubterranean houses. There are several such depressions outside the limits of the fortified site. Evidently they do not all belong to the fortified site. We have already mentioned that a Neolithic campsite lies beneath the culture-yielding layer of the fortified site; it is separated from the layer of the fortified site by a sterile interlayer and also includes houses. The depressions shown by dashed lines in Fig. 4 and the large depressions on the outer edge of the fortified site, which were partially disturbed when the ditch and embankment were constructed, evidently are traces of the houses of this campsite. The houses belonging to the period of the fortified hill site are from 80 to 150 m² in area. The fortified hill site was studied in 1931 and 1935, and its stratigraphy was determined and a certain amount of pottery collected (Plate XVIII, items 1–13) from the layer immediately beneath the turf.[124]

The Evi-Vozh fortified hill site is situated on a small cape formed by

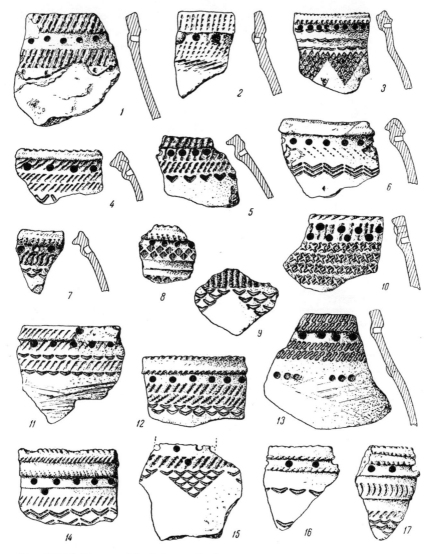

Plate XVIII. Pottery of the Zelenaya Gorka type.
  1 to 13–the Sortynya I fortified hill site; 14 to 17–the Kushevat fortified hill site on the Ob.

the junction of a rivulet with the Ob a short distance downstream from Kushevat on the right bank of the Ob. Unfortunately, no details are available on its layout or on that of two other sites (Khara-Patka and Salekhard II). In 1925–27 they were investigated by D. N. Redrikov, who gathered fairly abundant material, but left only a very brief description.

The Yamal Peninsula campsite was discovered by me in 1929. It is on the coast of the Kara Sea at 71°21′ north and is one of the northernmost Early Iron Age sites located 2 km to the southwest of the point of the cape, where the high and steep bank gives way to gentle dunes. These dunes evidently have been stationary for a long time and are now reinforced by grassy vegetation. The finds were made on the slopes of two hills facing the interior of the peninsula.[125] All objects were exposed. Bones of sea animals, fragments of clay vessels, et cetera were discovered. Walrus bones predominated among the bone remains; seal bones were found in lesser amounts, while bones of the reindeer and arctic fox were rare. The following stone implements were found: a scraper made from a thin piece of quartzitic sandstone, along the whole rounded edge of which one can see traces of retouching, smoothed from use;[126] a fragment of flagstone with a biconical drill hole (the fragment had broken off during the drilling);[127] a crudely flaked arrowhead of ironstone; and a corelike fragment of quartzite. Further, many pebbles and large stones were found on the hills. The presence of stone here must also be attributed to man's activity, as there is no stone elsewhere on the coast. The pottery of the campsite consists of a large number of fragments (Fig. 5), some of which were covered completely by a surface layer of sand.

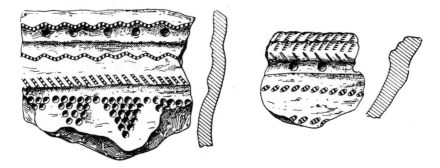

Fig. 5. Pottery from the dune campsite near Tiutey-sale [Walrus Cape].

The Zelenaya Gorka campsite was discovered during the operations of the Mangazeya expedition of 1946. It is situated on a small, vegetation-covered cape, whence its name, Zelenaya Gorka [Green Hillock]. This cape is on the steep right bank of the Poluy River, approximately 5 km downstream from Salekhard.[128] The Early Iron Age layer lies atop compacted soil and is covered by a layer of light-colored sand, in the upper horizon of which a vessel and implements of the Ust-Poluy type were discovered. The vessel is particularly important because it gives a very reliable indication of the relative dating of sites of both the Zelenaya Gorka and Ust-Poluy types. Abundant pottery material was collected at the Zelenaya Gorka site, from which a hitherto unknown form of Early Iron Age vessel was reconstructed. The material of the Zelenaya Gorka site is especially valuable for dating the sites enumerated in this chapter.

As we have seen, these sites are spread over a territory that stretches more than 1,500 km between the extreme points discovered thus far. The pottery of all these sites is highly uniform, despite the distances between the finds. The size of the territory indicates that the culture was well established and probably existed for a long time. We have called it the Zelenaya Gorka culture rather than period, in view of the importance of the site, even though the culture as a whole is not presently known.

The vessels of the Zelenaya Gorka culture are relatively short and have plano-convex bottoms.[129] They vary in size from 10 to 40 cm along the upper edge, with the largest diameter at the [slightly bulging] middle of the vessel. The neck, placed vertically or at a slight angle, usually blends smoothly into the body of the vessel. The rim was somewhat thickened by bending the edge in or by adding a ridge. This thickening forms a small cornice or collar, emphasized by a row of pits placed beneath it. This collar is one of the characteristic features of the Zelenaya Gorka pottery. Besides the vessels listed above, one finds shallow, straight-edge cups that are as much as 15 to 20 cm in diameter.

Among the ornamentation elements, one finds a small fine-toothed comb, often used for applying a vertical herringbone or zigzag pattern, and a smooth or a three- or four-toothed paddle used to incise parallel lines or as a stab-and-drag device. The flutings, found especially often under the collar of the vessel, were made with a smooth, curved paddle. The tiny, figured stamps which give a vessel an especially smart look are typical of the Zelenaya Gorka pottery. These stamps include a half-moon or angular stamp (smooth or toothed, sometimes double-lined); a wavy or S-shaped stamp; a rhombic, less often square and triangular, stamp, hatched in one direction or reticular; crosses, stars, or a crosslike rosette, and others.

The ornamentation is arranged and grouped very consistently. The neck along the collar and below the row of pits is covered with bands, chiefly of impressions applied with a comb, a paddle, or sometimes an S-shaped or other stamp, usually obliquely. Below this ornamental zone, in the transition zone between the neck and the body of the vessel, usually there is a row of triangles pointing to the base of the vessel. These triangles consist of rosette impressions made by rhombic, square, or half-moon (horns pointing upward) stamps. The lower part of the vessel is not ornamented (Plate XVIII, items 3, 9, 15).

The ornamentation, reflecting great care in the preparation and application of the stamp, gives the impression of being unusually elegant, rich, and unique. It is so characteristic and consistent that even a small fragment is enough to identify a piece of pottery as belonging to this type.

As we have seen, the relative dating of sites of the Zelenaya Gorka type has been established quite reliably, on the basis of the stratigraphic data of Sortynya I and Zelenaya Gorka, as between the Bronze Age and the Ust-Poluy period. The ornamentation of the pottery contains some typological signs that indubitably point to its connection with the ornamentation of the vessels from Salekhard I, Sortynya II, and especially Suzgun II. Contrarily, the early Ust-Poluy pottery preserves some motifs of the Zelenaya Gorka vessels which had disappeared in the second (developed) Ust-Poluy period.[130]

Some analogies can be drawn between pottery of the Zelenaya Gorka type and that of the synchronous Ural and Cis-Ural sites of this culture. For example, the ridge below the rim of the vessel is also characteristic of the ornamentation of that portion of the Gorbunovo bog pottery that Eding pointed out as having degraded Andronovo motifs.[131] The pottery of the Galkino fortified hill site on the Kama is somewhat closer to the Zelenaya Gorka type, especially the vessels that have eastern Ural features,[132] which are not typical of this Early Ananino site. The presence of a collar, the confinement of the decoration to the upper part of the vessel, and the rounded bottom bring the rest of the Ananino pottery somewhat closer to the Zelenaya Gorka vessels. We find the forms closest to the Zelenaya Gorka type in the pottery of the Bolshaya Rechka culture on the upper Ob. As far as we can judge from Gryaznov's data, low vessels with a rounded bottom and decorated on the neck and shoulders are also characteristic of the Bolshaya Rechka pottery; the band of triangles with the apex pointing downward and made with various figured stamps is also typical. Even a quite cursory comparison will reveal the similarity.[133] Flat-bottomed vessels of the type shown in Gryaznov's paper are not foreign to the lower Ob either.[134]

The sites of the Zelenaya Gorka type have not been studied sufficiently to give a full picture of the forms of the material culture and the communal life of that period. The only thing one may say with confidence is that the main occupation, as earlier, was hunting and fishing. In the northernmost part of the territory, on the Yamal Peninsula, the hunt was not restricted to land animals such as the reindeer and the arctic fox, but included the walrus and the seal.

The discovery of a campsite of the Zelenaya Gorka type at such a remote point in the north as is Cape Tiutey-sale again raises the question of the time of settlement and assimilation of the Arctic coast. Unfortunately here, too, the insufficiency of materials stands out quite sharply. Since identical pottery was found at the dune campsite and at sites on the mainland, one may assume that the material culture of both types of sites was quite similar. This could hardly have been the case if this remote portion of the Arctic had been settled during an earlier epoch.

Using Kushevat and Sortynya I as examples, we discern that fortified hill sites had already appeared on the lower Ob during the Zelenaya Gorka period. Evidently there were some changes in the communal life during this epoch that increased the frequency of warlike encounters. It is quite possible that this was facilitated to some extent by the development of metallurgy and by the attendant rise in the level of technology and productive forces, greater division of labor, and specialization, with an ensuing increase in interclan and intertribal exchange that afforded the possibility of amassing fortunes. The size of the houses (up to 150 m²), still very capacious, indicates the existence of multifamily dwellings and the retention of the primitive social relations. Perhaps during this epoch the population of the lower Ob was establishing the patrilineal clan organization, a process that took place very slowly here and was not completed for many centuries.

Earlier, we have noted the great stability of the pottery ornamentation, which was characteristic of this epoch. This stability could not have existed over such an extensive territory and in such a complexity of patterns unless the elements of the ornamentation had meaning and were not simply geometric designs. Ancient, meaningful ornamentation is a quite familiar phenomenon. The Zelenaya Gorka ornamentation is of special interest in this respect because by drawing on ethnographic data we may, to some extent, penetrate the thought and content of the patterns. Among the numerous artistic designs of the Ob Ugrians (the Mansi and the Khanty), a pattern pressed on a birchbark vessel with special stamps of reindeer or elk antler was widely used. A great variety of figures was carved on the stamps. If they are compared with the stamped patterns on the pottery of the Zelenaya Gorka period and the later patterns dated to the 1st millennium A.D., there is readily seen not only a similarity between them but, in a number of cases, an identity showing obvious continuity. Each of the figures stamped on the birchbark has its own name, indicating that the patterns are replicas of the tracks of different animals and birds. The tracks impressed on the vessels apparently were substitutes for the animals, whose sculpted images appear on the earlier pottery of the Ob region.[135] This substitution on the principle of *pars pro toto* was quite natural for hunters who constantly observed the tracks of animals and birds on snow and in soft earth. It was natural to associate these tracks with the animals themselves. Even recently, in the minds of the Mansi and Khanty a track was associated magically with the being that left it. It was held that if one pushed a staff into a fresh animal track or pricked it with a sharp stick, the animal would feel the prick and take to its heels. A woman, especially during periods when she was considered unclean, was forbidden to step on the track of the totem animal, because by so doing she would bring misfortune not only on herself but on her entire clan. To depict the track of an animal—a bear, an elk, or a reindeer—meant to depict the animal itself, to create its real, living double. The Mansi and Khanty avoided doing this, except in special cases.[136]

At first glance it would seem that two [stamped] figures depart from the rule—the snake and the duck. However, a snake track and the schematic representation of a snake are the same, and a duck, like any aquatic bird, has to be depicted in its entirety, because it leaves no track in the water.

The stamped patterns on pottery and on birch bark are associated not only by an external, formal similarity, but by the principle of application, that is, impressing the track of an animal into wet clay or pliable birch bark in exactly the same way as a track is left in nature. Both were representations of tracks which were substitutes for the animals themselves— a totemic apotropaism.

It is also interesting to compare the ornamentation of somewhat earlier pottery, namely, the ribbon ornamentation of the Bronze Age, which is well known from the more southerly sites of Andronovo culture. Recent finds (Suzgun, Zabolotye) show that it spread into the taiga zone as well. The ribbon ornamentation, with a very minor change of form, has been retained by the Mansi and Khanty on their clothing and their birchbark vessels. From the names of the designs of the ribbon ornamentation, we can gather that basically they depicted animals, birds, and plants.[137] Despite the vastness of the territory concerned and the dialectal and linguistic differences, the forms and names of the designs are very stable. The ribbon ornamentation is exclusively a woman's art and is practically never used by men; its role is primarily decorative, but to a certain extent retains vestiges of another meaning.

In each locality there is, among all the designs, one that is most characteristic and frequently encountered. The clothing and vessels have specific places for this design and from it one can almost always recognize whence the object came and even from which clan. For example, we find the design of the wing of the glaucous gull on the Bolshaya Ob upstream from its junction with the Kazym, the heath hen on the Kazym, the pike jaw on the upper Lyapin, the frog on the middle Sosva, the sable on the Tapsuy, and so forth. If we consider further that the common totem of the main Tapsuy clans is the sable, that the clans that settled along the middle Sosva are the "frog people," whose progenitor was the "great frog woman," that the principal clan of the upper Lyapin River, the Soynakh, considers its ancestor to be the pike, that the Kazym Khanty trace their descent from the great Kazym woman, the heath hen, et cetera, the meaning of the ornamentation of the clothing and vessels as portrayals of the totem ancestor becomes quite evident. Thus, the ornamentations of the birchbark and the ceramic vessels during the Bronze Age and the Early Iron Age evidence their totem-apotropaic meaning.

For a better understanding of the historical and ethnogenic processes in the lower Ob region during the Early Iron Age and subsequent ages, we must dwell briefly on the regions to the south, on the middle Irtysh and upper Ob. From an analysis of the data in the preceding chapters, we may project the existence of a broad ethnic community in the Ural and western Siberian regions, formed by the migration of tribes from the Trans-Caspian as early as the Neolithic period. The Andronovo culture appeared in the Bronze Age and was based on late forms of Neolithic cultures, probably tribal variants of this ethnocultural community. Evidently it was associated with the Ural and eastern Kazakhstan centers of ancient metallurgy, which set the forested-steppe and steppe tribes far ahead of their neighbors. The development of animal husbandry gradually led to economic differentiation, so that by the end of the Bronze Age the tribes of the middle Irtysh region had separated into sedentary groups with the rudiments of agriculture (of the type at the settlements of Alekseyevka and Bolshoy Log) and into groups where cattle breeding predominated and gradually led to a nomadic life.*

These changes in the economic structure apparently led, among the most mobile segment of the population, the cattle breeders, to new contacts with other ethnic groups, resulting in noticeable influences on their material culture. This explains the appearance of entirely new pottery shapes and ornamentations. In the wake of these contacts there appeared two different types of pottery, one of which may be regarded as characteristic for the cattle breeders, the other for the forest-dwelling hunting and fishing population.

* [The two paragraphs that follow were adjusted by the author in August 1968. Editor, A.I.N.A.]

The first type, which has fairly numerous analogues among the so-called Sauromat and Sarmatian ceramics of the steppe country flanking both the east and west of the southern Urals, is represented by rather crude vessels with a rounded bottom and meager ornamentation consisting of bands of pits or pearl-shaped depressions and sometimes incised triangles on the shoulders of the vessels. The second type is represented by vessels of rather diverse shape; the flat-bottomed vessels mentioned earlier were continued in part, for example, at Bolshaya Rechka,[138] the most recent layer of Sortynya II, and also included the Zelenaya Gorka type of vessel with a plano-convex bottom. This second type had an incomparably richer ornamentation than the just-mentioned nomadic type and is represented by the pertinent portion of the Gorbunovo site,[139] Bolshaya Rechka, and in part the Ivanovskaya fortified hill site. Its characteristic features are the development of a collar, a fairly rich ornamentation of the band on the neck, and rows of triangles consisting of impressions of fine stamps along the shoulders. Vestiges of Andronovo motifs are evident in the patterns. However, these are not just the humble everyday patterns, but also splendid ritual ornamentation; these are the "degraded Andronovo motifs" of the Late Gorbunovo pottery noted by D. N. Eding, the Zelenaya Gorka ornamentation entered onto some of the Suzgun forms, and others.

The differences in the pottery of the cattle-breeding nomads and the settled population probably arose from the retention of matriarchal elements by the latter. The nomadic life hardly favored the development of clay vessels; woman's industry was secondary, the social interests were dictated by the requirements of nomadic cattle breeding and the incipient military organization. With the transition to a patrilineal affiliation and patrilocal marriage, the women of the nomads were excluded from caring for the dead. This was manifested in the change from the splendidly ornamented burial urns of the Andronovo period to the casual, small burial vessels of the nomads. Evidently when the transition was made to the patrilineal clan, the rich ribbon ornamentation disappeared forever from the pottery. Probably this design was used chiefly for ritual purposes, particularly for a burial urn. Thereafter the design was used only on clothing (on which it probably originated) and on the birchbark artifacts and was made exclusively by women. The ribbon ornamentation survives in this form on the lower Ob to this day.

The ethnic and linguistic association of steppe and forested-steppe tribes of Kazakhstan and western Siberia, which was quite stable through the Neolithic period and the Bronze Age, survived some changes in the Early Iron Age resulting from the indicated changes in the economy and material culture as well as assimilation by their neighbors. The development of nomadism with continuous movements of the population over vast expanses inevitably must have smoothed out differences in language and material culture and facilitated the formation of more intimate and, at the same time, more extensive territorial communities than could have existed earlier. This process probably intensified, especially as tribal military organizations appeared and developed, thanks to which neighboring groups, including groups of the sedentary population, were drawn to some extent into the developing associations. This led to the formation of nationalities based on a community of tribes that were basically quite similar linguistically.

In the period under consideration, these Uralic- and Ugric-speaking tribes of the Irtysh region must have bordered in the south on the Aryan- or Iranic-speaking populations, which evidently assimilated the southernmost tribes to various degrees. This process was weaker to the north, but even there it may be seen in the diffusion of objects characteristic of the material culture of the steppe people of the Sacian-Scythian period. As examples, we have the bronze sword, and later the short iron sword, the bronze cauldron, stirrup-shaped bits and those of the Mayemir type, pickaxes of the Tagar-Ananino form, and others, in the Irtysh region. The forms inherent to the Ob and Irtysh regions are evidence of the ethnic unity that existed there. These include the hexagonal partitioned celts, undoubtedly associated with banded Andronovo-Seyma forms and reflecting the shape of the polished stone implements of the first stages of the local Bronze Age, the pickaxes and poleaxes with an eagle-head tip and with an animal maw on the butt, and finally, the stone sculpture in the round, not found anywhere outside the realm of the Irtysh tribes. We shall enter into a more detailed examination of this community of early Ugrian, or Savyr, tribes in the subsequent sections on the history of the Ob-Irtysh region.

PART II

THE MATERIAL CULTURE AND ECONOMY OF UST-POLUY

W. MOSZYŃSKA

The Material Culture and Economy of Ust-Poluy

Ust-Poluy is one of the key sites for the history of the Ob region. Our goal is not only to reveal the character of the Ust-Poluy culture and its material basis, but also to distinguish the various components which made it up and to pose certain questions on the ethnogenesis of the Ob Ugrians.

Among the materials gathered at the fortified hill (Fig. 6), there were arrowheads of various types, harpoons, bone endpieces of composite bows, and various artifacts relating to land- and sea-mammal hunting. The geographical position of the Ust-Poluy settlement promoted the

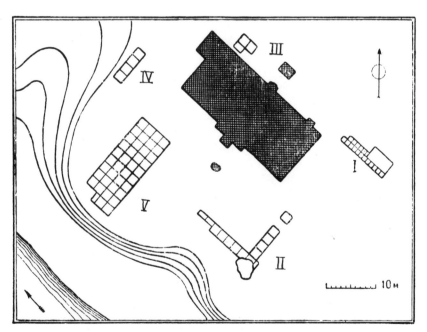

Fig. 6. Schematic plan of the Ust-Poluy excavations.
  I to V—sequence of excavations.

[Translated by Ethel and Stephen Dunn from *MIA*, no. 35, 1953, pp. 72–106. The first six paragraphs were omitted because they describe V. S. Adrianov's excavations of 1935 and 1936, which are described in Moszyńska's 1965 work, a translation of which is included in the present work (see pp. 251–325).]

development of hunting and fishing as the foundation of the whole economy. The Poluy River flows into the Ob at the Arctic Circle. At present, the landscape surrounding the site is typical wooded tundra, but as is evident from paleobotanical data, at the end of the 1st millennium B.C. and the beginning of the 1st millennium A.D., the forest extended considerably farther north, and pine forests grew around the mouth of the Poluy. Below Cape Angal, the Ob divides into numberless channels, which encourages the development of barrier fishing, and still farther down, it enters into the Ob Gulf—an extensive fresh-water bay of the Kara Sea, extending southward for many hundreds of kilometers. The Ob Gulf is rich in marine animals—seals and belugas which are attracted by the fish entering the Ob. According to I. I. Lepekhin, the beluga [white whale] in the past traveled as far as Berezov, that is, to the mouth of the Severnaya Sosva.

The abundant finds of fish bones and scales at Ust-Poluy and in other sites of the lower Ob relating to the same time and culture bear witness to the great importance of fishing in the economic life of the Ust-Poluy people. Of the fishing gear, only spears and hooks were preserved at Ust-Poluy. The Ust-Poluy spear points had three prongs, with the middle one having two barbs (Plate XIX, items 1–4). The construction of the fish spear may be compared with that of contemporary iron fish spears, which until recently were made of bone among the Khanty and Mansi. The prongs were inserted in a groove specially incised in the upper, broadened part of the shaft, which had the form of a spatula; they were attached with rosin and tied with a string.

Bone fishhooks are represented by single examples. The small number of fishhooks is to be explained to a certain degree by the fact that the wooden hooks, which as the ethnographic materials suggest, may have been more widespread than bone ones, have not been preserved; however, the principal point is that, at the time, just as now, fishing tackle with hooks was not widely used. From the ethnographic data we can deduce that the main form of fishing was by the barrier method, one of the early forms of collective fishing, using basket traps and wattle fish fences.[1] Nets were also used. This is shown by the presence in the material of spindles which could have been used in making nets and also by ethnographic and linguistic data. The nets of the Ob Ugrians, which were called by the Russian *Sibiryaks* [Siberians] *kaldan*, *syrp*, and *vazhan*, were net bags with two strings, an upper and a lower. Fishing was carried out by the following method:

Small poles are attached to both ends of the *syrp*, and serve to hold it down to the river bottom; a fine towline is tied to the upper drawstring, and the other end of it is attached to one of the poles. When sinking the net, the fishermen wind the middle of the towline once about the index finger, in order to know immediately when a fish gets into the *syrp*; usually the fish running into it pulls the net, and with it the towline. For each *syrp*, four boats with two men each are needed. Having noticed a school of grayling, all four boats station themselves in a row across the current, below the fish, the middle two which have the *syrp* moving forward together, and the other two at the same time

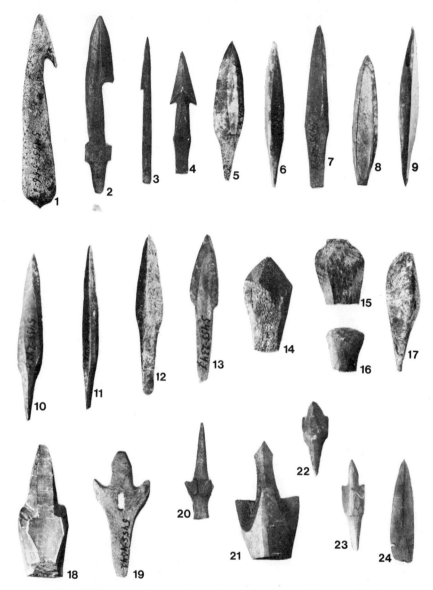

Plate XIX. 1 to 23–bone points and arrowheads; 24–shale arrowhead.

move with great speed above the net, beat on the water with sticks opposite the opening of the *syrp*, and the fishing is complete. Being occupied from childhood with this activity, the fishermen attain such experience and skill that, having seen the run of grayling from far off, they pursue each school until all are in part caught and in part driven off.[2]

Linguistic data compel us to assume that this type of net is derived from the basket traps. In Mansi, the *kaldan* type of net is called *pon*, while in Khanty the word *pon* signifies "creel," "snout," that is, a wattled trap.[3] We may suppose that the material used for making nets and traps was nettle fiber. In Mansi, nettle is called *ponal*, which is a derivative from the

79

word *pon*—net or wattle trap. In Hungarian, the verb *fonni* means "to spin," or "to plait."[4]

According to the data of Franz Belyavskiy, the Ob Ugrians, even at the beginning of the 19th century, made nets from nettle fibers and rose willow bark.[5]

Along with fishing, hunting was a basic occupation of the Ust-Poluy people. Of the tools for this activity, we know the bow and arrows. Bone arrowheads predominate in the materials; iron ones are completely lacking; bronze ones are known in small numbers, and are described in V. N. Chernetsov's work on the Bronze Age of the Ust-Poluy period.[6] For this reason, I will limit myself to the description of only the basic types of bone arrows (the variants conditioned by peculiarities of the raw material will not be cited):

1. Hafted points of flat-rhomboid cross section (Plate XIX, items 5–7), made as a rule from reindeer antler. The dimensions vary from 5.3 to 14.3 cm; the average length is 10–12 cm. In most cases they are made very crudely. Points of similar form, but made of iron, are known among the Siberian peoples and are universal. They are used chiefly in the hunting of animals and large birds (blackcock, geese).[7]

2. Hafted arrowheads of triangular shape in cross section (Plate XIX, items 8–13). These often are crudely polished fragments of the hollow bones of large animals, most frequently reindeer shinbones, which also determine their form. In size these points are not distinguished from those described above, and they are also the most widespread type in Ust-Poluy.

3. A large group is made up of the so-called blunt arrowheads (Plate XIX, items 14–17). The best known are those with sockets, although occasionally one does encounter hafted examples. The usual raw material was reindeer antler. Ethnographically, such points are well known. Called *tomar*, they are used chiefly for shooting birds and small animals, particularly sables and squirrels sitting in trees.[8] The *tomar* does not stick in the tree and is therefore not lost to the hunter.

4. Claw-shaped, socketed and hafted arrowheads chiefly of antler, usually five-pronged, with a perpendicular shank of half-moon shape (Plate XIX, items 18–20), which in a number of cases has not been preserved. A claw-shaped bronze arrowhead of excellent workmanship was discovered at Ust-Poluy. An iron point of the same type was found on the right bank of the Irtysh, near the city of Tobolsk, at the fortified hill site of Suzgun, which dates from the beginning of the 2nd millennium A.D. In the ethnography of the Ob Ugrians, claw-shaped points are just as well known as blunt ones. They are used chiefly in hunting waterfowl.

5. Less common are the hafted points, flat-rhomboid in cross section and subtriangular or sometimes elongated-triangular in form. In most cases, the angles are undercut and form sharp wedges. Usually these points are of antler and carefully worked. Their length is 10–13.5 cm and sometimes 6–7 cm (Plate XX, items 1–4).

6. Long-hafted arrowheads with elongated-rounded shanks and short points of flat-rhomboid cross section. Their total length is 14–15

cm, the length of the shaft being 8 cm, that of the haft 2.6 cm, and that of the point 3.9 cm. They are made of antler and carefully worked.

7. Socketed and hafted combat arrowheads with four-pronged points (Plate XIX, items 21–23). They are made chiefly of antler.

Single examples are representative of the following forms:

8. A bullet-shaped point of antler. Length 5.8 cm (Plate XX, item 6).

9. A three-sided point, with projecting socket, carefully made from walrus ivory. Its total length is 7.5 cm, and the length of the socket, 1.5 cm (Plate XX, item 5).

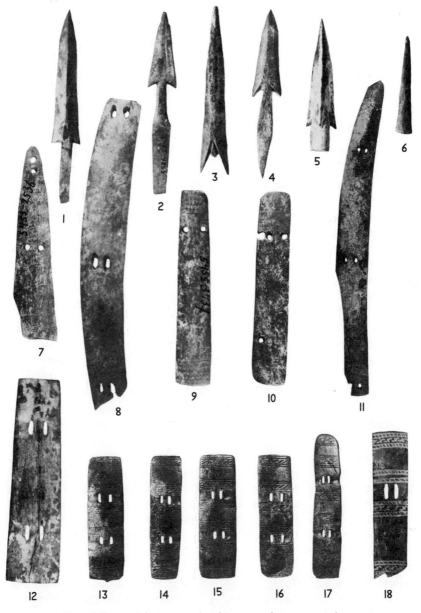

Plate XX. 1 to 6–bone arrowheads; 7 to 18–bone armor plates.

10. An arrowhead of flat-rhomboid cross section, with a projecting socket of round cross section. Total length, 8.8 cm.

11. An arrowhead of the same form as the preceding, but with an interior [recessed] socket; carefully made of antler. Total length 13.7 cm.

12. A peculiar point of elongated-triangular form. Unlike the others, it has neither socket nor haft, but only a rectangular notch in the base. Most probably the point was inserted into a corresponding notch or groove in the shaft, so that when the shaft was pulled out, the point would remain in the wound.

In Ust-Poluy, there is no clearly marked differentiation between hunting arrows and war arrows; however, the examples illustrated in Plate XX can probably be considered war arrows because of the care of their workmanship.

Analogues to the Ust-Poluy bone arrows are known from archaeological sites in Siberia and the Urals. The most frequently found are the more primitive and universal points, which we have assigned to the first and second groups. They occur widely in the Vyatka fortified hill sites and those of the Ananino culture (the Kotlov burial ground, the Konetsgorskoye settlement, et cetera).[9] They are found in great quantities at the fortified hill site of Potchevash, near Tobolsk (collections of Mameyev and Lytkin, kept in the Tobolsk Museum). Blunt arrowheads are also known from the Vyatka fortified hill site, and what is especially interesting, we know of a small arrow from the same place having neither haft nor socket.

The types of points assigned by us to the fifth group are found in the barrows of western Siberia, dating from various periods, beginning with the Bronze Age.[10] The presence of such points in the burial assemblage provides a basis for assigning them to the category of war arrows. S. K. Patkanov, in his work *Tip ostyatskogo bogatyra* [The nature of the Ostyak warrior], writes that for military purposes, bone and iron arrowheads of three-sided form (possibly like that illustrated in Plate XX, item 5) and of larger dimensions than hunting arrows were used. A war arrow with this kind of point was called *khakhray n'ot pete uryy n'ot*, that is, "an arrow edged by the likeness of the edges of a click beetle's beak."[11]

At Ust-Poluy and other sites deriving from the same period and culture, we usually find hafted arrowheads of shale, of willow-leaf shape, and usually of very small dimensions (Plate XIX, item 24).

About the construction of the Ust-Poluy bows we know very little, since nothing has been preserved except objects which can probably be considered as endpieces from bows. Objects of this type in our materials are in two forms. The first is represented by endpieces made from plates of antler; the blade is flat and wedge-shaped, and the upper end is sharpened. Grooves which may have served for the attachment of the bowstring are found on both sides of the upper part (Plate XXI, items 3–9). The second form is represented by endpieces consisting of two plates, the inner surfaces of which are flat, and the outer convex. The upper parts of the plates are of triangular form. In assembling them, an opening was made in the upper end, where the bowstring was attached.

Apparently such plates [or braces] covered the body of the bow. By analogy with contemporary models, we may assume that they were attached with the aid of rosin and birch bark (Plate XXI, items 1, 2). The owner's mark or, more rarely, a band of ornamentation is often scratched on the exterior surface of the brace.

Lacking corresponding material from burial grounds, we find it difficult to say whether these plates belonged to bows of different types or were attached to different ends of the bow. Bone endpieces of such forms are little known in archaeology. We were unable to collect any analogues for the first type. A bone endpiece consisting of two halves is close to the

Plate XXI. Endpieces of composite bows.

second; it was preserved in one of the Sargatskoye barrows, excavated in 1927 by V. P. Levasheva.

In the Ust-Poluy materials there is a group of objects constituting parts of reindeer bridles (Plate XXII). Objects similar to them are known from Middendorf's description of Tungus bridles for saddle reindeer.[12] Bone forehead pieces similar to those of Ust-Poluy but of larger dimensions are used in the harness trappings of the Reindeer Chukchi.[13] But there is no basis for assuming the existence of saddle-reindeer breeding at Ust-Poluy, since apart from a few finds of bridle parts, we have no remains of reindeer harnesses or saddles. The presence of highly developed dog

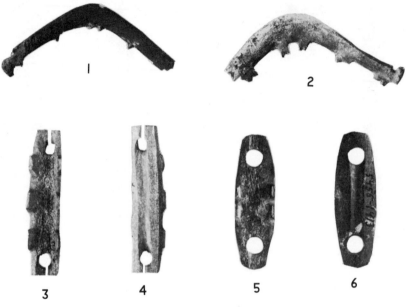

Plate XXII. Parts of reindeer bridles.

breeding at Ust-Poluy, which will be introduced later, also rules out the possibility of the existence of harness-reindeer breeding, as Shrenk [Schrenk] showed in his time, and as Zolotarev and Levin noted later in their paper on the question of the origin of reindeer breeding.[14]

We know of a way, among the Siberian peoples, of hunting wild reindeer with the aid of a decoy reindeer, which is kept at all times on a leash by the hunter. The following is a description of hunting with a decoy reindeer among the Tungus: "The decoy, a male or a female, should pass by its coloring for a wild reindeer. When the hunter notices a herd of wild reindeer, he releases the decoy to them against the wind. The decoy is at all times held by the hunter on a leash and the hunter crawls after it. The hunter directs the decoy with the aid of a thong, making it stop, lie down, and go in this or that direction. A good hunter with a skillfully trained decoy can kill many reindeer out of a herd before the other wild reindeer discover him. In these cases, a bow rather than a gun is usually used in hunting."[15] The Yukagirs and Evens also use this means of hunting with a decoy.

One can hardly doubt that the Ust-Poluy bridles were used for decoy reindeer. Their small size relative to Chukchi ones favor this view; the necessity to make the bridles as unobtrusive as possible resulted in the small size. Also, let us note the dissimilarity of the Ust-Poluy bridles to those of the Samoyed type, which appeared here later and are now universally distributed to the west of the Taymyr Peninsula. The wild reindeer was, apparently, the main object of the hunt. This is clear from the fact that it was reindeer antlers and bones which were the chief raw materials for the artifacts of the Ust-Poluy people. Among the osseous finds in the hearth stratum of the Salekhard semisubterranean houses, reindeer bones occupy the first place. We are of the opinion that hunting was carried out by means of decoy reindeer and also by spearing at river crossings in the autumn.

The wild reindeer does not fear expanses of water and easily swims across quite wide rivers. However, in the water it is not hard to overtake it in a light boat—the more so when, in the autumn, hundreds of thousands of reindeer come to the crossing at a definite time, and always at the same places. As Middendorf wrote, "The regularity which the animals observe in their 'crossings' is astonishing. All the skill of the hunter and all the gladness and sorrow of entire tribes and peoples of the Far North is based on exact knowledge of the exact times and locations for these crossings, at which they wait for the wandering animals in order to lay up provisions for the whole winter. He who wishes to clearly imagine to himself the scramble at this almost unbelievable slaughter should read the lively description in Vrangel's [Wrangel's] *Journey*. In just the same way and at precisely the same place as in the time of Vrangel and his companion Matyushkin, the reindeer crossed even in the past century."[16] It is difficult to conceive today the number of wild reindeer that accumulated at the river crossings. Suffice it to recall the statement of Pallas to the effect that "across the Anadyr, the herd of migrating reindeer for three days in a row so crowded each other that [even] while being killed they could not separate."[17]

The basic weapons at the spearing were the knife and a light spear, with a thin narrow blade, called in Russian *pokolyuga*. Thus armed, the hunter penetrated into the very midst of the swimming animals, and every moment risking being capsized and drowned, killed as many of the beasts as his strength would permit. The long (up to 25 cm) thin bone points from Ust-Poluy are reminiscent of such spears. In the winter, as was stated above, hunting of wild reindeer could be carried out by stealth, with the aid of a decoy reindeer.

Insofar as the finds of animal bones and the character of arrowheads permit us to judge, the Ust-Poluy people also hunted arctic foxes and small animals living in the trees—squirrels and sables—and also waterfowl, chiefly ducks and geese.

All in all, the picture was probably rather close to the descriptions of Franz Belyavskiy.

Fishing and the hunting of beasts, and in part the hunting of birds, constitute their only [economic] activity, and for this reason, the seasons of the year are utilized by them in accordance with these occupations. When the rivers open up, the Ostyaks leave their winter yurts and sail in boats with their families on the rivers, bays and channels, where, as we said above, they set up *balagans* and spend the summer, occupying themselves with fishing and at times also by hunting fowl. The fish they simply dry in the sun, leaving a part of it as provisions for the winter, and selling or bartering the rest. In the autumn, in October, they return with their catch to the winter yurt, and in the same month, or at the beginning of November, at the time of the small snow, all the Ostyaks in general (some even bring their families) set out in sleds to the forest to hunt animals, such as hares, foxes, otters, and occupy themselves with this until the deep snow, and then hunt sables and squirrels. In January, they go again to the yurts, and without delay, set forth in crowds after bear (to previously designated places), which they shoot with rifle bullets very skillfully; many also have tame dogs, with whose aid they kill these beasts with spears. Against bears, the Ostyaks use the same means as the peasants in the Russian *guberniyas*, who occupy themselves with this trade. In March, the men go out alone after reindeer, which they frequently take alive, but most often kill with arrows and also with rifle bullets. At the beginning of the thaw, they ride back to the yurts, bringing with them the reindeer meat, and then calmly await the opening of the rivers.[18]

The hunting of sea mammals played an important role in the economic life of the Ust-Poluy people. Some tools have come down to us, including large harpoons, various parts of which are found in the Ust-Poluy materials.

The Ust-Poluy harpoon points of various forms are all made of antler and are the hafted type:

1. Single-barbed harpoon; length 23.8 cm. In some cases, the blade was made of harder material and was inserted separately (Plate XXIII, item 8).

2. Harpoons of flat-rhomboid cross section with two symmetrical barbs, 11.5–12 cm in length (Plate XXIII, items 1, 2). Harpoon arrows of the same shape, 5.5–5.7 cm in length, are also known (Plate XXIII, items 3, 5, 6, 7).

3. Harpoon with two asymmetrical barbs; length 13.2 cm (Plate XXIII, item 4).

As far as we can judge from available materials, the Ust-Poluy harpoon had the following form: a [foreshaft] socket, usually made as one piece, was seated on the upper part of the [wooden] shaft (Plate XXIII, items 9, 13). The small socket in which the point [of the haft] was inserted was in the distal end of it. Compound foreshafts are also known: they are made of two tubular rings, which slide one inside the other, possibly with the aim of providing a smooth transition from the thick shaft to the thin point (Plate XXIII, item 10). To the lower end of the shaft was fastened a peg [harpoon ice pick] (Plate XXIII, item 16), the point of which served for digging into the ice while securing the harpooned animal. Like the points, the harpoon foreshafts and pegs were made of antler.

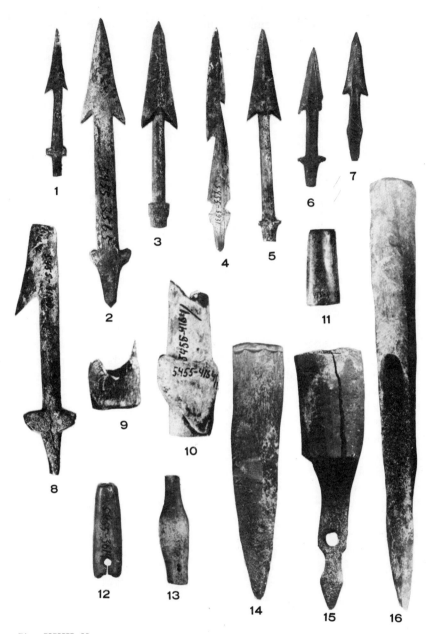

Plate XXIII. Harpoons.
    1, 2–of flat-rhomboid cross section and two barbs; 3, 5, 6, 7–harpoon arrows; 4–with two asymmetrical barbs; 8–single-barbed; 9, 13–foreshaft sockets; 10 to 12, 15– transitional (compound) foreshafts; 14, 16–harpoon ice picks.

Harpoon points and harpoon arrows of similar forms are widely disseminated. They occur in sites of the Ananino culture (for example, in the Konetsgorskoye settlement on the Kama), at Cape Potchevash near Tobolsk, and at other places. Harpoon points similar to those of Ust-Poluy were discovered by A. V. Schmidt in the burial ground of Oleniy ostrov.[19] Contemporary iron points for harpoon heads used among the

Ob Ugrians are not distinguishable in any way from some of the forms of the Ust-Poluy harpoons.[20]

The basic object of marine hunting was, in all probability, the beluga. According to Eyriye [Eyriés], they were hunted on the Ob as late as the beginning of the 19th century. "They . . . invariably appear after the fish about the middle of June, occupying at that time the entire width of the river for a length of five versts. They go up to Kunevatsk, at a distance of 260 versts from the sea. Even sturgeon fear their pursuit, and it is not surprising, for these monsters are from three to four *sazhens* in length. The frightened fish increase their speed, and thereby fall more easily into the nets set out. The [white] dolphins go back to the sea in September. . . . Some Ostyaks who make harness straps out of the skin of these monsters, know how to kill them both in the sea and in fresh water."[21]

It is possible that hunting for walrus also played a certain role. Walrus ivory is known in Ust-Poluy as raw material for making artifacts. Medieval writers tell us that the Ugrians paid tribute in walrus tusks. Sebastian Münster gives information to the effect that the Ugrians engaged in catching walrus and seals in the Ob Gulf.[22] Vasiliy Zuyev furnishes some data on the means of catching walrus. "Although the walrus are not more than three hand *sazhens* [spans], yet, according to the tales of the hunters, they are the greatest of all sea beasts. In their upper jaws they have two teeth about eight inches long, with the aid of which they crawl onto the shore or onto the ice, where, sleeping or resting, they are felled by spears with small barbs at the end. . . . When they find a sleeping [walrus], the hunters crawl up with spears tied to a long thong which is fastened to a stump or peg driven into the earth; and when the point penetrates the walrus, he frightened, goes into the water, and, having come to a certain depth, loses his strength and is pulled out onto the shore again and killed."[23]

The commentator on Zuyev notes that this method of hunting walrus has not been preserved to the present time, but its existence in the past is apparently connected with the developed marine hunting of the Arctic aboriginal tribes, afterwards assimilated by the Nentsy, who adopted some of their hunting methods.[24] The existence, in antiquity, of a maritime culture based on marine hunting on the shores of Yamal Peninsula and the Ob Gulf is attested by archaeological and folkloristic data.[25]

The presence of sled dogs at Ust-Poluy is confirmed by archaeological data. First, there is the find of a sculptured representation of a dog in harness, which forms a butt ornamentation of the handle of a knife (Plate XXIV, item 3). The dog is represented with a chest band, apparently similar in construction to those which Montandon-Levin assigns to the dorsal type.[26]

In the Ust-Poluy materials there is a group of objects relating to dog harnesses (Plate XXIV):

1. Guide buckles, that is, small rods with holes in the center for attaching straps. The buckles were made chiefly of antler (Plate XXIV, items 11–14). Their dimensions are rather considerable (10–16 cm), smaller ones being rarely found. As far as we can judge from the ethnographic

data, they served for fastening together separate parts of the harness—for example, attaching the lead rein.

2. Swivels (Plate XXIV, items 2, 4–10), which keep the straps, particularly the lead rein, from becoming entangled. In most cases they are made of antler. The Ust-Poluy swivels are identical to those used by the present-day Caribou Eskimos, which according to Birket-Smith, serve to attach the traces to the lead rein when the team is stopped.[27]

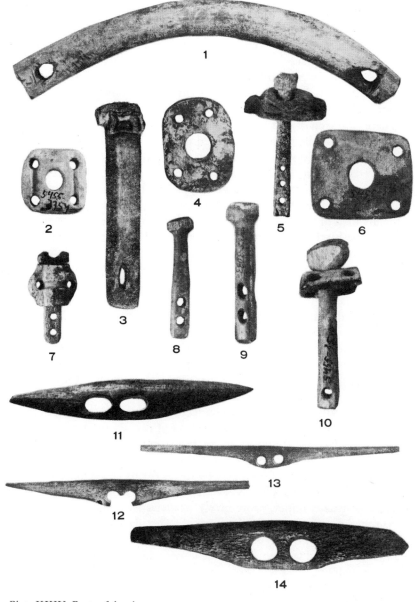

Plate XXIV. Parts of dog harness.
  1–tie rod; 2, 4 to 10–swivels; 3–representation of a dog in harness (from a knife handle); 11 to 14–antler guide buckles.

3. A piece of antler with holes at the ends (Plate XXIV, item 1). Similar antler or wooden artifacts are widely known over the entire north and are used for tying up dogs. They take the place of the chain and keep the dog from gnawing through the strap, which he is thus unable to reach.

4. Fids (marlinspikes) made from metacarpal bones. Such fids are used by present-day peoples of the North for loosening knots.

The existence of dog breeding in Ust-Poluy is confirmed by indications of dog sacrifice. During the excavations of Ust-Poluy by V. S. Adrianov in 1935, a large pile of bones, chiefly dog bones, was found in one of the squares of the excavated section, at a depth of 15–17 cm. The skulls had been put in one place.

Fifteen skulls were found in an area of 80 cm² of one of the rectangles of the excavation, in a stratum up to 20 cm thick. In none was the cranium intact, and the lower jaws lay separately. A scapula had been inserted into the temporal arch of one of the skulls. In the same place there was found a bone knife handle with a sculptured image of a dog harness.[28]

Information on dog sacrifice among the population of the lower Ob is preserved in Khanty folklore. In one of the heroic tales recorded by S. K. Patkanov on the Konda River, we read, "The head of a Samoyed came out of the lower reaches of a river and said: . . . As far as I am concerned, let many men of the Samoyed country bring here the bowls sacrificed to me and the birch vessels sacrificed to me; let there be brought here as blood sacrifices the dogs with tails, the furry dogs."[29]

Among the Nentsy clans, sacrificing of the dog is known only to the Yaptik clan, living on the northeastern shore of the Yamal Peninsula. There is reason to suppose that it is precisely in this clan that many features of the ancient aboriginal population of the lower Ob and the seashore have been preserved.[30]

In the religious worship of the Yukagirs, the aboriginal population of northern Siberia, the dog played a prominent role. The Nganasans had a special dog god (*baka-nguo*), and at the tribal festival of the "Clean Tent," the poles of this tent were smeared with the blood of a sacrificed dog.[31]

A considerable group of tools connected with the processing of skins and nettle fiber and also with the spinning of thread, the sewing of garments, pottery, and the working of bone and wood was gathered at Ust-Poluy.

The numerous finds of scrapers of various forms were connected with the processing of skins (Plate XXV). The material from which they were made was usually antler, more rarely whalebone. Sometimes a simple, untrimmed piece of antler in the form of a spatula was used as a scraper (Plate XXV, item 6). Usually the scrapers have straight, almost flat, handles and round working ends, the lower edges of which are serrated. On most scrapers, these serrations are retained only on the lateral surfaces, while the central part of the blade is polished smooth as the result of long use. The handles of the scrapers are fairly long, 8–9 cm on the average, with an overall length of the tool from 14.5 to 15.5 cm. Only in a few cases are larger or smaller ones found. The handles of the scrapers are

Plate XXV. Bone scrapers for the working of hides.
   1, 4–sicklelike scrapers; 2, 3, 8 to 10–spatulalike scrapers; 5, 7–T-shaped scrapers;
   6–bone serving as scraper.

often decorated with incised linear ornamentation (Plate XXV, item 10). On the spatula, in a number of cases, one can see the brand of its owner. The brands are of great interest, since analysis of them gives us the possibility of forming some idea as to the social structure of the Ust-Poluy people.

More rarely found are the small T-shaped scrapers of antler (Plate XXV, items 5, 7). Their blades are asymmetrical and the handles rather long and flat. The total length of the tool is 7–8 cm, and the length of the handle 5.5–6 cm; the working edge is thin and carefully sharpened. Such scrapers were used for working skins with a thin flesh side (such as squirrel or hare skins).

Unusual large tools of sicklelike form (Plate XXV, items 1, 4) were also used for working skins. As far as the ethnographic parallels permit us to judge, they were used for the initial processing of skins with a thick flesh side and of certain parts of reindeer hide—for example, that covering the shin.

In Ust-Poluy, we also often find scrapers made from split hollow bones. The majority of the Ust-Poluy scrapers have analogues in the ethnography of the peoples of the North. Until very recent times, scrapers made of antler were found among the Ostyaks (like that illustrated in Plate XXV, item 2); according to Sirelius, they were used by the Vasyugan Khanty.[32] Scrapers with rounded blades, now made of iron rather than bones, are found everywhere in the Ob area.[33]

No less plentiful are the finds of tools and objects connected with the manufacture of clothing. The most common of these are awls (Plate XXVI, items 5, 6, 7, 8). This small, widely distributed tool was made from fragments of hollow bones, or considerably more often, from other bone artifacts for some reason no longer used for their original purpose. We know of awls made over from endpieces of bows, from arrowheads, and the like. Sometimes metacarpal bones and the os penis of certain animals were used for making awls.

In Plate XXVI, item 4 depicts the handle of an awl, probably an iron one, the handle being made of antler; an item close to it in form is known from Cape Potchevash.[34]

Unfortunately, needles have not survived in Ust-Poluy, and there are only a few needle cases. These cases were made from the bones of birds, usually swans, and were whittled to a square cross section. The surface was very carefully polished, and in most cases decorated. The needle cases from the burial ground on Oleniy ostrov represent rather close analogues.[35] The needle case from the Glyadenovo ossuary is identical to those of Ust-Poluy, both in form and in decoration.[36]

Ethnographic data of the peoples of northern Siberia support the universal distribution of needle cases made from the [long] bones of birds, particularly swans. Unlike the needle cases of Ust-Poluy, the present-day ones are usually of round cross section.

Two small groups of finds are connected with the processing of nettle fibers. The first consists of small bones of reindeer and elk, the second of spindles.

Similar small bones of reindeer and elk were used by the Ostyaks living on the Irtysh, Konda, and Salym rivers, and also in the region of Surgut, for the initial processing of nettles. V. N. Pignatti, in reporting this, describes the process of working the fiber which he observed on the Konda River as follows:

Having taken a stalk of nettle in the left hand, and the bone in the right, [they] pierce the stalk near the root with the bone, the end of which lies on the index finger, trying meanwhile to make the two halves of the stalk approximately equal; moving the bone and the stalk, [they] saw the latter into two parts, the upper part being moved between the bone beneath and the thumb above. Then, leaving the stalk in the left hand, they break both halves of the stalk several times along the whole length, leaving about one-quarter *arshin* between the blades. They do this in order that the outer part of the stalk, the shive, and the inner part, the pith, be separated from the bast fiber, and this in a certain degree replaces the process of beating which is used in processing flax and hemp. The separated shive is removed with the same bone, beginning with the top of the stalk.[37]

Plate XXVI. Women's tools.
　1–mallet for breaking up pottery clay; 2, 3–spindle whorls; 4–bone handle for a metal awl; 5 to 8–punches.

Such bones are encountered very frequently among archaeological finds, particularly in Siberia. For example, they are present in great quantities in the materials from the fortified hill site of Potchevash (Cape Chuvashskiy), near Tobolsk.

The term *pon-fon*, common to Finno-Ugric languages with the basic meaning of "plaiting" or "basket type of fish trap" was mentioned earlier [p. 80]. This root appears also in the meaning of "to braid," "to twist," "to spin": Hungarian (*kendert fon; lent fon*)—"to spin hemp or flax"; Finnish—"to mend," "to braid"; Mordva—"to reel," "to coil."[38] In the Mansi language we find *pon*, "a fishing net," and *ponal* (*pon-al*, a denominative), "nettle." These words no doubt stem from the same root; hence it seems obvious that nettle was one of the earliest materials for the making of thread and twine.

The Ust-Poluy spindles (Plate XXVI, items 2, 3) are of small dimensions and flat. They were made of antler. No ornamented ones were found.

There is only one object relating to pottery, and that is a tool for breaking and mixing potter's clay, made of antler (Plate XXVI, item 1). Its working edge is highly polished. A tool of similar form, made from wood, is known from Yakut ethnography and [its use] was described as follows by V. I. Podgorbunskiy: "In making pots, good clay is usually mixed with chamotte, using one-third or one-half of the latter. Before this the dry clay is crushed into small pieces with a stone in a birch vessel or a wooden trough. To it is added the necessary quantity of chamotte, and it is mixed with a small wooden spade, first in dry form. . . . In order to make the mixture uniform, they beat it with a wooden mallet, *chokhochchu*, made from a segment of the trunk of a [small] birch tree, with a branch sticking out of it, serving as a handle."[39] The bone mallet from Ust-Poluy, apparently, fulfilled the same function.

The processing of skins and nettle fiber, the preparation of clothing and thread, as well as pottery making, were all in the woman's sphere. From ethnographic data we assume that the working of bone and wood was the work of men. The same was also true of metallurgy.[40] At Ust-Poluy, the tools of this type described in the following three paragraphs were preserved.

Antler wedges (Plate XXVII, items 1–4) of small dimensions (7–10 cm in length, on the average) were found. As a rule the working edge is greatly worn. Similar wedges are known from the ethnography of the Ob Ugrians. Sirelius writes that they are made of spruce or antler and are used for splitting trunks into planks or for dividing straight-trunked pine trees into so-called *zhalye* (lathing), which is used in huge quantities for building [fish] barriers and traps.[41] We propose that the Ust-Poluy wedges were also used for this purpose.

The finds at Ust-Poluy of iron knives (Plate XXVII, items 5, 6) and of a very large quantity of handles for them, usually bone ones, gives us reason to suppose that the iron knife was the basic instrument. This supposition is confirmed by the fact that aside from iron knives, only one fragment of a bronze knife has been discovered at Ust-Poluy. One knife made entirely of iron also has been found. It has a slender handle, ending in a ring.

Plate XXVII. Men's tools.

    1 to 4–antler wedges for splitting wood; 5, 6–iron knives with bone handles.

The knives are heavily corroded, and therefore it is difficult to judge the original shape of the blade and the means by which they were sharpened. The blade was inserted into a slender handle, usually fashioned from bone or antler, and of oval cross section. Its greatest diameter, on the average, is 1.5–2 cm. Small, round perforations were often drilled in the proximate end of the handle; the purpose of these is not entirely clear, since the supposition that they might have served to hang the knife on a belt is not confirmed by ethnographic data.[42] The handles of knives are usually very carefully worked, and often richly ornamented. Among the handles, two are surmounted by sculptured ornaments. One of these has been mentioned earlier—a handle with the sculptured image of a harnessed dog. Another one is decorated with the head of an eagle. These sculptures are distinguished by their realistic rendering.

The Ust-Poluy collections include a large group of household objects. Among them we find all kinds of knives, spoons, hooks for suspending objects, and so on.

Aside from iron knives, mentioned earlier, bone ones are also known. These knives, or more precisely, knifelike tools, made in most cases from shoulder blades of reindeer, make up a rather large group of finds (Plate XXVIII, items 1, 11, 12). Even today, such knives are used by the Ob Ugrians for cleaning fish. Several similar tools, made from antler and with well-finished and sharpened edges, were encountered. From their massiveness, it may be supposed that they were used for more varied purposes than the former.

Bone spoons of various forms and types are no less plentifully represented in the materials. Spoons made from the breastbones of large water birds may be assigned to the first group, which includes the largest number of finds.

The processing of the breast bones was limited to cutting off of the carina, levelling of the edge, and drilling of a hole through the base of the bone (Plate XXIX, item 1). Nenets folklore recalls such spoons to this day. In 1946, in the region of Salekhard, we recorded a folktale about Porne-ne. The principal character of the tale, half woman, half she-bear, uses "the breast bone of a swan" for a spoon.[43]

It is likely that such bones, originally used in place of spoons, served as a prototype for the more highly developed forms of spoons which began to be made, chiefly from antler but also from mammoth tusks and bones of marine animals. The handle of the spoon, which is sometimes somewhat bent (Plate XXIX, item 4), often has a round perforation at the upper end (Plate XXX, item 1) and is surmounted by sculpture, usually of some bird or beast (Plate XXX, items 2–6).

The second type includes spoons which are quite flat—essentially spatulas rather than spoons (Plate XXX, items 1, 4). The deeper spoons of the same form are a kind of variant of this type. The form and character of the workmanship of the handle is not at all distinguished from that described above. Besides sculptured decorations, we also find incised ornamentation, which will be treated in more detail below.

Plate XXVIII. 1, 11, 12–bone knives for scaling fish; 2, 3, 5, 6–antler back-scratchers; 4, 8–bone hooks; 7–bone belt buckle; 9, 10–stone pestles.

N. L. Gondatti relates interesting information on spatula-shaped spoo..s. In describing the burial ritual among the Mansi, he notes that they put wooden spatulas with the dead person in the grave. These take the place of spoons. In this connection is the especially interesting fact that similar spatulas are also used as sacrificial offerings, since according to Mansi belief, the gods eat food with spatulas, and not with spoons.

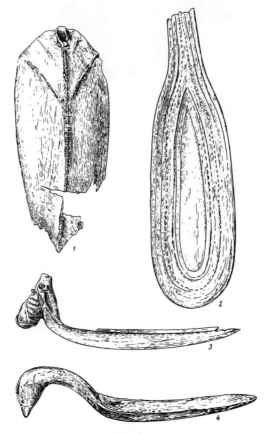

Plate XXIX. Bone spoons.

Thus, near each idol in a sacred depository or sacrificial place one might encounter many such spatulas brought to the gods with food.[44]

Consequently, ethnographic data lead us to consider the spatula-shaped spoon as an extremely archaic one, and further, that spatulas, together with the spoon-shaped breast bones of birds, represent the most archaic form of and are the prototype of all Ust-Poluy spoons.

Deep spoons with short handles, similar to the Ust-Poluy ones in shape, have been found at the fortified hill site of Sorochya Gora.[45] These are the only close analogues, unless we count the spoons from the Pod-cherem cache, which are, however, considerably different.[46]

At the present time, the Ob Ugrians use wooden spoons which re-semble those of Ust-Poluy chiefly in the decoration of the upper part of the handle by sculpture in the round. The use of spoons among the

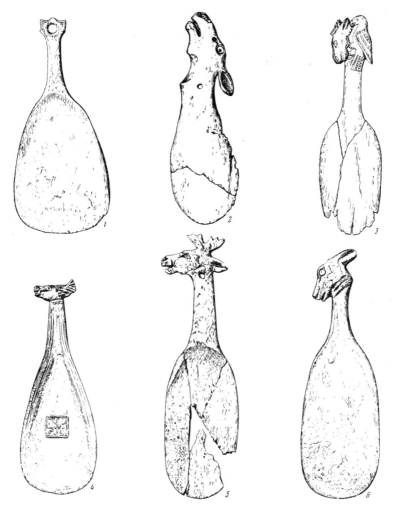

Plate XXX. Bone spoons and spatulas.
1, 4–spatulas; 2, 3, 5, 6–spoons.

Voguls and Ostyaks was limited, since they drank meat and fish broth from cups and used spoons only for thick porridge seasoned with berries or roots. It may be projected that the Ust-Poluy people used spoons in the same ways.

Bone hooks found at Ust-Poluy are illustrated in Plate XXVIII, items 4 and 8. Metal hooks, similar in shape, are well known among all peoples of northern Siberia. They serve to hang up preserved meat, birchbark vessels in which produce or articles are kept, and kettles over the fire. The Ust-Poluy hooks show no traces of soot, and it is probable that they served for suspending prepared articles of food.

Stone pestles of rather large dimensions are included among the household equipment (Plate XXVIII, items 9, 10). They are made of micaceous slate. The working surface is usually smooth and somewhat polished. The brittleness of the material from which they are made and the absence of signs of wear on the working surface give reason to suppose that the pestles were used for crushing some sort of soft substance like roots or berries.[47]

Besides the finds already listed, we believe that another category of artifacts, whose purpose at first glance seems unclear, belongs in the category of household equipment. These are small objects made of antler, with a socket for fastening onto a handle. Their working surfaces are often serrated (Plate XXVIII, items 2, 3, 5, 6). These objects recall hoes, and they gave V. S. Adrianov a basis for considering them votive hoes, which showed that the ancestors of the Ust-Poluy people had at one time practiced agriculture.[48] Such an explanation is not confirmed either by the shape of the objects or by archaeological data known to us from the Ob area and from western Siberia in general.

In the daily life of the peoples of the North, there is an object which very much recalls these "hoes"—the back-scratcher. It is known among both the Nentsy and the Nganasans as well as among the peoples of northeastern Asia, the Chukchis and Eskimos. In shape, the Eskimo back-scratchers are closest to those of Ust-Poluy.[49]

Trimmings for clothing and personal adornment are represented by buckles and combs.

Buckles were collected in considerable numbers. They were chiefly made from antler, more rarely from mammoth ivory. In most cases, the buckles are rectangular, with a double hook at one end and an opening for attachment of the belt at the other. Sometimes the hook is sculptured; for example, in the shape of two bird heads (Plate XXVIII, item 7). The buckles are often decorated. The center of the plate is usually free from ornament. Sometimes the owner's mark is scratched on it. Small rectangular clasps were found in smaller numbers—a few examples in all. They are 4.5–5.5 cm long and 2–2.5 cm wide. They are made of antler, and often decorated. Such small clasps probably served to decorate the belt or to regulate its length.

Probably the most impressive objects found at Ust-Poluy are the combs, most of which constitute true works of art. Their basic material is antler. Almost all the Ust-Poluy combs belong to one type—high, with long, wide, relatively sparse teeth. Only in a few cases is the upper part of the comb not decorated at all, or provided only with a round hole (Plate XXXI, items 2–4). It is usually ornamented or sculptured; sometimes the decoration covers the teeth as well. Birds and animals are the favorite motif (Plate XXXI, items 1, 5, 8), and it is only on combs that we find animals depicted in groups, which is unknown on other objects.

Two of the combs are distinctive in a somewhat different manner. One has rather different proportions from the others: it is shorter and wider. Its handle is decorated with three nail-like projections (Plate XXXI, item 7). The second, which does not differ in form from the others, is decorated with a rather complex composition, consisting of two highly elongated stylized heads of birds or fantastic animals (Plate XXXI, item 6). In treatment, these images are quite different from those found in the Ust-Poluy material. The excessively elongated proportions of the images, which recall the stylized figures of beasts well known from finds in the Urals (Podcherem, for example) and occasionally encountered in the Ob region (the finds on Cape Shaytan, near Berezov), place this comb among the latest in the entire group, and perhaps indicate that it is not of local but of Uralian origin. The same is indicated by brand marks, which are found on only two combs. The comb with the stylized heads of birds

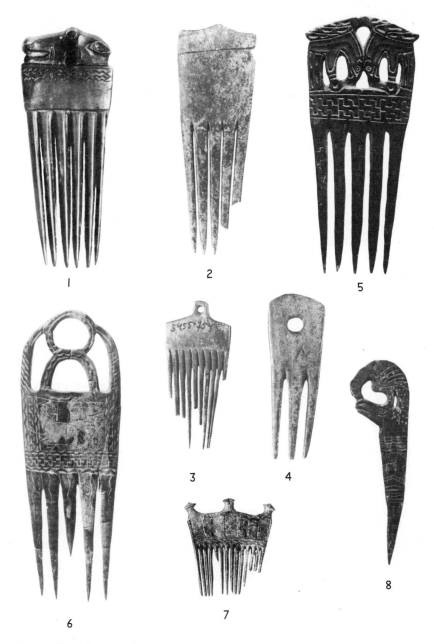

Plate XXXI. Bone combs.

    1, 5, 8—ornamented with representations of birds and mammals; 2 to 4—without ornamentation; 5—with ornamented teeth; 6—with stylized head of bird or animal; 7—with nail-like projections.

or animals has three different brand marks; two of them are similar to present-day Mansi marks belonging to the Bakhtiarov and Kurikov clans,[50] the first of which derives from the western slope of the Urals.

High combs for pinning the hair, with sculptured handles, are known in several territories distant from each other. The comb from the fortified hill site of Buy is close to the one from Ust-Poluy.[51] One may see a distant analogy to some forms of the Ust-Poluy combs in the well-known Solokha comb.[52] Finally, high combs close to the ones from Ust-Poluy in form, but constituting hair combs rather than pinning combs, are known from Eskimo archaeological materials.[53]

In analyzing the hunting equipment, we have concluded that, together with hunting and all-purpose arrows, there also existed in Ust-Poluy special war arrows. The more specialized weapons were hatchets and cleavers and also daggers and short swords, known in the Ust-Poluy culture from the finds described by V. N. Chernetsov.[54]

In the presence of offensive armor, it is natural to find the development of defensive armor, represented here by numerous parts of bone armor plate. These include the following:

1. Platelets (of which suits of armor were basically made up) of elongated-rectangular shape, with four holes in each plate, located in pairs (Plate XX, items 9, 10, 12–18). The platelets were tied together by thongs threaded through the holes, as in suits of armor plate widespread until comparatively recent times in northeastern Asia, China, and Japan.

2. Large plates, apparently breastplates. One of these, of whalebone, is very carefully made. On its edges are holes, serving to attach it to the other parts of the armor (Plate XXXII, item 1). Another, possibly unfinished, is made of a broad piece of elk antler and is similar in shape to the first one (Plate XXXII, item 2).

3. Elongated, slightly convex plates, used either for the vents of suits of armor or as sidepieces of the helmet. The holes in them, like those in the first type of plates, are located horizontally in pairs (Plate XX, items 8, 11).

4. Long plates, narrowed at one end, with four holes, the upper pair of which is located vertically. By analogy with Chukchi examples, these plates belong to a conical type of helmet (Plate XX, item 7).

In a number of cases, the armor plates are decorated with ornamentation consisting of bands of a linear and angular meander pattern, which is usual for Ust-Poluy. One of the breastplates is also decorated. Depicted on it is the figure of a warrior, apparently holding in each hand a sword similar in shape to one found on the Severnaya Sosva.[55] The warrior's head is ornamented with a crown of five arrow-shaped teeth. Around his neck is a necklace, the ends of which are shaped like the heads of animals, with open jaws. This figure somewhat recalls the cast bronze images known from Cape Potchevash and from Glyadenovo. Incidentally, the bronze armor plates from the barrows of Cape Potchevash are similar to those of Ust-Poluy, particularly in decoration.[56]

The figure on the bone breastplate and the scratched images on bronze

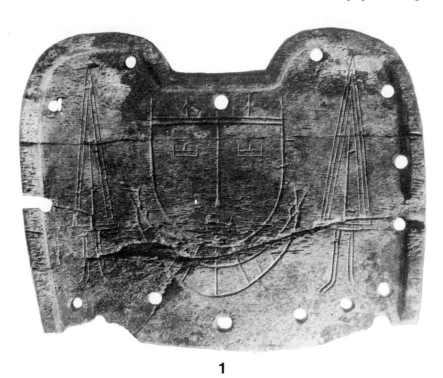

1

2

Plate XXXII. Armor breastplates.
1–of whalebone; 2–of elk antler.

plaques found at Ust-Poluy provide plentiful data on the engraved images which apparently appeared during the Ust-Poluy period. Without dealing with them in the present work, I will note only that the poses in which we see the figures on both bone plates and bronze plaques bear witness to the existence, even at that time, of war dances which are known from archaeological and ethnographic data.[57]

The general aspect of a suit of armor from Ust-Poluy can be reconstructed on the basis of engraved images on bronze artifacts from Ust-Poluy and from certain ethnographic parallels. Besides "shirts" made from bone or metal plates, skirts made from strips of walrus and bearded-seal hide were in use. It was mentioned earlier that suits of bone armor are known among the peoples of northeastern Asia, the Koryaks and Eskimos, and analogous ones of iron among the Chukchis. On the discs and plaques known from Ust-Poluy and other finds of the same period, one can find engraved images of people and mythical beings, whose clothing recalls in contour and even in some details the Koryak-Eskimo armor. The beings depicted are clad in shirts reaching somewhat below the waist and long skirts similar to the Paleo-Asiatic variety, composed of several wide bands. It is possible that the Ust-Poluy military clothing was similar to that of the Chukchis and Eskimos.

Bone armor plates are well known in Uralo-Siberian archaeology. Plates close to those from Ust-Poluy, differing from them only in method of attachment, have been discovered in the Kokonovka barrows.[58] The same are known from the barrows excavated by Zyryanov in Shadrinsk *uyezd*[59] and from the fortified hill site of Bolshoy Log, in the stratum of a settlement dating to the Sarmatian period.[60]

From the above we may judge how widespread bone armor plate was. This makes it more difficult to determine the origins of the Ust-Poluy armor, and only future finds will provide material for resolving this question. Only indirect data are available; these will be described in some detail and will connect the dissemination of armor plate on the lower Ob with the steppes to the south rather than with cultures of the Arctic littoral.

In summing up the material presented, we must conclude that the economy of the Ust-Poluy people was complex. It was based on land- and sea-mammal hunting, fishing, and the presence of highly developed dog breeding. The notable dominance of antler and bone as materials for making artifacts suggests that the hunting of wild reindeer was one of the most significant elements in the economic life of the ancient population of Ust-Poluy. The role of fishing, whose products apparently formed, along with reindeer meat, the basis of the diet, was also very significant. This is shown by the great quantity of fishbones in the Ust-Poluy pit house excavated by the Mangazeya expedition in Salekhard in 1946. The hunting of sea mammals, which certainly existed at Ust-Poluy (as indicated by the hunting equipment and the use of sea-mammal bones as material for artifacts), did not, it seems to us, have as great an importance in the economy as it had in that of the Yamal sites of the same period.[61]

We also assume that the population gathered nuts, berries, edible roots, and so forth, which continue to be of some significance among the population of the Ob district to this day. In order to dig roots, there must have been some tool like a spade or a mattock. The most massive of the points with sockets resembling harpoon ice picks seen in Plate XXIII (item 14) may be considered to have been the points of such tools.

Thus, in Ust-Poluy we have a culture of sedentary hunters and fishermen, among whom harness-dog breeding probably facilitated the development of these occupations and the exploitation of extensive territories.

The many-sided character of the economy is characteristic of primitive peoples, among whom the productive forces are still inadequately developed. An economy similar to the Ust-Poluy one existed in the recent historical past among many small peoples of the North, for example, the Gilyaks, concerning whom Shrenk [Schrenk] reported that the basis of their economy was fishing combined with sea-mammal hunting (chiefly seal and white whale), well-developed dog breeding, and to a certain degree, land hunting. However, Shrenk noted that hunting among the Gilyaks is primarily subsidiary in character, since they hunt mainly fur animals for sale.[62]

In economy, the Caribou Eskimos are even closer to the Ust-Poluy people; the basis of their economy was the hunting of the caribou, fishing, and sea-mammal hunting in combination with highly developed harness-dog breeding.[63]

In economy, the Ob Ugrians were also close to the Ust-Poluy people. Historical sources give us every reason to suppose that during the 1st and the first half of the 2nd millennia A.D., the Siberian tribes called Yugra [Ugrians] were ones of hunters and fishermen, utilizing harness dogs. Both Russian and Arabic sources and European travellers report this. A vivid description of travel by dog sled is found in the report *O sushchestvovanii Velikoy Vengrii obnaruzhennoy bratom Rikhardom vo vremya gospodina papy Grigoriya IX* [On the existence of Great Hungary, discovered by Brother Richard during the time of the Lord-Pope Gregory IX]. The monk Julian, who travelled [there] in 1237–38, wrote, "When we were still in Bascardia, there came a certain ambassador from the country of Sibur, which is surrounded by the northern sea. This country is full of food, but the winter there is so extremely severe because of the extraordinary amount of snow that almost no animals can walk there, except the dogs of that country; four large dogs pull a sled on which one man can sit, with the necessary food and clothing."[64]

The wide distribution of dog breeding in western Siberia is known as early as the end of the 15th century, when during the campaign of Prince Kurbskiy to Lyapin, his men-at-arms, according to the chronicle, rode on dog sleds. A unified opinion to the effect that reindeer breeding diffused relatively late among the Ob Ugrians—not earlier than the end of the 15th century—has now become established.[65]

The entire aspect of the culture and the remains of dwellings show that the Ust-Poluy population was sedentary. The basic dwelling, at least in the winter, was the pit house.

In Salekhard, at a distance of four kilometers from Ust-Poluy, the Mangazeya expedition excavated in 1946 a pit house which, on the basis of the excavated materials, was synchronous with the settlement at the mouth of the Poluy and belonged to the same culture. It was rectangular, almost square in shape, measuring 10 × 11 m. Its depth barely exceeded one meter. Directly opposite the entrance, which faces the bank of the river, there was a hearth of elongated form, extended along the house. On both sides of the hearth, along the walls, there were earthen sleeping platforms. Below the level of the floor, along one of the walls, there was a channel which, by analogy with the dwellings of the peoples of northeast Asia, was constructed for drainage and to improve the draft [for the fire].

V. S. Adrianov, who excavated Ust-Poluy, did not inspect the dwellings, but after we had studied the few of his field notes that had survived, and had repositioned the finds on the excavation sketches of 1935, we noticed that depressions containing the remains of hearth areas could be discerned. On the edges of such depressions, remains of birch bark and wood had been preserved. In one of them, a complete, pedestaled vessel was found. Plentiful finds of clay and slate models for bronze artifacts, and a casting mold, were also discovered in the depressions. This suggests that in Ust-Poluy the dwellings were also of the semi-subterranean type.

In interior plan and dimensions, the Ust-Poluy dwelling shows similarity to the contemporary summer *yurts*, which also have a central hearth on both sides of which benches are build along the walls.[66] A dwelling, which was probably close in type to those at Ust-Poluy, was described by V. Zuyev as follows:

> The hut has a quite peculiar construction and is built, as a rule, as a rectangle. For lack of large tree trunks, it is of necessity put together with small ones without moss being packed between the logs; some of the yurts have exits in the ground. In the yurts the space is divided among as many families as live in the yurt; and although, because of the multitude, the place is not large, each Ostyak woman with all her equipment and children must sit and work in the narrow place by the fire. . . .
>
> In such huts, are three, four and five families together, and if there are infants, then each mother has in front of her a cradle, into which dry-rotted wood is put for softness under the infant. On this they lay the infant, and having dressed him in a small fur coat, they tie him firmly and rock him. The other children sleep beside the father and mother. In the middle of the dwelling, there is a small fire, on which they cook the food, each one when she wishes, both for herself [the family] and for the dogs, which with their puppies, have their dens in the same yurts under the sleeping benches.[67]

The information which we have on the Ust-Poluy dwelling and also the data concerning owner's marks on various objects used by men or women suggest some facets of the social structure of the Ust-Poluy people. It is easy to discern that on the basis of form, the marks fall into two sharply different groups.

In one group we find rather complex marks constituting complicated versions of a crosslike figure (Plate XXXIII, item 1). They differ among themselves in details, but represent variants of one and the same symbol and are apparently family marks, deriving from a single clan mark. Brand marks close to them are found on certain celts of the Tobolsk group. V. N. Chernetsov finds analogues of them in northern China of Late Chou and Han times, and he suggests that the Ust-Poluy brand marks are imitations of Chinese characters and seals.[68]

In the second group the markings are incomparably simpler (Plate XXXIII, item 2) and bear close resemblance to the brand marks of the present-day Ob Ugrians (Plate XXXIII, item 3). While generally rare at Ust-Poluy, they are found more frequently on objects used by women.

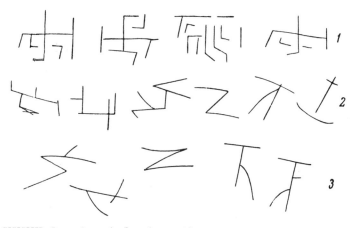

Plate XXXIII. Owner's marks found on artifacts.
1, 2–from the Ust-Poluy hill site; 3–those of present-day Mansi.

Hence we draw the conclusion that the complex markings, representing variants of a single one, belong to the Ust-Poluy people proper, while the others enter into the settlement either by chance on single objects or as a result of marital ties. Furthermore, this may be true of objects used by men or women, inasmuch as matrilocal marriage is to this day not a rare phenomenon on the Ob. The variants of the Ust-Poluy marks proper show that even during this era the clan was no longer a single economic unit there, but the extended family living under one roof was the economic and productive unit.

According to Zuyev, three to five couples lived in one *yurt*. Judging by the dimensions of the Ust-Poluy pit house, eight to ten people could have lived in it. Pallas vividly describes the life of a large group living in one house:

> For wintering, the Ostyaks choose high, dry banks near rivers, and build from thin young trees rectangular huts like the Russian ones, but lower, and almost half buried in the ground, and without roofs, in place of which they pile earth on top and leave in the middle a rectangular hole of moderate size, in which in winter, they place ice [to retain] heat and [admit] light. The door is usually, though not always, oriented to the west. In front of the door, they build storehouses (*labazy*) on both sides to store salvaged floatage [lumber] and other things. In such yurts or winter quarters, many families live

together, for which reason, the interior, is divided into as many cubicles as there are families living there; and however narrow these cubicles may be because of the multitude of people, the mother and children, with all her household supplies must find room in it and work by her own fire. From this one may imagine how they sleep in these barracks, and what order must exist there. Usually three, four and six families live in one house, but below Berezovo, there are yurts where up to 30 such families live together.[69]

Thus, generalizing the data on brand marks and dwellings, and using historical-ethnographic materials, we may suppose that the pit house dwellers, representing a group of very close relatives and affinals, constituted a single economic whole, the basic economic unit of Ust-Poluy society. The clan was apparently in decay, and there is reason to suppose that patrilineality already existed.

The Ust-Poluy culture of river-mouth hunters and fishermen dwelling in the forested tundra possesses elements foreign to cultures of similar type which connect it with the more southerly forested steppe and steppe regions. This has been repeatedly noted in works on the history of the lower Ob region.[70]

To the category of foreign elements found at Ust-Poluy are assignable, first, the fragment of the base of a bronze kettle, and the pedestaled clay vessels which imitate such kettles. Plate armor, although very widespread, should also be considered, at Ust-Poluy, as one of the cultural elements disseminated from the western Siberian steppe and forested steppe. We are convinced of this because of the similarity of Ust-Poluy armor plates and the bronze armor or girdle plates from the Potchevash barrows and the bone plates from the Kokonovka and other barrows of the middle Irtysh region. The representation of the dancing warrior on one of the Ust-Poluy bone breastplates (particularly if one regards the Sarmatian appearance of the sword) also provides a basis for connecting the armor with similar finds in the steppe regions of western Siberia.

However, it is the graphic art of Ust-Poluy which reveals most vividly the elements foreign to the culture of taiga hunters. Without setting for ourselves the task of describing Ust-Poluy art in the present work, we must at least briefly consider it, inasmuch as it reflects the complex ethnogenetic processes which led to the emergence of the Ust-Poluy culture.

The duality of style in the magnificent Ust-Poluy sculpture is obvious from the carved bone artifacts. Wide use of sculpture in the round was employed on everyday utensils. The most frequently decorated objects were combs and the handles of knives and spoons. The chief and sole subjects of representation were animals and birds. Two different traditions may be seen in the style. One of them is the primitive realism known from sites of the Late Neolithic and Early Bronze Ages in Siberia and the Urals and characteristic to no lesser degree to certain peoples of northern Asia—the Koryaks, Chukchis, and Eskimos. Representations in this style are found most frequently on spoons (Plate XXX). Usually it is the head or the entire figure of a bird or beast. It is chiefly water birds which are depicted, and of the animals it is most often the deer and the hare. The rendering is thoroughly realistic.

The combs are decorated in a different manner. A distinctively handled motif of battling animals was used, that of the eagle and the deer. The figures were rendered in arbitrary and stylized fashion, with ornamental handling of details. As time progressed, schematic and stylized figures of birds and animals, representing the details of an ornamental composition, were used. The depictions of animals on some combs yield in realism to the depictions on spoons (compare, for instance, the female elk on a comb [Plate XXXI, item 1] and on a spoon [Plate XXX, item 2]). The motif of the struggle of animals appeared, very rarely, on spoons as well. But here

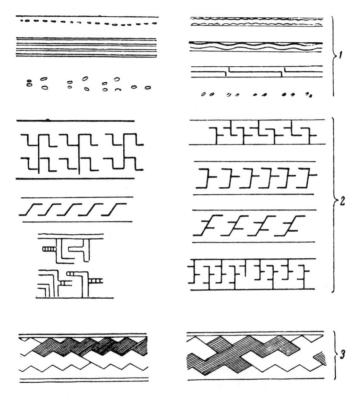

Plate XXXIV. Ust-Poluy ornamentation.

it is degenerate and transformed into a realistically rendered eagle, clawing the head of a dead reindeer (as can be seen on one of the spoons).

Thus the impression is created that this style, foreign to the northern hunting environment, was brought to Ust-Poluy together with the high combs for pinning the hair.

Also, there is no unity in the [geometric] ornamentation, which can be divided by formal indices into three groups. The first includes grooved and striated patterns, and also small pips and dots, which in some cases obviously imitate the tracks of animals (Plate XXXIV, item 1). The second group includes angular-linear, and the third angular-ribbon, ornamentation, which is found on bone in isolated cases (Plate XXXIV, items 2,3).

The ornamentation of the first group may be associated with hunting in the Ust-Poluy culture. Analogues to it are found among the present-day patterns incised into birchbark objects by the Ostyaks and Voguls. Something close to it is found in the ornamentation of scabbards from the Lozva valley decorated with representations of birds, fish, and animal tracks. Ornamentation of this type is apparently very ancient and goes back to early forms of art associated with hunting.

The second and third groups have a certain similarity and probably derive from a single source. The angular-linear ornament known from Andronovo ornamentations is found on the Ob only during the Ust-Poluy period, when it was widely used to decorate bone artifacts. Later it spread to pottery, and existed, as far as is known, over the entire territory long occupied by Ugrian tribes. Ornamentation of this type is also known in the Ust-Poluy period in the middle Irtysh (the Murlinsk cache).[71]

The angular-ribbon ornamentation is known on the territory of the Ugrian tribes as early as the Bronze Age and exists there to this day. It is rarely found on excavated objects, which may be explained by the fact that it was used primarily on soft materials, as it is today.

The closeness of the Ust-Poluy culture and that of the contemporary Ob Ugrians is very great. At Ust-Poluy we find practically all the components which make up the culture of the modern Ostyaks and Voguls. This is why it is so important to clarify the genesis of the Ust-Poluy culture.

One of its components is a culture of the Arctic type, found in rather similar forms over the entire northern coast of Asia and, in part, over the European North (as in the Oleniy ostrov burial ground on the Kola Peninsula). G. N. Prokofyev has noted that in the contemporary languages of the peoples inhabiting this territory, words relating to material culture—the names of the parka type of northern clothing, the panels of reindeer hide for the tent, game animals—are common to all the Paleo-Asiatics and are found in the languages of the Chukchis, Koryaks, and Eskimos, with similar or coincident meanings.[72]

The same closeness can be observed in the material culture. Thus, at Ust-Poluy, aside from general features whose origin can be explained by similarity of natural conditions, we should note certain particulars, for example, similar construction of dwellings (presence of an air-drainage trough) and similarity in the type of dog harness, with coincident details. Traces of the Arctic culture in the north of the Ob region appear most definitely among the population of the Yamal Peninsula. According to Nenets tradition, the "Sirti," as they call the bearers of this culture, disappeared from the northern part of the peninsula only in comparatively recent times.[73]

The Ugrian tribes of the middle Irtysh district, who brought with them to the lower Ob elements of the steppe and forested-steppe culture, stood socially and in terms of technology considerably higher than the local population. With their appearance in the lower Ob district begins the wide distribution of iron, traces of which have not yet been discovered in the earlier cultures. The same can be said of bronze. The high level of technology produced a flowering of material culture. Specialized military weapons of forms unknown in the north (battle-axes, three-finned bronze arrows, swords and daggers of Sarmatian type) bear witness to the introduction of new skills and probably higher forms of social structure.

It remains to direct attention to one further phenomenon, whose causes are as yet insufficiently studied—the features of similarity between the Ust-Poluy and the Ananino cultures. They are found in the similarity of form of many artifacts and in the ornamentation of pottery, the latter being particularly indicative. This compels us involuntarily to assume a connection considerably deeper than mere intertribal exchange and mutual influence. The solution of this problem will become possible only after profound study of the Bronze Age cultures in the Irtysh and Kama regions.

PART III

THE UST-POLUY PERIOD IN THE OB REGION

V. N. CHERNETSOV

The Ust-Poluy Period
in the Ob Region

The study of materials from Ust-Poluy and an analysis of sites at which objects analogous to the Ust-Poluy materials were found give us cause to state that they all belong to a culture having the same basic features and belonging to tribes of the same ethnic background. We have called this the Ust-Poluy culture.

We shall attempt to generalize the relevant data, to delineate the territory occupied by Ust-Poluy sites, and to characterize briefly the cultures that were synchronous with and akin to the Ust-Poluy.

We have been able to establish the chronological framework of the Ust-Poluy culture from the data we obtained by studying the bronzes of the Ust-Poluy period and from Moszyńska's analysis of the pottery and other artifacts that define the material culture of Ust-Poluy and the Potchevash fortified hill site. By drawing on the ethnographic folklore material, we have been able to determine the ethnic affiliations of the people who left the remains of this culture.

The sites can easily be divided into three basic groups: fortified hill sites and settlements, burial grounds, and sacrificial places.

A glance at the map will show that the territory of the Ust-Poluy culture can be traced clearly from Angalskiy Cape [Cape Angal], that is, from the point where the Ob crosses the Arctic Circle, up the Ob to its junction with the Irtysh. To the west of the Ob, the entire Severnaya Sosva basin, as far as its source in the snow-covered peaks of the northern Urals, falls within the sphere of the Ust-Poluy culture. Some parts of the Lozva basin and, as has come to light lately, the upper reaches of the Tavda are also to be included.[1] There is no certainty about the Konda, for not a single Ust-Poluy site is known from its vast basin. Besides, nearly impassable swamps lie between the upper Konda and the tributaries of the Severnaya Sosva. Indeed, the Konda territory is linked, to a considerable extent, with the Irtysh, Tavda, and Pelym rivers; this is clearly reflected in the language of the present-day Mansi. There are several indications that the Konda dialects of the Mansi language are more closely affiliated with the Pelym and Tavda dialects than with the northern ones. It is quite possible that further research will reveal that the

Translated by David Kraus from *MIA*, no. 35, 1953, pp. 221–41.

culture of the Early Iron Age of the Konda region was somewhat closer to the Potchevash than to the Ust-Poluy culture. At the same time there is no doubt that both were definitely allied. Both had a common type of pottery ornamentation and followed the same route of development. Many types of bone implements and bronze weapons, bronze celts in particular, were the same. To be sure, there were also some distinctions, mostly called forth by local conditions. For example, Potchevash arrowheads were rather small, of the Kluchevskiy (forested steppe) type, whereas the Ust-Poluy ones were long and heavy, well complementing the long woodland bows. Also, characteristically, the Potchevash does not contain pedestaled vessels—so typical of the Ust-Poluy sites. Only one is known; it is preserved in the Tobolsk Museum. According to its label, it came from the finds of V. K. Imsen in the Suzgun hill, 7 km down the Irtysh from Tobolsk. Pedestaled bronze kettles were scarce in the lower Ob, and hence there developed an imitative form in pottery. They were used more widely in the middle Irtysh, where they had religious significance. The forms of the Potchevash vessels are clearly associated with the ceramics of the Late Bronze and Early Iron Age cultures represented variously by the Ivanovskaya fortified hill site in the southern and by the Zelenaya Gorka site in the northern part of the region. The explanation of the similarities and differences of the Ust-Poluy and Potchevash cultures should be sought in the fact that although they were founded by related tribes, they were based on quite different economies—hunting and fishing in the north, agriculture and cattle-herding, with only some dependence on hunting and fishing, in the south.

Of course, the economy was not completely uniform even within the territorial limits of the Ust-Poluy culture. We have already mentioned the types of economy on the lower Ob; the specific forms of the economy must have been different farther upstream, that is, on the southern reaches of the lower Ob and its tributaries, where the natural conditions were somewhat different. For example, fishing, which must always have been very important on the Ob itself, could hardly have formed the basis of the economy deep in the taiga along the small streams not reached by the large runs of salmon. Elk hunting, and in the spring and fall, hunting of the wild reindeer during their migrations from the winter feeding grounds in the forest to the summer pastures of the open forested tundra and the mountain tundra must have played a larger role in the economy of such localities. Hunting fences with pre-set bows, or rigged spearheads, snares, pits, and other simple, easily prepared but highly effective and clever devices of the primitive hunter must have been used. We shall not describe these devices here, for they are familiar, in the main, from ethnographic material.

One may point out certain differences in the construction of the dwellings as well. The pit houses, which in the south were also constructed mainly on high river banks, did not have that special Arctic feature, the air-drainage channel, which apparently was not needed because of the absence of permafrost. Quite often one finds large village sites with a fairly thick culture-yielding layer, without trace of pit houses. Evidently here, in contrast to the Far North, dwellings could be built on the surface, owing to the milder conditions of the windless taiga winter. Probably there were also differences in the forms of some implements, the clothing, et cetera, reflecting in part specific tribal characteristics and in part regional economic specialties (like those which could be observed in the Ob region in historic times), but they did not disrupt the general cultural unity of the lower Ob.

To the south, along the lower Irtysh, the Ust-Poluy culture bordered on the Potchevash culture. The Urals, or perhaps the western slopes of the Urals, formed its western boundary, along the upper reaches of the basins of the Severnaya Sosva and the Lozva. The sources of the Pechora and its tributaries, the Ilych, Shchugor, and others, approach these places on the west and are separated from the rivers of the eastern slope by low passes and portages, which are quite passable in summer. The left tributaries of the upper Kama—the Vishera, Yayva, Kosva, and somewhat farther south, the Chusovaya—delimited the Ust-Poluy culture to the southwest.

Although the western slopes of the northern Urals are not too well explored archaeologically, there were individual finds made at different times which give us some idea of the characteristic features of the culture of this area. Among these finds are the objects in the caches of the Soples and of the Unya rivers. These caches quite clearly are the remains of small sacrificial places and sanctuaries similar to those known in the Ob region, and they contain complexes of different ages. Among these complexes, one finds flat-cast representations, in some cases not only similar to the eastern (that is, the Ob) ones, but identical to them. Such, for example, is the representation of an anthropomorphized frog with rays on its head, which appears in Spitsyn's papers (although it is not very well reproduced there).[2] A group of about twenty such representations, called *sopr-oyka* (old-man frog) and *sopr-né* (old-woman frog), was found in one of the Khanty sanctuaries. They are now in the Museum of Physical Anthropology and Ethnography in Leningrad.

These flat-cast representations are of a narrowly local nature. No image ever left the confines of the clan and perhaps included only its filial parts. The special image of each clan, however, was reproduced within that clan, but each time in a new form, so that the similarity of the flat casting within each group was determined solely by the clan tradition. Such a figurine could not be made outside the clan, nor could it be made of a totem group that included a number of filiate clans. Thus, one can be quite certain that the figure of the horned frog found on the Soples River was taken there from the Ob (or more exactly from its tributary, the Salym). If we consider the three-cornered and other representations from the Soples River, perhaps it would be even more accurate to say that the Soples River cache was left by a filiate clan that had once moved there from the Salym River. Let us recall that the objects of the Soples cache include a bronze arrowhead of the Ust-Poluy type. Ceramics very similar to the Ust-Poluy type were found on the Vishera River near one of the cliffs with ancient paintings during a survey made by the Perm University archaeological expedition under the direction of O. N. Bader. A very good collection containing pottery and bronze artifacts of the Ust-Poluy type was found in the Kaninskaya cave near the source of the Pechora by V. Kanivets in 1959–60.[3]

Finally, we must touch on the Glyadenovo sacrificial site, so widely known in archaeology. Without going into the question of its cultural affinity, because this would inevitably lead us far afield, we note merely that the finds from this site include objects that are not only similar to but actually identical with those of the Ob region, in particular with Ust-Poluy objects. Examples are a bone needle-case, arrowheads, and, what is particularly important, part of a form for copper casting which is identical to the Ust-Poluy casting form both in size and in the type of arrowheads cast in it. Representations of bears' heads found at Glyadenovo are not common for either the Ananino or the Pyanyy Bor cultures of the middle and lower Kama, but they are quite typical of the Ust-Poluy culture and of its synchronous and kindred western Siberian cultures.

One could propose that a culture of tribes closely related to the Ust-Poluy and Potchevash tribes existed in the western Cis-Ural region that includes the upper Pechora basin, the left tributaries of the upper Kama, and on the south, perhaps a part of the Chusovaya basin. Contrary to this, the archaeological materials from the lower Pechora are somewhat different from Trans-Uralian and Cis-Uralian ones. This may be seen in the Khaebidya-Peadera (Samoyedic for "Sacred Wood") site in the Bolshezemelskaya tundra near the shore of the Barents Sea, surveyed in 1947 by G. Chernov and excavated a few years ago by V. Kanivets. The excavation revealed an array of layers covering the Zelenaya Gorka, Ust-Poluy, and Yar-sale (post–Ust-Poluy) periods. The culture of Khaebidya-Peadera is closely related with those of the northern Trans-Ural and the lower Ob, but also differs in many respects, mostly in the forms and ornamentation of the ceramics. This culture also spread to the east of the Urals beyond the Arctic Circle, but only in the northernmost parts of the Ob region—the Yamal Peninsula, the banks of the lower Taz River, the Taz inlet, and perhaps the Ya-Vay Peninsula. Its western boundaries are not known. If the culture of the lower Ob region be regarded as ancestral for the Ob Ugrians (the Khanty and Ostyaks in particular), the culture of Khaebidya-Peadera may be connected with the ancient Lopars (Lapps), who were assimilated in this region by the Nentsy (Samoyeds) during the beginning of the 1st millennium A.D.

The sites characterized by the finds described by I. M. Myagkov adjoin the territory of the Ust-Poluy culture on the east, along the middle Ob.[4] Today, we know that similar types of objects are also encountered somewhat farther south, along the right bank of the Irtysh in the Tara region and to the east along the Chulym River as far as Achinsk. Undoubtedly, this territory can be assigned to still another culture, bordering on the Ust-Poluy and Potchevash cultures and very similar to each of them. We shall call this the Kulayka culture. In recent years this culture has been investigated more fully, and now we are in a position to suggest that it was probably associated with some of the woodland tribes of proto-Samoyeds or Ostyak-Samoyeds.

The list of cultures akin to the Ust-Poluy would be incomplete if we did not mention those of the upper Ob, middle Irtysh, and the Urals south of Sverdlovsk. We have only very preliminary indications of the upper Ob culture for the territory between the Tom River and the upper Ob. The middle layer of the Basandayka fortified hill site belongs to this culture. It has yielded objects of Late Tagar aspect and perhaps origin, as well as a flat-cast mask representing an animal (most likely a bear),[5] a bronze socket with meanderlike ornamentation,[6] and pottery of types well-known primarily in the Potchevash culture.[7] The disturbed burial ground farther up the Ob, near Novosibirsk, has yielded objects that can be dated to the 5th or 4th centuries B.C. Similar material has been discovered on the upper Ob at the Chudatskaya Gora fortified hill site at the mouth of the Kasmala River, where, according to Gryaznov, a lobed celt of the Tobolsk type was found with pottery similar to that of the Basandayka and Potchevash types.[8] Not far from Chudatskaya Gora, on the dunes near Bolshaya Rechka village, Gryaznov investigated a burial ground and a settlement, and on the basis of his findings he declared them to be of a separate culture, which he called the Fominskaya.

Materials similar to those described above have also been found on the middle Irtysh in Omsk *oblast*, in the middle layer of the Bolshoy Log [Big Ravine] fortified hill site on the right bank of the Om River, 6 km from its mouth. This site was discovered by a schoolboy, Vladimir Moroz, and was studied by us in 1949. The materials obtained at this site and described elsewhere give some idea of the culture.[9] It was a sedentary one, based on a complex economy that included stockbreeding, hunting, agriculture, and fishing. Judging by the bone finds, the inhabitants raised sheep, perhaps some large-horned cattle, and horses. The horse had religious significance. The agricultural aspect of their economy is demonstrated by an iron sickle, which B. N. Grakov's data show to be similar to the one found at the Kamenskoye fortified hill site. The shape and decoration of the pottery from the middle layer of this site is very much like that of Potchevash.

Pottery similar in ornamentation, but somewhat later than that of the middle layer of Bolshoy Log and similar to the post–Ust-Poluy pottery, was discovered on the left bank of the Irtysh opposite the mouth of the Om River.

Of the individual finds, one of the most important is a small bronze or copper figurine discovered in the autumn of 1949 at a depth of 0.7 m below the present surface, in the bluff of a ravine on the right bank of the Irtysh near a creek in the city of Omsk.[10] The figure, a flat-cast object, is a rather crude representation of a warrior holding a bow in his left hand and a spear in his right. On the head of the warrior is a bird, portrayed very schematically. The figure in general, as well as in its details, has very much in common with those known and described for the Ob-Irtysh region. The depiction of ribs is characteristic; they are indicated by raised lines exactly as they are on some objects from the Istyatskiy cache and especially the anthropomorphic figures of the Lozva type, indicating that they were cast in an earthen mold. The bird on the head of the Omsk figure also relates it to the figures of the Lozva cache. At the same time, its general outlines and technological features are very much like those of the representations from Lake Shigir,[11] while the weapons, not found on the representations from the forest belt, remind one of the figure from the Sapagova cache.

Although a considerable amount of archaeological materials has been collected in recent years from the middle Irtysh and upper Ob regions, it is not yet sufficient to outline the culture or cultures of this extensive area. All we can say is that one of them was founded by more or less sedentary tribes living in then forested river valleys. The forestation is attested to by the remains of bones of wild animals in the middle layer of Bolshoy Log, namely, those of the beaver, roe deer, elk, and stag, animals not indigenous to a steppe landscape.[12] It is very likely that there were local differences, particularly between the cultures of the middle Irtysh and the upper Ob. Although it appears that they had ties with one of the woodland cultures at the same time, they cannot be classified as forest cultures, because of the evidence of agriculture and stockbreeding, including small-horned cattle. Evidently, the cultures of the upper Ob and particularly the middle Irtysh occupied an intermediate position between typically forest and typically forested-steppe and steppe cultures. This latter type of culture occupied the forested steppes along the Ob and Irtysh. In the Irtysh it is well represented by burial mounds of the Kokonovka and Sargatskoye types, to the north of Omsk. The ceramics of these burial mounds differ considerably from those of Potchevash and are more comparable to Sauromatian ceramics of the southern Uralian steppes. Nevertheless, they have been found in some quantity at Bolshoy Log (Ravine) and in the mound graves of the Potchevash culture in the Tobolsk region. Ceramics from mound graves of the Barabinsk and upper Ob steppes present somewhat different features.

The forests and forested steppes of the Trans-Ural to the south of Sverdlovsk contain archaeological remains that are particular to it. Although the cultures of the Late Bronze and Early Iron Ages were here the same as they were in the more northerly reaches of the Trans-Ural, there developed during the 1st millennium B.C. several variant cultures. On the one hand, they were conditioned by contacts with the neighboring steppe cultures, and on the other, by the strong influence of the synchronous Amirabad culture of the Trans-Caspian area of Middle Asia.

Notwithstanding differences (which express themselves in the economy, mode of life, and shapes of vessels, weapons, and household implements), there are some traits which are universal to all the tribes which inhabited the territory of the Trans-Ural and western Siberia. One of the most significant ones was represented by the flat-cast objects with anthropomorphic and zoomorphic figures.[13] They occur in finds all over the territory—from the Urals to the Chulym River, from Ust-Poluy to Omsk and to the upper Ob beyond. One feature is common to all of these finds or caches. In each of them we find many flat-cast objects with a common theme, yet each of them cast in a different casting form. For example, on Karaulnaya Gora [Mountain] forty castings with birdlike figures were found; on Azov Gora, twenty-two were found and at Kuyash-Ognevskoye Lake, thirty. The Lozva cache contained about forty male and female figures with birds on their heads, the Kulayka find had many representations of bears and elks, a cache in the vicinity of Tobolsk had several representations of anthropomorphized trees with bear heads, and so on. Finds in the forested steppe also contained representations of female figures and warriors with swords, *akinakés* [short iron swords], or spears, with birds on their shoulders.

Certainly there must be an underlying cause for the similarity of the caches over this wide territory. Since the caches are of religious character, it is likely that their distribution indicates a unity of religious beliefs over the entire area. On the basis of investigations over the past few years, we are now able to conclude that all of these tribes were of Uralian origin. The eastern part of the territory, that is, the steppes to the east of the Irtysh, may be considered the homeland of nomadic proto-Samoyedic tribes. This is the position that M. Kosarev defends for the Bronze Age, and V. Mogilnikov asserts that Samoyedic groups existed on the upper Ob until the end of the 1st millennium A.D., when they were assimilated by Turkic-speaking peoples. The woodlands of the middle Trans-Ural were most probably the area of origin of the Ob-Ugrians, in particular the Mansi (Voguls). The wooded steppes of the Trans-Ural were very likely inhabited by Ugrian cattle-breeding tribes, among them the ancestors of the Magyars (Hungarians).

Having examined the territorial extent of the sites representing the Ust-Poluy culture and the cultures synchronous with and allied to it, we can now establish its chronological framework. The beginning of the Ust-Poluy culture is defined very reliably by the forms of objects very well known for the neighboring, already studied cultures, that is, the Ananino and the Tagar. At Ust-Poluy this group of early objects includes maces and poleaxes, both miniature and full-sized. As we have seen, both correspond to the forms characteristic of the later periods of the Ananino and Tagar cultures and may be dated not later than the 5th to 4th centuries B.C. The early objects from Ust-Poluy include a fragment of a celt of the second group,[14] which is synchronous with and similar to the Ananino celts, that is, those dating to the 7th to 4th centuries B.C., and a clasp fashioned to represent griffons, which has an exact analogue in the material from the Ufimskiy burial ground.

At the Katra-Vozh fortified hill site, where no examples of the earliest types of pottery were found and which must be regarded as belonging to the "developed" Ust-Poluy culture, a blue, eye-shaped bead was found which may also be dated to the 4th century B.C. The arrowheads found at the sites of the Kulayka culture establish the early date of that culture. Arrowheads of the Kulayka and Klyuchevaya types were found together in the large Konetsgorskoye village site on the Kama, which is 4th century B.C. This example may also be extended to the Ust-Poluy, if we consider that arrowheads of the Kulayka and Ust-Poluy types are found together at a number of sites, including Kulayka itself. The same date can be assigned to the complexes of Basandayka, the Ishimka cache, the Aydashinskaya cave, and the Novosibirsk burial ground on the basis of finds of arrowheads of the enumerated types and a large number of finds of Tagar objects: that is, figures of argali [wild sheep] and mirrors were found in Basandayka and the Novosibirsk burial ground, and figures of the onager and clasps fashioned to the likeness of the snow leopard were found in the Aydashinskaya cave and in the Ishimka cache. Arrowheads of the Kulayka type were found in the Novosibirsk burial ground together with dart points of a different type, which existed no later than the middle of the 1st millennium B.C. and probably went out of existence earlier.

The opinion has been expressed that the Tagar objects in the complexes of the so-called caches, which are, in most cases, the remains of ancient sacrificial sites, cannot be accepted as dating material, because the items could already have been "archaeological" objects when they found their way into the complex and were subsequently reused. This point of view may be correct if one is dealing with individual objects and what are chronologically more or less disparate objects. The bronze axe from Kulayka decorated with the figure of a bear in the ancient Tagar style is probably an object of this type. Chronologically, this axe, or the original after which it was fashioned, belongs to a considerably earlier period and must be disregarded in dating the complex. However, we have already seen that many Tagar objects are systematically repeated in all the other cited cases in the complexes of the Ust-Poluy sites and that they are chronologically more or less uniform. This enables us to establish the dating on the basis of contemporaneity. Our dating is further supported by the fact that not only have Tagar and perhaps Ananino objects been found in the Ust-Poluy complexes, but arrowheads of the Kulayka type have been found in one of the Ananino sites, the Konetsgorskoye village site.

Bronze cauldrons with a hollow pedestaled base also appeared in the lower Ob region in the middle of the 1st millennium B.C., the period of the founding of the Ust-Poluy culture by northward-moving Ugrian tribes. These cauldrons were imitated in pottery as vessels of the Ust-Poluy type.[15] A fragment of a similar copper cauldron was discovered at Ust-Poluy, and entire vessels were found at Tobolsk and several places in the Surgut-Narym region of the Ob.

The bear head resting on front paws as a subject of figurative art probably originated in this same period. This is the type depicted on the rectangular plaque found at Ust-Poluy or on the epauletlike clasp from the Yamal Peninsula. Although we do not have objects with figures of this type which could be dated to the 4th century B.C., we assume their existence, inasmuch as a similar figure was found in the Pokrovka II burial mound.

The birdlike figures with the head full-face or in profile, with straight, drooping wings and clenched claws, often depicted as small knobs, of the type found in the Istyatskiy cache, should be assigned to this early period. This type of representation had already appeared in the Ananino culture.[16]

The late stage of the Ust-Poluy period should be dated to the 4th and 3rd centuries B.C. It may be characterized by celts of the Tobolsk type (fourth group);[17] by iron daggers with bronze handles and with pommels of the Ust-Poluy, Lozva, and Ishimka types; by iron daggers with a straight crosspiece [guard] and a crescentic or straight pommel, for example, like the one from the Severnaya Sosva which has an exact counterpart in the grave goods of the Prokhorovka mounds and the

Pokrovka culture of the 4th century B.C.;[18] and by the hook type of iron knife. The magnificent development of decorations on implements and ornaments is a characteristic feature of this period.

Meandering and stepped patterns were the favorite ornamental motifs. We find them on the handles of Lozva daggers, on Nyaksimvol and Ust-Poluy rings, on the belt buckles and armor plates from the Ust-Poluy and Potchevash burial mounds, on a hand shield from the Aydashinskaya cave, on the edges of an openwork plaque from the Istyatskiy cache, and on many other objects.

The bronze figures with good relief work, made from models cut from clayey shale, existed in the late Ust-Poluy period, but evidently this technique appeared somewhat earlier, as indicated by Gryaznov's data on the technique of manufacturing the Minusinsk celts.[19]

On the basis of the finds in the settlement of Makar-Visyng-Tur, which yielded no Late Ust-Poluy pottery, we can determine that masks by the flat-casting technique (like those of Kulayka, Basandayka, and other sites) occur throughout the entire Ust-Poluy period. This group also includes small figures similar in form but with a disproportionately large head; these are, no doubt, derivatives of the earlier period (if we can judge by the treelike idols), which gradually disappeared by the end of the Ust-Poluy period.

The objects from the Lozva cache must be dated as Middle Ust-Poluy, judging by the dagger handles, and perhaps the Salym and some other figures also belong to this period. In general, however, it is quite impossible at present to make a detailed chronological classification of the flat-cast objects. For this, one must have incomparably more complete and systematic material than is available. Only the Sapagova figures can be classified with certainty as 4th to 3rd century on the basis of the form of the daggers depicted on them. These daggers are analogous to those of the Prokhorovka culture of the 4th century B.C.[20]

It seems very likely that the diffusion of representations, on bronze objects, of a bear with its head resting on its front paws belongs also to the 4th century. This is the same as those on the gold plaques from the Pokrovka burial mounds. Let us note that this motif is related in some way to the epauletlike clasps of the Yamal, Molotovka, Savina, and Fominskaya types, and subsequently the Ust-Poluy type as well. This relation was expressed in the exclusive preference at that time for representations of bears on the belt buckles and plaques, which lead to one of the names for the bear—"the buckle animal"—used in the Mansi language even today.

The end of the Ust-Poluy period is heralded by the disappearance of hollow-base vessels—imitations of bronze kettles. Chronologically the termination of this culture is established by finds at the Ust-Poluy site proper, as well as other sites. In one of the Ust-Poluy dwellings a form for copper casting for long and heavy arrowheads of the Ust-Poluy type was found.[21] The mold core was found with it. To all appearances, the form was ready to be used for manufacture. Other remains of the casting craft were also found—clay models and copper and bronze parts and fragments which would have been of value later on. One is left with the impression that activity at the fortified hill site was cut off suddenly and was never resumed. The date of this event may be determined by the span of existence of arrowheads of the type described, that is, they were not used later than the beginning of the 3rd century B.C. Since the Ust-Poluy materials also contain the latest type of pedestaled vessels, the date may be assigned to the entire culture, the chronological limits of which are thus from 500 B.C. to 200 B.C.

We find no materials to establish a late date for the neighboring Potchevash and Kulayka cultures, although I. M. Myagkov dates the Kulayka culture to "around the beginning of our era, but probably . . . later as well," or "to the period of the Pyanyy Bor burial ground, but not later than the Glyadenovo sacrificial site" (that is, according to his absolute dates, from the 2nd century B.C. to the 3rd century A.D.).[22] However, he arrives at this date from "the exclusive use of socketed bronze arrows which can be dated to the final stage of the Ananino burial ground. . . ." What is more, he accepts the obsolescent chronology of A. V. Shmidt—that is, for the Ananino culture, the 7th to the 2nd centuries B.C., for the Glyadenovo and Potchevash cultures, the 1st to the 3rd centuries A.D., and for the Pyanyy Bor culture, the 2nd century B.C. to the 4th century A.D.[23] If corrections are made in this dating, in keeping with the present chronology based on more complete study of the sites and cultures and on a more profound knowledge of the material (Ananino, according to A. V. Zbruyeva, is 8th to 3rd centuries B.C.),[24] we must move the chronological framework of the Kulayka culture considerably back and view it as synchronous with the Ust-Poluy.

Now that we have established the chronological framework of the Ust-Poluy culture, let us turn our attention to some characteristics of the period.

The material remains indicate high development of the productive forces and technology. Finds of spindle whorls indicate that the Ust-Poluyans knew the craft of spinning, most likely spinning of nettle fibers; the numerous scrapers of different form, in some cases similar to the present Khanty forms, indicate that the working of hides was an every-day occupation of Ust-Poluy women. Boneworking reached a high state of development (even today bone is widely used in the North as a raw material). From the unfinished pieces and the numerous [bone] handles, one may judge that the Ust-Poluyans already had a fair number of iron knives, but iron continued to be very valuable. The iron objects were used to the limit; when a knife had been ground as far as possible, its handle was split and the haft extracted. No wooden objects are preserved in the occupation layer and only the large bone wedges, which bear traces of wear, indicate that the Ust-Poluyans had techniques for splitting tree trunks.

One of the everyday occupations was the production of clay vessels. The layers of the fortified hill site contain a very large number of pot-sherds. Without going into the general characteristics of the pottery and its ornamentation, let us note just one form that is very characteristic of an Ust-Poluy settlement—the vessels on high, hollow pedestals. This form was not known in the lower Ob region either before or after the Ust-Poluy culture and is specific to that culture; it supplanted all other types of clay vessels for a time, but then disappeared completely. There can be no doubt that this form did not derive from any earlier known local pottery forms, but it copied the so-called Scythian bronze cauldrons with a ring base, which were widely used on the Ob in the second half of the 1st millennium B.C. Cauldrons of this type have been found near Tobolsk and on the middle Ob. They were also known to the inhabitants of Ust-Poluy. At any rate, there are several fragments of the base of a small bronze cauldron among the numerous copper and bronze artifacts of Ust-Poluy. A miniature bronze cauldron was also found at the Ust-Poluy settlement Makar-Visyng-Tur.[25] We still do not know whether such cauldrons were made on-the-spot on the lower Ob or whether they were imported from more southerly regions, but undoubtedly they were cast on-the-spot in the middle Ob region, as analyses of bronze objects from Kulayka have indicated.[26]

While we cannot say for certain whether the bronze cauldrons were made at Ust-Poluy, we can state that the art of bronze casting was on a high level among the Ust-Poluyans. We have noted that pit houses with clear traces of bronze casting were discovered within the Ust-Poluy fortified hill site: one was identified both stratigraphically and in a complex, the other only in a complex.[27] Not only implements but art objects were cast. For the latter, models were first cut out of soft shale, a material that is easily worked and provides a smooth, nonporous surface. The molding, one must assume, was done in clay, but we do not know any of the details of the production process. Rather complex copper forms were made for items of mass production, primarily arrowheads. Parts of a four-part mold of this type were found at the [Ust-Poluy] fortified hill site.

Evidently the Ust-Poluyans had sufficient metal; not only did they have copper, which is quite widely distributed in its native state in the Urals, but also the rarer metals, lead and tin. Undoubtedly the bronze with a very high lead and tin content was prepared intentionally, since we find such alloys only in specific objects. One may assume that the tin came from the south, from Kazakhstan, where according to S. S. Chernikov's research, it was worked in antiquity, beginning with the Bronze Age.[28]

The iron knife was already quite widely used at Ust-Poluy. These hooklike knives, whose shape is a vestige of the bronze knives, comprised a definite minority;[29] the most widely used knives were hafted and had a bone handle. Insofar as one may judge from the scanty finds, the most characteristic knives were narrow and, consequently, long, with a quite thick back and clearly defined unilateral sharpening of the cutting edge. Along with the narrow knives, one also finds other types, broader and flatter hafted knives.

Both types have their direct descendants today. The first of these is the presently used man's knife, narrow, sometimes broadening toward the end, sharpened on one side of the edge, usually the right, that is, in the manner in which scissors are sharpened. In some cases, these knives are so narrow, with a thick back, that they are almost trihedral in cross section. This is the *šoχri*, called *chukrey* by the local Russians; it is exclusively a man's knife and is highly suitable for working wood and bone. It is interesting that only knives of this shape are used for slaughter of the sacrificial reindeer and it is these knives that are sacred to clans that trace their descent from *šoχriŋjka*. The seven old brothers *šoχriŋ* ("the old knife men") are portrayed in folklore as seven smiths.[30] Their totem is the dragonfly, whose body is as narrow and as long as the knife *šoχri*. Evidently the ancient attitude toward metallurgy, in particular toward the smith's art and toward smiths, is fused with the traditional form of the archaic, narrow knife represented by the *šoχriŋ*. Thus, the narrow knife which appeared in the last centuries B.C. has been preserved to this day as a form sanctified by tradition and associated with the first smiths. The broad knife is also used widely today; it is a woman's knife with a broad rounded point, very convenient for cutting up skins and furs. It is quite possible that the broad knives found in the sites of the 1st millennium B.C. were women's knives and that the hooked knives of the Ust-Poluy type are their prototype.

We do not have enough information about the Ob region to judge when iron began to be produced there, since imported material may merely have been reworked at the early sites, including Ust-Poluy. Only in settlements of the 1st millennium B.C. do we find sufficient evidence of iron production, for example, the abundant cinders and slag at the Us-Nel fortified hill site on the Sosva, at the mouth of the Yalping-ya, the Us-Tolt fortified hill site, and others.

As is evident from our descriptions, most of the settlements of the Ust-Poluy culture were fortified hill sites. Apparently they first appeared on the lower Ob during the Zelenaya Gorka period; however, they did not reach full development till the Ust-Poluy period. This suggests that changes took place in the social structure of the northern Ob tribes during the Ust-Poluy period. These changes include an obvious increase in the frequency of military encounters, resulting from the whole chain of economic and social developments. Military attacks were now made for many more reasons than those characteristic of the earlier stages of primitive social structure, that is, blood feuds and the seizure of women. Only this increase in military conflict can explain the appearance of advanced and specialized weapons of attack and defense in the Ust-Poluy culture.

We shall not dwell on all the types of weapons, since they are described in special articles published elsewhere in this volume.* We shall merely list the basic types: bronze three-bladed arrowheads, certainly not inspired by hunting needs; bone lamellar armor and helmets; and spear points, among which the superbly made bronze three-bladed spear point merits special attention (Fig. 7). These spears come from territory of the Kulayka culture, which is adjacent and akin to the Ust-Poluy culture.[31]

---

* [The author refers to pp. 121–78 of *MIA*, no. 35, 1953. These articles have not been translated for the present work. Editor, A.I.N.A.]

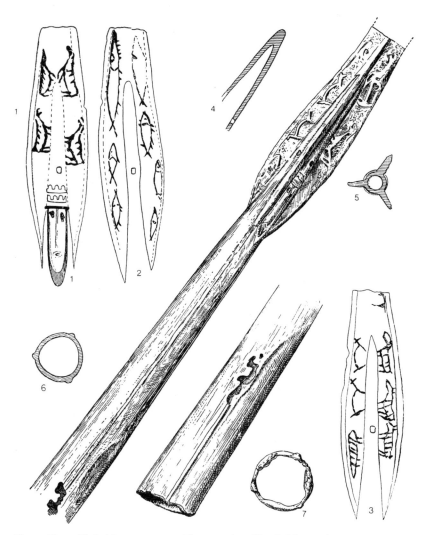

Fig. 7. Three-bladed bronze spear with engraving (Omsk Museum).
   1, 2, 3–tracings of the figures on the blades; 4, 5, 6–cross sections through various parts of the spear; 7–edge of the socket of the spear, somewhat reduced.

Besides the three-bladed form, which is not known outside western Siberia, there are figures of different animals and fish on the blades, which make this spear distinctive. Stylistically these figures are very much like those known from engravings and from the Ural pictographs. Furthermore, on the socket at the base of the blades there is the representation of a mask that is very similar to the Ob-region bronze masks of this period. These masks probably were associated with the idea of honoring an ancestor, an idea which developed with the increasing importance of the role of the military leader and which was expressed in skull-preservation rites, some features of which are similar to those of the Ananino culture. The possibility of this association leads us to view this spear as something extraordinary, but we do not know whether it was the property of a military leader or was used for some sort of ritual purpose. To grasp the meaning of this spear, it is interesting to cite Grigoriy Novitskiy's report on the sacred, perhaps ancient, spear worshiped in Pelym.

"In the black yurts several stadia from the city of Pelym, they worship a spear, to which is attached a small stone, and they keep it as a true idol, worshiped since antiquity by their elders; they, out of the darkness and ignorance of their ancestors hold it in high esteem. . . . When some animal, usually a horse, is brought for dreadful sacrifice to it, the priest, having raised this spear with only his hand, lays it lightly on the back of the animal and even if that animal be the strongest it drops to its knees and is oppressed by some invisible weight, even to the point of sweating and groaning, and cannot rise or straighten out, until the spear itself is raised: and the priest again takes it. . . ."[32]

The maces and poleaxes are even more specifically weapons. They are known both as miniatures and as true weapons, and they include a bi-metallic mace and a bronze poleaxe of superb workmanship found in the northern Ob region. Some investigators have held that the poleaxe is a ritual or ceremonial object because it is very light, being hollow-cast rather than solid-cast, has a very narrow socket, and is extremely gracile. Undoubtedly these ideas are correct; however, a military poleaxe with a sharp cutting edge does not have to be terribly heavy if it is set in a long enough handle. It is possible, though, as has been proposed with respect to the celebrated Pinega "axes," that a poleaxe of this kind could have been used on solemn occasions as a symbol of the achievements of a famous warrior or military leader, rather than as a weapon. However that may be, the following items are certainly of a military nature: the iron sword, or more properly, the long Sarmatian type of dagger from the Severnaya Sosva,[33] the small iron dagger discovered near Salekhard,[34] and the spears, both the iron spears from the Potchevash graves and the bronze spears.

The splendid weapons, some of which may have been used for rites and ceremonies, and the appearance of figures of warriors with swords (for example, the engraved image on the bone breastplate from Ust-Poluy) provide even more evidence than does the fortified hill site that the military relations were complex and, probably, that the role of the military leader had increased in importance. All the same, we still have too little material from which to judge the degree of development and the social character of the forest tribes of western Siberia during the Ust-Poluy period. From ethnographic data we know that among the Uralic family of western Siberian peoples there existed until recent times a dual system in which all the tribes of the Mansi (Voguls), Khanty (Ostyaks), Nentsy (Samodi), Selkups (Ostyak-Samoyeds), and others were divided in two strictly exogamous parts or moieties. Under these conditions a typical clan could not come into existence, since the local groups from which each of the two parts or moieties were composed were not inde-pendent in regard to exogamy but fully subordinated to a dual exogamy. Each local group was a collection of congeners forming an extended family, each family containing two to five (formerly more) married couples, living in a separate house. Filiation was patrilineal, marriage, as a rule, patrilocal, although matrilocal marriages were fairly common. Offsprings of matrilocal marriages bore the name of the father but at the same time were subject to the general norms of a given village and almost mechanically adapted themselves to the local group of the mother and, in the end, to her moiety. It may be projected that during Ust-Poluy times the system differed little, although there is the possibility that matrilineality and matrilocality were more emphasized.

Unfortunately, not a single burial ground has yet been found among the fairly numerous Ust-Poluy sites. Therefore, we do not have sufficient data to determine the physical type of the carriers of the culture. Such information would be of great value in answering questions on how this culture formed. Perhaps the numerous anthropomorphic images characteristic of the Ust-Poluy culture and represented by two forms, the three-dimensional and the flat figures, can serve as substitutes of a sort, albeit weak ones, for actual burials. The first type includes a bronze hollow figure of a man, carved models of clayey shale, some very realistic masks, and a superb stone sculptured representation of the head of a warrior found on the River Tuy.[35] Although from the territory of an adjacent culture, it is, just the same, interesting for tracing the physical type of the population of the lower Ob. Also coming into play is the anthropomorphic figure from Potchevash burial mound number 15,[36] which is highly reminiscent of the Glyadenovo figure and, in general composition, is similar to the figure carved on the bone breastplate from Ust-Poluy. The second type of representation includes the anthropomorphic figures scratched on bronze discs, less frequently on bone plates.

An interesting conclusion may be drawn from the information cited above. The figures from the southern edge of the forest zone, and even more from the forested steppe, show primarily Europoid facial features.[37] Similar features are displayed by the images of the Ust-Poluy period of the northern Ob, for example, the masks from Makar-Visyng-Tur, the small cast model from Ust-Poluy, and the masks in the Khanty-Mansi Museum. But among these, specifically in the north, there is a clear-cut, profoundly different Mongoloid type, represented by the bronze figure from Ust-Poluy and by the engravings on the plaques and discs from Ust-Poluy and the Khanty-Mansi *okrug*. All this confirms T. A. Trofimova's observation that the population of the Urals and western Siberia was a mixed type.[38] The sharp differences between the Europoid and Mongoloid features, we must assume, allows us to extend to western Siberia Trofimova's contention that the mixing of ethnic groups of different origin was incomplete in the Kama region during the Ananino epoch.

In considering the physical type of the carriers of the Ust-Poluy culture, it would be interesting to treat, albeit briefly, the elements that allow us to form some judgment of their external appearance. These characteristics include tattooing, which is depicted very clearly as vertical lines on the Khanty-Mansi masks and those of the Ishimka cache.[39] Tattooing was widespread among the Mansi and Khanty in historical times and disappeared in the Ob region only at the beginning of the 20th century. Another specific feature of external adornment was the wearing of braids, not only by women but by men as well, as can be judged by the Potchevash figure of a bearded man with braids. The custom of wearing braids, which was quite widespread in Siberia and which evidently appeared in the Ob region in the Ust-Poluy period, continued even longer, as may be judged by the engravings of the 1st millennium A.D. and by the ethnographic evidence. This custom persists even today among the Mansi and Khanty in some places. We have little to go on in regard to the clothing, and what is more, the clothing probably varied greatly from region to region. One should note merely the peculiar method of carrying a knife or dagger, a detail clearly expressed in the Sapagova figures. One end of the sheath was attached to the belt, the other was strapped to the leg. This unique and highly practical method is widely used among the hunters of the Ob region, that is, the Mansi and the Khanty.

The engraved figures provide a rich material for judging the religious concepts of the people of the Ust-Poluy period. We shall treat this problem when examining the materials relating to the 1st millennium A.D., but at present merely state the most characteristic and specific features. Among the engravings on the plaques and disks, we find figures with unique mixed anthropozoomorphic features. We also find anthropomorphic figures with added animal or bird heads and anthropomorphized representations of birds and animals, sometimes with human masks. If we compare these images with the mythical figures of the half-human, half-animal totem ancestors encountered in Ugrian folklore, we will have a firm enough basis for regarding these images as a graphic attempt to depict the complex images of the primitive totemistic attitudes. The figures scratched on the metal disks are grouped in part in specific compositions, evidently determined by some fixed concepts. In the upper part of the disk there are figures that depict a number of male and female clan totem ancestors. In the lower part there are representations of fish, snakes, and water animals, otters and beavers, evidently depicting the "lower world." The "upper," heavenly world is represented by the sun-bird Kars doing battle with the creatures of the lower world. Thus, in these compositions one finds that multisystem universe which is characteristic of the cosmogonic concepts of the peoples of Siberia, including the Ob Ugrians.

We have already had the occasion to consider the question of the content of the Ust-Poluy culture. My views of its origin and its role in the formation of the Ob peoples were outlined in a lecture and an article published in 1940.[40] The fundamental aspects of the hypothesis voiced at that time have been fully confirmed of late, on the basis of incomparably more material. As I said at the time, the most characteristic feature of the Ust-Poluy culture is its twofold nature. In describing the material, it was noted that the Ust-Poluy culture showed characteristics that are similar to both the ancient and the modern cultures of northeastern Asia. The similarity shows itself not only in the types of economy, which could easily be explained by the similarity of the ecologic adaptation, but also by the characteristics and details that could be the result of ethnic contact only. The specific details are the similarities in the construction of the dog harness, the bridles for the reindeer decoy (to those of the Tungus and the Chukchi draft bridle), and the details of house construction (to that of some proto-Eskimos). One is struck by the great similarity of the bone spade found at Ust-Poluy to the type widely employed among the Caribou Eskimos. Perhaps this is the place to mention the similarity in form of the Ust-Poluy and proto-Eskimo bone combs, although some of those from Ust-Poluy have sculpted decorations not found in the examples from Bering Sea graves. The Ust-Poluy culture and the cultures of northeastern Asia have an advanced, highly artistic bone sculpture in the round that is not found in the territory of the cultures neighboring on or akin to the Ust-Poluy, nor did this form exist in the Kama region, in Kazakhstan, or on the upper Yenisey.

Similarity with southern elements, the second characteristic of the Ust-Poluy culture, can also be followed in a number of traits mentioned in the analysis of the materials. We have already mentioned the diffusion of weapons of Scytho-Sarmatian types along the lower Ob during the Ust-Poluy period, that is, types which are characteristic of the steppe and forested-steppe cultures of that epoch. However, if these were the only examples of similarity to the south, they could be taken as random contacts only. Of much greater significance are the bronze cauldrons with ring bases, the dominant form of the Ust-Poluy pottery.[41] Studlike projections often found on the handles of the bronze cauldrons and frequently used as decorations on various everyday objects began to appear in the forested steppe and taiga, owing to the diffusion of ornamental motifs previously unknown in the north (for example, the cord) but typical of the forested steppe. Finally, the nature of these relations is evidenced by a find on the lower Ob, that is, a flat stone with a representation of a ram's head in relief. It was discovered in the Berezov region and is identical with the flat stones among the antiquities of the forested steppe of the southern and middle Trans-Ural region. P. A. Dmitriyev likened these stones to the small stone tables of Sauromatian (Sarmatian) Volga and the Cis-Ural slopes, and he dated them as Late Scythian–Early Sarmatian.

On the basis of his study of the small stone tables, which in turn are remotely analogous to the bronze altars of Central Asia, Dmitriyev concluded that the stones with the rams' heads were also altar stones.[42] Whether these are actually altar stones has not been clarified and requires thorough study, but there can be no doubt that they had ritual significance. It is also evident that a ritual object, in this case the sacrificial stone, was of great value to the members of the clan in whose religion it played a role. Such an object could not have any barter value outside the clan. Although such objects as weapons, ornaments, and metal vessels appeared in the long barter chains far from their place of manufacture, a sacrificial stone could only have been taken to the lower Ob, more than 1,500 km from its place of origin, by the northward movement of its immediate owners.

The coiled-animal theme is equally valuable for determining the nature of relationships during the Ust-Poluy period. This subject is very well known among the steppe cultures, in particular those of southern Siberia, where the early forms of the representations of a coiled animal date from the 7th to the 5th centuries B.C. In the ensuing centuries, the subject gradually degenerated, lost its realistic quality, and finally became the spiral rosette which can be seen on, for example, the handles of the Late Tagar mirrors.[43] The coiled animal engraved on the plaque now in the Khanty-Mansi Museum is very realistic, despite the highly primitive aspect of the image.

The representation of the coiled elk on one of the plaques from the Istyak cache is equally realistic and shows that the perception of the ornamental motif was not mechanical (the representations of coiled animals from the Ob are certainly not mechanical), but was a perception of the subject in its entirety, with its inherent content. This subject could scarcely have penetrated to the lower Ob later than the middle of the 1st millennium B.C., because after that time it had already begun to assume a purely ornamental character in the south. This is one more bit of evidence in favor of the date of formation of the Ust-Poluy culture stated in our analysis of the material.

We have summarized both the arctic and southern features observed in the Ust-Poluy culture. These features are such that we cannot attribute them to chance intercourse, but to firm ethnic ties. With what kind of ethnoses can these components of the Ust-Poluy culture be associated? The research of G. N. Prokofyev is of great interest in solving this problem; unfortunately, he left his work unfinished and we have only a very brief paper and lecture notes which he read at the Conference of the Commission on Ethnogenesis held by the Division of History and Philology of the Academy of Sciences of the U.S.S.R. on 28 and 29 May 1940.[44]

In studying the various languages of the Samoyedic group, Prokofyev concluded that "in addition to the thick stratum of vocabulary derived from the dialects spoken by the Sayan Samoyeds (Mator, Karagas, Tayginets, Soyot, Koybal, Kamasinets, and others) in the lexicon of the Nenets, Nganasan, and Enets languages, these languages have a considerable number of words not derived from the Sayan Samoyeds. These include, primarily, words relating to material production under subarctic conditions . . . and reflecting . . . the changes which occurred in the area of material culture of the Samoyedic tribes during their movement northward and their contact with the subarctic culture of the aboriginal population,"[45] which Prokofyev, on the basis of his analysis of ethnonyms, distinguishes as the "Tyan" group, which is non-Samoyedic in origin.

By linguistic analysis, he was able to outline the general features of the linguistic affinity of the Tyan ethnic group. He found that the names for the poncho[parka]-like arctic fur clothing, fur footwear, and fur coverings for skin tents, and the names for the walrus, seal, white bear, lemming, polar partridges, and so on that appear in the northern Samoyedic languages, that is, Nenets, Enets, and Nganasan (but that do not appear in the southern Samoyedic languages), have parallels and explanations in the Eskimo and Yukagir languages. This common lexical feature noted by Prokofyev can be traced in other areas of language as well: in the autonyms of the northern Samoyedic peoples and in the construction of the numeral system from 11 through 20.

For the 1st millennium B.C. in the arctic regions of the lower Ob, we know of cultures of littoral hunters who occupied pit houses and had a form of life evidently very close to that of the Eskimos. The earliest known site of this type is the dune campsite on the shore of the Kara Sea near [Cape] Tiutey-sale, which yielded pottery similar to that of Zelenaya Gorka. Pottery of this type was also discovered by G. A. Chernov on the Shchuchya River and farther to the west, in the eastern and northern parts of the Bolshezemelskaya tundra.[46] The middle and second half of the 1st millennium B.C. is represented by the pit house settlement on Tiutey-sale, a settlement whose remains were discovered in 1927 by Kols at the mouth of the Taz (also beyond the Arctic Circle), and one of the layers of the sacrificial place Khaebidya Peadera in the Bolshezemelskaya tundra.[47] Examples of the latest sites of the arctic littoral culture are the 16th and 17th century pit house settlements on Cape Khaen-sale, on the shore of the Malygin Strait at 73° north. This shows that despite the ethnic movements that took place in the lower Ob region during the 1st millennium B.C. as well as later (more about this later), the archaic Arctic culture continued to exist in polar regions at distances of hundreds of kilometers from the large river routes. The bearers of this culture, insofar as we can judge from a grave beneath the floor of a pit house at Khaen-sale, were tribes which retained their Mongoloid features. The remnants of these tribes, most probably proto-Lapp, were partially assimilated and partially annihilated by the Nentsy, who appeared in the Ob tundra and on the seacoast around the 10th century A.D. It was from these people that the Nentsy took the elements of polar culture reflected in their language. Nenets folklore offers abundant material for reconstructing the way of life of the ancient littoral hunters.

The profundity of the changes that occurred in the culture of the people of the lower Ob, demonstrated by the appearance of the Ust-Poluy culture on the scene, indicates that these changes were produced not only by the development of exchange with the south but by the appearance of a new ethnic element in the taiga region of northwestern Siberia, an element which brought with it customs entirely alien to the forest zone, that is, a tradition of Scytho-Sarmatian aspect. With what ethnos should these newcomers be associated? An examination of the ethnographic map will show that at present the entire Ob basin, eastward to the Narym area, westward to the Ural range, including the Chusovaya and upper Ufa rivers and some regions of the western slope of the Urals, and south-ward along the Lozva basin and the left bank of the Tavda, is settled by tribes of Ob Ugrians, the Mansi and the Khanty. If we consider the number of Ugrian tribes that were Turkicized and Russified and those in the east, in the region of the Tomsk-Narym [section of the] Ob, that were assimilated by Samoyedic tribes, the territory occupied by Ugrian tribes in historical times must have been very much larger than at present. In the earlier epochs, for example, in the 1st millennium B.C., their territory must have extended to the steppes of northern Kazakhstan and the southern Trans-Ural region, if we include the ancestors of the Baraba [steppe peoples] and the Magyars who lived there.[48]

Thus, one may say that about the beginning of the 1st millennium B.C., the steppe and forested-steppe regions to the south of what was then the limit of the western Siberian taiga were peopled by ancient Ugrian tribes which had progressed from pastoral cattle breeding to nomadic horse breeding. The whole forest belt and the tundra north of it to the Arctic coast was a region settled by mixed tribes which had come there in Neolithic times from the south and the east. In the taiga and the Ural range, the archaic Uralic element prevailed, perhaps already affected by the assimilative activity of the Ugrians in the southern taiga. Since at a later date we find an entirely Ugrian population throughout the forest region of the lower Ob, it is natural to assume that the sudden change which we have traced in the archaeological material was due to the appearance of the Ust-Poluy culture and kindred forest cultures in connection with the northward movement of Ugrian groups. We shall support this assumption with additional material.

In the folklore of the Khanty and Mansi, as well as in the clan and family names, and in the toponyms, we find one name that is of considerable interest for our problem: in Mansi it is *sipyr* (*š'ipər*), *syopyr*, *supyr*, *supra*; in Khanty it is *sebar* (*šebar*), *sopra*, *shaber*. B. Munkácsi translates it as a "clan name" (*nemzetség neve*). K. Papay reports that he heard the expression *shaber mu* ("land of the Shabers") in the region of Salekhard (Obdorsk), while A. Reguli, who traveled in those places before Papay, points to the *shaber maam* ("Shaber people") who lived there. To this we may add the names for the *sopra* clans: it is Sobrin for those near Salekhard, and Syopyr for those near Berezov. We also know of a Khanty leader Samar, who lived at what is now Samarovo on the Irtysh. On the Irtysh there was also a town called, in Khanty, *Tyapyr ush*, and in Mansi, *Syopyr-us*. The names *Supra, Sopra, Syopra* are very often given to settlements, streams, and landmarks throughout the lower Ob-Irtysh region. *Sipyr* (*sepyr, shapyr, shabyr*) emerges as the name of the progenitress of the moiety Moshch (Mon't'), one of the two Ugrian moieties. The word *sipyr* also appears as a synonym for the Mansi (Vogul). For example, in Khanty we have *sebar khul* or *mansi khul*, that is, the sebar of Mansi fish.* In a number of songs, the territory inhabited by the Mansi and the Khanty is called *lui vot asirm Sipyr makhum unlyn ma* ("the land populated by the Sipyr people of the cold north wind").

Finally, among the Tobol Tartars, according to S. K. Patkanov [Patkanoff], there is a legend about the Syvyr, or Sibyr, people who occupied the territory along the middle and lower Irtysh before the arrival of the Tartars. The Tartars ascribe to these people the burial mounds and the fortified hill sites which are named accordingly *Savyr-tuba* and *Savyr-kala*.[49] In the folklore of the Evenkis, we find a description of Savyr, the land to the west of the Evenki territory, populated by a horse people.

---

* [The "yelets," a small fish of the carp family. Translator, A.I.N.A.]

In historical sources of the beginning of the 13th century, we encounter the name "land of the Sibur," beyond the Urals.

Some investigators—for example, Florinskiy, Šafařik, and Patkanov—who have taken up the question of the Sipyr people (*syvyr, savyr, sibyr*) conclude that the Savyrs inhabited the middle and, in part, the lower Irtysh and regions adjacent. The similarity of the Savyrs and the Ugric-speaking peoples is indicated by the association of this name with the Magyar branch of the Ugrians. For example, Konstantin Bagryanorodnyi reports that the Magyars, while they lived in Lebediya,* were called Savartoy (Σαβαρτοι), which some scholars have explained as Σαβαρ τουτξοτοι 'ασφαλοι (Savars, that is to say, they are secure or fearless).[50] Patkanov [Patkanoff] considers it possible that the Siberian Sabars, or Sabers, were but a branch of the widely scattered Ugro-Finnic family.[51]

Some scholars hold that the Sabirs were of Turkic origin, and associate them, on the basis of information given by Procopius and Jordanes, with the Huns, in keeping with the theory that the Hungarians are of Hun-Turkic origin. However, this theory is not substantiated by the Hungarian language, which belongs, as everyone knows, to the Finno-Ugric family. B. Munkácsi's research is particularly interesting in this respect. He demonstrates that the horse-breeding terminology is a factor common to all the Ugric languages and that the terminology is not borrowed from the Turkic languages, as some researchers have assumed, but from the Iranian and Indo-Iranian languages. Munkácsi explains the very existence of the nomadic horse-breeding way of life among the ancient Ugrians by their proximity to the Iranian-speaking nomads, possibly the Sacae.[52] In view of the common horse-breeding terminology of the Hungarians and Ob Ugrians, we cannot place the ancient Ugrian tribes that became a component of the Mansi and Khanty farther north than the western Siberian forested steppe; indeed, we must place them in the immediate vicinity of the ancient ancestors of the Hungarians, at least during the nomadic horse-breeding epoch (that is, not later than the first half of the 1st millennium B.C.).

We shall not go further into this matter here, inasmuch as a separate paper should be devoted to the ancient history of the southern Ugrian tribes. We shall merely point out that the available information leads us to conclude that the ancient ancestors of the Ugrian peoples, whose common name was some variant of Sipyr-Savyr, were based on the ancient culture of western Siberia, the Trans-Ural, and in part, Kazakhstan. At the beginning of the 1st millennium B.C., the southern branch of the Savyr tribes experienced a profound and prolonged influence of the Iranian-speaking groups, possibly the Sacae. Traces of this influence are not limited, of course, to the few horse-breeding terms mentioned, but extend, in Hungarian and in the Mansi and Khanty tongues, to different areas of material culture, social structure, and ideology. Some words are of interest in that they characterize the time and medium in which these ties existed. Such words are as follows: Mansi, *kēr*; Khanty, *karta, karti*

* [By tradition located somewhere between the Volga and the Don rivers. Editor, A.I.N.A.]

("iron") // Avestan, *karĕta*; Pahlavi, *kart*; New Persian, *kard* ("knife");
Mansi, *käsi*; Khanty, *keši, kēže*; Hungarian, *kés (kēš)* ("knife") // Vakkh
(Pamir), *köž* ("knife"); Mansi, *sor*; Khanty, *sạr*; Hungarian, *sör* ("beer");
Sanskrit, *sūrā* ("intoxicating drink," "beer"); Mansi, *sāk* ("beads") //
Sanskrit, *saktá* ("pendants"); Mansi, *sorńi, sarəń*; Khanty, *sarńa*; Hun-
garian, *arany* ("gold") // Avestan, *zaranya* ("gold"); Mansi, *ɔtər* ("hero,"
"creature possessing superhuman strength"); Sanskrit, *asura* ("super-
human being").[53]

The examples cited may easily be expanded. On their basis we can
conceive of a society at a quite high stage of development and already
acquainted with ferrous metallurgy.

On the basis of the archaeological material, we may say that these
ancient nomadic Ugrian-Savyr tribes are represented in the cultures
reflected by the burial mounds of the Sargatskoye and Kokonovka type
in the middle Irtysh territory and by the Chelyabinsk mounds in the
southern Trans-Ural territory.

The archaeological material indicates that during the 1st millennium
B.C., as the nomadic Ugrian tribes developed and became stronger, their
influence on the sedentary tribes of the adjacent forest regions also
increased.

At a sharply defined boundary between the taiga on the right bank and
the forested steppe on its left bank, the Potchevash culture arose. It was
based on a complex economy of hunting and fishing, agriculture, and
cattle breeding. It was sedentary in nature, as can be judged by the
numerous fortified hill sites. The pottery of the Potchevash culture
undoubtedly belongs to the forest cultures and descends genetically from
pottery of the Zelenaya Gorka type. At the same time, the Potchevash
culture had mound burials, which are not characteristic of the forest
hunters and which contain, along with the Potchevash pottery, pottery
of the Sargatskoye steppe type. This mixture of pottery forms was already
noted in the early layers of the Ivanovskaya fortified hill site, a site
antecedent to the Potchevash culture. There can hardly be doubt that one
of the tribes of forest hunters and fishermen that inhabited the southern
edge of the forest in this part of the Irtysh region was in close proximity
at some period to the nomads who subsequently assimilated it, which in
turn explains the complexity of the forms of the Potchevash culture. It
is with these specifically Potchevash forms of material culture and art,
particularly engraving, that one finds a similarity to the southern
component in the Ust-Poluy culture.

Thus, in the final analysis, the Potchevash culture was the starting
point for the formation of the Ust-Poluy culture. At present we cannot
establish exactly the date of appearance of the Potchevash culture, but it
could scarcely have been earlier than the 6th or 5th century B.C.

The Ust-Poluy culture with its developed technology could not but
have exerted a profound influence in the neighboring littoral arctic tribes,
as evidenced by the pottery at the campsites of the Yamal Peninsula, the
Taz Inlet, and the Ya-Vay Peninsula, pottery which is rather similar to
that of Ust-Poluy in shape and decoration. What is more, in the folklore
of the Nentsy, who may be assumed to have spread through the tundra

along the lower Ob about the 10th century A.D., we find numerous legends about the "sirti" people, whom they found upon crossing the Ob [from the east]. The name of this people has been preserved in the toponymy in the form of the numerous *Siirti-yagas* (rivers of the Sirti), *Siirti-myads* (villages of the Sirti), *Siirti-nados* (Sirti Knoll), et cetera. Alexander Schrenk pointed out the parallelism he found in the names *sirti* or *sirti-ta* and *siber-ta*.[54] In the last variant, the similarity with the name *sipyr* is quite apparent. In all probability, some of the aboriginal arctic tribes, perhaps those whose territory was closest to the Ust-Poluy, were to some extent assimilated by the Savyr Ugrians, and thus they subsequently became known to the Nentsy under the general name Savyr.[55]

In concluding our description of the highly interesting Ust-Poluy epoch in the history of western Siberia, we draw attention to a phenomenon which is quite easy to trace, but which is far from clear, that is, the relationship between the cultures of the Ob-Irtysh and those of the Early Tashtyk period of southern Siberia and China. We had occasion to treat this problem earlier when we pointed out the similarity between the lobed celts of Tobolsk type and the northern Chinese celts of the Late Chou and Han periods. In addition to the shape of the celts, one may note the design widely used on them and the Ust-Poluy owner's marks which are, as it were, an imitation of hieroglyphs and seals, the similarity to which is strengthened by the fact that several of them are framed with cartouches. The widely used, elongated Z-shaped meander employed as an independent decoration or a border on the bone and bronze artifacts is a strong element of similarity, and another is the chessboard design found on the Ust-Poluy pottery and known both in the Chinese ornamentation of the Han epoch and in the wood carvings of the Tashtyk culture. Finally, there is the similarity of the Potchevash openwork plaques to the Chinese ones of the Han period. We could cite many more parallels, but the reasons behind such common factors remain unclear and their explanation is one of the tasks of future research on Savyr-Ugrian antiquity.

PART IV

THE REGION OF THE LOWER OB
IN THE FIRST MILLENNIUM A.D.

V. N. CHERNETSOV

Synopsis and Classification
of the Materials

It is only in comparatively recent times that a systematic archaeological study has been attempted along the lower Ob River; yet a considerable amount of material from the 1st millennium A.D. has already been collected. The greater part of this material, however, consists of chance finds which have come to a museum at different times, with no documentation except for the name of the place where it was found. Most of the large collections were obtained from the local population, and it is not always possible to associate them with any particular complex. A good deal of study has now been dedicated to the archaeological sites dating to the 1st millennium A.D. and the beginning of the 2nd millennium. The number of fortified hill sites, campsites, and graves reaches into the dozens, yet we have adequate, detailed information about few of them. There has been practically no scientific investigation of these sites, with the possible exception of the cemetery Barsov Gorodok, excavated by F. Martin in 1891. This is why it has been impossible for a long time to make use of the rich collections in the Tobolsk Museum, the State Hermitage [in Leningrad], and the State Historical Museum [in Moscow] even though these collections contain pottery and a large number of bronze artifacts.

It has been only in the last fifteen to twenty years that a well-documented, though small, amount of material has been processed, which made it possible to work out a basic time sequence for the sites of the 1st millennium A.D. on the Lower Ob and to define the principal stages in the history of the tribes inhabiting the area.

An additional difficulty encountered in working over the material of the 1st millennium is caused by the small degree of change observable in the material culture throughout this period. This continuity in form makes a typological analysis very difficult, and reliance on stratigraphy is indispensable for establishing a sequence of the cultural stages.

The absence of change in form is especially conspicuous in the large and significant ceramic collection. Over a period of more than a thousand years the basic pottery shapes not only scarcely alter, but they maintain their archaic appearance. The same can be said of the ornamentation, where only the most careful analysis reveals successive changes in its

Translated by Penelope Rainey from *MIA*, no. 58, 1957, pp. 136–245.

composition, with the ornamental elements for the most part retained exactly as they were in the 1st millennium B.C.

It is characteristic that T. J. Arne points to a return of patterns that are similar to Ananino ones when he describes the pottery from Barsov Gorodok, a cemetery dating to the end of the 1st and the beginning of the 2nd millennia A.D.[1] This conservation in shape and ornamentation is not limited to the Ob area, for M. V. Talitskiy notes the same phenomenon in the Kama River region. "Pottery making in the Kama region," he writes, "preserves very archaic features for a long time, almost until the 15th century. One can fairly easily sort out a series of pots extending from the Ananino to the Bolgar period which will vary only in details which are not apparent at the first glance."[2] A. P. Smirnov writes in connection with this conservatism in ceramic shapes: "The shape of the cup with a rounded, slightly thickened base which was typical of the Ananino, Pyanobor [Pyanyy Bor] and Lomovatovo periods is preserved even later into the 10th and 13th centuries A.D."[3]

The same phenomenon can be observed, but in a different degree, in other facets of the material culture; in the field of representational art it is present to an equal degree. The figures in bronze, considerable numbers of which are included in the archaeological materials, undergo changes both in style and subject matter during the course of centuries, but the changes are so gradual and difficult to perceive that it has so far been impossible to date the figures on the basis of formal analysis alone.

This extraordinary conservatism of form deserves our serious attention. The fact that it prevails over a very wide territory, in the Ob region as well as the Kama River basin, suggests that it is the result of historic processes common to the two regions. We shall attempt to discover some of these processes. In a preliminary way, we can state that they are basically due to the fact that, at the beginning of the A.D. era, in the Ob and Ural regions the formation of definite ethnic groups had already taken place, and their development was not disturbed by an intrusion of foreign elements during the greater part of the 1st millennium A.D. To this preliminary statement we may add that the resemblance between the material cultures of the Ob and the Kama areas (as observed in the succeeding stages of their ceramics and representational art) justifies the assumption that the tribes which settled in the Ob-Irtysh, Ural, and Kama regions are related.

For the reasons mentioned earlier, it has been extremely difficult to establish a time sequence for the Ob River sites of the 1st millennium A.D. This has only been accomplished after a detailed study of the multilayered fortified hill site of Us-Tolt, where a fortunate distribution of the material made it possible to distinguish three successive groups of pottery that covered in time the major part of the 1st millennium. After crosschecking of these groups with materials from several single-layered sites, the basic stages of the Ob material culture of this period could be established. At the present, the four basic stages that we have identified are as follows:

1. Yar-sale [Yarsalinskiy] stage (beginning after the Ust-Poluy): 200 B.C.–A.D. 200. The material of this stage, and particularly the ceramics,

ties it without a break to the preceding period, which is represented in the forest zone by the two interrelated cultures, the Ust-Poluy and the Potchevash. The Yar-sale archaeological materials are distinguished by novel and characteristic traits which define it as representing a distinct stage. The Potchevash and Ust-Poluy cultures correspond in time to the penetration into the forested Ob region of the Ugrian-Savyr tribes from the southern grasslands. The resulting period of intermixture with the local tribes of forest hunters and fishers is clearly reflected in the dual character of these cultures. It is only at this time that, in the ceramics of the forest zone, corded ware—so characteristic of the more southerly areas of the central Trans-Ural and western Siberia and hitherto unknown in the north—appears. The end of the Ust-Poluy period is marked by the disappearance of corded ornamentation and of ring-based pots (which were copied from bronze kettles). During the Yar-sale stage there occurred again a revival of stamped decoration characteristic of the forest pottery of the first half of the 1st millennium B.C.; it continued almost unchanged to the present day on the birchbark vessels of the Mansi and Khanty. At the beginning of the Yar-sale period the mixing of the newcomers and the indigenous tribes had been completed, the culture had lost its complex character, and all in all, this stage may be associated with the already-formed tribes reflected in the stages that follow.

2. Karym stage, A.D. 200–500, named after the village of Karym on the Yukonda River where the fortified hill site of Us-Tolt, which produced the pottery typical of this stage, is located. Although this pottery contains a number of specific traits, it represents only a sequential phase in the development of Yar-sale ceramics. A characteristic trait of the Karym stage is the development of the art of bronze figure casting. During this time motives in bronze decorative art, adopted from the southern jeweler's art, become widespread, particularly the imitation of medallions with almandine (garnet) inserts, as in the Podcherem cache. All told, the Karym stage is close to the Kharino one in the Cis-Ural area.

3. Orontur stage, A.D. 500–900. This stage is named after Lake Orontur in the headwaters of the Konda River, where a fortified hill site containing pottery that characterizes the stage is located. A number of sites has produced pottery which can be identified as transitional between the Karym and Orontur stages. The art of bronze casting retains a high level in the initial phases of the Orontur stage, but gradually degenerates toward the end of it. The material culture of the Orontur stage has much in common with the Lomovatovo; apparently both belong to interrelated groups of Ugrian tribes.

4. Kintusovo stage, A.D. 900–1200, named after the Khanty settlement Kintusovy Yurty on the Salym River. There is a cemetery nearby which yielded very rich material. The most characteristic trait of the ceramics of the Kintusovo stage is the widely used pattern produced with the stab-and-drag method using a small-toothed paddle. Figures of birds and animals cast in bronze almost disappear as ornaments and are replaced by palmate or digitate tinkling pendants for the most part imported from the Kama and Vychegda [on the western slopes of the Urals]. The common ornaments with small pearl-shaped studs and filigree work are

apparently also of western origin. The breeding of reindeer appeared in the Ob area toward the end of this stage, judging by the finds at the fortified hill site of Man-Nyaslan-Tur. Pottery fell into disuse at the same time, as its place was taken by imported copper kettles.

Chapter 1

The Yar-sale Stage
(200 B.C.–A.D. 200)

The most interesting of the sites dated to the 1st millennium A.D. in the area of the lower Ob is the fortified hill site of Us-Tolt, situated near the village of Karym (Kharom-Pavyl) on the middle reaches of the Yukonda River (Figs. 8 and 9).

The Yukonda is a left-bank tributary of the Konda River, joining the latter at the district town of Nakhrachi (in the Konda *rayon* of the Khanty-Mansi National *okrug*). This settlement was in former times a large tribal center, to judge from the evidence of history, folklore, and ethnography. It was a focal point for the Mansi who lived along the middle reaches of the Konda and its tributaries, the Tap and the Yukonda, that is, the population who spoke the Middle Konda dialect. It is this tribal center with which is associated the cycle of epic tales about the hero Vishch-Oter.[4] The settlements along the Yukonda, including Karym, belonged to the same tribe. The Yukonda is a typical taiga river, winding among swamps and hillocks overgrown with pine forest. The course of the river over its more than 500 km is interrupted by the countless logjams* so characteristic of rivers in the Konda valley, which flow through sandy terrain and are very difficult to navigate. As the banks are washed away, trees fall into the water, they cause jams during spring floods where the river narrows or curves sharply, and [eventually] earth will accumulate atop the logjam. In succeeding years more trees are heaped up, and eventually, over a space of 1, 2, or 3 km, the river disappears under an uninterrupted bridge of timbers and earth. Forests have already grown atop many of these logjams, and one can walk over them without suspecting that one is crossing the river.

In traveling on the river one must portage over these logjams—an easy task with a light craft but very difficult with a heavy load. Some of the logjams have had openings cut through them, but to go upstream or, even worse, downstream through these narrow passageways, between the wet, slippery timbers, especially with the very rapid current caused by the narrowness of the river at such places, is difficult and dangerous. This explains why in summertime the settlements along the middle and upper Yukonda and some of the other tributaries of the Konda are so very inaccessible, even though the distances involved are comparatively small.

* [*Zalomy*, in the original.]

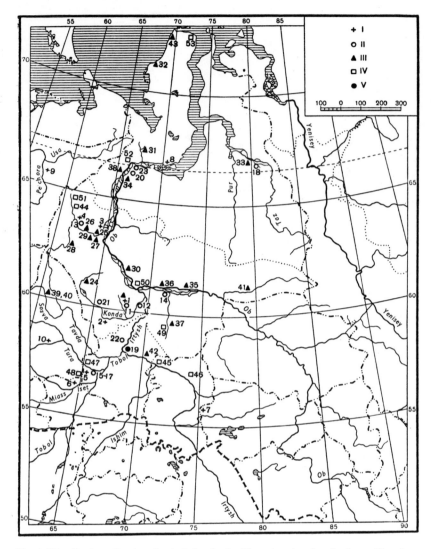

Fig. 8. Distribution of archaeological sites in the Ob region dated to the first millennium A.D.

I–the Yar-sale stage; II–the Karym stage; III–the Orontur stage; IV–the Kintusovo stage; V–the Potchevash culture.

I. *Yar-sale stage.* 1–Us-Tolt hill site at the village of Karym; 2–Leushinskoye hill site; 3–Sorovoy Cape hill site; 4–collections of D. I. Ilovayskiy on the Severnaya Sosva; 5–Slovtsov's hill site at Andreyevskoye Lake; 6–finds near Dalmatovo village on the Iset River; 7–Ust-Tartas *kurgans*; 8–finds at Yar-sale on the Yamal Peninsula; 9–find of scabbards on the Pechora River; 10–find of scabbards near the village of Koksharovaya on the Tagil River.

II. *The Karym stage.* 11–Us-Tolt hill site; 12–collections at Verbilskiy Cape on the Konda River; 13–collections of D. I. Ilovayskiy on the Severnaya Sosva; 14– collections near the mouth of the Salym River; 15–Kozlova cemetery; 16–Pereyminskiy [Pereyma] cemetery; 17–Zhilye hill site; 18–collections of R. E. Kols at Mameyev's winter campsite; 19–Tyukova (excavations of V. N. Pignatti; Potchevash culture); 20–finds at the Ishvar native village; 21–find of a representation of a deer on the Konda River; 22–finds at Filinskoye village; 23–finds at Salekhard.

III. *The Orontur stage.* 24–hill site at Lake Orontur; 25–Cape Shaytan (Yalping-Nël);

26–Sortynya III hill site; 27–Lyuli-Kar hill site; 28–finds at Khangla-Sam native village; 29–hill site Us-Nel; 30–finds at Bolshoy Atlym village; 31–finds on the Shchuchya River; 32–Cape Tiutey-sale campsite; 33–finds at mouth of Taz River; 34–Vozh-Pay hill site; 35–Barsov Gorodok cemetery; 36–Lenk-Ponk cemetery; 37–Vtorushin's collections at Kintusovo native village; 38–find near the Khara-pasl native village; 39–Shaytan caves; 40–Lakseya caves; 41–finds on the Vakh River; 42–burial mound finds near Aksenova village; 43–find near the mouth of Pyasyaday River.

IV. *The Kintusovo stage.* 44–Tān wārup-ēkwa hill site (near Lombvozh); 45–hill site and cemetery at Novo-Nikolsk village; 46–Bezymyannoye hill site; 47–Molchanova hill site and cache; 48–Bogandinskoye hill site; 49–Kintusovo cemetery; 50–Una-Pay cemetery; 51–Man-Nyaslan-Tur hill site; 52– Zelenaya Gorka campsite; 53–Cape Khaen-sale campsite.

The settlement of Karym is located about 200 km by river from Nakhrachi, on a low terrace of the right bank of the small river, the Kharom-ya (Karym-ya), a tributary to the Yukonda. The fortified hill site is in the immediate vicinity of the village and is located on a small hillock at which the small stream Vos-Kalteng-ya joins the Kharom-ya (Fig. 9). The hillock with its fairly steep slopes provides natural protection, which was further improved by artificial means. The narrow isthmus between the Kharom-ya and the Vos-Kalteng-ya was cut by two moats and another was dug around the monadnock. Presumably the earth from this moat was used to add to the hill. To the north the circular moat joined the Vos-Kalteng-ya, and thus the fortified hill site was surrounded by water on all sides.

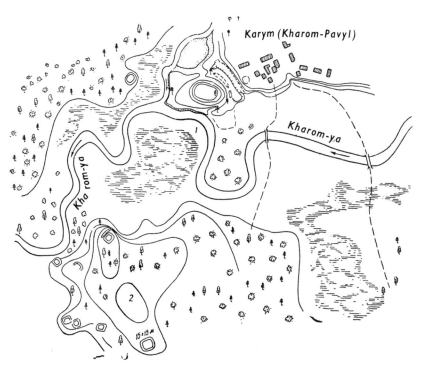

Fig. 9. Site of the fortified hill site Us-Tolt near the village of Karym.
1–Us-Tolt proper; 2–village of Mosryng-Vor-Nël.

Excavation showed that the area of the site was small, little more than 550 m², but densely occupied with pit houses. The crowding of the hill site apparently caused the settlement to spread beyond its limits; traces of pit houses were found to the northwest, beyond the boundary moats and on the right bank of the Vos-Kalteng-ya. In addition a settlement was found 200 m from the hill site on the left bank of the Kharom-ya, on a low, sandy rise overgrown with pine woods. Its pit houses are located for the most part along the edge of the rise on small headlands. Such locations obviously provided for good drainage, indispensable on the edge of the swampy floodplain.

Exploratory excavation disclosed a very thin and poorly yielding culture layer in one of the houses; it contained some unidentifiable pottery in a very fragmentary condition. The material obtained was not adequate for dating the houses with any certainty or for synchronizing them with any particular level of the fortified hill site.

There is a legend among the local Mansi that people from this settlement [on the sandy rise] were originally from the hill site, but that all later died of a sickness. This gave rise to the name of the place, Mosryng-Vor-Nël, that is, "Forested cape of the people who died of sickness." The hill site proper was called Us-Tolt, or "City Port," and figured in the legends of the Karym Mansi as the dwelling place of the ancestors of the tribe. Hence, until very recent times the site was held to be sacred, and sacrificial offerings were brought to its summit.

Investigation revealed that the strata associated with the place of sacrifice occupy the entire surface of the hill (Fig. 10, part 2, strata I, II, and V) and part of the side slopes (stratum IIa). The strata on the hill attain 1 m in thickness, those on the slopes, 0.5 m; they are composed of rotted chips, coals, and charred bones. No objects were discovered except on the very summit near a larch, where coins were found which dated to the 20th century.

Strata I and V were lighter in color and formed a lens on the summit of the hill. They must date to the latest period of the site in its existence as a place of sacrifice. Stratum II belongs to an earlier period; it is darker in color, and more amorphous. The wood is nearly decomposed. In the lower horizons of this stratum there are very occasionally found isolated fragments of pottery which apparently were transferred as a result of the stratification's being disturbed. A study of its profile indicates that stratum IIa is a displacement of stratum II due to sliding and erosion.

Below strata II and IIa lies a thin, sandy band, stratum IV, occasionally interrupted, which is distinguished by its light color and slight gumminess. Owing to erosion and deposition this band is somewhat thicker at the base of the hill. One may conclude that it was created by the last addition of earth to the hill when the trenches were deepened, shortly before the site was abandoned. This would explain why the layer was only faintly colored and contained no organic remains. Some time may have elapsed between the existence of the fortified hill site and the appearance on the hill of the place of sacrifice.

Stratum III is already associable with the site proper. It consists of very gummy [greasy] soil, strongly colored by its high charcoal content.

Pottery is abundant in the upper and middle horizons but sharply declines in the lower horizon and in the basic level is almost never encountered except in a few isolated cases which will be described later. Easily traced at this level, on the brow of the hill, are the rotted wood remains from the vertically set timbers that formed a palisade around the town site (Fig. 10, part 2, F). The lower ends of the beams were buried in the earth and for this purpose a trench was dug along the entire brow of the hill. On

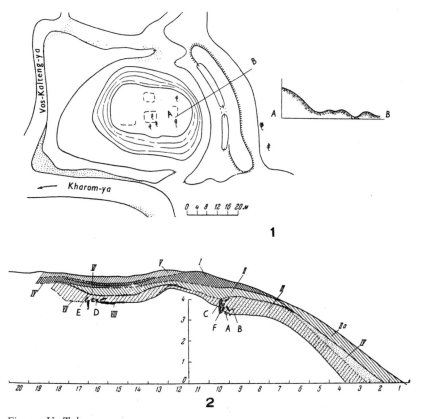

Fig. 10. Us-Tolt.
   1–sketch plan; 2–cross section.

the outer side this stockade was reinforced at the base by a double row of short poles or stakes which apparently did not protrude above the level of the ground. In addition the whole base of the wall was braced by a framework of horizontal timbers.

    Remains of pit houses were found in the flat area of the hill site, but a survey could not determine how many of them there were as the area was almost completely covered by the later levels of the sacrificial area.

    A small depression in the ground indicating the site of a former pit house was used in initiating the survey. The pit house, with its floor about 1 m below the former surface level, had a tentlike roof supported by posts at each of the corners of a centrally located hearth. In construction it was a duplicate of the semisubterranean hut which we had excavated in the village of Zelenaya Gorka near Salekhard[5] and of the dwellings so common on the lower Ob among the Khanty and Mansi until the beginning of the 20th century, described in detail by the investigators of that era.[6]

The pit of the Us-Tolt house was partly filled by the layer of earth which was once atop the [now collapsed] roof. The sandy layer, already described, sharply separated it from the more recent "sacrificial" strata above it.

The layer filling the hut, like layer III beyond the palisade, consisted of a rather gummy soil crammed full of pottery fragments. The presence of sherds in the roof layer is explainable by the fact that the earth used to cover the roof was taken not only from the pit dug for the house, but also in part from the culture layer of the hill site. The hearth consisted of a few thin layers of charcoal and the layers of reddish, burnt clay created by repeated coatings of the hearth.

The largest quantity of potsherds was collected from layer III, beyond the palisade, as well as in the area of the settlement proper.

The pottery of layer III is varied, and may be grouped basically into three types. The traits these three types have in common are the rounded bases and emphasized profiling of the neck and shoulders. Yet the profiling of the neck and rims and the ornamentation differ markedly among the vessels. Numerically, in this layer, the first and second types predominate; the third is encountered more rarely, though represented by larger fragments.

In addition, a few pieces of an entirely different appearance were found at point A in the layer directly under the settlement. They were fragments of flat-bottomed vessels which were covered near the base with comb stamping, but in the higher parts with bands of slanting, crosslike stampings, executed on a burnished surface (Plate XXXV, items 9–12). Judging by the fragments, this pottery from the layer underlying the settlement has some traits in common with pottery characteristic of the Suzgun culture, but it is more recent and belongs to the end of the Bronze Age. It is quite possible that there was a site of that period on the hill at the mouth of the Vos-Kalteng-ya, but that it was later destroyed when the fortified hill site was built.

The division of the pottery into three typological groups (not counting the flat-bottomed Bronze Age vessels) depends on stratigraphic evidence. All three types are encountered together in only two places: in the part of layer III which is on the slope outside the palisade, where slides and erosion from the fortified hill site resulted in an accumulation from all layers, and in the former covering of the roof which has been explained earlier.

Fragments from the first group were found separately at the very base of layer III and on the surface at the outer side of the palisade (Fig. 10, part 2, at A), that is, from a horizon which either preceded the time of the building of the hill site or which belonged to its very early period. In this same horizon were found a few sherds of Bronze Age pots. Small fragments of pottery of the first type, together with fragments of pots of the Suzgun type, were found below the horizon of the pit house floor (Fig.

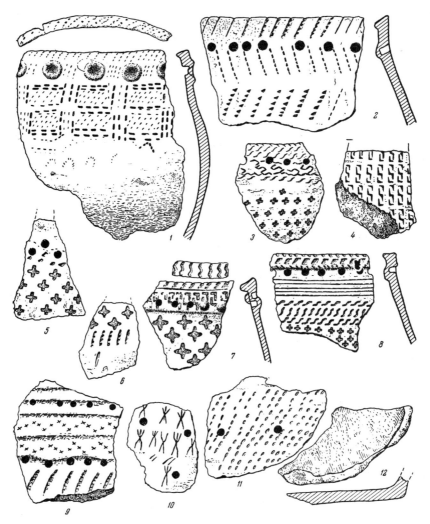

Plate XXXV. Ceramics from the fortified hill site Us-Tolt.
1 to 8–Yar-sale stage; 9 to 12–Bronze Age.

10, part 2, at E). The culture-yielding layer above this horizon, that is, the hut floor, contained few but large pieces of fourteen pots of the third type, which were apparently contemporaneous with the pit house.

Pottery of the second type was found separately in only one place, at the very bottom of layer III on the inner side of the palisade (Fig. 10, part 2, at C), where it appears to have been covered with earth when the fortifications were built and thus protected from admixture from layers which were deposited later.

Let us proceed to an examination of each of the pottery types. The pottery of Type I is round-bottomed, weakly profiled, with a smooth transition between the straight neck and the shoulder and main body of the pot. The profile of the rim is distinguished by a thickening of the edge, which thus forms a small, characteristic ridge on the inner side. As a rule the pots are made of clay with a slight admixture of coarse-grained sand and occasionally micaceous schist. The pots are usually decorated in the upper portion, but once in a while as much as two-thirds of a pot may be ornamented.

In examining the pottery of Type I, one easily sees strong resemblance to the pottery of the preceding, Late Ust-Poluy, period. This resemblance shows up especially clearly in many of the sherds (Plate XXXV, items 1, 2; Plate XXXVI, items 1, 5).

Typical of the third group of Ust-Poluy pottery are the checkerboard arrangement of ornamentation, the herringbone pattern executed with a coarse-toothed comb, and the meandering decoration of "ducklets."*

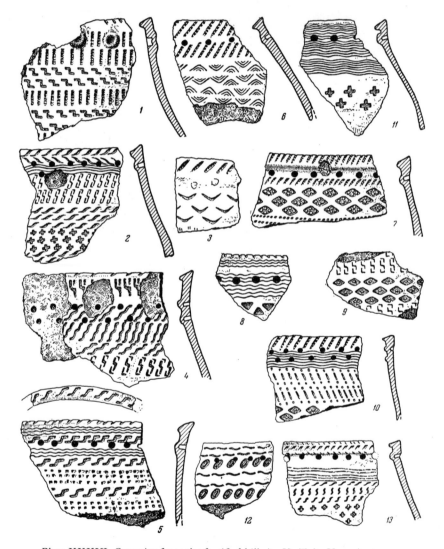

Plate XXXVI. Ceramics from the fortified hill site Us-Tolt: Yar-sale stage.

* [*Utochki* in the original. A stylized ornamentation suggesting ducklets swimming one after another. Editor, A.I.N.A.]

These elements are also characteristic of the Us-Tolt vessels, that is, Ust-Poluy Type I.

The only difference is in the small pits pressed into the interior surface of the pot to form a boss on the outer surface, which is then flattened by resmoothing the outer surface (Plate XXXV, item 1). This process is not known in Ust-Poluy, but it occurs quite often in Type I pottery from the Karym fortified hill site.

The decorative elements that have a wide distribution are those in the form of a small snake, or a letter S (Plate XXXV, items 3, 8; Plate XXXVI, items 2, 4, 13), occasional rather large crosslike impressions (Plate XXXV, items 3, 5–8), framed angles (Plate XXXVI, item 6), impressions of triangles (Plate XXXVI, item 8), and a lattice of oval or diamond-shaped impressions (Plate XXXVI, items 7, 9, 10, 12). These are all, with the possible exception of the nested angles, fairly well known from the late periods of the Ust-Poluy and especially the Potchevash ceramics. But here these impressions are far more numerous than all other types of ornamentation, which cannot be said about the Potchevash pottery.

An unusual decorative element on pottery of Type I is a three-part impression consisting of a combination of two angles and one "cleat" (Plate XXXV, items 4, 7; Plate XXXVI, items 2, 4, 9). This never occurs on pottery of the preceding periods in spite of the enormous quantity of material known to us from Ust-Poluy and the Potchevash fortified site. The finding of this three-member ornament on Type I pottery suggests that chronologically it should be placed immediately after the Ust-Poluy and Potchevash periods.

Type II is close to Type I but varies slightly from it in the profiling of the rims. Together with profiling characteristic of Type I, there is also a distinct variety (see Plate XXXVII, items 4, 5, 8), in which, instead of the flattened profile, there is a thin, slightly curving rim, occasionally reinforced with a small molding.[7]

In Type II, the stamped decoration almost, or entirely, disappears— the S-shaped ("snake"), the "cleat," the three-member impression, and the latticing which gave such definite characteristics to the pottery of Type I. Angular impressions, both simple and framed (Plate XXXVII, item 3), are preserved and widespread. For the first time semicircular impressions appear, both smooth and made with a comb (Plate XXXVII, item 8). Imitation of cording is very common. The stab-and-drag technique (Plate XXXVII, items 1, 4) becomes quite widespread; it was fairly rare previously, but achieves a broad distribution in the later periods.

New elements appear in the treatment and composition of ornamentation—for example, a broad band on the neck of a vessel which is filled with meandering slanting strips made with short stabs of a comb (Plate XXXVII, items 1, 2, 6). At times this meander pattern is made with light stabs of a fine comb (Plate XXXVII, items 4, 5, 7). More complex figures are not unusual, although these become more widespread in the subsequent period (Plate XXXVII, item 6).

The meandering type of decoration occurred before, but rarely (see for example Type I of Karym ceramics, Plate XXXV, item 3). It is also known during the later reaches of the 1st millennium A.D., but never was it as widespread or as finished as it was on vessels of Type II. Perhaps this was caused by simply transferring to pottery the decorations applied to bone objects, birchbark vessels, and articles of fur, as they had been in the past, in the Ust-Poluy period, or at the time.

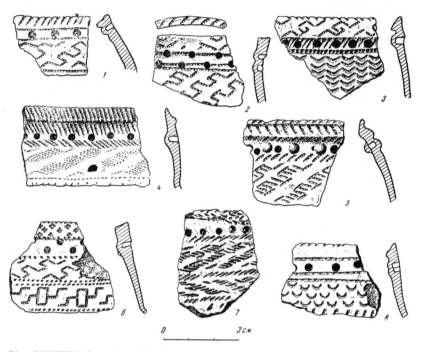

Plate XXXVII. Ceramics of the Karym stage.
1 to 6, 8–from the fortified hill site Us-Tolt (Type II); 7–from Verbilskiy Cape.

Type III of the Karym ceramics is characterized by pots with a more clearly defined, straight, or slightly slanting neck (see Plate XXXVIII). The distinguishing characteristic of the profile is an appliqué molding on the upper part of the neck which is always notched with lines that are either smooth or comb-impressed (Plate XXXVIII). In the ornamentation, motifs featuring slanted bands and strips on the neck continue (Plate XXXVIII, items 3, 6, 10, 14), but in the main their place is taken by bands of triangles formed by slanted strokes or hatching facing in two directions (Plate XXXVIII, items 1, 2, 7, 11). Sometimes this decorative band is complicated by interruptions of figured impressions (Plate XXXVIII, items 5, 7, 10, 12, 13, 15), and this gives the vessels a rich, elegant appearance. Another decorative element, the rudiments of which existed already in the Early Iron Age, comes into general use for the first time. It consists of bands of ribbons or decorations made usually with the stab-and-drag method or an angle stamp. These extend downward and to the lower third of the pot below an ornamental band on the neck and upper shoulders which is made with the angular impressions or framed impressions (Plate XXXVIII, items 4, 12).

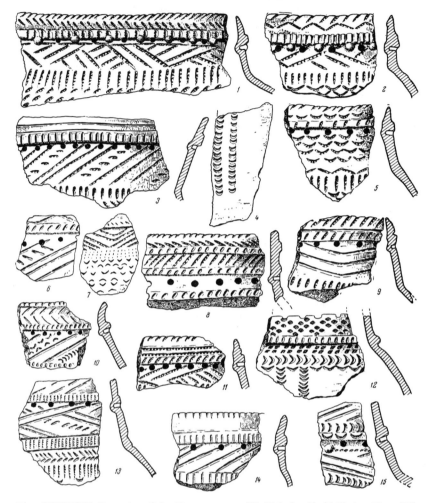

Plate XXXVIII. Ceramics of the Orontur stage (Us-Tolt fortified hill site; Type III).

In analyzing the chronological sequence of the types of pottery listed above, one must keep in mind that, with the exception of the mixed layer, Type III was found within the floor of the pit house. Here there were also found potsherds of other types, but only in very small numbers—two fragments of Bronze Age pots and a few small pieces from two pots of Type I—whereas Type III was represented by large fragments of fourteen pots. Such a disposition and relation of pottery indicate that Type III was contemporaneous with the last period of the site, while Types I and II refer to the period when the fortified hill site was being built, or to an earlier stage of its occupation. Type I pottery, discovered on bedrock under the embankment, reveals that the fortifications, in the form in which they were determined by the excavation, were constructed on the site of a settlement which had existed earlier.

In addition to pottery, the excavation of the site uncovered the following: an iron arrowhead (Fig. 10, part 2, at B), protruding from the base of one of the poles of the stockade, and an iron knife (Fig. 10, part 2, at D), lying under a beam near the hearth within the floor layer of the pit house. The knife blade, 10 cm long, is shaped exactly like those known in ethnographic records as "men's knives." It is fairly narrow, but broadens slightly toward the tip; it is sharpened on one edge only. According to the Khanty and the Mansi, this way of sharpening makes it very practical for woodworking.

In 1926, the Tobolsk Museum received from A. Safonov an anthropomorphic bronze figurine which had been found, according to the entry in the catalog, "in the mound of Karym." The figure represents a man in a conical helmet. His arms are hanging and are brought together below, where between the hands there is placed an article shaped like a pot. There is a rectangular strap on the man's chest, the "line of life," representing the inner organs.

Unfortunately we have no clue as to which layer contained this interesting find. Therefore, we shall leave the question of dating it open for the present and return to it later, when we will be able to compare it with a number of other analogous finds.

The three pottery groups established on the basis of the Us-Tolt materials are undoubtedly chronologically related. But it is essential to establish whether they are only local or reflect the development of pottery forms over a wider territory. To clarify this point it will be necessary to survey the distribution of pottery of each of the periods in the area along the Ob. In this connection, the sites containing only one stratum will be especially interesting. Among such sites containing pottery of Karym Type I is the Leushi fortified hill site, situated about 400 km upstream on the Konda River from Karym. This site became known through the investigations carried out by the geologist S. G. Boch in 1934; he collected a few pieces of pottery which are preserved in the Museum of Physical Anthropology in Moscow.

According to Boch's information, the Leushi site occupies a headland formed by the River Pava and the *sor** into which the Satyzhinskaya Channel empties. It is separated from the mainland by a broad and deep ditch about 50 m long, and today it is occupied by the graveyard of Leushi village [59°40′ N; 65°45′ E].

The sherds, which are found in great numbers on the surface (being thrown there when graves were dug), belong to round-bottomed pots of varying sizes. The walls of these are very thin, 2–4 mm, in spite of the considerably large diameter of the pots—over 35 cm.[8]

The pottery from Leushi is similar in many ways to the late Ust-Poluy and to Type I from Us-Tolt. With the latter it has in common an adaptation of the three-part decorative motif. It is also characterized by impressions of nested angles which often form inverted triangles arranged around the shoulders of the pot. This last trait was already known in the lower Ob region in the Early Iron Age (the Zelenaya Gorka culture), but on the Ob proper, in the territory occupied by the Ust-Poluy culture, it had disappeared entirely. However, back from the Ob and also along the

* [In the Ob River basin the underwater portion of a partly submerged valley. A lake formed by partial submergence of a valley. Editor, A.I.N.A.]

Irtysh it apparently continued to exist, since the inverted triangle is found fairly often on the pottery from Potchevash as well as from later sites.

On the basis of the three-member impressions on the ceramics of Leushi, this site may be synchronized, with reason, with Type I pottery from Us-Tolt.

In addition to pottery, Boch collected at Leushi eight bone arrow and spear points, some of them very carefully prepared and polished. Most of the heads are rhomboid and rhomboid or triangular in cross section. Only two are different: one is cylindrical with a flattened haft, the other is fairly large, triangular, with a notched base, and may be an arrowhead from an arrow used in a pre-set bow.

A bronze representation of a man's head comes either from the Leushi fortified site or from the area immediately adjacent to it. This Leushi "mask" markedly differs from those known to us from earlier periods, for example the village site of Makar-Visyng-Tur.* It is made of white bronze, very carefully fashioned, and represents the head of a man in a high, conical helmet decorated with an unusual hemispherical ornament.

Type I Karym pottery is also known from the fortified hill site Sorovoy Mys on the left bank of the Severnaya Sosva, 7 km upstream from Berezov.[9] This site has not been excavated and is known only from explorations carried out by S. G. Boch, by A. F. Palashenkov, the director of the Omsk Museum, and by ourselves in 1948.

The site has been nearly destroyed by the river, and the material, for the most part, is not in its original position. As far as can be judged by the finds and by the stratigraphy, Sorovoy Mys is a site with two layers which overlap only in part. The chronologically older [lower] layer corresponds to the second period of the Ust-Poluy epoch,[10] and the upper to the period of Type I Karym pottery. The pots are characterized by the same soft [smooth] profiling, by round bases, and the same typical profile of the rim, which is slightly flattened and hangs down on the inner side.

The most important ornamental trait is the three-part impression in all its variations. We also find patterns made with the stab-and-drag technique, rhomboid, eyelike stampings, and nested angles sometimes arranged to form rhomboids. Patterns made with a large-toothed comb and crosslike stamps are of secondary importance.

A singular specimen carefully cast in bronze was brought from Sorovoy Mys to the Omsk Museum by A. F. Palashenkov (Fig. 11). Judging by the socket, it was apparently used as a staff ornament. It is annular in shape and is somewhat reminiscent of the spear and dart heads with circular perforations. It is possible that this endpiece may be a survivor of similar heads that existed only until the middle of the 1st millennium B.C.

An interesting characteristic of this artifact is its decoration, which consists of two elongated and highly stylized moose heads fashioned along the edge. Stylistically they are comparable to similar figures widely known in the western Urals during the 1st millennium A.D., especially to the stylized moose heads from the Podcherem cache.[11] This comparison

* [A fortified hill site of the Ust-Poluy period investigated and described by W. Moszyńska. See p. 286 of this work. Editor, A.I.N.A.]

provides a basis for dating, but at the same time it poses the question as to what caused the penetration of such art so far east of the western slopes of the Urals. We will return to this question later.

The geologist D. I. Ilovayskiy found the same type of pottery (as described earlier) on the Severnaya Sosva or its tributary the Lyapin (Plate XXXIX). In shape and some specific decorative elements we see a correlation with Ust-Poluy, yet the presence of three-part stamp decoration combined with large "eye" stampings (Plate XXXIX, items 1, 6, 9) places the pottery found by Ilovayskiy, as well as Karym Type I, in the Yar-sale period.

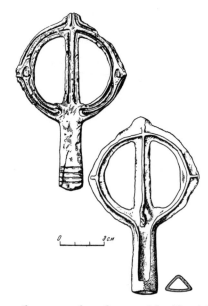

Fig. 11. Bronze staff ornament from Sorovoy Mys (Cape) fortified hill site.

Pottery with the three-part stamp is also known from territories considerably farther south. It is well represented in the materials collected by I. Ya. Slovtsov in one of the fortified hill sites at Andreyevskoye Lake near Tyumen. These finds were not included in his published work because he investigated the site later, after 1883.[12] The pottery collected by Slovtsov in the years 1885–87 is preserved in the Tyumen Museum (inv. no. 3873). The most characteristic pots in the group are usually of middle size with round bottoms and straight, well-defined necks. The decoration is, in most cases, on the neck and shoulders, not usually extending beyond the broadest portion of the pot.

In decorating, scant use was made of the comb, but figured impressions are widespread. Among the latter the "snake lines" were especially popular. They are well known from northern sites, including chronologically earlier ones, up to Ust-Poluy times. But nowhere was this motif so widely used as here.

Compared to other decorative impressions, the three-part stamp appeared numerically fewer times than it did on pottery of such sites as

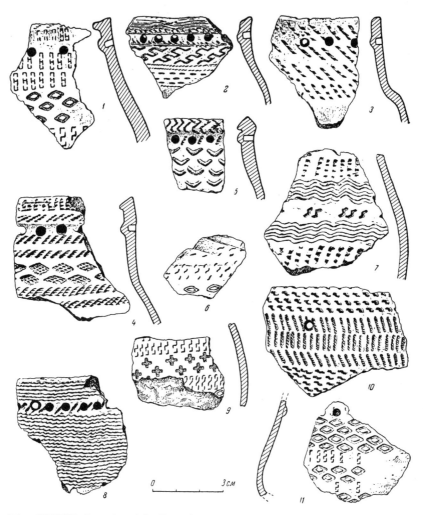

Plate XXXIX. Ceramics of the Yar-sale stage.
  1, 3 to 10–from the collection of D. I. Ilovayskiy on the Severnaya Sosva River;
  2–sherd from the Karym stage; 11–from Ust-Tartas on the Om River.

Leushi and Sorovoy Mys, or even Type I of Karym. Additionally, some specific forms of this stamp are discernible. Besides the three-part, classic type of stamp consisting of two angles with the cleat between them, we find variations with two cleats (Fig. 12, items 9, 10) or with a T-like figure which takes the place of the cleat, a three-part stamp with rounded elements, and so forth. These variations perhaps should be regarded as results of a gradual degeneration of the three-part stamp, as it is not found in later periods.

Along with the snake motif should be noted the equally widespread nested [or framed] angles and rhomboid "eyes." These have been encountered earlier, on pots of Karym Type I (Plate XXXVI, items 6, 7, 9, 10, 12) and on pottery from Sorovoy Mys, but then they were few in number or represented by single specimens among more dominant styles. On the pottery from the fortified hill site excavated by Slovtsov, the impressions of angles and rhomboid eyes are arranged in series like a checkerboard, forming broad bands of decoration. The angle impressions are oriented with bases alternately turned outward or inward, in which case they form nested rhomboids, giving this type of pottery a characteristic appearance. Angle impressions appear fairly early as pottery decorations along the Ob, but this particular arrangement develops only at the same time as the use of the three-part stamp or a little sooner, and then vanishes after flourishing for a rather short period.

It is a different story with the rhomboid stamps, (nucleated, ribbed, or trellised). They appeared also during the Early Iron Age and achieved a particularly full distribution at the beginning of the A.D. era; subsequently they continued to exist along with other aspects of the figured

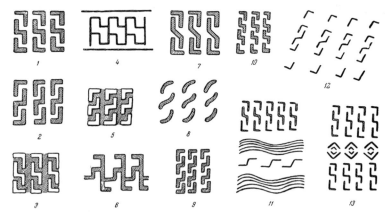

Fig. 12. Basic forms and variants of tripartite stamps.
1 to 3, 5, 7 to 13–on ceramics of the Yar-sale stage; 4–on bone, Ust-Poluy culture; 6–on ceramics, Andronovo culture.

stamping and survived on birchbark vessels until the present day. A characteristic trait of the Andreyevskoye ceramics (from the later collections of Slovtsov), which somewhat sets them apart from those described above, is the presence of ornamental bands on the necks and shoulders of vessels. At the first glance this could be considered a local development of ceramic ornamentation of this type derived from the south, yet this trait is also found in the north, although in the subsequent Karym stage. Thus this element may be considered a chronological index, and in this connection the fortified hill site investigated by Slovtsov should be dated as one of the latest sites within the limits of the Yar-sale period.

Pottery decorated with the three-part stamp is met with even farther to the south, on the Iset River. Fragments of pots, close to some of the Andreyevskoye ones, were found in the sand dunes in the Iset-Techin floodplain near the town of Dalmatovo (Fig. 13). The decoration was carefully done; it consists of alternate rows of unusually clear three-part stamping and nested angles [forming rhomboids]. One other find, far to the southeast, is known from Ust-Tartas on the Om River (Plate XXXIX, item 11). Here in 1895 S. M. Chugunov, while excavating *kurgans* [burial mounds], found a potsherd decorated with bands of three-part stamping and rhomboid eye impressions in the fill of one of the graves. The date of the burial itself was clearly determined by a Roman fibula and a blue, fluted, and glazed bead as not later than the 3rd century A.D. Since in later sites we find no pottery decorated with the three-part stamp, we may consider the Ust-Tartas find (ca. A.D. 200) as the upper limit for this type of decoration.

As can be deduced from the material described, Type I pottery from the Karym fortified hill site occurs over a very wide area, which not only includes the wooded Ob-Irtysh but extends farther into the forested

Fig. 13. Fragment of vessel from the dune near Dalmatovo village.

steppe along the wooded Irtysh valley. Naturally, over such a wide area of distribution we find variations such as the Leushi and Andreyevskoye ones, which could be explained as either local peculiarities or as due to differences in time. It is particularly the latter that is in most cases responsible for the difference among the sites. The basic traits that characterize the pottery of this group, although they are only decorative ones, are so characteristic and set it apart so clearly from the pottery of preceding and succeeding periods that we may look upon its style as an expression of a distinct cultural phase which is common to all the territory we have described. This phase is linked genetically, without interruption, to the Ust-Poluy and Potchevash cultures, and it emerges as the historically first culture specific to the Khanty. The chronological limits are set by the materials we have described. As has been stated, the Ust-Tartas finds date to about A.D. 200, and in sites which are later in time than the first century A.D., no pottery decorated with the three-part stamp has yet been found. Consequently A.D. 200 marks the terminal Yar-sale stage. Its beginning is determined by the end of the Ust-Poluy period, which was established by W. Moszyńska as 200 B.C. (see pp. 251–58 of this work).

In addition to the artifacts described, there are a few other finds which can be referred to the Yar-sale stage.

In the early 1930s a few objects were found during the construction of the Yar-sale sea-mammal hunting station on the Yamal. Of these a bronze scabbard, a perforated bronze plaque, and a bone spoon found their way to Salekhard and from there to the Museum of Physical Anthropology and Ethnography of the Academy of Sciences of the U.S.S.R.

The scabbard is the most interesting of these objects, although it has not been entirely preserved, the lower part being broken away (Plate XL, item 2). It (or rather the facing for it) is cast from copper or bronze in a mold made from a model.[13] The obverse side is open and spanned with only two crossbars made by means of setting two pieces of bronze in the finished form before the casting. The scabbard proper, which was enclosed in the facing, was made of two pieces of wood. Judging from

Plate XL. 1 to 3–finds from Yar-sale on the Yamal Peninsula; 4 to 12–from Mameyev's winter campsite on the Taz River.

the remaining oxides, it contained an iron knife with a bronze handle. The length of the blade barely exceeded 9 cm.

There are three triangular loops in the upper part of the facing on the inside which served for suspensions and which are highly polished by use. The face is ornamented with two animal figures. One represents a bear in bas-relief walking on the edge of the object. The figure is realistically made, and in the treatment of the snout it resembles the figure on the disc from Ust-Poluy. The joints of the feet are indicated with transverse parallel lines. Similar lines edge the hind paw where fur is indicated by a row of triangles. The suggestion of a tail turns into a thick, braidlike border running along the edge of the scabbard. Under the border the footsteps of the bear are indicated by small, elongated ovals. The significance of the [nucleated] eyes on the haunch, shoulder, and head of the animal is not quite clear.* It is possible that this is an attempt to carry over into realistic presentation the scrolls which are not appropriate to this style but are characteristic of the Ust-Poluy and Potchevash representations of fantastic beings, which is the category to which the other figure belongs. The latter is executed directly on the upper surface of the scabbard. It is flattish, curvilinear, filled in with parallel lines which are cut deep to give the impression of a rounded contour. A fantastic creature is represented, with the teeth and jaws of a carnivore, but with long horns. In spite of the schematic, conventional treatment, the figure is very dynamic and full of expression, achieved through the sharply turned head and the scrolls on haunch and shoulder. The figure reflects not only the Ust-Poluy–Potchevash artistic tradition, but also an earlier one, reaching back to the period of the fully developed Scytho-Sarmatian animal style.

Another object obtained at Yar-sale is an openwork, oval plaque, slightly arched along the long axis. The plaque is made in the shape of an animal in a spread-eagle position, seen from above (Plate XL, item 1). The spinal column is indicated by a double wavy line from which the ribs emerge, and on the right side some kind of internal organs are represented by an incomplete rosette. The showing of the skeleton and internal organs in zoomorphic and anthropomorphic figures is very common in the art of the Ob region in the various stages of its development. We observed this trait in an artifact of the Ust-Poluy period—for example, on the wolf figures from the Istyak cache; also, it persists in the drawings of the Khanty and the Mansi today.[14] The plaque has no ears or loops for suspension, but the inner edge of the braidlike border which encircles the animal figure is highly polished from use.

In all likelihood this object is a small wrist guard which was fastened to the inner side of the left wrist to protect it from the bowstring. Similar guards which existed until recent times over a wide area along the Ob were called in Khanty *yësh-kar*.[15] The figure and the surface finish of the Yar-sale *yësh-kar* are close in style to Ust-Poluy work, but the general composition of the object associates it with the broad group of

---

* [These nucleated circles suggest analogues in Old Bering Sea Eskimo art, or are perhaps suggestions of joints. Editor, A.I.N.A.]

open-work plaques and belt buckles widely distributed since the first centuries A.D.

The third article from Yar-sale is a bone spoon (Plate XL, item 3). The bowl is round, the handle elongated and rectangular. At the base of the handle is a fairly conventionalized figure of a bear. In general shape the spoon differs from the Ust-Poluy ones and is closer to those from Podcherem,[16] but actually most of all it resembles some of the Rodanovo spoons.[17] There is, however, no connection between the Rodanovo and the Yar-sale spoons as far as decoration is concerned. The two twisted lines that form the central strip on the Yar-sale spoon's handle seem to represent the backbone of the bear, and thus they correspond to the treatment of the spinal column on the *yësh-kar* described above. The edge strips of decoration form a chain of a complicated linking similar to that known on objects from the Podcherem cache.[18] The elongated moose heads, similar to those in Podcherem art, also appeared on the endpiece from Sorovoy Mys.

The Yar-sale scabbard is not unique. A scabbard very similar in many respects was found at the mouth of the Tsylma River on the Pechora.[19] The Pechora scabbards have only one [metal] side—the face. They are open at the back, with only three crosspieces. With the scabbard was preserved the knife handle, ornamented with the head of a griffon, while the lower end of the scabbard is decorated with the head of an eagle. The upper end has a triple band of ornamentation as in the Yar-sale scabbard, although here the decorative elements are different. On the Yar-sale scabbard the central band is made up of wavy lines bordered by two rows of triangles; on the Pechora one, the central band is filled with fairly large hemispheres with depressions, while the borders are composed of two rows of smaller hemispheres, "pearls." A row of similar pearls decorates the upper edge of the scabbard. Like the Yar-sale scabbard, the one from Pechora is decorated with animal figures and the arrangement of the figures is the same, but the stylistic treatment is quite different. Like the bear on the Yar-sale piece, the Pechora eagle and griffon heads are executed in the old tradition familiar to us from Ust-Poluy art, but the style of the animal figure posed along the edge of the Pechora scabbard is totally different. This figure is highly standardized, and a realistic reproduction of nature is sacrificed to symmetry. The eye figure [nucleated circle] on the hip and the rather feeble scroll on the shoulder are the last survivals of the old symbolic manner and are combined with another element, the pearl edging that follows the spine of the animal; this was never found in earlier artifacts.

All in all, the figure, both in elements of style and in the characteristic pose of the animal, belongs to a large group of molded figures which are well known in Lomovatovo art. At the same time, since this is the very earliest known example of the figures of this type, it indicates the necessity for a review of the old dates for figures in the round, with the idea of pushing back considerably the time when they first began to be made. This question will be treated later, in more detail.

In contrast to the detached figure, the bear figures in relief on the side of the scabbard are executed in a manner that is realistic but out of keeping with the pearl border. It becomes obvious when the scabbards are visually compared that on each one part is done in a realistic, another in a conventionalized, manner, but the relative position of the parts so treated is not the same.

There is an additional very important find that helps us understand the genesis of the standardized, molded animal figures and clarify the route by which scabbards like those from Yar-sale and the Pechora reached the Ob and Ural regions. In the 1840s D. P. Shorin, a student of local lore and a bonded serf in Demidov, obtained among other antiquities from the vicinity of the Nizhniy Tagil factory a "bronze scabbard of elegant shape" that had been plowed up at the village of Koksharovaya on the Tagil River. All trace of this scabbard was subsequently lost, and O. N. Bader has even suggested that the item referred to was really a find made near a *kurgan* [burial mound] on the Poludenka.[20] There is, however, a picture of the scabbard found near Koksharovaya in Shorin's manuscript.[21] In this very careful drawing it is easy to recognize the bronze scabbard from the collection in the State Historical Museum [in Moscow], where it is listed as a "chance find from the Altay." The scabbard was transferred from the Rumyantsev Museum, where it had been in the collection of Pogodin, to whom Shorin is known to have sent a copy of his manuscript and, apparently, the scabbard.

The Koksharovaya scabbard is in general similar to those described above, but it is decorated with only one representation of an animal, a figure on one side near the top (Plate XLI). The rest of the scabbard is undecorated except for smooth, raised circling bands and a pattern of arches at the lower end. The animal figure, that of a sable, is executed with great skill in a realistic style, with no added decoration. The surface of the scabbard is carefully polished.

The date of the Koksharovaya scabbard is difficult to determine, particularly as there is no other known that is exactly like it. One must assume that it is probably older than the Yar-sale and the Pechora scabbards, and perhaps it belongs to the 1st millennium B.C. In particular, the arched pattern which decorates the lower part and is generally rare in the Ob region is known from the Potchevash fortified hill site, which is dated to just this period.[22] A trait that is common to all three scabbards is the laterally positioned animal figure, which links them to the *akinakés** scabbards which had a characteristic "stub-wing" at the same place. This, for instance, is the case of the scabbards from the famous cache of Fettersfeld. It is quite possible that the resemblance we have observed is the result of southern influence on the highly individualized bronze scabbards of western Siberia. Undoubtedly contacts existed between some portions of the Ugrian and the Sarmatian tribes. Underlining this is the method, reflected in the Ugrian figurines from the Sapagova cache portraying booted warriors, of wearing the *akinakés* scabbard attached to the belt at the upper end and to the leg at the lower, which mode of wearing it continues to the present day among the Khanty and Mansi. It

---

* [A short sword of the Scythians and Persians used in close combat, 3rd–4th centuries B.C. Editor, A.I.N.A.]

Plate XLI. Bronze scabbard from near Koksharovaya village.

may be added that the modern Mansi scabbard, decorated with animal figures, slightly flaring toward the top and with a hole for a strap at the lower end, is no doubt genetically connected with the bronze scabbards described above.

As well as can be judged on the basis of the artifacts under discussion, the period to which they belong (200 B.C. to A.D. 200) is linked without interruption to the period preceding it. There are, however, new elements in the form and ornamentation of the ceramics and in the representational art which were not characteristic of the preceding era. Some of these were to become typical of the following periods. To return to the greatest mass of material, the pottery, one should note among these changes the complete disappearance of corded ornamentation, which was typical for the Ust-Poluy vessels. Cord decoration was not adopted for the ceramics of the lower Ob-Irtysh beyond the territorial limits reached by the Ust-Poluy culture. And in the latter we find that corded ornamentation was strongly represented only in the second group of ceramics, which represents the fully developed phase of the Ust-Poluy culture, in which we found examples that are practically the same as the corded ceramics of the Ural and Ananino types.[23] Later we shall examine the significance of this fact in order to understand the historical processes which evolved along the lower Ob. For the present, let us note that there is no cord ornamentation to be found north of the Tavda River either at an earlier or at a later period.

Among the characteristic changes in ceramics belong the introduction and wide distribution of the three-part stamp (Fig. 13). Yet this trait is not in itself entirely new in the decorative art of the ancient Ob region. There is a curious, steplike, belted decoration that is commonly found on the bone artifacts from Ust-Poluy (Fig. 13, item 4). In this connection, it should be noted that in the contemporary decoration of the Ob-Ugrian peoples, a characteristic is the so-called reversibility of the pattern, that is, the exact correspondence of the outlines of the figure to the background, which, especially in the bands of rhythmically repeated pattern, makes the pattern and the background indistinguishable except for color.[24]

This peculiarity of decoration, which is so characteristic of present-day art along the Ob, can be observed in the Ust-Poluy period (second half of the 1st millennium B.C.)[25] and even in the earlier Bronze Age [where it is associated with] the Gorbunovo peat bog.[26]

If one examines the steplike Ust-Poluy ornamentation, it becomes apparent that the background, which for convenience is shaded in two tones, corresponds exactly to the decoration which we called the three-part [or three-member] stamp. However, in considering the genesis of this trait we must not limit ourselves to the Ust-Poluy period. There is a closely related pattern known from Andronovo ceramics (Fig. 13, item 6), which served as a basic type from which the Ugrian ribbon type developed.[27] The three-part stamp motif, although only in certain variations, was known earlier but was not adapted to ceramics. The fact that at one particular stage, the post–Ust-Poluy period, it suddenly achieved a wide distribution undoubtedly emphasizes its significance in defining [the limits of] this period.

New traits appear in the representational arts as well as in ceramics. As we have seen, in the representation of animals, along with the archaic traditions preserved from the preceding stages, new elements, new methods, make their appearance and achieve a wide distribution in the succeeding period. The Yar-sale find is of especial interest. It not only illustrates clearly the conclusions we have drawn, but it shows how far northward the rich and luxurious culture of the Ob extended and how faulty were our theories about these apparently remote polar regions. The find on Cape Yar-sale is of an importance that quite justifies our naming after it the post–Ust-Poluy stage of the lower Ob culture.

Chapter 2

The Karym Stage
(A.D. 200–500)

In describing the second group of pottery from the fortified hill site of Us-Tolt, it was indicated that along with the preservation of some traits which link this group to the first, there appear entirely new ornamental methods and compositions. One of these methods is the application of decoration by stamps of checkerboard, latticed, or other patterns in a broad strip or belt on the neck and shoulders of a pot. This method arises during the Yar-sale stage and is found on pottery from Slovtsov's fortified hill site on Andreyevskoye Lake. This site, on the basis of an analysis of pottery ornamentation, should be placed late but within the limits of the Yar-sale stage.

New composition elements are seen in the pottery decoration of the second group which separate it from the preceding and subsequent groups—specifically, the filling of an ornamental band with diagonally placed strips of a meandering pattern (Plate XXXVII, items 1, 2, 6) or with strips filled with slanted hatching but, again, grouped into the same meander pattern (Plate XXXVII, items 4, 5). Sometimes, though rarely on pots from the Us-Tolt site, we find an ornamental band made up of even rows of scalloping or some other stamp ornamentation (Plate XXXVII, items 3, 8).

The pottery of this group which characterizes the second stage in the development of the Ob culture in the 1st millennium A.D. is named Karym, from the type site where it was [first] found, but it occurs at a few other points. On the Konda River it is known from the collections made at Mys Verbilskiy [Cape Verbil], about 300 km by river from Karym. Although the amount of material from this site is small, the ceramic decoration is so typical and so exactly like that from Karym (Plate XXXVII, item 7) that there can be no doubt that it belongs to this group.

Equally typical is the fragment of a pot, decorated along the neck with diagonal strips of a meandering pattern, in the collection of D. I. Ilovayskiy, from the Severnaya Sosva River (Plate XL, item 2). It is difficult to say what occasions the presence of a fragment of this type in material belonging basically to the Yar-sale stage. It is more than likely that the site where Ilovayskiy collected is stratified. The most significant aspect of the find is the distance from Karym at which this Karym type of pottery is found—not less than 1,300 km by river and nearly 600 km by overland winter trail. This gives us a valuable indication, if not of the limits, at least of the distribution, of the Karym culture.

As a result of the work of the Salym expedition of the Tobolsk Regional Museum in 1912, among other archaeological materials there was obtained a small ceramic collection from a site near the mouth of the Salym River, a left tributary of the Ob. Unfortunately, the exact location of the site is not known. The Salym enters the Ob about 100 km upstream from the latter's junction with the Irtysh. From Karym to the mouth of the Salym is about 300 km in a straight line, but by river at least twice that distance. In spite of the distance involved, the pottery is astonishingly close to that of Karym. The resemblance is in the general shape and in the profile of the vessels, in the arrangement of the decoration in a broad belt on the neck and shoulders, and even in the decoration itself. Especially significant is the presence of diagonally placed ribbons of a meandering pattern (Plate XLII, items 5, 6) which are identical to those of Karym (cf. Plate XXXVII, items 1, 2, 6). The resemblance between the very unusual knee-shaped decorations (at the two sites) should also be noted (Plate XLII, item 7, and Plate XXXVII, 6).

The fact remains, however, that at Karym the sherds with belts of decoration solidly filled by repeated imprints of the latticed or of some other pattern are isolated cases; at Ust-Salym they constitute the basic mass of pottery. Let us recall that this trait was present on part of the pottery of the preceding period, in particular on that found at Andreyev-skoye Lake. On account of its very wide distribution we have considered this trait as a chronological rather than a geographic indicator. This is supported by the fact that the trait recurs at a later period, but in lesser quantity. Its maximum distribution occurs in the second stage.

In a burial ground on Cape Kozlov at Andreyevskoye Lake we found pottery of the type described above, that is, decorated on the shoulders and broadest part of the pot by a belt of stampings placed in a checker-board design. Vessels from graves in the Kozlov cemetery have a thick-ened and rounded bottom and a short neck, either straight or slightly inclined inwards, and a smooth transition from neck to shoulder. This shape is very familiar in the Ob region; it appears during the Early Iron Age in Zelenaya Gorka pottery and continues with some slight variations through many stages. The resemblance of the pots from the Kozlov cemetery is emphasized by the presence of a [rim] collar on many of them, although in some cases it differs from the Zelenaya Gorka type. The rim collar is very rare in Yar-sale pottery, while it is absent from pots of earlier stages, that is, those close to the Ust-Poluy in form and decoration.

Such collars occur somewhat more often in sites belonging to the late Yar-sale period, as for example the Slovtsov fortified hill site, and are accompanied, for the most part, by the broad belts of decorations made up of stamp imprints in checkerboard formation. The rim collar is quite typical of Karym pottery: we find it on pots from the Karym site proper (Plate XXXVII, items 2–6) and on the fragment of a vessel from Ilovayskiy's material (Plate XL, item 2). In the Salym material the rim collar is found on a pot decorated in exactly the same manner (Plate

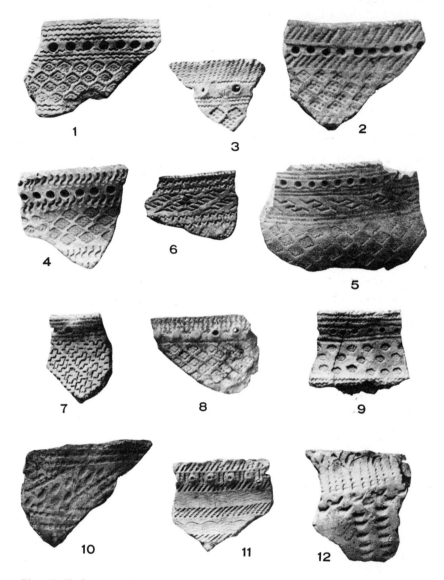

Plate XLII. Ceramics of the Karym stage, from finds at the mouth of the Salym River.

XLII, item 2). The specimens excavated from the Cape Kozlov cemetery fully uphold its identification with the Karym period.

The Cape Kozlov cemetery was discovered in 1950 during our reconnaissance of the Andreyevskoye Lake region. It is situated on a raised bank at the foot of Cape Kozlov, opposite Bolshoy Ostrov, which separates the Bolshoy [Big] Andreyevskoye Lake from the Maloye [Little] Andreyevskoye Lake. The cemetery consists of a large number of small hillocks which are becoming indistinct. Some of them are more or less round in shape. The diameter of the hillocks averages 4–5 m; the greatest height is 0.3–0.4 m. The excavations, which were begun in 1952, revealed that each of these little mounds was a miniature *kurgan* with fill about 0.2 to 0.4 m deep. However, in the course of circumstances, the separate but closely placed heaps of fill ran together, causing the undulating appearance characteristic of the entire burial ground. The burials were subsurface ones. The skeletons were extended, face up, with head toward north. The depth of the burials ranged from 0.7 m to 1.25 m, as measured from the base of the fill. The burial pits measured 0.7–0.9 m by 1.8–2.5 m. Frequently remains of a hearth were found on the surface directly under the fill in line with the pit. In some burials the remains of a timber frame in which the deceased was placed can be observed. In the best-preserved burial, no. 2, the inner measurements of the framework were 0.6 m × 2.15 m, with a skeleton measuring 1.65 m in length. The frame was made of timbers from 15 cm to 30 cm in diameter. The grave inventory, what was preserved of it, was small, although judging by the size of the timber frame in burial no. 2 (which considerably exceeded the size of the body), one might suppose that a large quantity of objects had been placed in it.

In most of the burials excavated there was a pot, usually just one, placed to the left of the head. Sometimes the bones of a horse lay beside the pot and to the right. Small copper buckles with long, bent tongues were also found. There were two to a belt, one in front and one behind. Similar buckles occurred over a wide area in the late Sarmatian period,[28] and they are particularly characteristic of sites of the Kharino type in the Cis-Ural, dating to A.D. 200–400. In graves no. 2 and no. 4 remains of iron knives which had been hung from the front of the belt were found.

In burial no. 1 there was a neck ornament made of thin, round, copper rod. The ends were flattened and small openings pierced in them, presumably for a cord or wire fastening. Analogues to this neckpiece are found among the Late Ananino women's neckpieces in the grave goods from the Zuyeva and Kotlov cemeteries.[29] In later times such neckpieces disappear altogether, and for the first half of the 1st millennium A.D., the date of the Kozlov burial ground, neck pieces with a catch are typical.[30] There is also the possibility of a different date for this burial than that for the rest of the cemetery. It is located a bit to the side, directly at the edge of the lake. It is impossible to determine whether a mound once existed on top of it because the surface was disturbed at this point by a modern turf house. There was a layer of white sand under the skeleton. The small pot found next to the head differs from others found in the Kozlov cemetery. It is smaller and the bottom is more pointed. Decoration is limited to notches on the rim and a series of pits at the neck. At half a meter from the burial were the remains of a hearth, and at the distance of 1 m, the fragments of several pots of the usual Kozlov type, described earlier. As the connection is not clear between these fragments and the burial, it is better to leave open the question of the date and affiliations of the burial until more work is done in the area.

The rim collars on the pots from the Kozlov cemetery and the broad, checkerboard belts of square and diamond-shaped stampings duplicate the pottery of the end of the Yar-sale stage at Slovtsov's fortified hill site on Andreyevskoye Lake and of the Karym stage (Plate XL, item 2; Plate XXXVII, items 2–6; Plate XLII, item 2). The pot, analogous to the

Kozlov one which was found in the Kintusovo cemetery, is to be dated considerably later. However, there is no rim collar on this pot; its place is taken by ribbed molding, which is characteristic of the Orontur stage of A.D. 500–900. The slanting strips [of ornamentation] on the neck, made with the stab-and-drag method, also testify for a later date. The vessel from Kintusovo demonstrates how widespread pottery of the Cape Kozlov cemetery type was; it also makes it possible to see this type in transition and to judge at what period it ceased to exist.

On the basis of the pottery found in the Cape Kozlov cemetery and by its comparison with sites contemporary to it, as well as with earlier and later ones situated along Andreyevskoye Lake but belonging to a different though related culture group, it becomes clearly evident that Kozlov is assignable to the early part of the Karym stage (A.D. 200–300).

One of these sites, the Pereyminskiy cemetery, was found on a terrace above the floodplain opposite a second narrows [*pereyma*] about 2 km from the Cape Kozlov cemetery. It consists of poorly defined, circular mounds of various diameters stretched along the edge of the terrace. The one lying farthest to the west measured 8 m × 6.5 m. When it was excavated, a small hearth was found at a depth of 0.4 m from the surface under the central part of the fill. At the same level two burial stains [patches] were uncovered on either side of the hearth. They were parallel to each other and oriented from south to north. Between them and alongside the hearth was found a complete undecorated cup with thick walls and a conical base. One of the burial patches measured 1.7 m × 0.65 m, the other, western one, 1 m × 0.9 m. In the larger grave, a poorly preserved skeleton 1.65 m long was found at a depth of 1 m; it was extended, face up, with the head pointing north. At the right side of the skull lay the bones of a large hoofed animal, too poorly preserved to be identified. The skull of the deceased had been penetrated at the base by some sharp instrument. The face bones were crushed. On the right arm was a poorly preserved bracelet made of two twisted loops of copper wire. In the vicinity of the pelvis were two beads, one of carnelian and round, the other gilded. Beads were also found between the knees: a biconical one of rock crystal and two blue ones, one round and one faceted. At the skull there were round ones and cut ones, both blue. A rusted iron knife lay by the left thighbone. Among the bones of the left hand there was a ring with a socket for a jewel which, however, was missing.

In the smaller grave a crushed round-bottomed pot was found at a depth of 0.7 m. It was decorated with a band of imprints of a coarse-toothed comb. A little to the north of it, on the same level, were some bones of a human skeleton heaped together—two scapulae and a jaw-bone, together with one bone from some large hoofed animal. To the side were the remains of a small hearth. As the grave had clearly not been disturbed, the position of these bones indicates a secondary burial. Furthermore, the entire skeleton had not been placed in the grave—a fact undoubtedly deserving of our attention.

Three meters from the first mound was a second, so faintly outlined that it was difficult to determine its shape. A slight depression could be observed in the middle of the fill. The burial had probably been disturbed. At a depth of 0.3 m cranial fragments and the lower jaw of a man were found; at a depth of 0.7 m, there was an iron buckle with a tongue.

A third mound was located 10 m from the second. It could be traced quite clearly on the west side, where it was bordered by a scarcely definable trench, but on the east the edge of the fill had been completely obliterated. The height of the fill did not exceed 25–30 cm; the diameter was at least 10 m. When the mound was opened, three clearly visible burials came into view at a depth of 0.5 m. They were in a row, east to west, and oriented south to north. In the westernmost burial, no. 4, which measured 2 m × 1.1 m at the depth of 0.65 m in the northwest part, there was discovered a skull, face down, and the lower jaw bones of three men. Below lay a confusion of bones from several skeletons, among them a child's placed beside the left arm of one of the skeletons. The bones were in a poor state of preservation, and this made it impossible to reconstruct the positions of the skeletons. The difference between the depth at which the skulls were lying and the depth of the rest of the bones can be explained by the bodies being buried in two levels, which could have caused the bones to settle. Among them was found a buckle with a guard and a whetstone.

The next burial plot, no. 4, was placed 2 m west of grave no. 4; it measured 2 m × 1.5 m. Three skeletons were found at a depth of 1.25 m: two were of adults, and between and above them, that of a child. The adult skeletons lay face up, heads pointing north, half turned toward each other (Fig. 14, I). The heads were slightly raised. The right (eastern) skeleton was slightly smaller, and judging by the ornaments, of a female. On the fingers of both hands of the female were rings of white bronze with diamond-shaped panels—one on the left and two on the right. On the man's belt there was a bronze buckle.

Burial no. 6 measured 2 m × 2 m and was located 1.3 m west of burial no. 4. At 1.3 m below the surface there was again a group burial containing the skeletons of no less than four persons (Fig. 14, II). The arrangement of the skeletons rather resembles that of the burial just described. Two of them, a woman's on the right, to the east, and a man's on the left, lay face up, half turned toward one another. Above them and closer to the man was placed the skeleton of a child with its head resting on the man's breast. Below these skeletons lay a fourth, also in an extended position, on its back. The skull was missing.

Due to the poor preservation of the skeletons and the confusion of the bones caused by the multiple burial in very loose, sandy soil, it is far from possible to tell in every case to which of the skeletons the objects found with them belong. The most plentiful objects were associated with the female skeleton. Near the skull, on which there was still a strand of dark hair, were four round beads of rock crystal and a blue glass bead. A biconical carnelian bead which lay somewhat to one side should probably be included with this skeleton. On its chest there were bronze ornaments which were apparently sewed on to the leather or fur clothing. Above and below them were annular bronze fibulae. The tongues of these were probably of iron, judging from other similar finds, but were not

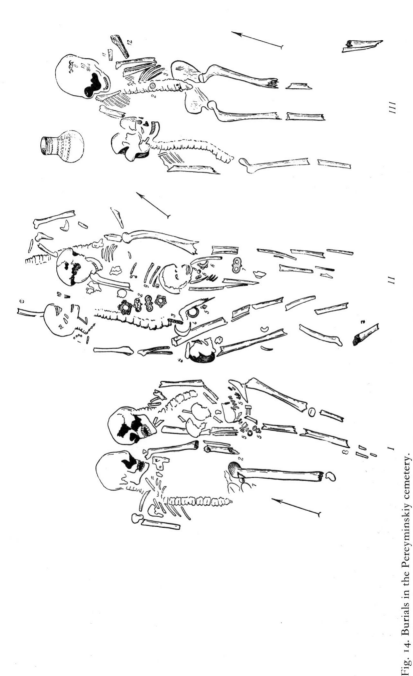

Fig. 14. Burials in the Pereyminskiy cemetery.
I–burial 5; II–burial 6; III–burial 8. The numbers indicate the place of the following finds: 1–beads; 2–brooches; 3–knives; 4–bracelet; 5–rings; 6–pendants; 7–buckles; 8–inset; 9–birch bark; 10–hair; 11–bone brooch; 12–whetstone.

preserved. Between the fibulae were two brooches or buckles formed by pairs of discs. A piece of leather strap still remained in one of them. One was decorated with a ram's head, the other with that of a lion. Judging by the subject and surface treatment they are imports. On the skeleton's left arm was a bracelet and a ring with a diamond-shaped panel quite similar to those found in burial no. 4. The remains of an iron knife, almost completely rusted away, lay at the pelvis.

A small bronze buckle with a guard and remains of an iron tongue probably belongs with a male burial, as it was found near the waist of the man's skeleton. On the chest, directly under the jawbone of the child, were two small bronze pendants and an oval, shallowly convex one, of rock crystal or glass. Below these, a wheel-like fibula and a double disc buckle were just like those found associated with the woman's skeleton. In addition, in burials nos. 4 and 5 there were numerous fragments of shattered, small, round beads of gilded glass.

Hearths were found north of the row of burials and at a distance of 3–4 m from it, that is, on the edge of the fill described above which covered the graves. The hearths lay at a depth of 1–1.1 m, that is, about 20–30 cm above the level of the burials. One hearth was situated opposite burial no. 4 at the depth of 1 m. Pieces of a vessel were found in it, intermingled with the bones of large, hoofed animals which could not be identified due to the poor state of preservation. The second hearth, at the depth of 1.1 m, was opposite grave no. 4; it also contained fragments of pots and bones, and a third, similar one, lay at a distance of 6 m to the NNE, opposite the same burial. Opposite burial no. 6, at a distance of 5 m from it, in a small, dark patch outside the limits of the fill, fragments of a man's cranium were found at the depth of 1.5 m. And finally, opposite burials nos. 4 and 5 and on the same level, two more patches which contained no material were found.

The absence of pottery in the graves attracts attention. The pots as well as the hearths are set somewhat to one side; they were located on the natural surface of the ground before the fill was added. It is possible that the several collective burials under one fill reflect a social phenomenon, that is, the house with many hearths inhabited by several families, which existed in the Ob region, according to ethnographic evidence.

Although there were no signs of fill on the dunes, the excavation was extended to the west and east on the line of burials nos. 4 and 6. A burial without inventory (no. 9), was found 3 m west of no. 6, and two additional ones, nos. 7 and 8, east of no. 4 (see Fig. 15). One of these, no. 7, was at the very edge of the dune. Here, at a depth of 0.5 m, the poorly preserved long bones of a skeleton were found, the tibial and scapular, and on top of them the fragments of a skull. Below these bones, at a depth of 0.75 m, the remains of a second skeleton were uncovered; they consisted of fragments of the skull lying on shoulder blades, and under these were pelvic bones. The pieces of a crushed pot were found 1 m to the north of the aforementioned burial at a depth of 0.25 m. It was not possible to sketch a plan of the burial owing to the decayed condition of the bones. It may be supposed that the body was buried (at the lower level) in a seated position; the confusion of bones in the upper level suggests a

Fig. 15. Burial no. 8 in the Pereyminskiy cemetery.

secondary burial, perhaps of only a partial skeleton, as was the case with
the secondary burial in the first mound described above.

Two meters west of grave no. 7 and at a depth of 0.35 m two narrow-
necked, round-bottomed pots were found (Plate XLIII, items 3, 4). A
little lower, at a depth of 0.75 m, were two skeletons lying extended, face
up, oriented to the NNW. The pots were placed over the head of the
skeleton on the left. At the feet of the skeletons and, as in every other
instance, at 35–50 cm above the level of the burial were two shattered pots
(Plate XLIII, items 1, 2). On the forehead of the skeleton on the left was a
pendant in the shape of two joined horse heads. Associated with it were
bright green stains of copper oxide which had preserved a strand of
straight, dark hair. A bone disc and whetstone lay at its left shoulder and
on its chest a hemispherical bronze ornament. To the left of the pelvis
were remains of an iron knife. Two meters to the west of burial no. 8, at a
depth of 0.35 m, still another pot was found, similar to the preceding ones
(Plate XLIII, item 5). There may be another burial on a line with this one,
but a tree prevented excavation of the three meters of connecting ground
toward burial no. 4.

In its inventory, the Pereyminskiy burial ground resembles that of the

Bakhmutinskiy cemetery and is close to it chronologically. The buckles found in burials nos. 4–6 closely resemble the Bakhmutinskiy buckles. Medallions from the latter with oval, glass inserts are similar to the inserts found in the child's burial, no. 6. There are pendants with horses and wheel-like plaques from the Bakhmutinskiy graveyard which are reminiscent of the fibulae from burial no. 6. Chronologically the Pereyminskiy cemetery barely exceeds the limits of the period of the first Bakhmutinskiy group, that is, the 4th–5th centuries A.D.

Plate XLIII. Vessels from burial no. 8 in the Pereyminskiy cemetery.

A comparison of the Pereyminskiy materials with those of the second Bakhmutinskiy group reveals some very real differences. Various beads, characteristic of this second group—carnelian with incrustations, ones of flattened amber, many-faceted blue glass ones, small, flattened ones of blue glass, and gilded cylindrical ones—are not represented by a single example in the Pereyminskiy cemetery. Contrarily, the second Bakhmutinskiy group has none of the rough-cut and round blue glass beads that were present in the Pereyminskiy cemetery, and the gilded ones which are so well represented here are rare in Bakhmutino.

The shield buckles from burials nos. 4–6 are similar in general outline to the Bakhmutinskiy ones. The latter, however, have a hollow arcuate with a depression for the tongue, which gives it the form of a letter **B**. Those from the Pereyminskiy cemetery have a narrow arcuate guard and are closer to the buckles from the Kharino cemetery. The pendants from the child's burial, no. 6, are almost exactly like the Kharino pendant, which is a round disc with a flat elevation in the center, surrounded by ten flat circles attached to its edge.[31] The pendant with horse heads from burial no. 8 also differs from the Bakhmutinskiy pendants and is practically the same as a find at Grudyata,[32] which Smirnov is inclined to date to the 4th–5th centuries A.D.[33]

For purposes of comparison, the wheel-shaped clasps from both cemeteries are especially useful. The resemblance between the Pereyminskiy and the Bakhmutinskiy ones seems striking at first glance, but diminishes when studied in detail. On the Pereyminskiy clasps, distinguished by their fine workmanship, the ring is made up of three rows of imitations of large pearls; its outer edge is embellished with six clusters, each made of three balls. The Bakhmutinskiy fibulae are more crudely executed. The rings do not have the three clear subdivisions, and the imitation of the pearls is done with notches. In place of the well-modeled, three-ball clusters, there are small, badly executed, slightly convex, double discs. All in all, the Bakhmutinskiy clasps give the impression of being a degenerate form of those which are represented in a better version in the Pereyminskiy finds.

According to V. F. Gening, wheel-shaped objects similar to the Bakhmutinskiy plaques were being used during the Lomovatovo period, not as buckles, but as plaques at the end of belt pendants. In this version a thong was originally threaded through the loop designed to hold the tongue, and the double curve of the flange opposite became extended into a hollow tube. This constitutes not only degeneration of form, but the putting of things to a use for which they were not originally intended, with complete disregard for their shape. The transition from the three-ball cluster to the double disc is in itself significant for dating.

In his excellent substantive analysis of the Podcherem cache, V. A. Gorodtsov wrote, "In the disc-cluster pendants there is a curious artistic treatment of the cluster in the shape of a three-ball pyramid. This motif is absent in later Chud [Finnic] art, and is not observed in the earlier art of the Uralian Chuds; obviously it was introduced from without."[34]

Articles stylistically associated with Podcherem are to be found outside the Podcherem complex in such finds as those at Ples hamlet, Grudyata village, Mikhaleva village, and others. A. P. Smirnov dates these convincingly to the 4th–5th centuries A.D.[35] Nothing of the kind is found in later sites. This gives us confidence in determining the age of the Pereyminskiy fibulae. The double-disc plaques from burial no. 6 correspond to the Podcherem material more closely than do the wheel-like buckles. The plaque cited in Gorodtsov's report is its closest analogue.[36] In dimensions, form of the disc, and ornamentation the plaques are almost identical, with the only difference of the pearls on the Pereyminskiy discs being larger than the convex dots on those of Podcherem. The basic difference between the artifacts is that the pendant grapelike clusters are absent in those from the Pereyminskiy cemetery and small animal heads replace the wing-shaped crosspieces. The central crosspieces are identical in both plaques (see Fig. 27 in the cited work of V. A. Gorodtsov).

The appearance in the Cis-Ural of grape-cluster pendants, of pendants in the shape of flies or cicadas, and of the oval medallions apparently imitating ornaments with almandine (garnet) inlays is ascribed by Gorodtsov to imports dating to Roman times. The double-disc plaques should be associated with this same group of objects that imitate the medallions with inlays and that, to judge by the materials from the Pereyminskiy graveyard, served as everyday ornaments on clothing— not as cult objects, as Gorodtsov supposed.

Actually it is not difficult to find specimens in artifacts from the northern shore of the Black Sea dating to the first centuries of our era which conform fairly closely to the pieces we have been describing. Thus among the analogues which can be dated with certainty are objects from the Kerch catacombs on Gospitalnaya [Hospital] Street, dated by heraldry and coins of the Emperor Constantine II (A.D. 317–361) and of Valentinian III (A.D. 425–455).[37] Among the artifacts are earrings that in shape and pseudofiligree border[38] closely suggest the Podcherem pendant,[39] which differs only in that it substitutes smooth panels for the inlaid stones. Let us recall that a ring with a round setting, close to those known in collections from Olbia, Chersonesus, and Kerch, was found in burial no. 1 of the Pereyminskiy cemetery, and an oval glass inlay from an ornament, in burial no. 6. The disclike plaques from the Pereyminskiy cemetery and the Podcherem cache call to mind the round platelets from Kerch with a border of pearl filigree and with inlaid stones.[40] There is a particularly close analogy to the disclike plates reported, for example by Gorodtsov,[41] in the gold medallion decorated with garnets which was accidentally found on the Taman Peninsula near the former colony of Mikhaelsfeld.[42] It has been suggested that this medallion belongs with the cache found there earlier and dated by a coin of Justinian I (A.D. 527–565).[43]

In describing the Pereyminskiy cemetery we noted the double-disced plaques decorated with animal heads on the bridge (crosspiece). It is a very interesting find, because lions' heads adorn one of the plaques and rams' heads the other. These figures, from the point of view of both subject matter and iconography, are foreign to the art of tribes living in the Cis-Ural and in western Siberia, and nothing analogous has been found locally in any period. There can be no doubt that they are imported. They are hardly local copies of an imported model. [If they were], in preparing a clay impression of the original, the delicate, detailed work, such as the lion's mane (which we find in the figures), would inevitably have disappeared; nothing of this sort of detail is found in the bronze figures of local workmanship.

In analyzing the objects from the Podcherem cache, Gorodtsov noted that in the Cis-Ural the place of the Scytho-Sarmatian forms is taken by new forms arising from the influence of the Roman empire and the Indo-Parthian kingdom. At the beginning of the 4th century A.D. "their place in relation to influence on the Cis-Ural is taken by the powerful kingdom of the Sassanids."[44] This somewhat simplified but essentially accurate observation is especially valuable in setting an upper date for the Pereyminskiy cemetery. It is quite obvious that the Pereyminskiy plaques cannot be associated with the applied art of the Sassanids: they clearly express a Greek tradition, even though it be in the form of a survival. Stylistically they are close to the products of the jeweler's art of the first centuries A.D. Thus the date established by Gorodtsov for a shift in imports and influence, which he uses for determining the date of the Podcherem cache, is entirely applicable to the Pereyminskiy burial ground.

The place of origin of Pereyminskiy and Podcherem imports is still a matter of conjecture. Even after all the study that has been made of the material from the northern shore of the Black Sea, we know nothing from that area that has the specific character of the Pereyminskiy plaques. It is obvious that the production center for ornaments imitating the jeweler's art of that period for export to the country of the "barbarians" was not there. Gorodtsov's reference to the Parthian kingdom is a reasonable one. Actually in pre-Roman and Roman times, imports from the west did not penetrate east of the Cis-Ural, where authentic Roman objects are still being found. Beginning with the period of the Achaemenids, importing from the Middle Asiatic kingdoms into both western Siberia and the Cis-Ural was fairly well established. The intensity of these ties with the Middle Asiatic south is also indicated by the presence in the language and folklore of the Ugrian tribes of a number of borrowed words which testify to influence of the eastern Iranian-speaking peoples as early as Scytho-Sarmatian times.[45] In the folklore we meet with not only reflections of the myths about the bird Garud and the World Tree (which are fairly widespread), but also a modified form of the Chorasmian myth about Siyavush ~ Siyavarsh. Even more interesting is the fact that we find in the folklore mention of the name Pärap-arsykh, the second part of which is considered by B. Munkácsi to be a local version of the Parthian name for the Arshakid [Arsacid] dynasty.[46] All these considerations lead to the assumption that the origin of these ornaments is not in the area immediately north of the Black Sea, but in the Hellenized kingdoms of Middle Asia and to some extent of Asia Minor.

Having defined the possible chronological framework for the Pereyminskiy cemetery as within the limits of the 4th–5th centuries A.D., let us now return to a consideration of more immediate interest to us—the pottery from this site. On the basis of isolated fragments and vessels that have been reconstructed, a fairly complete picture of pottery shapes may be established. The Pereyminskiy vessels are customarily made with a round base and a fairly clearly defined, straight neck. Their height varies; often they are so low that the diameter exceeds the height. In shape they are similar to what we described earlier as characteristic for the Karym stage, but there is a striking difference in ornamentation. The design of it is poor, occurs only on the neck, not even reaching down onto the shoulder. It consists of cord, comb or toothed-paddle impressions, and pitting. Figured stamp impressions are not used.

 Similar to the Pereyminskiy ceramics (except for vessels from burial no. 8, which will be dealt with later) are those found at the fortified hill site "Zhilye," situated about 150 m from the cemetery. Here also are round-bottomed vessels decorated almost exclusively with cord and comb. While there is a small number of pots decorated with a diamond-shaped impression, the number of these in proportion to the whole is insignificant. Perhaps if we had at our disposal a greater number of vessels from the cemetery, we would find among them some that were also decorated with diamond impressions.

 It seems that the hill site lasted somewhat longer than the cemetery. In the general mass of pottery there was a sherd decorated on the shoulder with triangular imprints, a motif familiar in early Iron Age pottery along the Ob, and as a survival continuing to exist there until the first centuries A.D. On the fragment this decoration already reveals a decadent form.

 Somewhat more often one finds bands of pitting or the imprints of the stab-and-drag paddle, which descend from the neck to the base of the pot, and ribbed moldings on the neck. Both these traits become diffused in northern pottery at a somewhat later time, in the subsequent Orontur stage, but it is also possible that they occurred earlier in the type of pottery we have just described.

 At present we cannot define exactly the time brackets for the hill site Zhilye. Two pertinent circumstances should be pointed out, however. First, the pottery from most of the graves in the Pereyminskiy cemetery belongs to the same group as the pottery from Zhilye and is very likely in part synchronous with it. Second, in the immediate vicinity as well as farther afield, in the Tyumen region, there are sites with pottery similar to that of Pereyminskiy cemetery, but belonging to an earlier or a later period. Among these may be mentioned the site at Andryushin Gorodok,[47] the Bogandinskoye fortified hill site on the Pyshma River, the Molchanova hill site on the Tura, and others. The Molchanova pottery will be described later; here we shall only mention that its ornamentation belongs to the same comb and/or cord type and that in general it is very close to the pottery of Andryushin Gorodok, the Pereyminskiy cemetery, and Zhilye but that it should be dated not earlier than the following Orontur stage.

 In addition to the ceramics, a clay figurine was found that is superior in the care with which it was made (Fig. 16). It represents a man in a crouched position, dressed in a parka with the hood pushed back. The face is conventionally represented by a small circle. The decoration on the clothing is done with a small stick, using the stab-and-drag method. The hair is indicated by longitudinal lines on the head, done similarly. In

Fig. 16. Clay anthropomorphic figurine from the fortified hill site Zhilye.

cut and arrangement of decoration the parka is close to the modern Mansi and Khanty parka. The sleeves are broad at the base but end in narrow cuffs ornamented with stripes. A piping of similar bands goes around its lower edge. Considering the obviously accurate rendering of the figurine, it is very significant that the arrangement of decoration on the breast emphasizes the absence of an opening [slit]. Here we have a "closed" parka, of the pullover type, rather than one that opens in front. Consequently, the find provides valuable evidence that the [closed] parka type of garment was distributed much farther south than it was in historic times. A figurine similar to the Zhilye one was found at fortified hill site no. 4 on Andreyevskoye Lake (Fig. 17).

The pottery from burials nos. 7 and 8 of the Pereyminskiy cemetery proved a surprise. These burials are synchronous with the others, are contiguous to no. 4, and form a continuation of one of the rows. Yet, the

Fig. 17. Clay anthropomorphic figurine from fortified hill site no. 4 on Andreyevskoye Lake.

vessels found in them have nothing in common either in shape or in decoration with those which have been described thus far. They are all shaped more or less like a jug [without a handle], with straight or slightly flaring necks, and round, in some cases bomb-shaped, bodies. The ornamentation is confined to two areas: on the neck, almost always just at the rim, and on the shoulders. The decoration consists of comb-stamped or smoothed hatching which forms checkerboard, herringbone, or diagonally crosshatched bands. On two pots (Plate XLIII, items 1, 3) there is a row of small triangles on the shoulders, dented in their centers with the point of a little stick, and on one the neck is circumscribed with five parallel narrow moldings imitating cords (Plate XLIII, item 3).

The vessels also differ in technological execution. While a clay analysis has not been made, or the way of firing examined, the light orange color of the surface and of the clay where there is a break clearly indicates a different manufacture.

This was the first time we encountered pottery of this type, and no chronological or distributional analogues to it can be pointed out. An only approximate parallel might be seen in the pots from Nevolino cemetery on the Kama, dating to the Lomovatovo period. Actually, the only thing these have in common with the Pereyminskiy vessels is the tall and straight neck; the decoration, proportions, and shape of the body and base are different.[48] A good deal closer to the Pereyminskiy vessels in shape and decoration are those from the burial mound [*kurgan*] at the village of Tyukova near Tobolsk[49] and from the Sargatskoye and Nikolayev *kurgans* near Omsk. In particular we note the characteristic band of triangles filled with hatched lines or twisted [made by twisting] depressions. However, the Sargatskoye and Tyukova *kurgans* belong to a considerably earlier period, the 4th–3rd centuries B.C., and the resemblance to the Pereyminskiy pottery may be simply genetic. As yet pottery has not been encountered which could be considered remotely developed from the Sargatskoye-Tyukova prototype; for this reason the ceramics in Pereyminskiy grave no. 8 are particularly interesting.

The finds on Andreyevskoye Lake suggest a region where boundaries of three cultural areas had met, and that they differ from each other in pottery ornamentation. The first of these, to which basically this work is devoted, is characterized by pottery with comb-stamp type of decoration. Its distribution is principally in the taiga part of the Ob-Irtysh, to the north of the Tura River and the mouth of the Tobol. Also, this type of pottery is found much farther south, in the wooded valleys of the Irtysh and the Ob as far as the mouths of the Om and the Bolshaya Rechka. The second area is defined by the presence of pottery with comb and corded decoration and is localized in the central Urals and Trans-Ural [that is, eastern slopes of the Urals] area. Unfortunately, this territory has been very little investigated up to the present, particularly as regards sites of the 1st millennium A.D.* Therefore, we cannot yet trace the limits of distribution of the comb and corded pottery. Its study should certainly

* [At present (1968) this territory is being intensively investigated. (Personal communication from author.) Editor, A.I.N.A.]

be undertaken in the immediate future. At present we can only say with reasonable certainty that the spread of this type of pottery can be traced to sites of the so-called Trans-Ural Ananino epoch,[50] which is tentatively dated to the 8th–4th centuries B.C.

Our information is equally scant about the limits of distribution of ceramics characterized by the vessels from grave no. 8. One can only say that it is not found at sites in the forest belt. It can most likely be associated with the nomadic tribes of the Trans-Ural and the steppes along the Irtysh.

Actually not one of the three groups of pottery listed represents anything new. The development of each can be traced more or less clearly to the 1st millennium B.C. and may be linked with ceramics of that period which are already known to us. On the basis of conclusions we have already indicated, we assume that these three pottery groups belong to the three interrelated groups of Ugrian tribes which had already been formed by the 1st millennium B.C. In this connection the steppe and forested-steppe tribes should be regarded as basically proto-Magyar and later including the Turkicized Ugrian ancestors of the Barabinets and Bashkirs. The group of comb and corded pottery from the Ural and Trans-Ural should, it appears, be associated with the proto-Mansi tribes, and the comb-stamped with the ancient Khanty. Later we shall return, and in more detail, to the question of the ethnic characteristics of these groups. At the moment it is significant that the relationship between them may be explained by their proximity on the shores of Andreyevskoye Lake.

Let us return to the material associated with the northern group and examine the bronze artifacts which on the basis of typology are synchronous with the Karym period.

In 1926 a small amount of very interesting material was collected by R. E. Kols, leader of the Taz expedition of the Russian Geographical Society, on the left bank of the Taz River near Mameyev's winter camp.[51] The collection was then turned over to the Anthropological Museum of Moscow State University (see Plate XL, items 4–12). Conspicuous in the collection for its fine workmanship is the handle of a knife in white bronze, with the haft of its iron blade still in position (Plate XL, item 4). Also found was what appears to be the lower part of a similar handle. In the same style and executed with the same care is the perforated piece representing an eagle (Plate XL, item 5), a piece with perforated bulges (Plate XL, item 6), and some small crosslike plaques with a crossbeam on the obverse (Plate XL, items 7–9, 11). Three of the plaques were strung on a sinew thread.

It is difficult to say if these finds were associated. There is no stratigraphic information about them, nor does an analysis of the composition give any clear picture. The crosslike plaques were in use for a very long time, and there is no clear idea of the dating or duration of the artifacts with perforated bulges, like the one illustrated in Plate XL, item 6. One can state with greater or lesser assurance that the handle and the bird figure belong to the same period and the same classification of objects: they are close in style and identical in the manner of cutting the pattern with deep lines, which have clear-cut edges. Very close analogues to Mameyev's winter camp handle may be found among those of the Podcherem cache. They were incorrectly called mace-heads by Gorodtsov.[52] One of these, published by Gorodtsov, is similar in design, with the only difference being that it is crowned with the head of an animal rather than a bird and it has a smooth socket at the lower part rather than a faceted one.[53] Faceted sockets are present on handles crowned with heads of moose and deer,[54] indicating this to be a type familiar to the Podcherem masters. Not quite so close but still very comparable is the handle from Kharino to which Gorodtsov refers and which he dates to the 4th–5th centuries A.D.[55] This date, which we have accepted for the Karym stage, appears to be entirely appropriate for at least a part of the artifacts from near Mameyev's winter camp.

From the forested section along the Ob there are several chance finds in addition to the sites we have enumerated. Particularly interesting among these are the detached, cast figures of birds and animals. Lack of sufficient study of the region and a lack of an adequately worked out typology makes it impossible for us to date these figures. In the absence of stratigraphic information we must limit ourselves to a very tentative estimate of the chronology. Nevertheless these chance finds are of great value: they display clearly the stylistic peculiarities of the representational art in the Ob region during the 1st millennium A.D., and also to a certain extent they permit an analysis of the ethnic composition of the area, particularly when the Ob materials are compared with those of neighboring areas.

The majority of the objects illustrated (Plate XLIV) belong to the group of hollow figurines. This group, principally based on materials from the Kama region, was analyzed by A. A. Spitsyn, who also pointed out some of its most characteristic decorative traits. He noted "edging like a beaded strip or like cording; notched bands; a corded edging sometimes becomes a band made up of squares; or even of dentates."[56] Spitsyn ascribes the hollow figurines to the Lomovatovo period, which he dates as the 8th–9th centuries A.D. A. V. Shmidt expanded and completed the list of characteristic traits started by Spitsyn. Shmidt's category of hollow figurines includes "numerous animal figurines embellished with the typical dotted-line decoration which follows the natural form of the animal. The rounded contours, with nothing in them of the geometric or conventionalized, proclaim their realistic style. . . . The entire collection of the figurines is stylistically homogeneous and is datable to about the same period."[57]

Besides the group of figurines described above, Shmidt noted another group made up of "highly conventionalized little ducks and cocks decorated with shallowly incised bands."[58] According to him, the hollow figurines of the first group did not prevail later than the time of the Lomovatovo culture, "but it is likely that they did exist in the preceding periods," judging from their undoubted successive associations with the hollow Glyadenovo figurines. At this point, Shmidt also came to the conclusion that the date proposed by Spitsyn for the Lomovatovo culture should be changed to the 6th–8th centuries A.D.[59]

After his investigations of the Podcherem cache, Gorodtsov reached

Plate XLIV. Hollow-cast representations of animals.

1, 3–from Filinskoye village; 2–from the Konda River; 4, 5, 7, 10, 12–from the former Tobolsk *guberniya*; 6–from the vicinity of Ishvar native village (Kunovat); 8–from vicinity of Tyukova village; 9–from Severnaya Sosva River; 11, 13–from Salekhard.

the conclusion that the casting of hollow bronze figurines may well have existed at an earlier time, beyond the limits of the Lomovatovo period. In discussing the period of the greatest flowering of representational art in the Cis-Ural, embodied in the cast bronze artifacts, the period which Spitsyn called "the golden age of Chud art," Gorodtsov stated that "if this art really had a golden age it must have existed not in the 9th and 8th centuries as Spitsyn supposed, nor in the 8th and 6th centuries, as Shmidt preferred to date it, but rather at a still earlier age."[60] In conclusion Gorodtsov even points out that after the 6th century the Chud art progressively starts to decline.[61]

Smirnov came to similar conclusions and found it desirable to change the dating of individual figurines and also of a number of sites which had been classified as Lomovatovo ones—the finds at Ples village, the Georgiyev cache, the finds at Vish-Palnik, Grudyata, and other places.[62] These he transferred to the last period of the Pyanobor [Pyanyy Bor] culture, that is, according to the chronology he suggested, to 4th–5th centuries A.D.[63]

Now that we have examined the views of investigators about the hollow figurines from the Kama area, let us see how well we can transfer their stylistic traits and chronology to the Trans-Ural and western Siberian finds. Spitsyn relies on the specific characteristics he has established and thinks it possible to consider as one unit all the material relating to the bronze figurines from the Cis-Ural and western Siberia. He wrote, "The area of distribution of the shamanistic figurines is the joint drainage of the Ob and Irtysh and that of the Kama basin with adjacent parts of the basins of the Vychegda and Pechora. Shaman's articles were not made on the Yenisey: they arrive there from the direction of the Chulym," and further, "Only a limited number of these articles has so far been found in the Ob basin. The majority of them were in the Kama, and to some extent the Pechora, basins. Whether the major workshops were on the east or west slopes of the Urals it is at present impossible to determine."[64] Apparently Smirnov upholds a similar position, because besides depending on extensive ethnographic material in the Trans-Ural, he thinks it possible (though without emphasizing it) to view the Kama materials and the Siberian ones in the same light, particularly those from Skripunova village, that is, from the area of the Lenk-Ponk cemetery on the Ob.[65]

A. V. Shmidt also admitted a close connection between the bronze figurines of the Cis-Ural and western Siberia, although with reservations. In his opinion the western Siberian animal style was in many ways related to that of Perm [on the Kama], but also, in many ways it differed from it.[66] Leaving aside the question of subject matter, which of course displays specific characteristics for both the Cis-Ural and western Siberia, let us dwell on Shmidt's observations about the style of the figurines. In his opinion, "In Siberia there is a great deal of punctate decoration with very small, *not* large, dots; on the Kama, as we know, it is present only in the post-Lomovatovo epoch. . . . What is especially important, in western Siberia there is little of the realistic Lomovatovo stylization, and the figurines, particularly on the plaques, usually have an unimaginative character."[67]

Now that thirty years have passed since Shmidt wrote his work, it is possible to say with confidence that his opinion was basically incorrect. As far as one can judge from his subsequent work, the error in his appraisal of western Siberian art style was due to the fact that he rejected for some reason all the material known up to that time which related to figurine and hollow casting and focussed on a group of figurines in flat casting, very specific in their form and cult significance.[68] It is not surprising that this one-sidedness in the selection of material resulted in the opinion that "the Trans-Ural masters had no interest in real, living forms" and had in their work no "place for the reflection of true, living forms."[69]

There is also actually no basis, even if one judges by the figurines published by Spitsyn, to insist on the diffusion, in Siberia, of small, punctate decoration. Considering the material we have at our disposal at present, introduced in the present article, and in my previous work on the bronzes of the Ust-Poluy period,[70] as well as in the publications of T. J. Arne,[71] it is easy to discover that small punctate ornamentation is as little typical for western Siberia as it is for the Cis-Ural. On the early figurines of the Ust-Poluy period there is no ornamentation except for occasional cordlike edging. The details, such as fur, feathers, and contours of folded wings are indicated by raised or sunken lines which fairly accurately, although sometimes in a slightly conventionalized manner, reproduce the characteristic natural features. Contrary to Shmidt, the style of the representational art is chiefly realistic, though in combination with fairly complex symbolism.[72] In this group may be included the figurine of an eagle (Plate XLIV, item 8), from the Tobolsk Museum, obtained by V. N. Pignatti from the vicinity of Tyukova village. Unfortunately, there is no detailed documentation in the museum, but it is quite likely that this figurine comes from the Tyukova *kurgan*, which belongs to the Potchevash period and was excavated by Pignatti.[73] The pose of the eagle, the way its talons are indicated, the realism of the figurine, and its close resemblance to some of the Ust-Poluy figurines—all strongly point to this dating. The figurine of an owl must be close to it chronologically; it comes from "somewhere in the Tobolsk province" (Plate XLIV, item 10).

To this group belong both stylistically and chronologically those figurines from the Kama region which were set apart by Shmidt as being earlier bird figurines.[74]

The realistic style continued to some extent into the first centuries A.D., judging by the hollow bronze castings from the Kozlova cemetery (four bear figurines resembling those from Glyadenovo,[75] a bird and an animal figurine datable to the 4th century A.D.) and also in all likelihood the admirable figurine of a goose from Filinskoye village (Plate XLIV, item 1). Along with these and not later than the 2nd–3rd centuries A.D. (as can be judged by the figurines on the Pechora scabbard and objects from the Podcherem cache), decorative details appear on the bird and animal figurines (particularly the hollow-cast ones) and with them a more clearly expressed stylization, perhaps as a result of the increasingly decorative role played by these objects. To these objects could be added from our materials those from Mameyev's winter camp, which belong to the Podcherem period, the figurine of a bird from the Ishvarskiy *yurts* [native village] (Plate XLIV, item 6), which resembles the Podcherem ones in style, and possibly several other bird figurines (Plate XLIV, items 7, 12).

While the imitations of cords and the linear divisions of the surface are retained, those motifs described by Spitsyn make their appearance:

edgings of beaded bands, as for example in Plate XLIV, item 9, and bands filled with squares and diamonds that are so common over a wide area on bronze articles from the Cis-Ural and western Siberia until the 8th or even the 9th centuries A.D. More specific for the Trans-Ural and Siberia are the bands of large beads or hemispheres (Plate XLIV, item 4) and the flat, protruding circles which we already saw on the belt buckles of the Ust-Poluy period. This motif first appears on figurines of the Yar-sale period and survives with few changes until the end of the Orontur period, since we find it on a figurine from burial no. 20 at Barsov Gorodok,[76] which has a secure date of the 9th century A.D. It is, of course, possible that we are dealing with an object which is being used for the second time, considering that it is the only specimen of its kind present in this cemetery.

Very often the flat, protruding circles are framed in a cartouche shaped like a teardrop or a comma and are placed on the shoulder or hip of an animal as, for instance, on the deer figurine (Plate XLIV, item 2). This, as well as the scrolls on the hip and shoulder of the animal depicted on the Yar-sale scabbard, may be considered the reflection of a stylistic process for emphasizing the muscles—a process so familiar in the art of the Sarmatians and Huns. Even though the portrayal of a deer denotes a change in subject matter, it is still very likely related to the art of the steppe cultures. In the course of time, the process in question underwent some changes. On later figurines we find the teardrop cartouche usually replaced by concentric circles and ovals, sometimes cordlike, as for example on the horse figurine from burial no. 20 at Barsov Gorodok,[77] or replaced simply by meaningless bands, as on the horse from Filinskoye village (Plate XLIV, item 3).

An oversupply of ornamental details which are so little in accord with nature (Plate XLIV, items 11, 13) seems, in the art of figurine casting in the Ob region, to be a sign of decay just as it was in the Cis-Ural. This process of decay was materially abetted at the end of the 1st millennium A.D. by the development on the Vychegda and the Kama of bangles for trade. This created a new fashion in ornaments and supplanted the production of decorative figurines, a complicated process under domestic conditions.

Chapter 3

The Orontur Stage
(6th–9th Centuries A.D.)

In the upper reaches of the Konda River more than 900 km from the point where it joins the Irtysh, the pure and sparkling waters of Orontur Lake spread among sandy hillocks overgrown with forests of pine. The lake is joined to the river by winding channels that flow through swampy valleys, and its shores must always have appealed to man as a convenient place to settle. Investigators who had visited Orontur Lake—Nosilov, Infantyef, Boch—repeatedly noticed the sites of former habitation along its shores. Some of these sites, as for example the sacrificial places, obviously date to recent times, but others may well have their origins in earlier periods.

According to S. G. Boch, there are pine forests growing out of the sandy gravel along the left bank of the stream that joins the lake to the Konda River, and the soil has a clayey surface. One of the hills is circled by a trench 1 m in depth; the circular rampart built up from the [soil on the] inner side of the trench has a diameter of 20 m and a height of as much as 2 m above the bottom of the trench. A culture-yielding layer with charcoal is found at a depth of 0.25 m inside the circle contained by the wall.

Another town site, also circular, is situated on the south shore of the lake. Here Nosilov collected a considerable amount of material, which is now being kept in the Museum of Physical Anthropology in Moscow.

The pottery of the Orontur fortified hill site consists basically of fragments of pots which are the same in form and decoration as those in the upper level of the Karym site of Us-Tolt (Plate XXXVIII). In this ornamentation we see the characteristic sharp-angled bands and ladders; triangles, hatched in different directions; bands and ribbons executed with the stab-and-drag method and reaching to the bottom of the pot. Stab-and-drag ornamentation done with a dentated paddle is widely represented; the edges were either straight or curved. There are rhomboids stamped with the same kind of paddle, and zonal bands are also made with these. The molding with transverse hatching at the base of the neck, characteristic of the ceramics of the third Karym group (Plate XXXVIII, items 1–4, and others), is clearly represented on the Orontur vessels.

The resemblance between Orontur and Us-Tolt ceramics suggests a synchronization of the former with the late period of the Karym fortified hill site.

To the Orontur period also belong the finds at Cape Shaytan, situated on the left bank of the Severnaya Sosva River 25 km upstream from Berezov. Apparently there was once a sacrificial place here, judging by the Mansi name *Yalping-Nël*, that is, "Holy Cape." Recently, when areas of the cape were plowed for vegetable gardening, several bronze objects were found. They were given to the Tobolsk Museum. In 1911 the geologist D. I. Ilovayskiy collected pottery on Cape Shaytan which is now kept in the Museum of Physical Anthropology at the Moscow State University. Despite the small amount of material found, the ornamentation is so clear and definite that it can with certainty be identified as belonging to the type which we have described from the upper level of the Karym hill site and from that of Orontur. This is particularly the case of the sherds with characteristic molding and crosscutting.

In addition to sherds, many bronze annular pendants, fragments of neck rings and bracelets, and a round bronze plaque with the figure of a griffon were found. I do not know of any existing close analogues to this figure, but on the basis of information contributed by K. V. Trever, it may be dated to the middle of the 1st millennium A.D., or a little later.

There is another find which deserves special attention; it is the rather imperfectly cast buckle with representations of hares and moose heads. An analogous type of buckle is known from other finds which will be discussed in detail later.

The find of the griffon plaque at Cape Shaytan was not unique. A plaque that is magnificent in execution was acquired as a chance find from the Kintusovo *yurts* on the Salym River and is kept at present in the Tobolsk Museum (Plate XLV, item 1). Judging by the small suspension loop which is cast in one piece with the object, it is a local copy of an import.

Some of the characteristics expressed in the figure of the griffon indicate that the original may have come from the east, and in Mr. Trever's opinion, also could be dated about the middle of the 1st millennium A.D. and certainly not later than the 6th century. A plaque closely resembling this one in the representation of the griffon, and in particular the position of its wings—one from "somewhere in Siberia" which is illustrated in the work of A. A. Spitsyn, "Shamanskiye izobrazheniya" [Shamanistic Representations]—itself has not been preserved, and Spitsyn used the drawing of Medvedev (which is in the collections of the Archaeological Commission) in publishing it.[78]

It is very likely that Cape Shaytan also yielded a plaque (Plate XLV, item 2) which is in the Tobolsk Museum and was published by Spitsyn with the following description: "A cast plaque with the representation of three warlike figures; the shoulders point inward and the legs are short as in a child or a bear, with creases at the knees and ankles; the figures wear belts and necklaces, the eye-sockets are semi-lunar and each figure has three ears on the top of its head; the swords are like broad knives with short hilts. There are two openings for suspension . . . white bronze or silver."[79]

1

2

Plate XLV. Bronze brooches.
  1–from the vicinity of Kintusovo; 2–from Berezov region.

It is difficult to agree with Spitsyn's theory that this object is imported. In its casting technique it is not superior to many other articles known to us (see Plate XLIV), while in subject matter it is closely allied to local Ugrian representations. The figures on the plaque represent three *menkvs*, that is, spirits of the Por moiety, in a characteristic pose of the sacred dance with swords which Castrén described in his time and which I also was able to observe on the Ob. In a traditional representation of *menkvs*, which are beings with a mixture of human and bear attributes, the three digits which are mentioned by Spitsyn, the bearlike quality of the figures, and the sharply pointed and many-pointed heads are characteristic. In Ugrian folklore, the *menkvs* appear as one-, two-, or three-headed, and even in more modern Khanty wood sculptures the triple heads are indicated by the three-toothed occiput. Spitsyn also misinterpreted the detail, which he called "eye-sockets in semilunar shape." The bronze mask from the Kintusovo *yurts* (Plate LIV, item 10) and, even more clearly, the wooden mask with silver facing in the Tobolsk Museum reveal that these are not eye sockets but the visor of a helmet.

Pottery of the Orontur type is found in another place on the Severnaya Sosva River, in the fortified site of Sortynya III, which is situated on the left bank of the river, 3 km upstream from the village of Sortynya. The fortified site is on a small promontory bounded by a deep moat and protected by a system of banks and ditches. The bounded area was small and entirely occupied by dwellings placed close together (Fig. 18). These were arranged in two rows with a corridor between them connecting the separate lodgements. The Sortynya III site is interesting in that it represents a type of many-roomed collective dwelling. Such sites are not known in earlier times, but later they occur fairly frequently.

There is another site on the Severnaya Sosva which may, although with some reservations, be assigned to the Orontur period. This is Lyuli-Kar, which was investigated in 1946 by the director of the Omsk

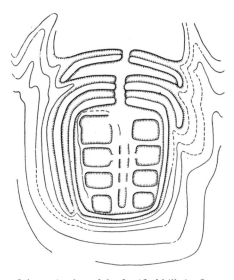

Fig. 18. Schematic plan of the fortified hill site Sortynya III.

Museum, A. F. Palashenkov. It is situated 90 km upriver from Berezov, not far from the Lyulikary *yurts* [village], 2 km from the point where the Usyng-Ya [River] joins the Severnaya Sosva. On one side the hill site is bordered by a small ravine, on another by a deep gully, and on the open side by a rampart and ditch which even today is as much as 2 m deep. The town rises 12 m above the floodplain, a fact which obviously gives rise to its local name, *Lyuli-Kar*, or "High Place," in the Mansi language.

The pottery from Lyuli-Kar has a number of traits that are characteristic of the Orontur stage. Notable are the presence around the neck of a molding notched in vertical or slanting lines (Plate XLVI, items 1, 2, 5) and the frequently recurring decoration which consists of a pendant band filled in with imprints of smooth or pitted angles or half-moons (Plate XLVI, items 3, 4). Also typical of the Orontur period is the wide distribution at Lyuli-Kar of rhomboid impressions, expecially nucleated ones (Plate XLVI, items 1, 2, 4) and those transversely ribbed (Plate XLVI, items 2, 7). The number and variety of stamped impressions on the Lyuli-Kar ceramics, however, far surpass those known to us from the upper level of Us-Tolt and from the Orontur hill site and tend to associate the pottery with that from an earlier period. Such an association is emphasized by the presence on Lyuli-Kar pottery (in addition to the notched [ribbed] molding) of a small collar similar to that seen on pottery of the Karym period, but here almost invariably decorated with oblique lines (Plate XLVI, items 3, 4, 6). Apparently such a collar was the starting point for the development of the ribbed molding which is characteristic for the Orontur period. Finally, it should be noted that the band of triangles made by cross-hatching is not present on the pots from Lyuli-Kar; it is a trait unknown during the Karym stage but widely distributed in the Orontur, especially toward its close.

All these considerations lead us to date the Lyuli-Kar site to the very beginning of the Orontur period, since we can identify in its pottery a number of traits which characterize the transition to this period from the Karym.

There is pottery which in decoration closely resembles that from Lyuli-Kar in the culture level washed out of the right bank of the Severnaya Sosva near the village of Khangla-Sam, and on the right bank of the Ob similar pottery was found near the village of Bolshoy Atlym (about 300 km north of the mouth of the Irtysh) by N. Kozhina, a student at the Geographical Institute of Leningrad University.

Pottery typical of the Orontur period and having, like that of Lyuli-Kar, a number of specific traits, has been found not only in sites in the taiga but also in the Far North, in particular as a result of the explorations of G. A. Chernov on the upper reaches of the Shchuchya,* near 67° of northern latitude.[80]

Even more interesting are the finds of similar pottery in the hamlet of Tiutey-sale. This little settlement, which I found in 1927, is at 71°30′ N, on the west coast of the Yamal Peninsula. It is at the junction of the rivers Ser-Yaha and the Tiutey-Yaha, near the point where the latter empties

---

* [A left-bank tributary of the lower Ob, Editor, A.I.N.A.]

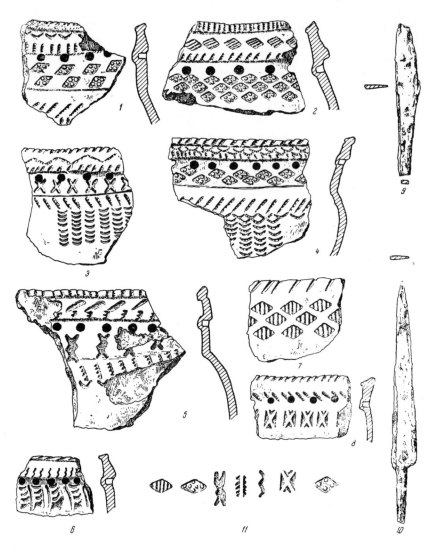

Plate XLVI. Finds from the fortified hill site Lyuli-Kar.
  1 to 8–ceramics; 9, 10–knives; 11–examples of vessel ornamentation.

into the Kara Sea. Unfortunately, the excavation of the site was not completed, because news of the death of my expedition companion, N. A. Kotovshchikova, obliged me to abandon my work and leave for the other coast of the peninsula.

Tiutey-sale is located on the edge of a high and narrow cape which is delimited by the rivers mentioned above and the sea coast. It consists of three pit houses built on narrow promontories located on the steep coast, which is being washed away by the sea. Such a location probably provided good drainage indispensable under the swampy conditions of the adjacent tundra.

The largest pit house was discovered on the tip of one point of land, a smaller one at the base of the same point. A third hut, also small, was on the next elevated point of the shore. A few steps from the steep shore edge was an irregularly round pit, long since filled in.

The layout and mode of construction of the huts could be established only in part, as they had been thoroughly disturbed by the Nentsy, who dug there repeatedly in a search for bronze objects and bone artifacts. It can be stated only that the houses were round, one of them 7 m in diameter, the other two somewhat smaller; the hearths were located in their centers.

At the edge of the houses were remains of vertical posts, but it was impossible to determine the construction of the roofs. In the largest house, in the few places where large pieces of the fallen roof remained undisturbed, a thickness of 0.4 m was measured, testifying to the thoroughness of its construction.

There was an abundance of animal bones scattered in and around the buildings. Among these were the bones of walrus, seal, whale, polar bear, fox and reindeer. In addition there were many small bones of birds and rodents which it was impossible to identify owing to the poor state of their preservation. The great majority of the bones belonged to sea mammals, especially the walrus. Dozens of walrus skulls were found around the houses, but bones of land animals occurred less frequently. In the solid, hard-packed floor of the house, which was up to 0.2 m thick and made up of charcoal, bones, wood chips, and bits of baleen, there were fragments of clay pots and various objects. The pottery included sherds from a great number of pots. The material used in their manufacture came from clay deposits and was plentifully admixed with coarse-grained quartzitic sand and mica. The pots were hand-modeled from slabs of clay, and the inner surfaces were apparently smoothed with grass, while the outer surface remained rough; the firing was poor (Plate XLVII).

Due to the fragmentation of the sherds it was difficult to determine with any degree of accuracy the shapes of the pots. Apparently they were shallow basins and bowls, most of them with round bottoms. The rim profiles varied. There were some pots with almost straight rims, that is, with a very gradual transition from neck to rim. Others had a well-defined neck with a noticeably thicker and somewhat flaring rim. The edge of the rim was usually flattened. A thickening or appliqué molding just below the rim was rather typical. The basins, which apparently had flatly rounded bottoms, also had thickened rims and flattened edges.

In addition to the round-bottomed pots there are fragments of pots with low, collarlike bases. However these collars have no resemblance to the well-defined bases of the Ust-Poluy pottery. The collections of R. E. Kols from the mouth of the Taz River or those of G. A. Chernov from the sacrificial site at Khaebidya-Peadera may contain some parallels [to those of Tiutey-sale]. Probably these bases express a faint survival of the erstwhile influence of Ust-Poluy pottery. This influence was more strongly felt in earlier cultures, contemporaneous with the Ust-Poluy. It is all the more interesting to note such long survival of a tradition once invoked in the culture of a tribe in a remote corner of the Arctic. In comparison with the Ust-Poluy bases, the bases of these arctic pots were

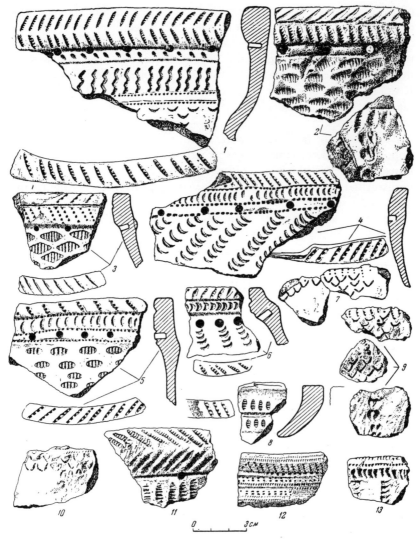

Plate XLVII. Ceramics from the pit house on Cape Tiutey-sale.

more functional, as they gave stability to the round-bottomed vessels. This probably is the explanation for their long-continued use.

The size of the Tiutey-sale pots varied, ranging from the very small to those with a diameter of 25–30 cm. The thickness of the walls ranges from 4 to 14 mm, with the majority between 7 and 8 mm; the basins are usually thin-walled—4 to 6 mm. The decoration as a rule is limited to the upper parts of the vessels and covers the neck and shoulders, but only in isolated cases reaches lower. The rims and edges are usually decorated. The basins are decorated on the inside with a narrow band near the rim, along its thickened edge, and, rarely, with a thin band on the outside, also near the rim.

The resemblance, mentioned earlier, of this pottery and that of the Orontur type lies chiefly in the composition of the ornamentation and partially in the decorative details. Typical of the Tiutey-sale pottery is molding with transverse grooving made with a comb or with a stab-and-drag paddle, and a broad band on the neck also made with a comb or various stamps, among them ones with a "snake" motif. Often this band, as on Orontur pottery, is replaced by diagonally placed curved impressions, usually made by the stab-and-drag method. Below the decorated zone of the neck, just as in the pottery from the taiga sites, we find vertically positioned stab-and-drag or stamped ornamentation.

But together with the resemblances one must note the differences, as for example the very much thickened lip on the fragment shown in Plate XLVII, item 1, which cannot be compared to the appliqué molding mentioned earlier for the Orontur type.

Among the stampings characteristic of the pottery from Tiutey-sale, along with the angular or semilunar ones which are widespread in the southern areas, there are others unknown in that region—the "hoof-print," the "arrow," and rare and nontypical forms of oval or oval-rhomboid, ribbed stampings.

In details of shape and ornamentation of the pots under discussion, there are parallels in other sites of the polar areas. In reference to the bases, it already has been noted that identical forms are known from the mouth of the Taz River (Mameyev's winter camp), and closely allied forms were reported by Chernov among the finds from Bolshezemel-skaya tundra.* At sites along the lower course of the Kolva-Vis River, a right tributary of the Kolva (also in the Bolshezemelskaya tundra), were found pots very similar in rim profile and, in decoration, with identical forms of ribbed stampings. The ribbed oval stamp was also widely used on pottery in Zhuravskiy's collections at sites of an earlier period in the same area.[81]

The question of similar pottery found in the subpolar and transpolar regions to the east and west of the Ob deserves the closest attention, but unfortunately it cannot be reviewed at present owing to the lack of adequate materials.

In addition to pottery, a large quantity of metal objects was found at Tiutey-sale. Bronze and copper were found in the form of small sheets, and iron artifacts included forked arrowheads, a knife fragment, a ring, scrapers, and some shapeless pieces. Of course, the huts had been dug over by the Nentsy to obtain bronze artifacts.

In spite of the remoteness of Tiutey-sale, which lies 600 km in a straight line and over 1,000 km by river beyond the Arctic Circle, metal had become an integral part of the material culture of the local inhabitants. This fact goes far toward refuting the popular conception of a so-called bone culture for tribes of the Far North, who are presumed to have retained a Neolithic mode of life incredibly long, in some places almost until the present day.

The form of knife used at Tiutey-sale may be judged from a small wooden knife. It is impossible to decide whether it is a toy or had some

---

* [In northernmost European Russia, along the Arctic Circle between the Pechora River and the northern reaches of the Urals. Editor, A.I.N.A.]

ceremonial significance,[82] but in shape it must be close to the knives that were in actual use. The wooden handles found in the deposit support this idea. Knives were sharpened with whetstones of slate or sandstone.

The pit house dwellers seldom used stone. Only a quartzite scraper was identified. Judging by the conical form of the drillhole on a piece of antler, however, we suspect that stone continued to be used for drilling at least on occasion.

The hunting equipment included crudely fashioned points of antler with sockets, a point, also of antler, in the shape of a thin stick, oval in cross section, 13.4 cm in length, with its base flattened for fixing in a slotted shaft, and arrowheads for the hunting of birds.

Articles in everyday use include a chisel-like instrument of antler, sharpened on both ends. The original surface of the antler is retained at one end and has acquired a fine polish from long use. It is probable that this tool was used for working hides or for smoothing seams.

Among the finds were a beautifully made spoon and scoops of antler. Similar scoops of antler or bone may be interpreted as scrapers for cleaning hides; scrapers identical in shape were reported by U. T. Sirelius for the [present-day] Khanty.

Mention should also be made of a wooden punch, two baleen plaques, and three indeterminate objects which are alike in shape, two being of wood and one of bone. Likely these are handles for a drawknife, that is, a sort of plane in which an ordinary knife fills the role of the planing iron. Such planing tools are widely known from ethnographic studies made along the Ob.

Some important articles made of antler were found. They have the appearance of oar grips or handles and suggest that the hut dwellers used some kind of boat.

Also, there was a thin board with a hole in the center—a fragment of a mask. Judging from the width of the opening it could not have served as sun-glare goggles, so it may have been a cult object.

Although the excavations at Tiutey-sale were unfinished, we may conclude that the settlement existed for a fairly long period. This is indicated by the thoroughness of construction of the houses and the thickness of the culture-yielding layer as well as by the quantity of bone refuse, which indicated that sea mammals, the walrus in particular, were the base of the local economy, while land animals and birds were of secondary importance.

The fortified hill site of Vozh-Pay, on the right bank of the Ob near the village of Kushevat, also belongs to the Orontur period. It was excavated by Redrikov in 1925, and the material and a description of the site were given to the Museum of Anthropology and Ethnography of the Academy of Sciences of the U.S.S.R. in Moscow. According to Redrikov the site is stratified, with many layers. At the bottom are strata belonging to the Late Bronze period. These are covered by a layer of the Ust-Poluy period, and above it is a deposit containing pottery which is decorated on the neck with slanting bands and triangles crosshatched in different directions, reminding us of the upper, Karym-pottery level at Orontur. Finally, on the very surface of the Vozh-Pay site, there are a few potsherds which are obviously not of local manufacture. They are undecorated, with rims that flare sharply outward. It is probable that they belong to an early Russian settlement. Redrikov also obtained a fragment of a thin-walled crucible in the shape of a small glass with rounded bottom which resembled the Bolgar ones found at the Rodanov hill site.

Although the pottery from Vozh-Pay and that from Orontur resemble each other, there are very marked differences in ornamentation. At Vozh-Pay the patterns filled in with stamped impressions are absent; it does not possess the elegance characteristic of Orontur pottery; one does not find the incised molding characteristic of Orontur and Karym sites. In severity of decoration this pottery resembles that from the burial ground at Barsov Gorodok and recalls the pottery of the succeeding Kintusovo period.

The burial ground of Barsov Gorodok was excavated in 1891 by the Swedish archaeologist F. Martin. He did not publish the results of his work, and it was not until 1935 that a report on this very interesting material based on Martin's notes was published in Stockholm by T. J. Arne.[83] The cemetery lies on the banks of a stream about 10 km downriver from Surgut and 0.5 km from the westernmost of six hill sites which are situated along a stretch of 4 km. The central one of these is called Barsov Gorodok, but judging from Martin's information there is no basis to suppose that the cemetery is associated with this particular hill site. Thanks to the map systematically drawn up in 1925 by N. Pavlov and brief notes preserved in the archives of the Tobolsk Museum,[84] the information left by Martin about the location of the cemetery and hill site, although not very clear, may be amplified and clarified.

At a distance of 11–12 km west of Surgut and 2 km from the new village at Belyy Yar, there is a steep bank called Barsova Gora which stretches along the northern bank of the stream Utopla. N. Pavlov noticed many sites along the edge of the steep bank, most of them nearly washed away by the stream, as Martin had also reported. One of these sites, which is situated at the southernmost point of the bank (between stakes nos. 51 and 53 on Pavlov's chart), is actually associated with the name of the Khanty leader Bars, who perished with his warriors at the stream after the destruction of their citadel in the 16th century. Near the site are two boulders marking the sacrificial place of the Khanty. Here in 1889–91 Kazakov, S. Chugunov, and later F. Martin carried out excavations with no yields. Somewhat to the west of the point which is formed by the bank of the stream and a small ravine (in the Khanty tongue, *soym*), Martin discovered and partially excavated a site located between stakes nos. 57 and 58 on Pavlov's chart.[85] To the west, on the other side of the ravine, is located the burial ground about which Martin writes that it lies "to the west of the last fortified site, is about 100 m long and is bounded on both sides by ravines which descend to the river from the north."[86] Pavlov followed the bank as far as Gusevaya Rechka [Goose Creek], and in this area he also reported a number of sites. In one of these, situated immediately past the second ravine, he noticed house pits.

On the north, the area of the cemetery is bounded by a small "two-meter-high" rise, apparently an upper river terrace. Graves are scattered over the whole area between the ravines, with no apparent order, and perceptible only because of shallow depressions in the loose sand.

Of the graves excavated by Martin, 108 contained material—clay pots, iron knives and arrow points, bronze ornaments and pendants, a pair of iron S-shaped bridles, flint and iron assemblies, and so on. The pots are round-bottomed, with the neck more or less well defined. The average height is 8–10 cm, the diameter 10–12 cm, but there are some which do not exceed 4 cm in either diameter or height. Decoration is arranged zonally in the upper part, but below the neck there are occasionally vertical or slanting bands that sometimes reach right to the base.[87] Comb stamping is the most common; there are also semilunar imprints and patterns filled in with the stab-and-drag method.[88] Frequent use is made of bands composed of triangles hatched in different directions.[89] However, notched [incised] molding is absent. Generally speaking, even with its local peculiarities the pottery from Barsov Gorodok is close to that from Vozh-Pay, and, in part, actually synchronous with it.

To avoid going into details of the material from Barsov Gorodok, I shall cite only a description of one of the graves, which will enable us to date the pottery: "The skeletal remains were positioned face up with the legs bent at the knee and pulled tight up against the chest (The arms were also bent at the elbows and pressed tight against the chest, thus giving the impression that the body had been tightly bound.—Author), the head oriented to the north. On the right, or west, side of the skull stood a clay pot and on the left or eastern side was an iron knife. Around the neck was a horse-shaped pendant and bronze beads."[90]

The horse-shaped pendant closely resembles one from Mikhaleva village on the Kama. A. P. Smirnov dates this pendant, with the entire Mikhaleva complex, to the Lomovatovo period.[91] The pendant from the burial we have described differs only in the shape of the pendants at the ends of the chain links and in the absence of a human face.

It is difficult to ascribe without reservations the pottery from Vozh-Pay and Barsov Gorodok to the Orontur type. A number of traits characteristic of the Orontur pottery is absent. Apparently this material should be classified as a separate Vozh-Pay chronological group within the limits of the Orontur stage or perhaps as transitional between the Orontur and Kintusovo stages. Relying on dating established for the burials at Barsov Gorodok, we think that pottery of the Orontur type proper did not exist later than to the end of the 8th century A.D., at which time it was replaced by this transitional type, which lasted apparently through the greater part of the 9th century.

A classification based on the ceramics of these transitional groups such as the Lyuli-Kar (a transition between the Karym and Orontur) and the Vozh-Pay (between the Orontur and Kintusovo) is entirely justifiable since all the material from the 1st millennium A.D. presents an uninterrupted picture of the development of a single culture: within the limits of this culture the stages we have identified are functional in establishing a chronology, but they reflect no basic changes and certainly no breaks in the history of the tribes about the lower Ob.

Let us review materials from other sites which may be referred to the Orontur period, that is, the 6th–9th centuries A.D.

In 1887, S. I. Patkanov, who was then a doctoral candidate at St. Petersburg University, on a mission for the Ministry of State Properties in the northern part of the Tobolsk *guberniya*, carried out there, in addition to his mission, a number of interesting archaeological investigations which provided an extensive collection which is now divided between the State Historical Museum and the State Hermitage. According to Patkanov's field notes (which are preserved in the archives of the Leningrad branch of the Institute of Archaeology of the Academy of Sciences of the U.S.S.R.), almost all the objects secured were found "in a small, water-washed burial mound or kurgan (*sopka* ["hillock"] in the local speech), situated on the banks of the Ob between the villages of Skripunova and the Apriny yurty about 60 versts from the large village of Samarovskoye." This hillock, which the local inhabitants call Lenk-Ponk, "consists of a low mound which was used by the earlier inhabit-ants for a burial ground. Here and in the immediate vicinity were found all the metal artifacts I brought to the Commission, the animal figurines, etc."

A large collection from the Lenk-Ponk cemetery was obtained by the Salym expedition of the Tobolsk Guberniya Museum under the direction of L. R. Shults and B. N. Gorodkov. Today it is in the Tobolsk Regional Museum.

In the main, the Lenk-Ponk collection consists of a group of bronze and silver ornaments, among them bangles (Plate XLVIII, items 1–11), paw-shaped pendants (Plate XLVIII, items 12–27), crosses (Plate XLIX, items 6–8), and pendants in the shape of birds (Plate XLIX, items 17–24) and of small animals (Plate XLIX, items 15, 16, 25–34). A pendant shaped like a bird and the animal figures published by Spitsyn should be included with these.[92] The peculiar perforated object with horns should also be noted (Plate XLIX, item 10), and a round, convex button (Plate XLIX, item 1) as well as other artifacts.

The majority of these ornaments are specific to the Ob region, and all the bangles belong to a fairly widespread type, with the possible excep-tion of the one illustrated in Plate XLVIII, item 9. The closest analogues to them appear to be pendants reported in A. P. Smirnov's work[93] and the horse-shaped pendant from the cemetery at Mikhaleva village on the Kama, mentioned earlier. The rest of the artifacts in the collection, with the exception of a small group, belong to the same period, the 6th–9th centuries, which corresponds to the Lomovatovo period in the Cis-Ural. The figure of a hare published by Spitsyn also belongs to this period.[94] In pose and technical execution it is fairly close to the figure from burial no. 25 of the Arkhiyereyskaya Zaimka ["Bishop's Home-stead"]. The latter may be dated to the first half of the 8th century A.D.,[95] and in general style it resembles the figure of a mountain goat from burial no. 20 at Barsov Gorodok, which is clearly dated by a bronze vessel of the 9th century.

The majority of the zoomorphic pendants are highly stylized, in which they differ from the other pendants known from the sites of the preceding

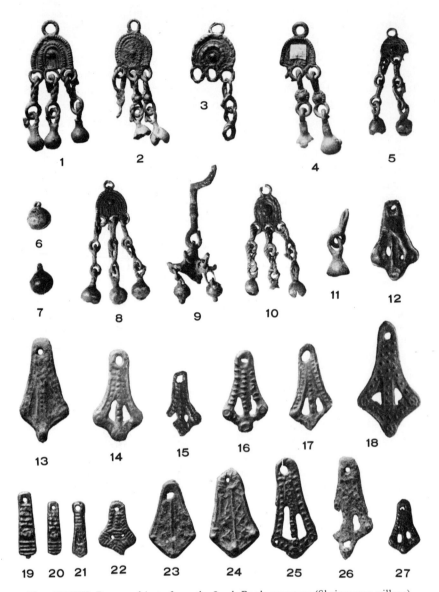

Plate XLVIII. Bronze objects from the Lenk-Ponk cemetery (Skripunova village).

period, which can be traced to the bear figure on the bronze scabbard from Pechora. The zoomorphic pendants existed practically throughout the 1st millennium A.D., gradually drawing away from the realistic treatment of the prototype and taking on a more and more stylized shape until they develop into the open-worked, bell-shaped pendants (Plate XLIX, items 25–34). In the beginning of the 2nd millennium they vanish.

In addition to the ornaments described above there is a broad, flat, open bracelet cast of white bronze. The ends are decorated with stylized bears' heads (Plate L, items 1, 2). We shall return to a more detailed discussion of this type of bracelet presently.

Among the finds at Lenk-Ponk one distinctive group of objects differs from the rest in origin and in time. These are the silver ear and head rings with granules [shaped like small pearls], a silver pendant, also with granules and carnelian inset, and local imitations of similar ornaments. It is quite likely that later, from the 10th to the 12th centuries, interments were also made at Lenk-Ponk as they had been at Barsov Gorodok. Moreover, it is possible that these artifacts do not come from the burial mound at Lenk-Ponk proper, but from a place "in the immediate vicinity," mentioned in Patkanov's account.

Some of the artifacts from another collection date to the 6th–9th centuries A.D. They comprise Vtorushin's collection from Kintusovo on the Salym River. Among the objects are two broad, flat bracelets

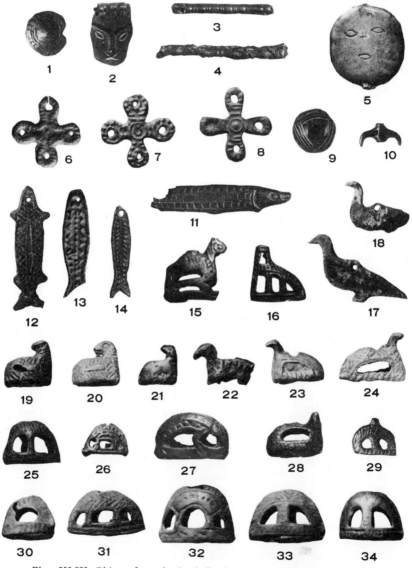

Plate XLIX. Objects from the Lenk-Ponk cemetery (Skripunova village).

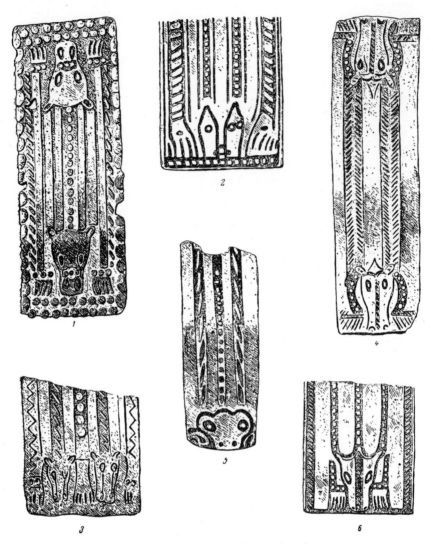

Plate L. Ornamentation on bronze bracelets.

(Plate LI, items 1, 4) analogous to those from Lenk-Ponk. Similar bracelets are widely known along the lower Ob. In addition to those mentioned, there is one from the cemetery at Una-Pay on the Ob, one, a chance find, near Ishvarskiy *yurts*, another chance find from the lower Ob, and six from the cemetery at Barsov Gorodok. One of the Barsov Gorodok bracelets differs from the rest in that it is not decorated with bears' heads but with the figure of a man in relief. Besides this there are three bracelets from Usov's collection which are in the State Hermitage,[96] and four known from a cache found not long ago at Molchanova village on the Tura River near Tyumen. Bracelets of this type are not known beyond the limits of the Ob-Irtysh basin, with the exception of one fragmentary example from Zarodyat,[97] and T. J. Arne rightly considers them specific for the Ob, which seems to mark the center of their distribution.[98]

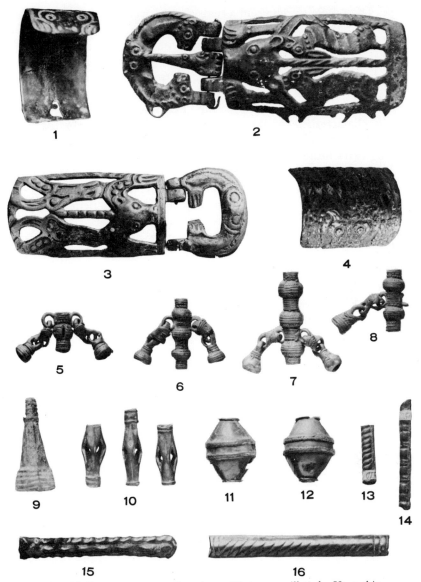

Plate LI. Bronze ornaments found near Kintusovo village by Vtorushin.

Other objects, just as specific for the Ob, are the large bronze buckles which are represented by two specimens in Vtorushin's collection (Plate LI, items 2, 3). Such buckles may be divided into two types according to the preparation of the head, or hasp. The first kind is as a rule wider and shorter with a broad, usually undecorated, hasp which is cast as one piece with the buckle. Of this type is the chance find near the native village Khara-pasl (Fig. 19, item 3) and the buckles from graves nos. 20, 80, and 82 at Barsov Gorodok.[99] The second type includes those mentioned from the collection of Vtorushin, the chance find on the Ob (Fig. 19, item 2), and the buckles from grave no. 31 at Barsov Gorodok and from the Glyadenovo ossuary.[100] Besides these we can pick out two buckles that seem to represent a transition between the two types. One is from burial no. 21 at Barsov Gorodok.[101] In proportions and in the animal figure executed on it, it is very close to the chance find on the Ob (Fig. 19, item 2), but differs from it in the stationary hasp. The other one, described earlier with the material from Cape Shaytan, is also similar to buckles of the second type in proportions and outline, but has a stationary hasp like the preceding example.

It is characteristic of these buckles that they are decorated with animal figures which often consist of complicated combinations, including extra heads. In this characteristic, Arne sees a survival of the tradition of Scythian representational art. This theory seems to have some justification, especially if we have in mind not specifically Scythian art but the art of the Ob region in the Scytho-Sarmatian period as represented in the Ust-Poluy, Potchevash, and other related Ugrian cultures. Here it suffices to point to the openwork plaques from the Istyak cache and the Aidashinskaya cave which have figures of fantastic creatures in the form of a moose but with the features of a carnivore, and the epaulettelike clasps with bear figures, as for example the one from the Aidashinskaya cave.[102] The shape of the hasp on the Kintusovo buckle (Plate LI, item 3) shows the relationship between the buckles described above and these epaulettelike fastenings: the Kintusovo specimen has an *en face* orientation of a bear's head resting on its front paws, which though stylized, in treatment is essentially similar to many of the epaulettelike fastenings from the Ob basin.[103]

The traits we have enumerated lead us to suppose that the buckles under consideration, or at least their immediate prototypes, may have made their appearance at an earlier period than we can establish for them on the basis of available materials. Support for this theory may be found in the general resemblances between these buckles (if we take into account a different technique of execution) and two early specimens—one, a gold buckle found in a Sarmatian cemetery in the Davydovskiy *rayon* of Voronezh *oblast* which A. P. Smirnov dates to the 1st–2nd centuries A.D.[104] and the other a 1st-century A.D. buckle from the Kerch Peninsula. Another argument for dating these buckles earlier than within the chronological limits of the Orontur stage, synchronous in general features with the Lomovatovo period, is provided by the close resemblance of the creatures represented on the buckle shield from Khara-pasl and the pendants in the shape of cicadas from the Podcherem cache.[105] This resemblance is heightened by the identical dotted-line ornamentation.

Significant in a consideration of the origin of these buckles may be their resemblance to the [decorated] strap holders and small plaques of the so-called Hun type (for example, the buckle from Gorbunyat)[106] and to specimens of a still earlier period that are decorated with figures of animals (for example, the buckle with a panther from Aidashinskaya cave).[107]

However, in spite of all these comparisons, it seems impossible to find complete analogues of these buckles we have been discussing beyond the limits of the Ob basin. The closest to them are buckles from a period

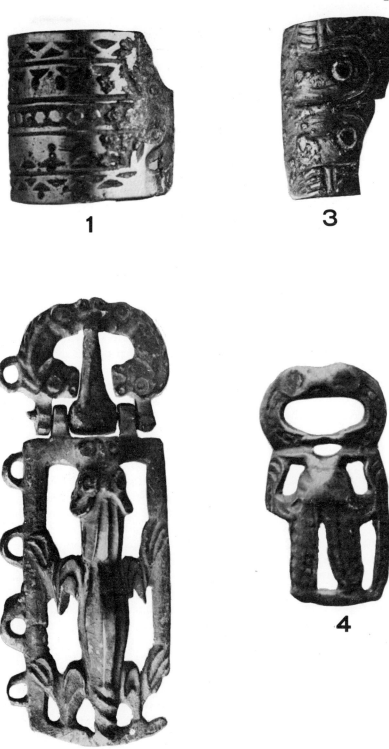

Fig. 19. Chance finds on the Ob River.
1, 2–middle Ob; 3–from Khara-pasl; 4–Ishvar native village.

synchronous with the Orontur in the burial ground at Suuk-Su in the Crimea. The hasps of these have similar shape and construction, and the face of the buckle is often embellished with animal figures. Yet, we should not consider the possibility of direct connections between buckles from areas so far removed from each other, and therefore the reasons for this resemblance and the question of origins of these buckles must be left open. Nonetheless, we may consider the buckles as specific for the Ob, especially if we consider the animals depicted on them and their semantic associations. Bear figures appear on the majority of the buckles, sometimes in combination with hares or moose, or just the heads of these animals. On one of the Kintusovo buckles (Plate LI, item 2) there is a bear's head flanked by two hares, the [elaborate] hasp containing two heads of hares and that of a bear. There is a buckle with an identical arrangement of figures from Barsov Gorodok and from Glyadenovo.[108] Figures of a bear (and apparently a hare) appear on the buckle reported by Arne;[109] there are bears, in very stylized form, on the hasps of buckles from Khara-pasl and Barsov Gorodok.[110] A bear figure in conjunction with moose heads is known on another Kintusovo buckle and two hares with two moose heads on a buckle from Cape Shaytan.

These animals—the bear, moose, and hare—are known to us in the role of totems among the Ugrian tribes. The bear figures most widely, in fact almost universally, and it is the totemic ancestor of the Por moiety. The female hare is one of the totemic versions of the mythical ancestor of the Moshch moiety and is called Sovyr-Nay. She is usually localized among the Khanty and the northern Mansi. The moose was the moietal ancestor among the northern Uralian groups of tribes, which have now disappeared but which once inhabited the area from the Pechora to the Slyva, on the western slopes of the Urals and the left tributaries to the Kama. Why the representation of the moietal totems should appear on the buckle is a special problem not appropriate at the present. At this point we shall simply note the close association of these buckle figures with Ugrian mythology and emphasize at the same time the intensely local character of this class of object. Exceptional among the figures on buckles are the rams' heads in association with two birds' heads on a buckle from Barsov Gorodok[111] and the diminutive heads, which appear to be those of horses, on the hasp of a buckle from the Ob River region (Fig. 19, item 2). The horse, the ram, and the bird are not, however, foreign to Ugrian mythology. The goose and eagle were held to be totem ancestors of the *moš~moń* moiety among the southern Ugrian steppe tribes of cattle herders and horse breeders. In contemporary Ob-Ugrian folklore, which combines elements typical of the forest hunters and horse breeders (who appeared later in this area), the goose image represents the son of the ancestress of the Moshch moiety, Sovyr-Nay, who takes her place in the cult and is represented in his anthropomorphic form as a heavenly rider on a white horse. The cult of the horse was also important with some tribes, the southern Mansi in particular. The ram was also well known among the Ugrians in antiquity, but on the so-called stone sacrificial tables which P. A. Dmitriyev has good reason to associate with the culture of the ancient Ugrians, the Savyrs.

Other artifacts from Vtorushin's collection which may be ascribed to the Orontur are the perforated, bell-shaped objects (Plate LI, item 9) known from the finds at Zobachevka[112] and from the Georgiyev cache, which Smirnov dates to the end of the Pyanobor [Pyanyy Bor] period[113] (these are also known from the Rozhdestvenskiy burial ground),[114] perforated pieces (Plate LI, items 13, 14), a needle case (Plate LI, item 16), a bronze knife handle similar to the one from burial no. 83 at Barsov Gorodok,[115] and perhaps an openwork piece (Plate LI, item 10), which somewhat resembles a piece from Grudyata with similar diamond-shaped outlines but without the perforations.[116] The perforated tinkling pendants (Plate LI, items 5–8) belong to a much later time and have counterparts in burial no. 16 at Barsov Gorodok, which Arne dates in the 11th–12th centuries. We find further examples of such pieces in the Kintusovo period, which follows the Orontur.

The sacrificial place in Shaytan [Devil's] and Lakseya caves on the Ivdel River may also be dated to the Orontur period. As far as I know, there are numerous sacrificial, bone-yielding caves in the basin of the upper Lozva and its tributaries, that is, in the surroundings of the town of Ivdel in Sverdlovsk *oblast*. The Lozva Mansi made offerings in some of these caves in comparatively recent times. Not one of the caves has yet been studied, however, and there is not even so much as a simple description of one. We know of small collections from only two of these caves; these were made by the local student of antiquities, G. Leshchov, in 1928–29. His material was partially published by Ye. M. Bers, although the publication leaves much to be desired. Obviously Bers was poorly versed in ceramics of the 1st millennium A.D. and refrained from discussing the pottery beyond a statement that "the pottery with pitted, comb-stamped decoration found at the top of the cliffs on the Ivdel River in association with animal bones is known on the east slope of the Urals in the Bronze and Iron Ages through the 2nd and 1st millennia B.C.; as nothing else was found with it, this pottery cannot be more accurately dated."[117]

The places along the Ivdel River are fairly well known to me, but I was there many years ago, and at the time I had unfortunately little knowledge of archaeology. Later on, in 1938, I was able to visit the Shaytan cave, but it was so late in the fall that no work could be undertaken. However, I have a little information in my possession to add to Bers's scanty data about the location and character of the cave.

The cliff mentioned in the quoted passage is on the right bank of the Ivdel at the mouth of the Shaytanka River.[118] The cave is located a short distance upstream from the river mouth, in the middle of the river slope. The opening is in a narrow ravine which ends in a rocky precipice falling straight to the Ivdel. The only way to approach the cave is from the top of the ravine. The entrance is broad and high. The cave is dry and extends, gradually narrowing, for about 15 m; it ends in a cracklike "chimney" which reaches to the top of the cliff (Fig. 20). Small "burrows" lead off sideways from the main cave for a distance of a few meters. The floor of the cave is covered with bones, principally those of bear, deer, and horse. Near the wall toward the front of the cave there is a large hearth covered by a huge stone fragment that had fallen from the ceiling, apparently as a result of the unequal heating.

I was able to examine only a few buttons from the collection of objects found in the cave by one of the local antiquarians. These buttons are in the shape of a shallow cone with a crosspiece on the obverse side, and they are cast in white bronze with a high zinc content, to judge by the oxydization. Of the four buttons I saw, one was decorated with a leafy figure like a four-petalled rosette (Fig. 21, item 1), another with a rope-like band (Fig. 21, item 2); on the third were depicted two bears' heads facing in opposite directions (Fig. 21, item 4), and the fourth was decorated with four wavy lines (Fig. 21, item 3).

Three buttons, of the same appearance as those just described, were

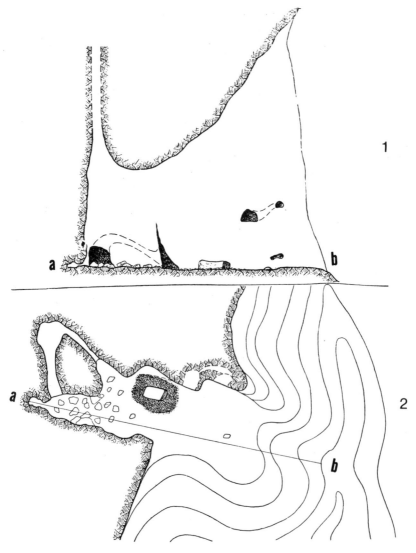

Fig. 20. Schematic drawing (1) and cross section (2) of Shaytan cave.

found in burial no. 87 at Barsov Gorodok.[119] On the basis of an ornament for the forehead found in the same grave, Arne dated these buttons to the 10th century A.D. and considered them imports. However, we have every reason to suppose that they appeared in the Ob basin earlier than this, not to mention various prototypes which already existed in the Ust-Poluy period.[120] Arne based his theory of importations on the fact that there were so few of them, but this is no longer true. In addition to some twenty buttons from the Shaytan cave, they are known from the finds at Lenk-Ponk, the village of Aksenova, the settlement of Novo-Nikolsk on the Irtysh, and the Vakh River (Fig. 21, items 5, 6).[121] In addition to the frequency with which they occur, their local origin is shown by the bears' heads depicted on them, which are of the type so well known from the epaulettelike clasps and from the buckles described above for the 1st millennium A.D.

E. M. Bers dates the finds from the Shaytan cave to the 6th–8th centuries A.D., and in general we can agree with this. Unfortunately the drawings and descriptions in Bers's memorandum leave much to be desired, and it is difficult to gain from them a clear idea of the material. It is, however, possible to conclude that the detached figure of a hare[122]

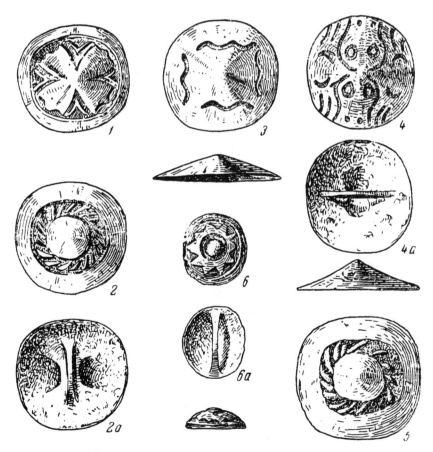

Fig. 21. Bronze buttons.
1 to 4–from Shaytan cave; 5, 6–from Vakh River.

and the hare from Lenk-Ponk are identical and that the shape of the middle panel of the "knife cover" is certainly similar to that from Vtorushin's collection (Plate LI, item 15). These artifacts may belong to an earlier period, perhaps the first half of the Orontur period or even to the middle of the 1st millennium A.D. As for the bronze plaque with a bird figure, as far as can be judged from the poor drawing, its stylization and a certain excess of decoration place it at the end of the Orontur period.

As was explained, Shaytan cave on the Ivdel once belonged to the Mansi clan of Pershin, part of whom died off and part became Russianized more than eighty years ago. It is known from literary sources that the Khanty and the Mansi at the end of the ceremonies that accompany the killing of a bear carry the skull and bones of the animal to a special place. Here they hang the skull on a tree as a symbol of the burial of the bear, and they bring a horse or deer as sacrifice, and leave little pieces of bright cloth near the skull, coins, brass buttons, et cetera. In former times, according to the Lozva Mansi, caves were used as burial places for the bear bones, and here sacrifices were performed. Shaytan and Lakseya were such sacrificial caves.

The Lakseya cave is also situated on the right bank of the Ivdel, but farther upstream, about 1 km from the mouth of the small Lakseya River. The cave is very large, and in the depths of it the floor reaches below the level of the river, and thus the cave ends in an underground lake. G. Leshev obtained his collection right at the entrance. It is hard to judge how long the sacrificial place on the Lakseya was used. A date can be fixed to a certain extent by the horse-shaped pendant illustrated by Bers.[123] It resembles the pendant found in burial no. 39 at Barsov Gorodok[124] and is almost exactly the same as the Mikhaleva one, which Smirnov places in the Lomovatovo period,[125] which corresponds to the Orontur period in the Ob basin.

In concluding the description of material pertaining to the Orontur period, let me mention the limited finds near Aksenova village on the Irtysh and those from the Pyasyaday River.

The collection from Aksenova is in the Tobolsk Museum and consists of two pear-shaped pendants, buttons of the type described earlier, and the fragment of a bronze object decorated with the figure of a bear. This fragment is probably from the sidepieces enclosing a small bag for carrying flint, similar to the bone pieces I have seen among the Mansi. There is a very similar object in the materials from the Kalinskoye hill site on the Kama,[126] which apparently belongs in the middle Lomovatovo period.

The second collection was found by the Samoyeds on the north shore of Yamal Peninsula between the rivers Tiutey-Yaha and Pyasyaday-Yaha, near 72° north. It consists of bronze, perforated objects shaped like small tubes with a slight swelling (Fig. 22, items 2, 3), and one fairly stylized representation of a bird. This little figure is rather unusual in the singular addition of extra wings onto the shoulders of the bird (Fig. 22, item 1). Perhaps these constitute the vestiges of a supplementary image of the bird similar to those often met on objects cast in flat molds. This similarity is emphasized by adding the ribs and heart into the figure,

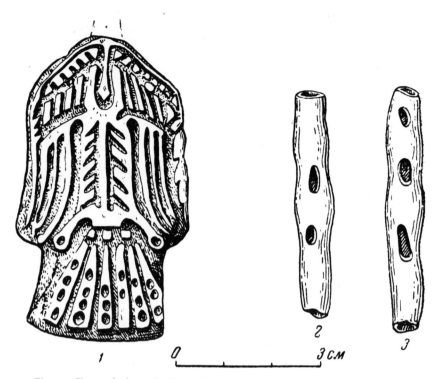

Fig. 22. Chance finds on the Pyasyaday River (northwestern Yamal Peninsula).

but this practice seems to have disappeared, and it is unknown in bronze objects of the 1st millennium A.D. The treatment of the ringlike claws is also archaic. But since the pitted decoration on the tail, the way of portraying the feathers, and the general outlines of the figure do not permit us to give it too early a date, we place it, with some reservations, in the Orontur period. In such remote parts of the Ob region as the north of the Yamal Peninsula, there could exist local traditions in the representational arts which would retain archaic features longer than in the south. So far this is only a supposition. We should emphasize, however, that the fact that this sort of object has been found so far to the north is in itself very interesting.

Chapter 4

The Kintusovo Period
(10th–13th Centuries A.D.)

As we have seen, toward the end of the Orontur stage, the stamped decoration on pottery began to disappear gradually and was being replaced by patterns made by the stab-and-drag method and comb impressions. The decoration became sparse and monotonous. Such is the appearance of pottery from sites dated from the 10th–12th centuries, particularly, for instance, the late stages of the cemetery at Barsov Gorodok, where we can be fairly certain of the dating of graves nos. 1, 48, and 67.[127]

Among other such sites are the fortified hill Tān wārup-ēkwa, which is situated on the left bank of a tributary to the Severnaya Sosva, the Lyapin River, near the village Lopom-Vozh. The site is badly disturbed and it is impossible to determine its stratigraphy. In the culture-yielding layer, in addition to pottery, links of iron chain armor were found and an iron axe which dated the site clearly in the 11th–12th centuries. Interestingly, according to V. P. Levasheva,[128] axes of this shape are characteristic of the Novgorod *pyatinas** and the [neighboring] Baltic area. According to archival sources, the expeditions of the Novgorodians to Ugria began in the 11th–12th centuries, and it was apparently in connection with these that Novgorod and Baltic types of objects were introduced to the Ob basin.

As at Barsov Gorodok, the pottery at Tān wārup-ēkwa consists of round-bottomed pots with very distinct profiling: the straight neck described a sharp angle with the rounded body. However, in contrast to the pots of Barsov Gorodok, these are thin-walled and carefully made. The decoration consists almost exclusively of zones of stripes made with the stab-and-drag method, either smooth or dentated. The pottery of Tān wārup-ēkwa contrasts sharply with that of the Orontur stage; the slanting ribbonlike or ladderlike decoration and the crosshatched triangles, which were so characteristic of the preceding stage, disappear altogether. Pottery from the Novo-Nikolsk hill site on the Irtysh is basically the same as that just described.

In 1913, N. I. Bortvin was sent by the Archaeological Commission to "find in the Tara *okrug* a place on the Irtysh called *Golaya Sopka* ["Barren

* [*Pyatina*, literally "fifth", a generic name of a district, of which Novgorod had five during medieval ages. Editor, A.I.N.A.]

Hill"], reported as a place where interesting objects were often found and forwarded to the Commission through the peasant Usov." According to Bortvin's account, "the hill proved to be a fortified hill site near the mouth of the Ishim River, 7–8 *versts* down the Irtysh from the settlement of Ust-Ishim, at Novo-Nikolsk on a hillock which is gradually being washed away. The height of the hill is about 40 *sazhens*. The area of the site proper is in shape of an irregular oval bounded on one side by a rampart and ditch and sloped toward a river spit on which there is a low terrace. . . . The rampart appears to have been built of earth from a culture yielding level, with potsherds and bones, perhaps during a second period of occupation."[129]

Bortvin worked more than 375 m² of the site and found a culture-yielding layer from 0.7 to 1.75 m thick. As a result of this work he concluded that the site, composed of two levels, represented "two cultures, the older one corresponding to the last of the local Copper Age, and a Tatar culture of the 14th–15th centuries. . . . The older culture is represented principally by a large amount of pottery. The pots were manufactured with a fine, plastic clay; they were round-bottomed and were ornamented with a quantity of incised lines as well as with rich stamping typical of pottery from early fortified hill sites in western Siberia; the most common form is a wide-mouthed cup."[130]

Before and after Bortvin's field work, the sites in the Novo-Nikolsk area were repeatedly visited by amateur students of local lore. Among these was S. Usov, who acquired a number of artifacts. Part of these are now in the State Historical Museum [in Moscow], part in the Tobolsk Museum. Collections of pottery and of bone artifacts from this area also reached the Omsk Museum. In 1948, V. Korti visited Novo-Nikolsk and later kindly forwarded invaluable information about the location of the sites. And finally, in recent years geologists have collected pottery, which they have turned over to the Leningrad branch of the Institute of the History of Material Culture of the Academy of Sciences of the U.S.S.R.

As far as we know there are two sites at Goloya Sopka, near Novo-Nikolsk: the fortified hill site and the cemetery which contained Usov's collections. The pottery from the hill site is monotonously repetitious and close to the pottery from Tān wārup-ēkwa, and in the main, it is assignable to the Kintusovo stage. The cemetery contains pottery that is the same as that at the hill site, but also a few differing vessels belonging to a considerably earlier period. The most prominent decorative patterns are made by the stab-and-drag method, which, as noted above, was typical of late sites; the arrangement of the decorative details, however, is strongly suggestive of the Orontur stage. Some of the pots resemble those from Barsov Gorodok.

In all likelihood the cemetery at Novo-Nikolsk dates to the very end of the Orontur stage, or even to the period of the Vozh-Pay group. Materials known to come from the cemetery support this view. Thus the figure of a hare (Plate LII, item 1) and a button (Plate LII, item 5) are quite similar to those from Shaytan cave, while the figurine of a horse (Plate LII, item 3) is the same as that from burial no. 20 at Barsov

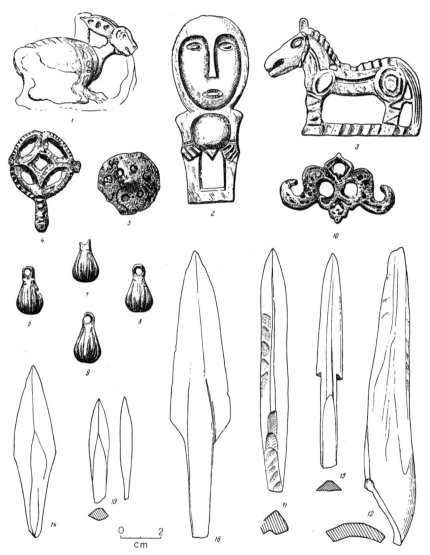

Plate LII. Finds from the cemetery at Novo-Nikolsk village (Golaya Sopka).
1 to 10–bronze; 11 to 16–bone.

Gorodok,[131] which is dated by a bronze cup with an Arabic inscription from the beginning of the 9th century A.D.[132] The anthropomorphic figurine of similar workmanship (Plate LII, item 2) may be ascribed to the same period.

The hollow, pear-shaped pendants from Novo-Nikolsk cemetery (Plate LII, items 6–9) are similar to the pendants from Aksenova village and are differentiated only by being fluted. I can think of no close analogues beyond the limits of the Ob basin, with the exception of the pendants, or as N. A. Prokoshev calls them, "little half bells," known from a burial on the Chusovaya River which is dated to the 11th century.[133] The Chusovaya pendants are round rather than pear-shaped, however, and they are three-lobed rather than being subdivided by flutings; they are decorated with a thin molding below the loop and, all told, they do not appear to be contemporaneous with the pendants from Novo-Nikolsk.

Analogues to the openwork plaques (Plate LII, item 10) were found in the Saltovo cemetery, and this would agree with the date quoted above for the horse figurine. The earrings—the loop is missing from one (Plate LII, item 4), the tear-shaped pendant from the other—are to a certain extent similar to the type in use during the Saltovo period.

The bone arrowheads, which are fairly numerous among the finds, are represented by ones that have the outline of an elongated rhomboid and are triangular or rhomboid in cross section. They are characteristic of the period and as a rule are crudely made with heavy strokes which indicate that an iron tool was used. This contrasts them sharply with arrowheads of the Bronze and Early Iron Ages, which were made with scrapers and were carefully polished.

The fortified hill site of Bezymyannoye ["Nameless"], situated on the Irtysh, 6 km downstream from the large village of Yekaterininskoye in Tara *rayon*, can be dated to the Kintusovo period on the basis of its pottery, which is of the same type as that from Novo-Nikolsk. This site, consisting of an inner, middle, and outer town circled by trenches and embankments (Fig. 23), was found by me in 1945 on a high promontory formed by the entrance of a nameless stream into the Irtysh.

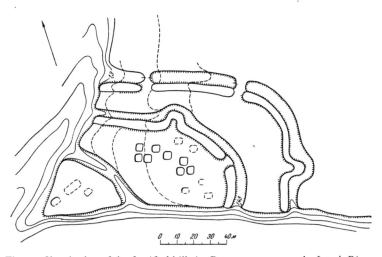

Fig. 23. Sketch plan of the fortified hill site Bezymyannoye on the Irtysh River.

The peculiarity of the fortifications consisted in the projection of the ramparts on both sides of the gates of the outer and middle rings of walls, which permitted a flanking fire along the trenches. The fortifications of the inner city were especially strong. This trench was 6 m broad and 3 m deep, and apparently there was no permanent structure over which it could be crossed.

The surface of the site was very uneven, and it was impossible to find clear traces of houses except in the center, where depressions 5 × 5 m square seemed to indicate pit house remains. The extremity of the site, projecting onto the point of the headland, was also protected by an abrupt escarpment, some 4 m high.

The culture-yielding layer was thin in the lower parts of the site but reached a thickness of 0.7 m in the interior. It was filled with bone and pottery fragments. The bones included those of moose, roebuck, and fox. In addition to the pottery, a bone spearhead and an iron point were found. The pots were round-bottomed with well-defined shoulders and straight necks inclined slightly inward at the top. There were also fragments suggesting cup or flat bowl shapes very similar to Ananino ones. The pots from the Bezymyannoye site were made by first forming the pot by uniting slabs of clay and then thinning it by beating. The clay was purified by sedimentation and used without any perceptible admixture; the firing was average. The ornamentation was placed in bands and was limited to the neck and shoulders. The stab-and-drag method was widely used, with both dentated and ribbed paddles. This ornamentation is very similar to that at the Tān wārup-ēkwa hill site and at Novo-Nikolsk.

The decoration is placed in bands composed of herringbone, ribbed or dentated stampings positioned vertically or obliquely. Often this design is complemented by a series of triangles made with comb or paddle-edge impressions. From the triangles emanate vertically, more rarely obliquely, positioned ribbons. Sometimes the triangles are absent and the ribbons descend directly from the lower edge of the band.

There is another type of pottery found at the site in small quantities, on which the decoration is limited to a series of irregular impressions. This pottery is analogous to that found in the upper layer of the hill site Bolshoy Log near Omsk and also to the pottery described by Levasheva for the Voznesenskoye hill site on the Om River; it belongs apparently to an entirely different, that is, a Tatar, culture.

As in previous times, the towns and cemeteries containing pottery that was characterized in the Orontur period by stamped decoration and in the Kintusovo period by decoration done with the stab-and-drag technique, with either paddle or comb, are contiguous along the southern limit of their area of distribution (in the Tobolsk *rayon*, on the Tura River) with sites yielding cord-impressed pottery. One of the latter sites, the Molchanova fortified hill site on the left bank of the Tura, is about 20 km north of Tyumen. The site has been almost completely destroyed by the river, which is constantly undercutting the steep bank. The remaining parts of the culture-yielding layer were not sufficiently extensive to establish a stratigraphy. Yet an amount of the pottery, characteristic for the site, was collected.

The Molchanova pottery is quite close in shape and decoration to that described above for the hill site at Zhilye [Andreyevskoye Lake] and for the Pereyma [Pereyminskiy] cemetery. Characteristic for the pots is the bulging, round-bottomed body and clearly defined neck, either straight or sloping slightly inward. The decoration is only on the neck, except for rare cases when it extends a little way down the shoulders. The great majority of the pots is decorated with cord impressions and a few with the imprint of a small-toothed comb. However, there are also some stab-and-drag decorations made with a small-toothed paddle; these are unknown at the earlier Zhilye site, which contained corded pottery. This type of decoration relates the Molchanova pottery with that of the Kintusovo period. The Molchanova pottery ornamented with a very small comb is also analogous to Kintusovo ware. Connections with northern pottery types may be noted in the sherds, which are apparently associated with the early period of occupation at the Molchanova site; these include decorative elements which are well known to us from the sites at Orontur and Us-Tolt.

The Molchanova hill site may be dated from the cache which was found a few years ago in close proximity to it and which is now kept in the Tyumen Museum. The cache consisted of broad bronze bracelets with bear figures of the type described above, brass plaques with loops riveted onto them, and some riveted copper kettles. Plaques such as these apparently do not occur before the 10th century A.D., which sets a limit for the dating.

There is a fairly large number of hill sites along the Tura containing pottery of the Molchanova type, but almost none has been studied. Only a few small collections of pottery from these sites are known.

At this point it is difficult to have any clear conception of the culture typified by the corded pottery or of the area of its distribution. One can only say, after comparing material from the individual sites, that southwest of Tobolsk the corded pottery existed from the middle of the 1st millennium B.C. until about the 10th–12th centuries A.D. In the early portion of this extensive period there is a close resemblance of this corded pottery to part of that of the so-called Trans-Ural Ananino, and even of the Ananino proper. It is quite probable that it is from the area (where this pottery was distributed) that the movement of some Ugrian tribes started toward the lower Ob region in the second half of the 1st millennium B.C.—thus the temporary presence of corded pottery there during the Ust-Poluy period, which disappears again during the Yar-sale period. A study of those sites containing cord-impressed pottery which reflect the culture of the Ugrian tribes of the Central Trans-Ural is a task demanding our attention in the near future.

Among sites of the Kintusovo period, the cemetery situated near the Kintusovo *yurts* should be mentioned. It is located on the upper reaches of the Salym River, a left tributary to the Ob.

In addition to Vtorushin's collections from this area, described earlier, materials from the cemetery proper were obtained by the Salym expedition of the Tobolsk Regional Museum. According to B. N. Gorodkov's description the burial ground is situated on the shore of a lake near the Kintusovo *yurts* and is bordered on one side by the lake and on the other by a trench, now almost obliterated. The uneven surface of the ground is overgrown with an old stand of birch and aspen. Decorated potsherds were found in quantities along the shore of the lake, or *sor*; in some places they were actually heaped in great quantities. Occasionally, some metal ornaments were found among the potsherds.[134]

At the time of the investigation of the Kintusovo cemetery, tinkling pendants were found (Plate LIII), also the neck circlet (Plate LIV, item 1), the silver head circlets embellished with decorated granules (Plate LIV, items 2, 3), a silver earring damaged by fire but retaining traces of decorative pearl-like granules (Plate LIV, item 8), bronze and silver embossed beads (Plate LIV, items 4, 6), a bronze mask of a man in a conical helmet, and the figure of a man holding a horn in his right hand (Plate LIV, items 10, 7). The last-named is undoubtedly an import; figurines similar to it are known from a great variety of sites, none of which is connected with the Ob region.

In addition to the bronze artifacts there are many iron arrowheads characteristic of the beginning of the 2nd millennium A.D. and an amount of pottery. Three of the pots were complete. One was very simple and without ornamentation, another was decorated in stab-and-drag fashion

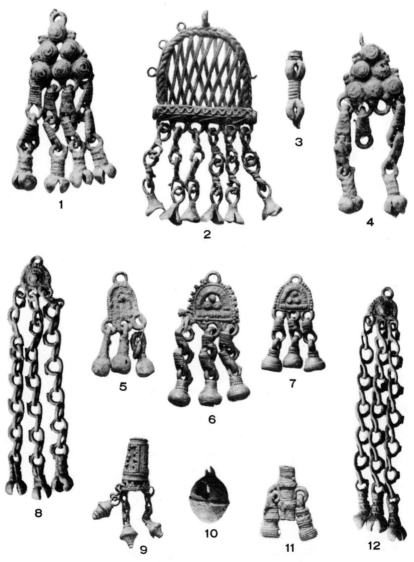

Plate LIII. Bronze ornaments from Kintusovo cemetery.

Plate LIV. Finds from Kintusovo cemetery.
1 to 4, 6, 8–silver; 5, 7, 10–bronze; 9–clay.

with the semilunar edge of a paddle, with the characteristic slanting bands hanging from the neck. The third is decorated with a broad band of latticework made up of rhomboid impressions. This pot is very reminiscent, at least at first glance, of the pots present at the end of the Karym stage, but the incised molding and the slanting bands on the neck with a stab-and-drag paddle imply a later period. Nevertheless, this pot was hardly made earlier than toward the end of the Orontur period, since, as we have seen, the notched molding disappears completely soon after this period. This also applies to the aforementioned pot, on which the same semilunar stamping was found.

An early period in the Kintusovo cemetery is represented by the pendants illustrated in Plate LIII, items 5, 6, 7, and perhaps 8 and 12. All the other finds belong to the 10th–13th centuries. Thus the pendant with a latticework panel (Plate LIII, item 2), by analogy with the pendant from Kiprusheva village on the Kama,[135] may be dated to the 11th century, as can the pendants labelled as items 1 and 4. The perforated pieces (Plate LIII, item 11) have analogues in the Rozhdestvenskiy cemetery[136] on the Kama and at Barsov Gorodok in burial no. 16, which Arne dates to the 10th–11th centuries A.D.[137] This date is verified by the presence of bronze beads (Plate LIV, items 4, 6) which are analogues to those known from a burial on the Chusovaya River,[138] in the Kostroma *kurgan*[139] and the Narva *kurgan*, which N. N. Gurina ascribes to the 12th–14th centuries.[140] And finally this is the period indicated by the silver ornaments with granules which are probably of Bulgarian origin (Plates LIII and LIV).

Another site which in part belongs to the Kintusovo period is the cemetery of Una-Pay on the Ob, near the mouth of the Irtysh. The collections from this site were made by students from Khanty-Mansiysk and were brought to the Tobolsk Museum. Judging from the materials, the site also includes the Orontur stage. To this period belong the paw-shaped and crosslike pendants, the earrings of the Saltovo type, the pendants decorated with a conventionalized bear's head, parts of hollow figurines of birds, and some tinkling pendants.

To the 10th and 12th centuries belong the horned pendants, which have analogues on the middle Kama, pendants in the shape of bells, made of copper plate, which are comparable to the pendants from the Pustoshinskiy cemetery of the 11th century, and the articles decorated with pearls or granulelike imitations of them.

Among the late and clearly dated sites may be numbered the unique fortified hill site of Man-Nyaslan-Tur, situated on the lake of the same name, near the settlement of Saranpaul on the Lyapin River.

At one time this site may have occupied a headland on the river, but at present it is situated on high land between two lakes. It is surrounded by a barely perceptible rampart and ditch which encompass the remains of a large rectangular dwelling consisting of connected pit houses (Fig. 24). The floor space of this many-roomed dwelling is about 600 m² and includes not fewer than eleven or twelve pit houses or rooms. This type of settlement house has never been encountered by us at earlier sites and is apparently characteristic of only the end of the 1st millennium A.D.

The excavation of one of the pit houses revealed that its depth was inconsiderable; it was about 5 m square, with a central hearth and broad earthen platforms along the walls. On either side of the entrance were piles of coals, bones, and small pottery fragments. Among the latter were three pieces apparently from a flat-bottomed Russian pot made on a handwheel or plank, some pieces of a very thin-walled, undecorated pot, and one sherd which may be compared with the pottery of the third Karym stage. This latter find may have gotten accidentally into the culture-yielding level of this site and should not be considered in connection with the dating, which can easily be determined by the find of an iron key of Bulgar style with a lumen in the shape of a cross. Such keys are widely known in the Kama region and can be dated quite accurately to the 11th–13th centuries.

In addition to the key, pieces of iron knives were found, also arrow points, fragments of a clay crucible, an unfinished blank for a large bone spear point, and an artifact of antler that remotely suggests part of a modern reindeer bridle. The resemblance is expressed in the placing of the openings and the general form, but the measurements of this piece somewhat exceed those known to us as components of the harness.

If the hill site of Man-Nyaslan-Tur belongs to the 13th century, then the presence of a reindeer harness is quite permissible chronologically. If it could be determined positively that the find is a component part of a harness, it would fix the time for the introduction of reindeer herding into the basin of the Severnaya Sosva. To the same period may be

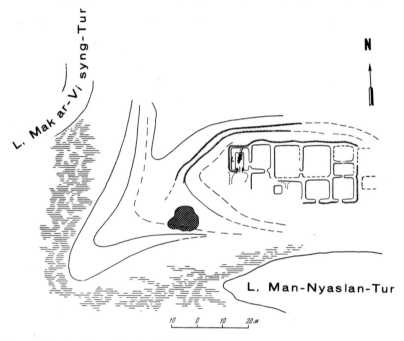

Fig. 24. Sketch plan of the fortified hill site Man-Nyaslan-Tur, near the village of Saranpaul on the Lyapin River.

ascribed the settlement of Zelenaya Gorka, near Salekhard. We found this site in 1946 but, unfortunately, had not the time to excavate it fully. We were able to excavate only one hut adequately, but we obtained nevertheless some quite interesting material.[141]

Zelenaya Gorka is the name of a small headland delimited by a steep ravine; it rises about 12 m above the level of the Poluy, not far from the point where the former joins the Ob. The surface of this headland is hammocky and slopes steeply toward the river. At the foot of the headland is a shallow ditch and embankment; from this point the ditch descends the steep incline to the foot of the ravine.

The platform of the hill site is partly disturbed by cultivation of a vegetable garden, but in the remaining space there are three or four perceptible depressions of pit houses. We excavated one of these.

It was possible to reconstruct the floor plan to the hut in its entirety. The center was occupied by a hearth, which was somewhat raised and consisted of a rectangular framework made of beams 10–15 cm in diameter, filled with sand. On both sides of the hearth there was a passageway about 1 m wide and beyond it a platform positioned along the walls. The height of the platform was about equal to that of the hearth and was just a little lower than the surface surrounding the pit. In front of the hearth was the beginning of a short passageway 0.5 m deep, which probably had led into an entryway. Beyond the hearth and in the passage areas on both sides of it the height of the floor was the same. Large quantities of stones were found here, many fire-cracked, and animal bones, principally of fox and reindeer.[142]

The hearth and the whole living area of the pit house were covered with the remains of the collapsed roof. There was a rectangular frame to hold up the roof; the frame rested on four posts placed in the central part of the pit house. The proximate ends of four beams rested on the corners of the frame, the distal ends being secured at the outer corners of the pit house. The roof covering consisted of light slanting timbers, the lower ends of which rested on the edge of the pit and the upper ends against the central frame and the main beams. The roof was covered with a lathing of poles covered with birch bark; over this was placed a layer of fir branches, then a layer of coals, and finally, an earth covering.

The multiple layers of the roof and the employment of different materials had the purpose of keeping out water and keeping in the heat, alike indispensable in the rugged polar climate. The coals and evergreen bows were supposed to preserve the wooden construction of the roof from dampness and rot. A little back from the hearth, at the four corners, four upright beams were set, apparently also attached to the frame, and presumably serving as supports for hanging kettles, drying fish, and so on.

Unusual about the materials from Zelenaya Gorka was the complete absence of pottery, and this in spite of the undoubtedly permanent nature of the settlement. This is interesting and significant in that it helps fix a date for the disappearance of pottery on the lower Ob.

Among the various artifacts found were articles of daily use and ornaments. There is a very interesting bone brace of a [composite] bow which in no way differs from those which we see in the modern bows used widely among the Khanty and Mansi until two decades ago. Arrow points are represented by one three-sided bone specimen and by the one flat, iron, rhomboid point. There are two blanks for arrows—one made from antler, the other from a tubular bone.

Near one of the walls of the hut an iron knife was found with a narrow, slightly curved point showing some signs of retouching on the right side. This knife differs in shape from those known to us from earlier archaeological sites or from ethnographic observations. The Khanty and Mansi knives have a straight back and a straight cutting edge only slightly rounded at the distal end. They are sharpened on one side only and [the facet is] quite abrupt. Such knives were to be found in the Ob basin not later than the middle of the 1st millennium A.D. Knives analogous to that from Zelenaya Gorka are known only from the cemetery of the 18th–19th centuries on the Khalas Puhor [Island of the Dead] in the Ob. To judge by the embossed brass handles, they are undoubtedly imports. The same is probably true for the Zelenaya Gorka knife.

Among other finds in the hut, the following are of note: a flat bone spoon, a small whetstone for sharpening needles, a small piece of copper leaf doubled over and flattened, which may have been used as a scraper for cleaning fish, a binding of copper leaf with two rivets, which probably reinforced the sprung rim of a wooden pot, and an antler artifact. For the latter there is an ethnographic parallel in the net holder to which the first loops of the net being made are tied.

Among the ornaments is a paw-shaped pendant of white, tin-plated bronze and two blue porcelain beads, one of which is flattened and ribbed, the other shaped like a keg and decorated with slanting, crosslike depressions. A. P. Smirnov limits the existence of these beads to the 13th–14th centuries,[143] and they may therefore fix the date for the Zelenaya Gorka settlement, making it contemporaneous with the hill site on Lake Man-Nyaslan-Tur, which was dated by the Bulgar type of key and where, similarly, no pottery was found. Apparently the spread of metal ware in the Ob region reached such proportions by now that it crowded out ceramic ware. It should be noted that a great quantity of foundry slag was found at Zelenaya Gorka, testifying to the extensive development there of metallurgy.

To the same period or to a slightly later one may be dated the pit house settlement near Cape Khaen-sale on the Yamal Peninsula, where again no pottery was found. This settlement (which I found and excavated in 1929) is situated at 73° north on the coast of Malygin Strait not far from Cape Khaen-sale. Here the coast is in places steep and abrupt; in places it descends fairly gently to the sea. Along the shore, in the lower levels, are sticky, blue [vivianite] clays, and in the upper horizons, sands. In places where it is well drained there is almost no vegetation to bind it. At this latitude bushes do not grow, and the tundra near the shore takes on the aspect of a semidesert. Yet, there is one factor that makes the eastern shore of the gulf liveable, and this is the enormous quantity of driftwood cast upon the shore every year from Cape Drovyanoy to the mouth of the Yady River. West of the Yady-Yaga [River] there is very little driftwood, but near Khaen-sale some parts of the shore are thickly covered with it for a distance of 100 m and more from the water.

The remains of the settlement are located 1.5 km east of Cape Khaen-sale. The small cape had been formed by a stream that enters the sea at this point. The cape was an excellent site for building pit houses owing to the fine drainage and dry, sandy soil. The entire settlement consisted of six or seven huts, which had not been disturbed. This allowed, to a degree, the determination of the construction of the buildings even though the wooden portions preserved poorly in the sand. As at Cape Tiutey-sale, the dry ground had made it possible to build the houses in other places besides the very edge of the bank; some were as much as 20 m from it.

All of the pit houses were round, 7–8 m in diameter. The pits did not reach more than 0.7 m or 1 m below the surface. The entrance was a small, apparently covered, passage about 2 m long. It was easy to trace the passages during the excavation: they began level with the floor and, gradually rising, came to the ground surface. Usually the entrance faced south. The fireplace was in the center of the house, and driftwood was used for fuel.

As far as can be judged from the poorly preserved pieces of wood in one of the huts, the roof was made of beams set up to form a cone. There were the remains of supporting posts at the corners of the hearth. It is probable that the roof was supported by a rectangular frame that rested on these posts, as in the case of Zelenaya Gorka. A layer of earth was spread over the top of the roof.

From the distribution of articles found on the floor some conclusions can be drawn about the inner construction. Most of the finds were near the entrance or near the back wall behind the fireplace. The space on either side of the hearth usually produced nothing, which seems to indicate that this area was occupied by sleeping platforms. At the entrance to some of the huts there were piles of ashes and small, charred bones. Most of the articles of domestic use were found near the fireplace and the back wall.

Of the abundant remains of bones found in all the houses, the most numerous were those of seal and fox; there was a large quantity of polar bear and deer bones, and those of whale and walrus also occurred. There were a great many bird bones, but in most cases these were too poorly preserved to be identified; all the identifiable ones belonged to the long-tailed duck.

It was quite interesting that the bones of the different animals found in the huts were deposited separately. Along the wall at different points there were bones and skulls of foxes in neat piles; the seal bones and skulls were apart from these, and the bird bones were also separate. Thus, in one of the houses, against the wall beyond the fireplace there were more than thirty complete fox skulls and a great number of fragments. An explanation of such practice must be sought in religious festivals on the order of the festival for the resurrection of animals, which is known to us from ethnographic studies of the Chukchis and Eskimos.

A typical feature of the Khaen-sale materials is the preponderance of iron over bone and antler for the manufacture of artifacts for which antler and whalebone were normally used.

Among the interesting finds were whalebone wedges apparently used for splitting wood, a net weight made of a thick piece of whalebone perforated near one edge, another piece of the same material that looks like the section of a sled runner, and a tool that is a flattened oval in cross section, 48.5 cm in length, and has a paddlelike, broadened portion at one end with sharp edges—possibly a [snow] shovel or hoe.

There was a piece of whale jawbone in house no. 3; it was 1 m long and 25–30 cm broad. The jaw was placed with the flat side up, and on it lay a narrow, much-sharpened iron knife. On the opposite side of the same house were found two fragments of a whale shoulder blade. On the surface of these, as on the jawbone, are the marks made by a sharp cutting tool, such as can be seen on women's cutting boards used among northern peoples.

Among the artifacts made of antler were several knife handles, three articles similar to those found at Tiutey-sale and tentatively classified as planing blocks, bird arrowheads, very close in shape to the modern ones which the Nentsy use in hunting partridge, peg-shaped arrow-heads, and two slabs carefully fashioned from antler, one of them decorated and with traces of lashing at the narrow end. These slabs may be interpreted as bone braces for a composite bow. According to ethno-graphic data, such braces were widely used among tribes with an Arctic culture, as the scarcity of good wood necessitated the use of bone and sinew in the manufacture of composite bows. Bow bone braces were found by A. P. Okladnikov also in one of the Kitoy burials [west of Lake Baykal]. The folklore of northern peoples, including the Nentsy, abounds in references to bone bows. Without pursuing any further possible parallels, it seems safe to assume the existence of the composite bow with bone braces among the inhabitants of Khaen-sale.

Iron artifacts were found in great numbers in the huts. Among these were knives, all more or less of the same type—narrow, with the cutting edge sharpened from the right. There are remains of wooden handles on the hafts of some of the knives.

In house no. 4 a knife with a gently curved tip was found. This shape of blade, unique among the others, recalls its analogue found in the Zelenaya Gorka house and suggests the same source from which knives of this type found their way to the north. Also in house no. 4 were found a knife with a curving blade similar to that used for carving spoons and a *palma* with the haft and point broken off.[144]

Two types of arrow points were found: bifurcate, and elongated rhomboid ones. There were a few [simple] harpoon heads triangular in shape, all more or less alike. Two of these lay at the right hand of a skeleton found in a burial (to be described later). Such harpoon heads were set in a bone or wooden foreshaft, which in turn was affixed to the shaft proper.

In house no. 3 near the wall opposite the entrance were found bits of coat of mail; the rings were completely rusted through and disintegrated on being touched. Many axes were uncovered during the excavation, most of them broken. Many damaged and formless pieces of iron were found in house no. 4, where apparently a blacksmith dwelled. Two complete axes were found: one in house no. 1, very accurately made and beautifully preserved, the other in the burial. The second axe was of crude workmanship, quite irregular in shape and with a rounded butt. Both axes were sharpened from the right, a practice popular with many Ob-Ugrian and Samoyedic tribes even today.

Also in house no. 3 were found two semicircular bits such as are used today in a bow drill, and a flat file with a coarse cut.

There was no trace of pottery in any of the pit houses, but three handles from copper or iron kettles were found, a rim of a copper kettle, and a copper lug from a kettle of large dimensions. Evidently, at the time the houses were occupied, metal ware was present in such quantities that it displaced the imperfect pottery.

The ornaments found consisted of an openwork specimen made of twisted sheet brass, an iron ring 28 cm in diameter, in shape the same as the belt fibulae used by Nenets women, and a fragment of an imported bronze pendant.

In house no. 4 to the left of the entrance, a burial, to which we referred above, was uncovered. It was about 25 cm below the culture-yielding layer. The skeleton lay on the left side, with the legs flexed and the head toward the north. Two harpoon heads lay by its right hand, and at its head there was an axe and a semicircular iron bit. At the feet were the remains of a wooden object, probably a bow.

Under the skeleton one could discern remains of planks set crosswise, and planks positioned parallel to the skeleton covered the burial. The skeleton was poorly preserved. Judging from the closeness of the cranial sutures and the excessive abrasion of the teeth in the lower jaw, it must have belonged to an elderly person.

There were no traces of clothing except for a few seal hairs adhering to the bones of the feet; this gave a clue to the material from which the boots may have been made.

Next to the burial, to the southwest, a thin stratum of charcoal indicated the location of a hearth. A few centimeters above the level of the grave lay a small sandstone whetstone and two seal vertebrae wrapped in birch bark.

The grave inventory consisted of an axe, drill points, and harpoon heads which were identical to, and hence contemporaneous with, those from the house. Apparently the deceased was placed in a shallow pit in the floor of the hut and was then covered with planks and earth.

The question arises, Was occupation of the house continued after the burial? It is impossible to say definitely, but the absence of objects on top of the grave save for the whetstone and seal vertebrae (which were likely part of the burial complex) seems to indicate that the house had been abandoned after the burial.

On the basis of the finds at Cape Khaen-sale it can be established that this area was occupied for a considerable period of time by a group whose basic occupation was the hunting of sea mammals, especially seal. Wild deer, fox, and birds also occupied an important place in the economy.

The shore of Malygin Strait is well suited for reindeer hunting. The deer gather along the shore in great numbers twice a year. In the spring they cross on the ice over Malygin Strait from Yamal Peninsula to Belyy [White] Island and in the fall they return. Their favorite place for the crossing is the narrowest, western part of the gulf near Cape Skuratov.

Judging from the presence of a sinker in one of the pit houses, one might deduce that the people were fishermen, though it is impossible to say this with certainty, since the sinker may have been used for a seal net. Nothing else was found that could be associated with fishing.

It is likely that all houses were not built at the same time. The wooden portions of house no. 1, for example, were in a better state of preservation than the others, and its outlines on the surface of the ground were more easily traced. Thus, we may suppose that it was built later.

The period of the settlement near Cape Khaen-sale can be determined quite accurately. The bronze pendant with a decoration of plant forms found in one of the houses has its exact counterpart in pendants found by V. N. Pignatti while excavating Isker. Axes were also found at Isker which resembled those from a burial in house no. 4.[145] These analogues as well as the very shape of the axes—without a flange, but with an oval butt—suggest the probable period of habitation as the beginning of the 16th century.

The traditions of the Yamal Nentsy may also be of help in dating this settlement. They figure with only five or six generations since their arrival to the northern extremity of the peninsula, and they figure the six generations on the basis of the graves of their ancestors in the tribal cemeteries. The number may be somewhat increased if one takes into account the probability that the early arrivals to northern Yamal may have carried their dead back to their former tribal cemetery. Thus, even the folkloristic data to an extent concur with the archaeological findings in establishing the dating.

Conclusions

The aims of the present work have been an initial systematization of the archaeological material and an establishment of the periodization and chronology which could serve as a basis for working out the history of the Ugrian tribes of the Ob basin during the 1st millennium A.D. Such a history can be written only when work similar to this has been carried out in other territories inhabited by Ugrian tribes, that is, the Ural and Trans-Ural, and the valleys of the Tobol, Vagay, and Ishim rivers, and when full use has been made of all the available linguistic, folkloristic, and ethnographic data. In the meanwhile we are limiting ourselves to the material in our possession and attempting the most basic report possible, with the hope that it may serve as a foundation for future work in the history of the tribes in the Ob region.

When the material of the 1st millennium A.D. is summarized, the existence of a single culture can be established for the lower Ob region. The exact limits of its distribution cannot be defined at the present, but apparently in the south the boundary did not reach far beyond the left bank of the Irtysh between Tara and Tobolsk; west of Tobolsk it reached as far as the Tyumen region. To the east the lower Ob culture reached into the Narym valley, where it met a related culture which we may call Early Selkup. Existing in antiquity as a close variant of the lower Ob culture, apparently, since the beginning of the Christian era, it became differentiated and developed along its own lines into a separate culture. We have excluded the Early Selkup culture from the present study because of insufficient materials.

The lower Ob culture, which may be viewed as an Early Khanty culture, derived its principal characteristics at the beginning of the Christian era from the Ust-Poluy culture. In the succeeding 1,000 years its development was not disturbed by perceptible outside influences. This peaceful development is especially conspicuous in the ceramic material. At the end of the Ust-Poluy period the corded ware which had appeared on the lower Ob with the arrival of the Ugrian-Savyrs disappears, and its place is again taken by stamped decoration, which indicates the end of a reciprocal process of assimilation. In the Yar-sale stage, still close in many respects to the Ust-Poluy, the stamped ornamentation typical of the lower Ob forested area again becomes widespread, reaching its maximum development in the middle of the 1st millennium A.D. Later, stamped ornamentation disappears from the pottery, but the technique survives on articles of birch bark until modern times.

In the course of several thousands of years of pottery ornamentation on the lower Ob basin, two parallel processes are observable: stamped ornamentation and the ribbon pattern. As was mentioned earlier, the figured stamp develops in a hunting economy and is typical of it. All the figures on birch bark have names, which indicate that they represent the tracks of different animals and birds. Tracks imitated on vessels apparently took the place of the entire animals which we found sculptured on vessels in the earlier Ob basin ceramics. This substitution on the principle of *pars pro toto* came naturally to hunters who were constantly watching the tracks of birds and animals on snow or damp ground. The tracks became associated with the animal itself.

The stamped decoration on pottery and on birch bark articles becomes associated not only by outward, formal resemblance but also by the principle of application involved—the imprint of the track of the animal in soft clay or sufficiently pliable birch bark, just as it occurs in nature. The imprint was the substitution for the animal, the totemic averter of evil.

The other technique of decoration involving the ribbonlike geometric motifs presumably developed first on soft materials rather than pottery. It became widespread on pottery during the Bronze Age, but later, during the Early Iron Age, it practically disappeared. The two processes, stamped and geometric, can be found side by side during the Karym and Orontur stages; at the end of the Orontur the stamped process disappears and is replaced by combinations of the meander and the triangle elements, which survive almost to the end of the 1st millennium A.D. In some cases these resemble quite closely the modern ribbon type of decoration, but they are usually limited to a belt made of crosshatched triangles and to slanting steps and meanders, which closely resemble those combinations which D. N. Eding called decadent Andronovo motifs in connection with the pottery from the Gorbunovo peat bog.

In the course of the 1st and the beginning of the 2nd millennia A.D., the shape of the pots remains the same. Basically it is similar to that from Zelenaya Gorka, which appeared in the Ob basin at the beginning of the 1st millennium and disappeared temporarily during the Ust-Poluy period.

At present it is impossible to deduce an accurate picture of the economy of the population during the 1st millennium A.D. Even though we are certain of the unity of the culture, the basic traits of the organization on which the economy was based must have varied over such a wide territory. In the south a role was played by agriculture and cattle herding which already existed in the preceding Early Iron Age. In the sites of that period (Andryushin Gorodok and Potchevash), bone hoes were found repeatedly, and when A. I. Dmitriyev-Mamonov excavated the Potchevash *kurgans* he uncovered many charred grains.

According to the analysis of the horticulturist Krylov of Tomsk University, the large majority of the grains were barley, one of the first grains to be cultivated. Grains of oats, buckwheat, and false flax are less numerous; the last, according to Krylov, were growing as weeds in the barley fields.[146]

The fact that the Ugrians were acquainted with agriculture in fairly ancient times is supported by certain linguistic evidence. Thus the Mansi *tep*, "barley," literally means "food"; *tepkan* is "field" or, literally, "the place for food." This certainly indicates that barley occupied an important place in the diet of the ancient Ugrians.

Agriculture can scarcely have spread very far to the north, and probably extended no farther than the mouth of the Demyanka River, a right tributary to the Irtysh. We can also be fairly certain about cattle breeding; we find clear indications of its existence in Early Iron Age sites. The representations of rams' heads on one of the Barsov Gorodok buckles suggests the possibility of sheep herding in the Surgut region.

Horse breeding, which was certainly highly developed in antiquity, continued to be practiced to some extent even after the arrival of the Ugrian-Savyrs to the north. This is indicated, in the areas reaching from the mouth of the Irtysh to the Sosva and Kazym rivers by the existence of a special breed of horses called *vogulka*, to distinguish it from the breed used by the Russian populace. The S-shaped bridles found in burial no. 68 at Barsov Gorodok certainly point to horse breeding.[147] They are dated by F. Martin, with the oldest part of the cemetery, to the 8th century A.D. A. Popov contributes proof that horse breeding survived in parts of the lower Ob basin with his statement that "the Narym Khanty killed wolves with whips, chasing them on horseback."[148]

Hunting and fishing were the chief means of livelihood in the taiga belt. At the same time a special type of life and economy was developing in the Arctic among the coast dwellers of the Yamal Peninsula. The archaeological material presented above from the settlements at Tiutey-sale and Khaen-sale confirms the accounts of the travelers in the middle of the 2nd millennium A.D. who found settlements on the shores of the Kara and Barents seas where the population lived in pit houses, used primitive wood, bone, and stone tools, and lived off the sea.

De la Martiner wrote as follows about the coastal people near the mouth of the Pechora: "All their tools consist of sharpened sticks of very hard wood, wooden bows strung with bark fibre, quivers full of arrows and a stone knife which cuts like a razor and is worn on the belt. The Novaya Zemlya native wore on his shoulder a quiver-full of arrows. . . . The war axe made of fish bone (walrus ivory?—Author) he carried over his shoulder holding it with one hand while in the other he held his bow. . . . The needles they sewed with were made of fish ribs and the arrow- and spear-heads of fish bone, as indeed were most of their tools. The shafts of their spears were made of heavy wood of a reddish-brown color, the arrows of a much lighter wood and of lighter color, and all was covered with decoration."[149]

The coastal people lived in semisubterranean houses which were apparently of the same construction as those found on the Yamal. "All the houses are very carefully made of fish (whale?—Author) bone, covered also with fish bones, packed on top with moss and surmounted so well with sod that no wind can penetrate to the interior except through the door which is built like the opening of an oven, and through the roof in which a little window is built."[150]

The clothing was made of bird skins and seal furs. The women, according to de la Martiner, were tattooed in a manner suggestive of Chukchi tattooing. One of them "wore her hair in two braids reaching to her shoulders; there were blue lines drawn across her chin, and three or four lines reached the forehead. The ears and nostrils were pierced and blue stones were hung from them in little rings made of fish bones; the [stone] ear pendants were as big as large forest nuts, those which hung from the nose were the size of peas."[151]

The coastal people made skin boats similar to the Eskimo kayaks, with a framework of bone and wood, and they used harpoons. Stephen Barrow mentions such kayaks, which he saw in 1556 on Vaygach Island.[152] De la Martiner wrote about them in much greater detail when he visited the Barents Sea a hundred years later. "We got them to our ship together with a small boat made like a gondola, 15–16 feet long and 2–2.5 wide, made very cleverly of fish bones and hides; within the skins were sewn in such a way that they formed a bag from one end of the boat to the other. Inside such a boat they were covered to the waist in such a way that not a single drop of water could get inside and in this way they could hold out safely in every weather."[153]

A letter from a Dutch merchant, Johann Ballak, to Gerard Mercator in 1581 indicates that skin boats had been in use along the Ob at the end of the 16th century,[154] and they were used there until the 1830s. Franz Belyavskiy describes such a kayak in detail and accompanies the description with a drawing. "The boat of the Ostyaks and Samoyeds is made like the usual Russian boat with this difference: a) there is no difference between the bow and the stern, b) the boat is fitted on top with a cover of worked whale intestines which is gathered together by a drawstring in the middle of the boat like a lady's drawstring handbag. The natives at times of high water or storm or when they are hunting seals or whales, which requires the greatest speed, agility and skill, sit in the boat, pull up the draw-string which girds them about the waist, and then go not only down the rivers but even out into the Ob Gulf and along the Arctic coast. Here they plunge like a dolphin and are not afraid to pursue whales and kill young walrus, convinced that they are safe and cannot sink."[155]

Reflected in the folklore of the present-day tundra dwellers, the reindeer-herding Nentsy, are memories of the coastal houses that looked like mounds on the headlands that jutted out into the sea:

> Three brothers
> The headmen of three turf-covered pit houses
> Three brothers live on three headlands.
> The brothers hunt sea animals,
> Whales, walrus and seals.

According to tradition the coastal hunters did not live in the pit houses through the year. These were used only in winter; in summer the people went away into the heart of the tundra to hunt wild deer and molting geese and to fish in the lakes and rivers. The campsites we have described on the shores of the tundra lakes and on the dunes of the Taz and Ob gulfs are the records of these wanderings.

The economy, material culture, and way of life of the ancient inhabitants of the Yamal coast were close to those of the Eskimos and sedentary [Coastal] Chukchis. Apparently, in all of the Arctic ecumene, given the similarity of conditions and a similar level of technology, there could develop very closely related forms of material culture and economy. We are interested not only in the problem of the regularity of convergent development, but also in the question of how close ethnically the people on the different parts of the Siberian coast were. Unfortunately we have very little material to go on. On the basis of some linguistic and archaeological evidence we may deduce that there existed a close relationship between the early Uralic population of the Arctic reaches of the Ob basin and some of the ethnic groups on the Arctic coast of eastern Siberia, most likely the ancestors of the present-day Yukagirs. This evidence is upheld by a number of analogues in the area of material culture, which refer to various small details, the agreement of which points to cultural proximity rather than convergence. Such are the same forms of the dog-harness swivel and the bone [shoulder blade] snow-shovel edges at Ust-Poluy and among the Eskimos, the resemblance of details in the bridles for decoy reindeer known from Ust-Poluy and among the tribes of eastern Siberia, and others. The population of the Yamal coast was already assimilating from the Ugrian-Savyrs during the Ust-Poluy period.[156]

Judging by the pottery from Tiutey-sale, this assimilative influence continued during the 1st millennium A.D., since the Arctic coastal culture remained basically unchanged until it was replaced by the sled-using, reindeer-breeding culture which appeared on the tundra as an improved form of economy for the given stage of technical development. This supplanting of cultures did not occur at the same time in all parts of the territory under discussion.[157]

The Samoyed tribes practicing this type of economy must have appeared in the tundra regions of the lower Ob in the 10th–12th centuries, but in the more remote parts, for example the tip of the Yamal Peninsula, Belyy Island, and others, the Samoyeds probably arrived only after A.D. 1500. According to their traditions, when the Nentsy arrived on the Yamal they found sea hunters who lived in pit houses, whom they called *Siirtya*. War was carried on between them, but cases of mixed marriages between the newcomers and the aborigines are also mentioned.[158]

The Samoyed tribes assimilated the remains of the earlier, aboriginal population but also were themselves influenced by the local people, which explains some of the specific traits of the Yamal Nentsy. The Samoyeds are also known to have exerted their influence on the Ob Ugrian tribes, whose northern representatives had adopted reindeer breeding by that time. But these events exceed the chronological limits of this work.

The greatest advances made during the 1st millennium A.D. were in the field of metallurgy. By the end of the Ust-Poluy and Potchevash periods, copper was no longer used for tools and weapons.

In western Siberia, celts of the Tobolsk type were the last to be developed in a series of copper-bronze hewing tools and could only be supplanted by the more perfected iron ones. Admittedly, west of the Urals this process took place somewhat earlier; in the sites of the Pyanobor [Pyanyy Bor] period there are no bronze celts. It is possible that the lack of raw materials in the Kama region, particularly tin (which made a hard casting possible), resulted in the more rapid adoption of iron metallurgy.

Although at the present we do not have direct evidence on the type of cutting tool used in the Ob basin during the post–Ust-Poluy period, it seems highly probable that it was an adzelike tool with a socket of hammered iron, like the type of celt found in a burial of the Fominskaya culture datable to the terminal phase of the Ust-Poluy and, in part, to the Yar-sale period.[159] It is difficult to say how long the socketed adze existed as the basic cutting tool; along with the axe it is readily utilized on the Isker and in the Ob basin to the present day. The modern hewing tools* used for hollowing out boats and making grooves in beams have the same appearance. Evidently, by the end of the 1st millennium A.D. the "lugged" iron axes appeared in the Ob basin. They are known from the hill site Tān wārup-ēkwa, the Kintusovo cemetery, et cetera. Some of these are obviously imported; others, which closely resemble those from Isker, were perhaps made locally.

As we have seen, iron knives were quite widely distributed during the Ust-Poluy period. At that time, the curved knives, survivals of the Bronze Age ones, were in a minority; the most widespread ones were hafted, with a bone handle. Judging from the few finds made, the most typical shape was narrow with a comparatively long blade having a fairly thick spine. We find knives of the same shape in much later sites, such as the Kintusovo cemetery, Lyuli-Kar, Barsov Gorodok, and others. Owing to the better state of preservation and the greater number of specimens, the unilateral sharpening of the blade can be readily seen. In these sites and others of the same period we find broader knives along with the narrower ones, and flat, hafted knives. Both types can be clearly traced through to the present.[160]†

Of particular interest is a type of knife-dagger and sword occurring during the 1st millennium A.D. Artifacts of this type, as a rule double-edged but sometimes single-edged combat knife-daggers, are usually made of one piece of iron. What differentiates them from other artifacts similarly used is a bifurcation of the upper end of the handle, which ends in volutes or antennae twisted outwardly. A similar "heavy iron sword with a bifurcated handle" was mentioned by Gorodkov, who observed

---

* [*Pazniki i tikavki* in the original. Editor, A.I.N.A.]

† [The three paragraphs that follow were inserted by the author in 1968. Editor, A.I.N.A.]

it in one of the sacred places [groves] of the Ostyaks on the Salym River, a tributary to the Irtysh.[161] A fellow traveler of Gorodkov, L. Shults, opined that "the iron sword with a bifurcate handle reminds one of early Scandinavian ones." At the same place there was a "heavy knife which served, according to tradition, for the scalping of enemies."[162]

According to information supplied to me by V. Mogilnikov, a young archaeologist specializing in western Siberia of the 1st millennium A.D., a single-edged long knife or knife-dagger with a bifurcate handle was found on the Parabel River, a tributary to the Ob in its middle course. Additionally, a sword with a bifurcate handle and twisted ends is known from the Yerykayev cache, and there is another one found somewhere on the middle Ob and now deposited in the City Museum of Kolpashevo on the middle Ob. In Mogilnikov's opinion the swords may be dated to approximately A.D. 500–800.

A similar type of sword, found on the lower Ob, is now in the Salekhard (formerly Obdorsk) museum. This is no doubt a very old sword, although it does not give the impression of being an archaeological specimen, because of its excellent state of preservation. A drawing of the sword reveals a bifurcate handle ending in volutes turned outwardly, with each volute embellished with two rings made of thick copper wire. The rings may have been a later addition. Incidentally, the preservation of the sword may be accounted for by its having been deposited in one of the Ostyak sacred places, where one may not rarely find objects dating to an earlier period than the 1st millennium A.D. It is quite likely that such swords were at one time used in combat, but after the arrival of the Russians to the north, they were kept as objects of tradition and used only on occasion of the sacred sword dance, similar to those described by Castrén, who witnessed such a dance in the 1850s.[163] This type of sword is very probably of local origin, as was suggested earlier. Because of the shape of the handle, it would be difficult to compare these swords with those used in the sacred dances and the *akinakés* of the so-called Scythian-Sarmatian type, which always have the volutes turned inward. Unfortunately we do not possess swords of the described type obtained under controlled field excavation conditions, and thus we are unable to fix the time of their appearance. However, we cannot exclude the possibility that they were present as early as the Ust-Poluy period, if we consider the find, at Ust-Poluy, of a breastplate of whalebone on which was engraved a representation of a soldier holding two daggers or swords with bifurcate handles and outwardly turned antennae.[164]

The Ob region has not been studied thoroughly enough for us to determine the time at which iron was first produced there, since in the early settlements, including Ust-Poluy, there may have been only the reworking of imported iron. Yet, at Ust-Poluy the comparatively large supply of iron makes this proposition improbable. We are more inclined to believe that iron metallurgy developed in the region almost as early as it did on the Kama. This is supported by a number of finds: the blacksmith's tongs at the site of Us-Nel, apparently from the Karym period, iron slag at Lyuli-Kar, and numerous pieces of smelted iron from local bog iron at Andreyevskoye Ozero (Lake) adjacent to sites datable to the last centuries B.C. and the first centuries A.D. But the production of iron apparently never developed enough locally and died away in the 10th–11th centuries with the appearance of a multitude of iron products from the west and later with the arrival of the Tatars on the middle Irtysh. The early historical sources report a great demand for iron articles on the part of the population of the Ob region.

Copper and bronze casting in the 1st millennium A.D. was limited to figures; the maximum development took place during the Yar-sale, Karym, and in part the Orontur periods. To this time span belong the innumerable little figurines, in particular those of birds and deer, which are outstanding for the care with which they are executed and for the technology involved and which surpass in quality even the best of the Ust-Poluy period. The technique of casting apparently remains the same, with carved molds being used. However, the later figurines are more carefully smoothed, so that the traces of heavy, angular cuts that were characteristic of many objects from the Yar-sale period are no longer in evidence.

The numerous engraved representations on plaques and metal utensils, which are already known from the Ust-Poluy period, have great significance in our studying of the way of life, clothing, and even some aspects of religion.

Bronze casting begins to diminish toward the end of the Orontur period. Large objects practically disappear and are superceded by numerous plaques of different shapes—wide, flat bracelets, buttons, pendants, openwork pieces, small birds and animal figures in the round, all progressively more and more schematic.

A great number of imported bronze and silver objects appear in the Ob region about the 10th century and later, such as moon-shaped pendants, diadems decorated with pearls, wire earrings and bracelets with keglike appendages—in other words, a complex of ornaments well represented among Russian and Bulgarian antiquities. These ornaments inspired local copies, most of them clumsy ones. The technique of handling pearl-like ornaments was apparently never mastered, and on local objects we find only imitations, the "pearl" being replaced by small cone-shaped, cast pellets.

Copper working probably disappeared at the same time that ironworking did, that is, during the first half of the 2nd millennium A.D. Apparently this was brought about by the importations of Russian and Turkic-speaking peoples. Their ready-made objects gradually crowded out the local ones. Local production never developed to the point of manufacturing goods for trade. Pottery disappears also at this time, probably owing to the importation of metal ware, particularly riveted kettles, made of copper leaf. Such were found, for example, in the Kintusovo cemetery, at Molchanovo, and Barsov Gorodok. Badly fired clay vessels could not compete with copper kettles, while birch bark and wooden ware fully satisfied all other household needs.

Of all the metallurgy that existed in the past among the Ob Ugrians, only tin casting remains today. Some cult objects are made: magical and curative figures, figures on which oaths are taken, in some cases images of the dead, and ornaments. It is flat casting and is done in forms cut out of pine bark, or more rarely out of soft slate.

Imported articles and ornaments indicate to some extent the main sources of cultural influence and trade. Thus the majority of tinkling pendants are identical to those from the middle and upper Kama and the Vychegda basins.[165] Pendants of the type illustrated on Plate LIII, items 1–4, are similar to those known from the Sarsk hill site and the Mikhailovo cemetery in Yaroslav *oblast*, while the beads (Plate LIV, item 6) are analogous to those from the Kostroma and Narva *kurgans*. An axe found at Tān wārup-ēkwa originated in Novgorod or the Baltic area. And finally the innumerable circlets for the head, the moonlike objects, and the rings decorated with pearl-like granules probably also came from the Russians to the west.

All this demonstrates that the basic cultural and trade relations of the lower Ob were directed toward the upper and sometimes the middle Kama, the Vychegda, and the upper Volga. To a lesser degree one can postulate ties with the lower Kama region and with the Bolgars. These contacts in all likelihood were stopped at the end of the 1st millennium A.D. by the movements of the Komi-Permyak tribes from the Vychegda to the Kama and subsequently by the beginning of the Novgorod campaigns, which followed for the most part the same route.

PART V

ARCHAEOLOGICAL ANTIQUITIES OF
THE NORTHERN PART OF
WESTERN SIBERIA

W. MOSZYŃSKA

Introduction

The Ob basin, particularly its middle and lower parts, has not yet been studied sufficiently from the archaeological point of view. Nonetheless, the work conducted there in recent decades has yielded material which indicates that this territory is of exceptional historical importance. It has natural features conducive to the intensive development of human society: the river routes, which are meridional and which connect the Ob basin with the southern part of Siberia and Kazakhstan, the ore deposits of the Urals and Kazakhstan, the wealth of fauna in the area, and the historical processes that occurred there influenced peoples and cultures territorially remote from it.

Those who study the cultural history of the Eurasian and American Arctic are faced with the problem of explaining the numerous cultural features common to the peoples of the Far North, a culture which has been termed circumpolar.

The complex problem of a circumpolar culture has long attracted the attention of many authors—F. Boas, K. Birket-Smith, G. Hatt, and G. Gjessing, to name a few. Among the Soviet investigators, only V. G. Bogoraz and A. M. Zolotarev have given attention to this problem.

F. Graebner was the first to specify "hunting cultures of the arctic and subarctic zone." Taking their peripheral location as his basis, Graebner assigned these cultures, along with the Tasmanian and the "boomerang culture," to the most ancient stratum. The uniformity of the geographic conditions and the great similarity of the economic forms in the subarctic zone led to the assumption that it developed by convergence, owing to the common geographic medium. This was pointed out vividly by Bogoraz: "Man in the North lives wholly under the power of nature, and if we take three groups of cultural phenomena—the material, the spiritual, and the social, we notice that all of them are influenced with great force and strictness by several groups of (natural) conditions."[1] However, in noting the convergent occurrence of a number of phenomena in the cultures of the peoples of the arctic and subarctic zones of the Old World and the New, convergence due to nature, Bogoraz attempted to discover the ancient ethnic stratum underlying these cultures. He

Translated by David Kraus from *Svod Arkheologicheskikh Istochnikov*, no. D3–8, Institut Arkheologii AN SSSR, Moscow, 1965, 88 pp.

based his attempts primarily on folkloristic data, because in those days no archaeological material was available.

W. Thalbitzer and F. Boas attempted to delineate and explain individual coincidences in the cultural phenomena. In particular, Thalbitzer did much to establish Eskimo-Lapp parallels in their spiritual cultures.[2] Boas, acknowledging the convergence of development in the uniform geographic medium, noted that just a few of the cultural elements of circumpolar distribution can be explained by identical geographic conditions. In his opinion, another explanation was required for features common to the circumpolar zone, such as the use of dogs as draft animals, birch bark for dishes and boats, subterranean dwellings with the entrance through the roof, the flat drum, and armor plate.[3]

The work of the Danish ethnographer G. Hatt had a great influence on the further study of circumpolar culture.[4] Hatt advanced the hypothesis that two components of different age form the basis for the culture of the peoples inhabiting the circumpolar regions. These components are manifested, in particular, in two types of clothing.

According to Hatt, most forms of clothing employed widely in the arctic and subarctic regions may be divided into six groups:

1. Clothing developed from the poncho type
2. Clothing developed from a loose mantle, originally a simple deerskin
3. Trousers developed from leggings, in some cases probably from leggings combined with a triangular genital cloth
4. Trousers developed from breechcloth (that is, a piece of skin or cloth drawn between the legs and fastened before and behind by a waistband)
5. Boots and shoes developed from a [combination of a] stocking and sandal boot
6. Moccasins, and boots developed from moccasin boots

Further, Hatt established that the first, third, and fifth groups of clothing were widely used among the peoples of the eastern and western Arctic, while the peoples inhabiting the intervening area, which includes most of Eurasia, made wide use of clothing of the second, fourth, and sixth groups. If this is true, the first, third, and fifth groups represent an older type of clothing, while the second, fourth, and sixth groups represent a chronologically later type. Rejecting the proposition that these types could have developed independently of each other, Hatt concludes that they penetrated to America from the Old World at different times. The more ancient type is best represented by the Eskimo. Hatt called this the "coast culture." It developed along the rivers and lake shores and must have reached the Arctic before the appearance of skis. Hatt called the later stratum the "continental culture," because only after the appearance of skis was it able to overcome the vast continental expanses between Lapland and Labrador. The value of Hatt's work is that in making a comparative analysis of the culture of the many northern peoples, he was able to distinguish the common elements of these cultures and to group them into entire complexes. Hatt's hypothesis was accepted and developed by a number of North American and Scandinavian scholars, including the prominent Eskimologist K. Birket-Smith, who announced himself a proponent of Hatt's hypothesis and acknowledged the complexes differentiated by Hatt, but proposed that they be given other names because the terms "coast" and "continental" are ambiguous and lead to misunderstandings that make their application difficult. In their place, Birket-Smith proposed the terms "ice-hunting and fishing culture" and "ski culture," which, in his opinion, would accentuate the characteristics of the winter life in the circumpolar region.[5]

Birket-Smith's study of the Caribou Eskimos led him to conclude that their very primitive culture is a vestige of an ancient continental culture once widely distributed through the circumpolar zone, namely, the "winter ice-hunting culture." Birket-Smith was inclined to see in this hypothetical culture some common basis for the cultures of the circumpolar zone. In speaking of it, he pointed out that it coincided with W. Schmidt's cultural circle, which had its origin in the northern regions of central Asia.[6] Later, Birket-Smith's ideas about this culture changed somewhat and became more specific: he held that it was possible to view the continental circumpolar culture as Paleolithic or Epipaleolithic, and he even began to associate it with the Late Aurignacian cultures of Siberia, stating that the Denbigh flint complex is related to the Folsom and Yuma complexes and to the Old World Mesolithic and Upper Paleolithic.[7]

In using the term "ice-hunting and fishing culture," Birket-Smith had in mind chiefly lake hunting and fishing. A. M. Zolotarev, who accepted Birket-Smith's hypothesis in its general form and also his terminology, considered it possible to expand this concept to include sea-ice hunting and fishing near the coast.[8]

The Norwegian archaeologist G. Gjessing made a special study of the circumpolar culture, based on archaeological material.[9] Noting that at present this culture covers a vast territory, from northern Fenno-Scandia to the eastern coast of North America and Greenland, inhabited by various peoples, in whose cultures one may trace a similarity in both the general phenomena and the individual elements such as the shaman's drum, cradle, needle case, et cetera, Gjessing considers two questions to be of major importance: (1) Is this similarity due only to the specific natural conditions, or can one establish cultural connections for this entire vast territory? (2) How far into antiquity can one trace these relations and determine where the Arctic culture began?[10]

In contrast to Birket-Smith, Gjessing distinguishes two ancient synchronous circumpolar cultures, coastal and continental. In Gjessing's construction, both these cultures are outlined by zones, or as he calls them, belts, in which cultural ties have existed since the most ancient times. The coastal belt, or the coastal sea hunting culture, stretches along the Arctic coast across the Bering Strait into the New World, while the continental culture extends across the zone of coniferous forests of Eurasia and North America. He establishes the Arctic coastal belt on the basis of three elements: the use of slate for making artifacts, the skin boat (umiak), and the seal harpoon. Gjessing's three elements are not syn-chronous. Skin boats are known only from the materials of the 16th–19th centuries, and even Gjessing doubts that they can be connected with the problematical Stone Age boats of the cliff paintings.[11] In most cases, socketed harpoons cannot be traced further back than the 1st millennium B.C.[12] The diffusion of the slate industry is datable to a considerably earlier period. This disparity in chronology does not allow us to view these phenomena as a complex of indicators.

Gjessing lists a somewhat larger number of common cultural elements for the subarctic belt of the circumpolar zone. He selects five basic groups of elements: (1) some forms of stone implements (rectangular stone adzes, crescentic flint implements, arrowheads with a notched base); (2) a bone industry (bird darts); (3) pottery (comb-impressed and textile-impressed); (4) underground dwellings; and (5) art (the similarity appears both in the animalistic round sculpture and in the rock sculptures and rock paintings, in which some details are common, such as the "lifeline" on the animal images). The ancient sculpture in the round in Scandinavia is expressed chiefly by representations of the elk, the bear, and waterfowl. In most cases, a bird or animal representation adorns the handle of a slate knife, or a comb, or an antler spoon. These same motifs are found in the sculpture of Finland. Finnish wooden spoons are decorated with representations of elk, bear, and bird heads. Gjessing opines that the home of the Eurasian animal style lies to the east of Perm, and he traces all the round sculpture of this style to Ural sculpture, that is, that of the Shigir and Gorbunovo periods.[13]

Such, according to Gjessing, are the common elements of the conti-nental cultures of the subarctic belt. He traces some of them, particularly the dwellings and the common features of art, to the Paleolithic. He assumes that the cultures of the western European Upper Paleolithic and the Eskimo culture developed out of the same base, which must be sought in the "ancient Asiatic Stone Age culture."[14] We have already noted that he envisioned a unified circumpolar culture, "a continuous belt of cultural phenomena." However, these phenomena do not coincide chronological-ly, and their localization in most cases goes far beyond the limits of the circumpolar region, even in the broadest possible sense of the word. The main factor in the development of the culture, according to Gjessing, was diffusion; he allows convergence only in the case of identical geographic conditions. The territorial remoteness of the phenomena observed in different geographic circumstances thus becomes a priori evidence of diffusion. The second major premise of Gjessing amounts to a recogni-tion of the "limitless vitality of the cultural impulse, which is unlimited in time and space." This frees him from the need to date and synchronize the phenomena and allows him to draw on materials of different ages. All this, combined with insufficient analysis of the material in a number of cases lends an air of speculativeness and lightness to his constructions.

The question of a circumpolar culture again became the subject of lively debate in connection with the study of the Ipiutak site in Alaska.[15] Larsen's and Rainey's search for parallels for the Ipiutak materials led them to the very remote area of northwestern Siberia, the Trans-Ural and

Cis-Ural regions. On the basis of some similar features, they proposed that the Ipiutak culture originated in western Siberia. They considered it possible to associate this culture, which they assumed to be older than the Ipiutak culture, with the proto-Eskimos, who were, in the opinion of Larsen and Rainey, most probably reindeer hunters and fishermen living in the northern part of the forest zone of Eurasia. They also were of the opinion that groups of forest hunters moved out along the Arctic coast as early as the Neolithic period and that this movement began in Siberia, whence it extended westward as far as northern Scandinavia and eastward to America where, according to Larsen and Rainey, the Eskimos are the last survivors of an ancient circumpolar Arctic hunting culture.[16]

Treatment of the complex problems of the origin and development of Arctic cultures should be based on a detailed and universal study of ethnographic data and archaeological remains. Among the latter, the Early Iron Age remains of the lower Ob region occupy an important place. The material from these sites has been summarized, essentially, in the works of V. N. Chernetsov.[17] Using as his basis a complex of rather unique pottery found together with a uniform complex of other artifacts, he concluded that these archaeological sites belonged to a single culture, which he called the Ust-Poluy. He established that this culture was of a two-component nature, in which the features of an Arctic hunter-fisher way of life was combined with elements characteristic of a more southerly culture. He did not associate the penetration of these southern elements solely with the development of barter, although he did attribute some importance to it, but with the appearance of a new ethnic element in northwestern Siberia, an element which brought with it customs and traditions of a steppe culture. The blending of this new element with the aboriginal population, which can be observed in the Ust-Poluy culture, played a substantial role in the formation of some groups of Ob Ugrians, principally the northern Khanty. In Chernetsov's opinion, the Ust-Poluy culture existed in the second half of the 1st millennium B.C.[18] His views, which he developed most fully in his survey papers,[19] evoked criticism from a number of specialists. The principal critique came from M. P. Gryaznov, who investigated the archaeological sites of the upper Ob region. Having differentiated an upper Obian culture and having period-ized it, Gryaznov held that his upper Obian Iron Age sites should be taken as standards for determining the chronology of other Obian cultures. He proposed, in keeping with the periodic system he had worked out, that the Ust-Poluy period be dated to the "Fominskoye stage," that is, to the 7th–8th centuries A.D.[20] Gryaznov's viewpoint was not generally accepted in the archaeological literature. L. R. Kyzlasov upheld the dating proposed by Chernetsov and noted parallels between the Ust-Poluy and Late Tagar materials.[21]

Gryaznov's main argument is based on some features of external similarity between the material cultures of the Fominskaya and the Ust-Poluy sites: identical elements of the pottery ornamentation (tri-angular, S-shaped, oval, and other stampings) and its composition, the spherical form of the vessels with a round bottom and a lip character-istically inverted, the presence of vessels with a hollow base such as had been found in the villages of the Fominskaya stage on the Irmen River; the "geometric ornamentation of the cast scabbards [having] very similar counterparts in bone artifacts from Ust-Poluy"; and similar bone arrows and heads in the Fominskaya burials and in those of Ust-Poluy.[22]

Gryaznov holds that his proposed dates (7th–8th centuries A.D.) are not in conflict with other materials from the Ust-Poluy site for the following reasons: "bronze objects of the Lomovatovo type" were found at Ust-Poluy; bone spatulas and *spoons of the same sizes but somewhat different shapes* were discovered at the Rodanovo fortified hill site; the Ust-Poluy bone arrowheads are very similar to the 10th–11th century Cis-Uralian arrowheads; the distinctive ornamentation of the Ust-Poluy bone and metal artifacts is quite similar in form, in general and specifically, to the ornamentation of bone artifacts from the Rodanovo fortified hill site; and there are ownership markings, which did not appear in the Cis-Kama region until the 1st millennium A.D.[23]

We intend to analyze Gryaznov's arguments in detail in a separate paper, so we will dwell only on the basic issue here. The concept that the Fominskaya and Ust-Poluy pottery were identical was the result of incomplete publication of the Ust-Poluy material. This incomplete publication was Gryaznov's only source of information on the subject, and he did not undertake a study of the collection on his own. In the appropriate section of the present paper, we will indicate the characteristics of the individual groups of Ust-Poluy pottery, the results of typological analyses of them, and the tallies made in processing the pottery of different sites of the Ust-Poluy culture.

The characteristic shape of Ust-Poluy pottery is the cauldronlike vessel with a hollow pedestal and, generally, a short everted neck and very sparse ornamentation. Figured stampings appeared in the late stages of the Ust-Poluy culture. They were used much more widely in the succeeding period. Vessels on pedestals, it should be noted, are a familiar form in the Tagar and Tashtyk sites. Therefore, a comparison of vessels on pedestals from the Irmen villages and the Fominskaya graves with similar objects of the Ust-Poluy culture cannot serve as the basis for their dating. The Ust-Poluy complex of bone arrowheads is incomparably richer and more diverse than the Fominskaya. Among the many hundreds of specimens of Ust-Poluy alone there are, of course, counterparts of the few specimens published for the Fominskaya burials, but such analogues may also be sought in the materials of the Ananino and Dyakovo sites.[24] Therefore, this type of comparison does not constitute sufficient grounds for dating the Ust-Poluy culture. An important factor in dating it is the fact that in its various sites one finds bronze arrowheads and ornaments that are analogous to specimens found in the Ananino complexes. We have summarized the material of these finds in Fig. 44, which indicates that the Ust-Poluy and Ananino cultures were synchronous. This summary provides the basis for more exact dating of the Ust-Poluy culture, and we can now set its limits within narrower bounds, namely, the 5th to the 3rd centuries B.C.

The foreign literature contains criticism of Chernetsov's second thesis, that is, his ethnic interpretation of the Ust-Poluy materials. D. B. Shimkin, in summarizing the results of Soviet research in western Siberia, concluded that the archaeology of western Siberia, and the lower Ob in particular, reflects the history of the Samoyed peoples, not the Ugrians.[25] Without denying the similarity of the Ust-Poluy and Ob-Ugrian materials, Shimkin points to the elements of similarity found in the Nganasan culture and holds that the Ust-Poluy culture should rather be associated with the Samoyeds, inasmuch as the "Ugrians came late to this territory." This position is based on the traditional but outdated concept that the ancestors of the Finno-Ugric peoples came from the Volga and the Kama, a position we cannot accept.

   The present monograph unifies the data on the archaeological sites of the Ust-Poluy culture in the northern forest belt of western Siberia (see Fig. 25). Recently, after the aforementioned papers on the archaeology of western Siberia had been published, new materials were obtained, and collections were made available which could not be included at the time of publication of the earlier works because of the difficulty of processing museum materials during the war. The present paper is based on materials in the Museum of Physical Anthropology and Ethnography in Leningrad, the Sverdlovsk Regional Museum, the Omsk Museum, the Archaeological Institute of the Academy of Sciences of the U.S.S.R. in Moscow, and the Museum of Physical Anthropology of Moscow University. Thus, I have the opportunity to present more fully the northern aboriginal component of the Ust-Poluy culture without

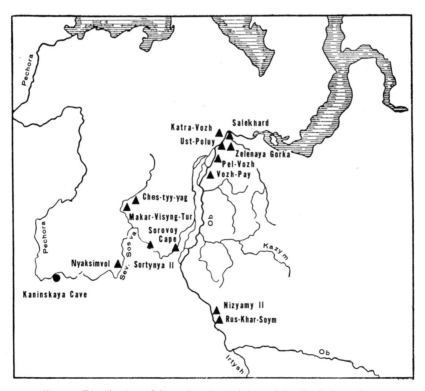

Fig. 25. Distribution of the archaeological sites of the Ust-Poluy culture.

exaggerating the role of the southern elements, which were given the main attention in previous publications,[26] with the result that one perhaps formed the impression that the Ust-Poluy culture was unique, apparently having nothing in common with the other cultures based on more complete data than have been available hitherto on the antiquities of the Ust-Poluy culture. Inasmuch as the material is very extensive, not all artifacts could be illustrated or described. Only those specimens are included which characterize specific series of objects, and these, in turn, are classified according to purpose and type. The plates of principal types and synchronizing finds, together with the published data, have allowed us to establish the place of the Ust-Poluy culture among the cultures of Eurasia and to attempt to indicate its role in the history of the cultures of the circumpolar zone.

Chapter 1

Description of the Sites

UST-POLUY (Tyumen *oblast*, Yamal-Nenets [National] *okrug*), Plates LV to LXIX. A fortified hill site on the right, high bank of the Poluy River, Ust-Poluy is 3.5 km from the city of Salekhard and 4 km from Angalskiy mys [Cape Angal], upstream from it. On the landward side, the hill site was protected by a ditch and rampart that are scarcely discernible now. There was a sacrificial place within the site.[27]

The first information on this site was obtained in 1932, when bronze and bone objects were found during construction works. Some of these objects were subsequently turned over to the Museum of Physical Anthropology and Ethnography of the Academy of Sciences of the U.S.S.R. During the two field seasons, 1935 and 1936, an expedition of that museum, headed by V. S. Adrianov, made excavations at the site (see Fig. 26). For a number of reasons, the work was never completed, and a considerable part of the documentation of the 1936 excavations was lost. Only the field notes of the 1935 expedition are preserved, together with a schematic map of the excavations, and some cross sections. In addition, there are descriptions of the collections which contain data on the distribution of finds by square number. In 1935 the work was concentrated in five sections.

Excavation I (see Fig. 27) involved squares 1–17a, with an area of 17.5 m², and was carried out directly adjacent to a cellar pit (2 × 4.5 m). During excavation, some bone and pottery objects were uncovered. The area was divided into 1 × 1 m squares. The few cultural remains were found immediately below the turf. Accumulations of ashes and charcoal occupied all the exposed area of squares 10–11.

Square 6 contained a considerable accumulation of pottery, part of which consisted of fragments of a single crushed vessel (MAE 5331–141).* In the immediate vicinity, in square 5, two iron knives and an armor breastplate were found; a bronze anthropomorphic representation was found in square 17a, and a spoon with a sculptured handle was found in square 4.

Excavation II included squares 18–31, with an area of about 22 m² (see Fig. 28). It was discontinued at the clay pit, 1.5 m deep. A culture-

---

* [MAE, Museum of Anthropology and Ethnography of the Academy of Sciences of the U.S.S.R. in Leningrad. Translator, A.I.N.A.]

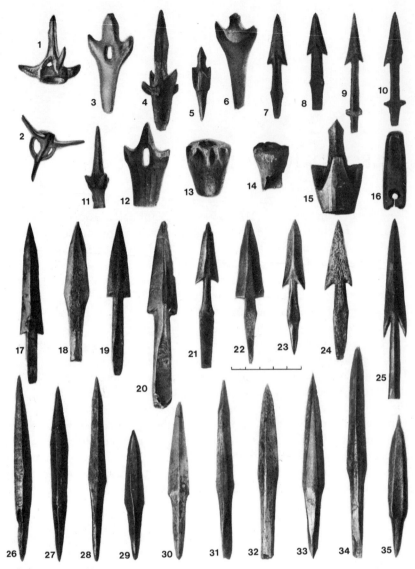

Plate LV. Ust-Poluy. Implements for land hunting.
1 to 4, 11, 12–spiked arrowheads with side blades; 5, 6, 13 to 15–blunt arrowheads; 7 to 10–heads of harpoons; 16–socket of a harpoon; 17 to 35–hafted arrowheads. Materials: 1, 2–bronze; 3 to 35–reindeer antler.

yielding layer containing several artifacts could be traced only at the northern wall of the pit. The surface of this sector was much littered with construction debris and mounds of earth dug out in preparing the foundation of a building. Part of the surface was greatly disturbed by small pits, and the turf layer of squares 23–31 had been turned over. Squares 21–25 contained a large amount of ash. The finds were very unevenly distributed among the squares. Beginning with square 26, finds were more and more rare, and the culture-yielding layer thinned out altogether in squares 30 and 31. Material was most abundant in squares 21–24, in which there were an armor breastplate with the representation of a warrior, a bronze ornamental plate, a bronze anthropomorphic representation, a forehead bone piece of a reindeer bridle, a bronze casting of an owl, a bronze anthropomorphic representation, sheet copper, and finally, a mould for casting bronze arrowheads. Stone pestles were found in squares 28 and 29.

Excavation III, squares 32–34 (see Fig. 27), was made in the immediate vicinity of the building foundation, whose excavation in 1932 produced the first finds. The 4.75-m area of the excavation stops 0.5 m from the

Plate LVI. Ust-Poluy. Implements for land hunting and fishing.
   1–bullet-shaped arrowhead; 2–three-bladed socketed arrowhead; 3, 4–bone forehead pieces for a reindeer decoy; 5–side barb of a [composite] fish spear; 6 to 10–planoconvex lamellar blades; 11 to 18–flat, sharp-pointed lamellar blades. Materials: 1, 3 to 18–reindeer antler; 2–walrus ivory.

Plate LVII. Ust-Poluy. Implements for sea hunting.
    1–harpoon head with side blade; 2 to 6–harpoon heads; 7 to 10–socketed harpoon foreshafts; 11, 12–harpoon socket pieces; 13 to 16–ice creepers. Material: reindeer antler.

Plate LVIII. Ust-Poluy. Dog-harness parts.
1 to 5–strap buckles; 6–two-part swivel; 7–pipelike swivel; 8, 9, 11 to 13–two-part swivel plates; 10–shaft of two-part swivel; 14 to 17–two-part swivel plates. Material: reindeer antler.

foundation wall. The surface was greatly disturbed by the construction work. The culture-yielding layer was immediately below the turf. Square 32 yielded very little material and the culture-yielding layer became noticeably thinner toward the southeast. On the other hand, square 33 and the part of square 34 immediately adjacent to square 33 yielded many finds, among which special attention should be called to nine bone handles of iron knives, bone scraper-spatulas, an iron knife, four bone fish knives, a bone dart head, two flat bone spoons, and bone tweezers for plucking hair.

Excavation IV, squares 35–38 (see Fig. 28), was made at the edge of the slope of a ravine and was divided into four squares 2 × 2 m each. The culture-yielding layer, which contained artifacts in extremely poor condition, lay immediately below a very thin layer of turf. In square 37 there was an irregular oval, ashy spot whose greatest diameter was 65 cm. It was 4 cm thick. Among the finds, the ice-creeper shoe from square 37 is worthy of note.

Plate LIX. Ust-Poluy. Spoons with straight and curved handles, decorated with sculptured representations of bird and animal heads. Materials: 1 to 4–mammoth tusk; 5, 11–reindeer antler; 6–walrus ivory; 7 to 10–bone.

Excavation V, the main excavation, included squares 39–76 (see Fig. 29). In it an area of 76.5 m² was exposed. The culture-yielding layer lay at a depth of 15–50 cm from the present surface. The excavation uncovered a large campfire area occupying all of squares 45–52, 59–62, and 68–70 and running into squares 71, 63, and 53. In square 50 the ash spot with charcoal was directly below the turf layer, about 20 cm from the present surface. Spots with ashes were also observed in the lower horizon of the

Plate LX. Ust-Poluy. Flat spoons with simple straight handles.
Materials: 1 to 3, 9, 10–bone; 4 to 8, 11 to 13–reindeer antler.

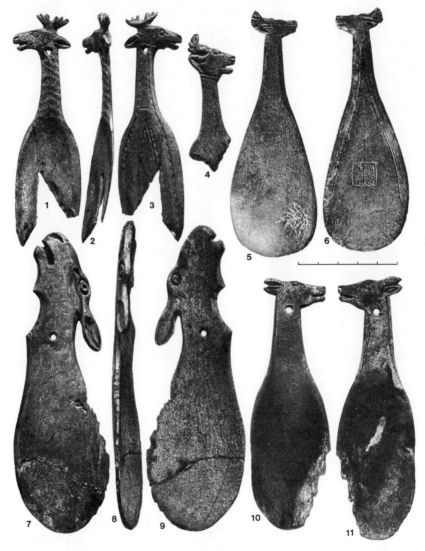

Plate LXI. Ust-Poluy. Flat spoons with handles decorated with carved representations of animal heads. Material: reindeer antler.

layer. The diameter of these spots in square 53 reached 18 cm with a thickness of 8 cm. In square 73, the charcoal spot was 45 cm in diameter and on bedrock. This sector also contained several accumulations of pieces of birch bark; in square 74 there was a large deposit of fish scales. Square 47 presented an interesting picture. About 20 cm below the present surface there was a large accumulation of animal bones. In a sector of just 0.7 m², fifteen dog skulls were collected; all the crania had been pierced. Two dog skulls with broken crania were discovered in square 48 at a depth of 30 cm from the present surface. In square 46, at approximately the same depth, a bone knife handle with the sculptured representation of a dog in harness (MAE 5331-1183) was found in addition to an antler punch decorated with the sculptured head of some animal. In squares 60 and 62,

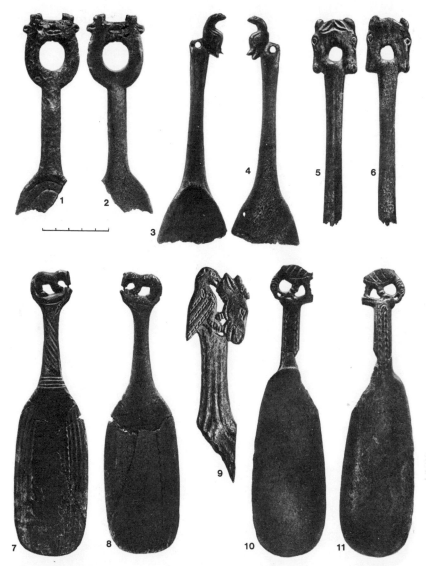

Plate LXII. Ust-Poluy. Flat spoons with handles decorated with carved representations of birds and animals. Material: reindeer antler.

human skeletal remains were found: a tibia, two clavicles, three ribs, and a lower jaw. In square 62, in addition, two back-scratchers were found, together with a flat spoon with a sculptured handle and the sculptured representation of an animal; not far away, in square 61, a comb was uncovered. Besides these, the following were found within the campfire area: slate models with anthropomorphic representations, an epaulet-shaped bronze clasp, a bone wrist guard, a belt hook, a needle case, several spoons with sculptured handles, a comb, and snow-shovel blade edges. One should also note the finds in square 72, outside the campfire area in Excavation V. Here a comb, the sculptured representation of an eagle, and two bronze anthropomorphic figurines were found.

In 1936, the expedition of the Museum of Physical Anthropology and Ethnography, under the direction of Adrianov, continued the excavations at Ust-Poluy, concentrating on two areas, Excavations IV and V. Excavation IV was extended eastward, and 14 additional 2 × 2 m squares were worked. Excavation V was extended in all directions, uncovering an area of 117 m². Northeastward the excavation was extended to the air terminal building, that is, to the place where the first finds were made in

Plate LXIII. Ust-Poluy.
    1 to 7–needle cases; 8, 9, 11 to 15–back-scratchers; 10–spoon; 16, 17–knives. Materials:
    1, 2–tubular bones of aquatic birds; 3 to 7–metapodium of Artiodactyla; 8, 9, 11 to 15–reindeer antler; 10–bird sternum; 16, 17–seal scapulae.

1932. The field documentation of the work of 1936 has not been preserved, except for the schematic diagram of the excavation squares, but this diagram shows the square numbers of Excavation IV only, and we do not know how the squares in Excavation V were numbered. Therefore, although we have a square-by-square description of the excavations of 1936, the distribution of finds can only be indicated in part of the plan. Nevertheless, we do get the idea that the composition of the finds in the squares of Excavation V differed little from that determined by the

Plate LXIV. Ust-Poluy. Scraperlike implements.
  1 to 4–T-shaped scrapers; 5 to 12–scraper-spatulas. Material: reindeer antler.

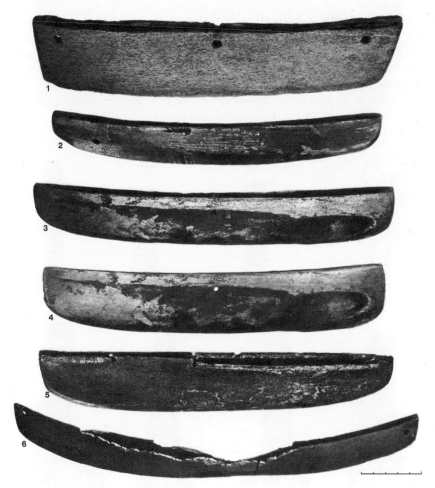

Plate LXV. Ust-Poluy. Snow-shovel blade edges. Materials: 1–whalebone; 2 to 6–mammoth ivory.

excavations of 1935. Let us note that a comb (square 92) was discovered in Excavation V in 1936, as one had been in 1935. Square 99 abounded in finds.* Bronze plates with engraving, slate molds of anthropomorphic representations, a bronze plate with the representation of two animals, a bronze arrowhead, five spoons, including sculptured ones with handles, a representation of a bird in flight carved from an antler, back-scratchers, ten knife handles, and many bone arrowheads were found in square 99. Excavation IV yielded a large number of finds, among which one should note harpoon parts (blade, socketed head, and socket pieces), snow-shovel blades, and an ice creeper. It should also be noted that several bronze plates and brooches, a slate model of a form for casting ornaments, and a bronze celt were found in this section.

A large number of bones was collected during the excavations. The

* [Squares 92 and 99 are not included in Fig. 26. It is assumed that these squares are extraneous to the site proper. Editor, A.I.N.A.]

Plate LXVI. Ust-Poluy. Pieces of armor plate.
  1–fragment of a wrist guard; 2 to 6, 8, 10 to 14–armor plates; 7, 9–helmet plates.
  Material: reindeer antler.

Plate LXVII. Ust-Poluy. Armor breastplates. Materials: 1—whalebone; 2—elk antler.

osteological material from Ust-Poluy is in the Zoological Institute of the Academy of Sciences of the U.S.S.R., where it has been analyzed by V. I. Gromova. According to her, the bones belonged to the following animals:

Canis familiaris   *Alces machlis*
Castor fiber   *Martes zibellina*
Lepus timidus   *Sciurus vulgaris*
Vulpes vulpes   *Rangifer tarandus*
Vulpes lagopus

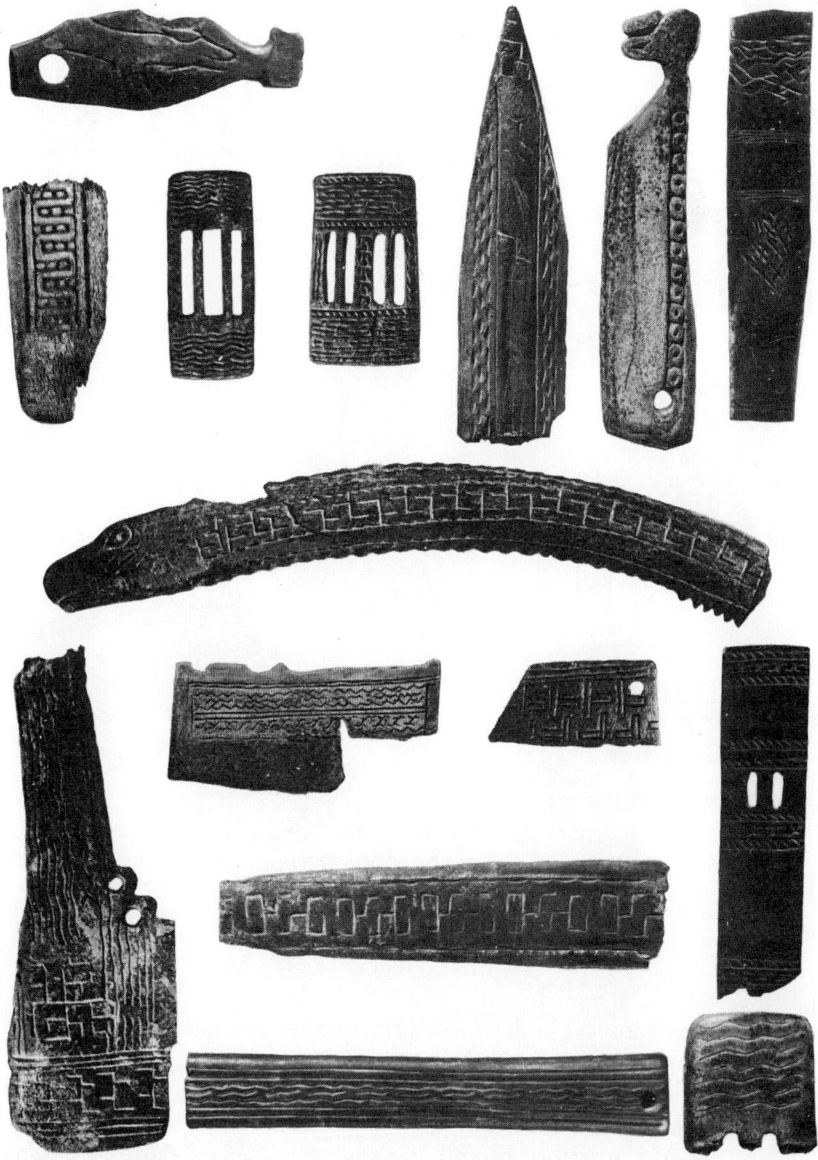

Plate LXVIII. Ust-Poluy. Ornamentation and graphic art. Material: reindeer antler.

Plate LXIX. Ust-Poluy. Figured casting and slate models.

1, 2, 6–partially worked blanks of anthropomorphic representations; 3 to 5–anthropomorphic representations; 7–cast of a fantastic creature; 8–cast of a bird sitting on a bear; 9, 10–partially worked blanks of zoomorphic representations; 11, 13, 14–birdlike representations; 12–partially worked blank of a birdlike representation; 15–signet ring; 16–partially worked blank of an umbonate badge. Materials: 1, 2, 6, 9, 10, 12, 16–clayey shale; 3 to 5, 7, 8, 11, 13 to 15–bronze.

The archaeological collections were turned over to the Museum of Physical Anthropology and Ethnography, where they are kept among the holdings of the Archaeology Section (Collection 5331, nos. 1–2512, and Collection 5455, nos. 1–4839).

We used the field books and the square-by-square descriptions to compile maps of the excavations, which show the individual finds as well as the quantities of materials. The quantitative plots for Ust-Poluy include pottery (6,372 potsherds), bone arrowheads (428), antler handles of iron knives (181), antler and bone scraper-spatulas (106), knives for cleaning fish (91), dog-harness swivels (93), spoons made from the sterna of birds (31), and flat antler and bone spoons with simple handles (31). Both the individual finds and the bulk material were distributed very irregularly over the excavated area. The distribution of the finds leads us to believe that the excavations at Ust-Poluy uncovered a number of complexes. In addition to the habitation layers (Excavation III), layers were discovered

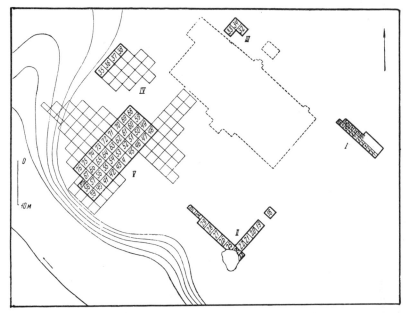

Fig. 26. Plan of excavations at Ust-Poluy. The excavations of 1935 are shown in heavy lines.

that were associated with a bronze-casting industry (Excavation II). I will not dwell on the latter, since this problem has been treated in sufficient detail in earlier research on Ust-Poluy.[28]

The picture presented by Excavation I was quite distinctive. Here, in addition to an accumulation of ashes and charcoal, were found a vessel on a hollow base, a bronze anthropomorphic representation, and an armor breastplate. Possibly this excavation revealed a burial, although this is highly hypothetical in view of the incomplete documentation. Excavation V had the most abundant finds, even if we consider only the area excavated in 1935. There was an enormous accumulation of various objects in some sections of this excavation. For example, square 62 yielded 273 different objects and 160 animal bones, square 63 yielded 208 objects and 184 animal bones, square 71 yielded 284 objects and 103 bones, and square 47 yielded 502 bones of animals and birds. Such accumulations in a small area, especially if we consider the finds of dog skulls and human bones, provide the basis for assuming that Excavation

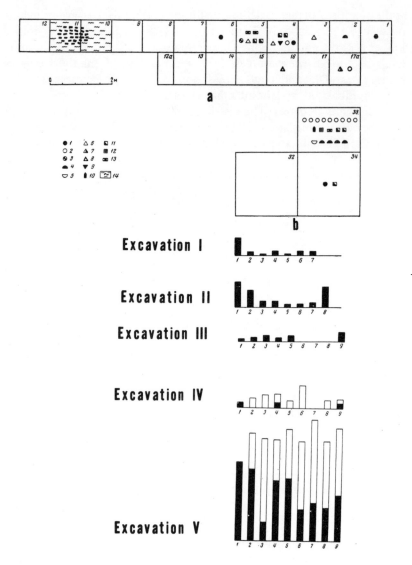

Fig. 27. Distribution of finds in Excavations I and III (a and b, respectively) and diagrams of the distribution of materials by quantity and by excavations at Ust-Poluy.

Explanation of symbols: 1–accumulation of pottery; 2–bone handles of iron knives; 3–armor breastplates; 4–bone knives for cleaning fish; 5–flat spoons with simple handles; 6–swivels; 7–bronze anthropomorphic representations; 8–stone pestles; 9–deep spoons with handles ornamented with round sculptures; 10–tweezers for plucking hair; 11–antler and bone scraper-spatulas; 12–dart heads; 13–iron knives; 14–ashes with charcoal.

In the bar graphs: 1–pottery; 2–bone arrowheads; 3–antler handles of iron knives; 4–antler and bone scraper-spatulas; 5–bone knives for cleaning fish; 6–swivels; 7–armor plates; 8–spoons made from bird sterna; 9–flat spoons with simple handles.

The total number of finds of a given category of objects at Ust-Poluy is shown as a [relative] percentage (the number of artifacts in the excavations of 1935 are shown in black, 1936 in white).

V disclosed a sacrificial site. This assumption is supported by the presence of the campfire area. The large number of finds of antler and bone artifacts, decorated with carving, the zoomorphic sculpture and figured bronze castings, and the concentration of very many objects in very small areas, including objects such as bronze brooches and arrowheads, slate figure models, bronze zoomorphic representations, those of birds made from antler, and a very large number of bone arrowheads, as in square 99, also support this assumption. To verify it, let us examine the ethnographic

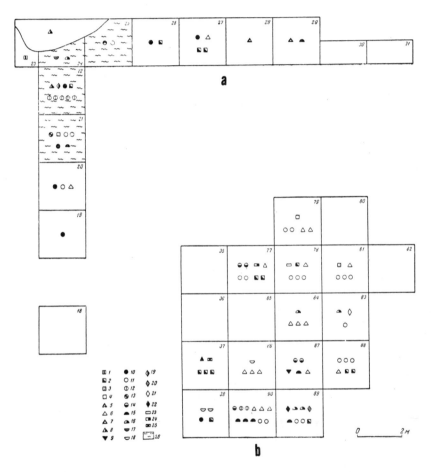

Fig. 28. Distribution of finds in Excavations II and IV (a and b, respectively) at Ust-Poluy.

Explanation of symbols: 1–bronze castings of birds; 2–antler and bone scraper-spatulas; 3–small bronze brooches; 4–snow-shovel blade edges; 5–ice creepers; 6–swivels; 7–stone pestles; 8–bronze anthropomorphic representations; 9–deep spoons with handles decorated with sculpture in the round; 10–accumulations of pottery; 11–antler handles of iron knives; 12–spoons made from bird sterna; 13–armor breastplates; 14–harpoon parts; 15–bone knives for cleaning fish; 16–copper casting molds for arrowheads; 17–sheet copper; 18–flat spoons with simple handles; 19–forehead bone piece of decoy reindeer harness; 20–bronze celts; 21–slate models; 22–combs; 23–flat spoons with sculptured handles; 24–bone belt buckles; 25–iron knives; 26–ashes.

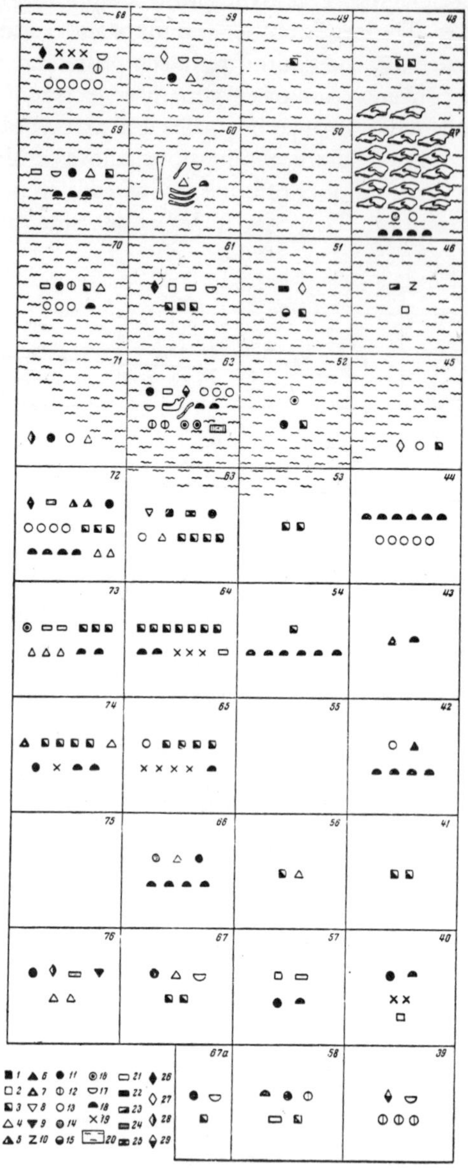

Fig. 29. Distribution of finds in Excavation V, Ust-Poluy.

Explanation of symbols: 1–wrist guard; 2–snow-shovel blade edges; 3–antler and bone scraper-spatulas; 4–swivels; 5–bronze anthropomorphic figurines; 6–ice creepers; 7–stone pestles; 8–belt hooks decorated with carved representations; 9–deep spoons with handles decorated with round sculpture; 10–punches with sculptured handles; 11–accumulations of pottery; 12–spoons made of bird sterna; 13–antler handles of iron knives; 14–needle cases; 15–harpoon parts; 16–back-scratchers; 17–flat spoons with simple handles; 18–bone knives for cleaning fish; 19–armor plates; 20–ashes; 21–flat spoons with sculptured handles; 22–epauletlike clasps; 23–sculptured knife handles; 24–sculptured representations of animals; 25–iron knives; 26–combs; 27–slate models; 28–forehead bone piece of decoy harness; 29–accumulations of bone arrowheads.

data pertaining to sacrificial and ritual places—their location, external appearance, nature of inventory, possible orientation, nature of offerings, and in part the concepts associated with them.

A. Kannisto's data indicate that sacrificial places may be subdivided into two types, *mãń kan* (small sites) and *janij kan* (large sites).[29] The former are situated in a village and serve a few inhabitants only. Kannisto is very vague about the location of the latter, that is, the ritual, sacrificial places proper. According to his data, such places are located either near settlements or far from them, on river banks, in forests, and in caves.[30] One can scarcely say that specific sites were chosen for sacrificial places, the more so since in the 18th and 19th centuries, there has been a tendency to move them to the most out-of-the-way places. At present, according to V. N. Chernetsov, they are often found on floodplain islands, in the upper reaches of taiga rivulets. Often ritual places are found in old fortified hill sites, usually medieval ones, with which are associated the traditions of some social group and which are regarded as places of ancient habitation.

One can get an idea of the physical appearance of a ritual site from the description of one of the Sampiltal family visited by Chernetsov in 1935. It was some distance from the mouth of the Lepla River on a ridge overgrown with fir and pine. Among the trees stood four small [storage] sheds (1 × 1.5 m) on pilings about 1.5 m high; near them were pilings that had belonged to earlier sheds at this site. In one of the four sheds were vessels used for the offerings, three trays, several wooden basins for meat, axes for cutting firewood, and a special axe for chopping off the heads of elks brought there by the hunters. Beneath this shed were inverted kettles. Another shed contained a small wooden anthropomorphic image with silver eyes (the son of *Lēp-tit-ɔjka*) dressed in a great number of robes and several sharp-pointed cloth hats. Next to him was *S'ak-ɔjka* (old-man hammer), the comrade-in-arms of *Lēp-tit-ɔjka*, represented by a 17th century battle mace. *S'ak-ɔjka* was also wrapped in shawls and clothing. In this shed there were arrows with iron tips and many robes worn during dances. *Lēp-tit-ɔjka* and his sword were not at the sacrificial site, for the keeper of the site had them in his own special shed in the village. *Lēp-tit-ɔjka* is an elk cast from lead with eyes encrusted with gold and an old silver coin inserted in his right side. Somewhat aside from the building in which the images were kept was a place for offerings, which consisted of a primitive narrow table and three felled trees placed behind it. Among the small sheds were several campfire sites. In addition to the sacred images, clothing, swords, and spears used during dances, there were implements of industry.

The above is in good agreement with the information on sacrificial places supplied by F. Belyavskiy, who wrote, "To the altars, in the middle of a hollow formed by three trees, the Ostyaks and Samoyeds take the best of the skins acquired in the hunt as a gift to the gods. They shoot the arrows which were most successful in the hunt into the trees; also, after a good catch of fish, they wrap the trees with their favorite net, whose deterioration bears witness to the service it has given."[31]

In such sacred places both bloodless and bloody offerings were made.

Among the Ob Ugrians the animal most commonly sacrificed was the reindeer.[32] Also they offered wild animals and birds taken in the hunt. There are many reports of this by various authors: "All the offerings to the idols are taken into the forest. The peoples form a circle around the idol, the priest, and the animals destined for sacrifice: reindeer, small game, and waterfowl."[33]

The absence of reindeer skulls at the Ust-Poluy sacrificial site can easily be explained if we consider the late appearance of reindeer breeding among the Ob Ugrians. A more significant difference from the above description is the presence of dog skulls and human bones. Kannisto's indication that dog and human sacrifices were made in the past among the Voguls is particularly interesting in this respect: he notes the equivalence of dogs, humans, and horses as sacrifices.[34] And Bogoslovskiy observed, "They hang the skin of the horse, as well as its skull, on a tree near the sacrificial site. They work the other skins and bury the bones of the sacrificed birds and animals."[35] While the bones were buried, the skulls of the sacrificial animals, as well as those killed in the hunt and taken to the sacrificial site, usually were hung on trees or, those lacking, on poles driven into the ground especially for the occasion. Probably the dog skulls were mounted in the same manner at the Ust-Poluy sacrificial site. One may merely assume that they were not simply hung on branches or poles, but were first placed in some kind of birch bark receptacle, in such a manner that they lay breast down on a very small area.

There is considerable evidence that the Voguls and the Ostyaks practiced human sacrifice. Besides historical documents that tell of human sacrifice, mention is made of it by authors who studied the population of the lower Ob.[36] Similar indications are given by Finsch, who got his information from "a shaman." According to this shaman, "formerly even human sacrifices were taken to Ya-y-mal." Finsch, although he gives this evidence, treats it as very dubious, proceeding chiefly from his own moral and ethical convictions.[37] However, Yu. I. Kushelevskiy does not doubt the authenticity of such stories. He cites a quite detailed account of such a sacrifice.[38] In 1938, Chernetsov, while among the Mansi, recorded a story about the former custom of human sacrifice among the Voguls. He began his story as follows: "On the Konda, the Konda hero was worshiped as a *pupij* [ancestral guardian]. Every seven years, or three times seven years, they would buy a human being. Each time they took a youth for sacrifice. Whether it was from the Lozva, or the Sosva, wherever they could get one, they took him." Further, he tells how a young man was acquired and kept in the village. In this village there was a large dwelling that housed many people. In winter, after the fall's work had been done, they would bring a large anthropomorphic image, the size of a man, into that house. He said further that they would kill a man before that image, after which they would cut him up and cook him in a kettle. Then they would spread the contents of the kettle in a metal basin which they would place on a table before the central figure. After the ceremony was over, they would carry that basin into the forest and throw the contents of the bowl into a large container made of logs.[39]

Now we shall examine briefly the social groups and phenomena with which these sacrifices can be associated. The clan sacrifices before and after the hunt were the most widely celebrated rite.

Larger, regular festivals dedicated to an ancestor were also held, as were periodic tribal festivals. These latter, to all appearances, were the most expressly military in nature. Such festivals consisted of sacrifices to the ancestors of the participating clans, dances in which the ancestors were depicted, and finally war dances, in which all participated. Such festivals were held on fixed dates by tribes of the lower Ob. A festival of this type was described by Castrén as follows: "The most solemn of these festivals is held in the fall, when the nomadic Ostyaks with their spoils of the hunt move from the tundra to their fishermen-bretheren on the Ob. This fall festival is held in specified years by the different clans; however, the festival is not restricted to the members of these clans. The Ostyaks gather for the festival with all their clans and bring with them their idols to greet the gods of their neighbors and to accept their hospitality. All 'outsider' idols are placed in a special yurt, where the clan keeps its own idols; however, clans which do not have a special [permanent] yurt for the idols construct a spacious hut for the occasion."[40] Next, Castrén describes the war dances performed at these festivals and the sacrificing of reindeer, whose blood is used to smear the lips and face of the images of their ancestors.[41] According to Castrén, as well as to Finsch and Brehm,[42] similar rites were performed in sanctuaries of this type for other, extraordinary reasons. Castrén writes, "Such sacrificial rites are carried out in many other circumstances as well: at the beginning of some undertaking, before an imminent long journey or nomadic foraging expedition, et al."[43] We find such information in Finsch and Brehm as well.[44] In this connection we should also recall the story cited by Kushelevskiy concerning a human sacrifice at the conclusion of peace between the Ostyaks and the Samoyeds: "From among them they chose a Samoyed by lot, killed him, cooked him, and ate him. Afterwards they cut off the top of a larch and on the cut-off place set the trough from which they had eaten the human flesh. This rite was a faithful warranty of eternal agreement between them, and the larch still stands, not far from the Pashertsevye yurts and the village of Obdorsk."[45]

The abundance and variety of finds at the Ust-Poluy sacrificial site leave doubt that it belonged to just one clan. The remains of a human sacrifice also give us cause to believe that we are dealing here with one of the larger centers. We may assume that the fortified hill site Ust-Poluy was a refuge used by the population of the nearby unfortified settlements. The remains of such settlements have been found both at a distance and in the immediate vicinity of Ust-Poluy, on the banks of the Poluy River, for example, at Salekhard. It is natural that such a site should have a sacred place belonging to a social organization larger than the clan, namely to the population of the territory. Thus, there is reason to assume that there was some sort of tribal center at Ust-Poluy, at which rites were celebrated in connection with certain periodic festivals and extraordinary events involving the entire tribes, such as preparation for military action, the end of a war, the conclusion of peace, and the like. Such tribal centers, in which periodic festivals were held, are known for the lower Ob and have been described by many investigators. For example, there are indications that such tribal centers existed quite recently in Labytnangi and Aksarka.[46]

SALE-KHARD [Salekhard] (Tyumen *oblast*, Yamal-Nenets [National] *okrug*). A settlement on the right, high bank of the Poluy River on Obdorsk Hill, Salekhard is at the southeastern extremity of the large cape on which the city of Salekhard is situated.[47] On the hill, whose maximum height is 15 m, there is a culture-yielding layer containing abundant archaeological remains of various periods. The first news of archaeological finds at Salekhard came in 1926, when D. N. Redrikov made a large collection of pottery assignable to various periods. This collection contains many fragments of cauldronlike vessels on hollow pedestals. The collection and the account accompanying it are preserved in the Archaeology Section of the Museum of Physical Anthropology and Ethnography [in Leningrad] (Collection 3632).

In 1946 the Mangazeya expedition of the Arctic Institute for Scientific Research under the direction of V. N. Chernetsov made excavations on Obdorsk Hill at Salekhard. They uncovered a dwelling belonging to the Ust-Poluy culture. The material has been completely published.[48] The collection is preserved at the Archaeological Institute of the Academy of Sciences of the U.S.S.R. [in Moscow].

KATRA-VOZH (Tyumen *oblast*, Yamal-Nenets [National] *okrug*). Katra-Vozh is a settlement on the left bank of the Ob at the mouth of the Sob River, 50 km from Salekhard.[49] It was investigated in 1936 by the expedition of the Museum of Physical Anthropology and Ethnography under the direction of V. S. Adrianov. The expedition made some small excavations which established the presence of a culture-yielding layer. The exploratory excavation, which was divided into 10 squares of 2 × 2 m, uncovered a layer which yielded bone arrowheads, the bone handle of an iron knife, a bone wedge, dog-harness swivels, two antler combs, an armor plate, cast bronze birdlike images with a mask on the breast, bronze ingots, and an iron knife. Three hundred and forty-four potsherds were taken from the excavation. Adrianov maintained that the excavation partially uncovered an underground dwelling. In addition, several pits were dug and some materials were collected: a stone pestle, a blue glass bead, a bronze celt, a bone knife handle, bones, and pottery. The collection is in the Museum of Physical Anthropology and Ethnography (Collection 5455, nos. 4856–4999; see Plate LXX).

PEL-VOZH (Tyumen *oblast*, Yamal-Nenets [National] *okrug*). This site was investigated in 1936 by the expedition of the Museum of Physical Anthropology and Ethnography headed by V. S. Adrianov. Surface material was collected: pottery (198 sherds), a black glass bead with a white pattern, a bone armor plate, and pieces of slag. The collection is in the Museum of Physical Anthropology and Ethnography (Collection 5455, nos. 4843–55).

Plate LXX. Katra-Vozh.
    1–plano-convex blade; 2–two-part swivel plate for dog harness; 3–hafted tip of a bird arrowhead; 4–celt; 5–two-part swivel plate; 6–birdlike representation; 7–knife handle; 8, 9–combs; 10–flat spoon. Materials: 1 to 3, 5, 7 to 10–reindeer antler; 4, 6–bronze.

ZELENAYA GORKA (Tyumen *oblast*, Yamal-Nenets [National] *okrug*). This site may be the remains of a burial. An intact vessel on a [hollow] pedestal, of the Ust-Poluy type, was found in the culture-yielding layer of this Early Iron Age campsite. A bronze three-bladed [tri-fluted] arrowhead was found not far from it, but in a sector disturbed by the construction of a 10th or 11th century dwelling.[50] The collection is preserved at the State Historical Museum.

VOZH-PAY (Tyumen *oblast*, Yamal-Nenets [National] *okrug*). A settlement on a cape on the right bank of the Ob, Vozh-Pay is between the villages of Evi-Vozh and Seugort-Soym in the Kushevat *rayon*.[51] This site was investigated in 1927 by D. N. Redrikov. He gathered the archaeological material chiefly at the foot of a ravine in a secondary deposit. According to Redrikov, who investigated the summit of the hill, the settlement located there was multilayered. Below the turf was a 30 to 60 cm thick culture-yielding layer, separated by a sterile stratum from a lower culture-yielding layer which was up to 1 m thick. A considerable portion of the pottery collected by Redrikov at Vozh-Pay consisted of vessels on [hollow] pedestals similar to those found at Ust-Poluy. A collection of Redrikov's finds is preserved in the archaeology section of the museum of Physical Anthropology and Ethnography (Collection 3632), where his account of the work conducted in the Kushevat *rayon* of Obdorsk *kray* is also kept.

SOROVOY MYS (Tyumen *oblast*, Khanty-Mansi [National] *okrug*). This site is situated on a cape, on the left bank of the Severnaya Sosva, a short distance to the south of the city of Berezov. There was an undisturbed cultural layer up to 1 m thick in the upper part of the escarpment of the cape, which is washed by the Sorovaya River. Part of the material was found as a secondary deposit on the broad beach that circles the cape.[52] The site was investigated at different times by S. G. Boch, A. F. Pala-shenkov, and V. N. Chernetsov. Boch and Palashenkov collected surface material. The pottery collection made by Boch is stored in the Museum of Physical Anthropology at Moscow University; Palashenkov's finds (pottery and the cast bronze representation of a bird of prey with extended wings) are in the Omsk Regional Museum.

SORTYNYA II (Tyumen *oblast*, Khanty-Mansi [National] *okrug*). This is a fortified hill site at the mouth of the Sortynya River, a left tributary of the Severnaya Sosva, 2 km upstream from the village of Sortynya and 0.5 km farther upstream from the fortified hill site Sortynya I. It was studied in 1937 by S. G. Boch and V. N. Chernetsov (at different times).[53] Chernetsov amassed a large collection, a considerable part of which consists of pottery and crucible fragments, as well as many animal bones. The collections made by Chernetsov are preserved in the Museum of Physical Anthropology and Ethnography (Collection 6074, nos. 7–24; Collection 4456, nos. 33–78).

MAKAR-VISYNG-TUR (Tyumen *oblast*, Khanty-Mansi [National] *okrug*). A settlement situated on the second terrace of the left bank of the Lyapin River, 0.5 km from the river, this site is on the shore of the floodplain lake Makar-Visyng-Tur, which is 3–4 km from the village of Saranpaul.[54] The culture-yielding layer was located along the high shore of the floodplain lake. Easily discernible large dark spots, within which large accumulations of pottery were found, had been revealed by shallow ploughing. Perhaps these spots were traces of surface or shallow pit houses. This site was investigated in 1935 by V. N. Chernetsov. Surface material was collected: a large amount of pottery, fishing sinkers, slag, flint scrapers, and chips. The collection is among the holdings of the archaeology section of the Museum of Physical Anthropology and Ethnography (Collection 6074, nos. 25–49). In 1937 the settlement was studied by A. F. Palashenkov. The surface material he collected is in the Omsk Museum.

CHES-TYY-YAG II (Tyumen *oblast*, Khanty-Mansi [National] *okrug*). Ches-tyy-yag II is a site on the left bank of the Lyapin River near the village of Saranpaul, 50–100 m north of the Neolithic campsite Ches-tyy-yag; a culture-yielding layer was discovered on the shore of this flood-plain island. The layer was traced along the shore for 50 m and almost that far in from the shore. The cultural remains lay at a depth of 30–40 cm from the present surface. In 1948, L. G. Dolgushin, a fellow of the Geographic Institute of the Academy of Sciences of the U.S.S.R., collected surface material here. The collection, consisting of pottery, is in the Archaeological Institute of the Academy of Sciences of the U.S.S.R.

NYAKSIMVOL (Tyumen *oblast*, Khanty-Mansi [National] *okrug*), Plate LXXI. A fortified hill site on the left bank of the upper Severnaya Sosva, near the village of Nyaksimvol. The site, surrounded by a ditch and a bank, is situated on a cape formed by the Severnaya Sosva and a swamp in a former bed of the Neys River.[55]

In 1930, A. K. Trapeznikov, a student of local lore, collected surface material at the Nyaksimvol site. The collection, which contains pottery, bronze plates, a bronze ring, bone artifacts, and a fragment of the handle of a copper vessel, was given to the Sverdlovsk Regional Museum (inventory no. 1027). A second collection made at Nyaksimvol, by F. S. Rogalev, was given to that museum in late 1932 or early 1933 (inventory no. 1138). It consists of pottery, eleven metal plates, iron knives, bronze arrowheads, and numerous bone and antler artifacts, including armor plates, spatulas, et cetera. In 1932 the site was investigated by V. N. Chernetsov, who discovered that the culture-yielding layer which contained fragments of vessels on [hollow] pedestals lay immediately below the turf. He made a collection of pottery that is now in the Museum of Physical Anthropology and Ethnography (Collection 4456, nos. 1–8). In 1936 the leader of the Severnaya Sosva Geological Prospecting Group presented the Sverdlovsk Regional Museum with yet another collection of archaeological objects gathered at the Nyaksimvol fortified hill site (inventory no. 1821). It includes pottery, bronze artifacts, bone and stone objects, and a metal anthropomorphic representation.

Among the upper Sosva Mansi there are legends associated with *N'ajš'am wōl ŭs*, "city at the mouth of the Neys River," that is, with the Nyaksimvol fortified hill site. These legends tell of a woman ancestor and of the unsuccessful matchmaking overtures toward her by an ancestor of the Sampiltal clan, *Lēp-tit-ōjka*. The Nyaksimvol site we have described is situated at the mouth of a former bed of the Neys River. There are

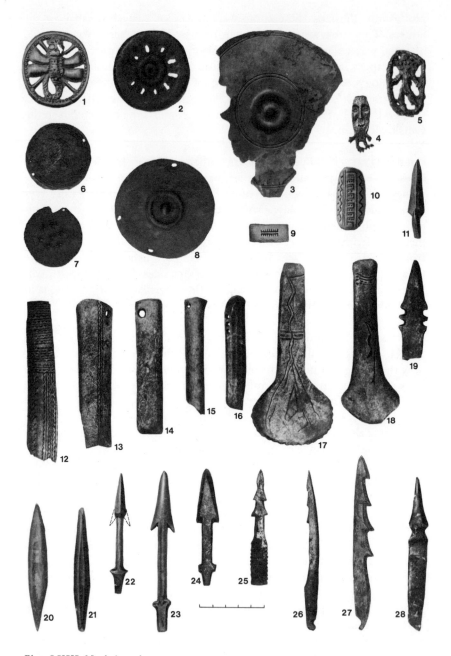

Plate LXXI. Nyaksimvol.

1–openwork, cast brooch; 2–cast brooch with slits; 3, 6 to 8–cast brooches; 4–anthropomorphic castings; 5–cast of a fantastic creature; 9–cast ornamental plate with serration; 10–signet ring; 11–arrowhead; 12–blade with incised ornamentation; 13 to 16–knife handles; 17, 18–scraper-spatula; 19–sharp-pointed, flat blade; 20, 21–arrowheads; 22, 24–harpoon head points; 23–harpoon head; 25 to 27–fish-spear barbs; 28–plano-convex blade. Materials: 1 to 11–bronze; 12 to 19, 22 to 28–reindeer antler; 20, 21–fragments of tubular bones.

fortified hill sites at the mouth of the present stream as well. This fact, and the fact that the legends are usually associated with later, generally medieval sites, leaves it uncertain that they refer to the Nyaksimvol site described above. However, the composition of the finds there does not exclude the possibility that a large sacrificial place once existed, the one with which the legends of the Mansi are associated.

NIZYAMY II, fortified hill site (Tyumen *oblast*, Khanty-Mansi [National] *okrug*). This disturbed site is on the right bank of the Ob, near the Nizyam-skiye *yurts*, on a small cape at the mouth of the Nisan-Iogan River. The fortified site was disturbed by later building and by modern installations. In a cut of the river bank a clearly defined culture-yielding layer was evident. It contained fragments of vessels on [hollow] pedestals, of the Ust-Poluy type. This site was studied by the expedition of the Archaeo-logical Institute of the Academy of Sciences of the U.S.S.R. under the direction of V. N. Chernetsov.[56]

RUS-KHAR-SOYM (Tyumen *oblast*, Khanty-Mansi [National] *okrug*). A culture-yielding layer containing fragments of the Ust-Poluy type of vessel on [hollow] pedestals was discovered on the right bank of the Ob, upstream from the Nizyamskiye *yurts*, at the mouth of the rivulet Rus-Khar-Soym.[57]

Chapter 2

Description of Objects
of Material Culture

The finds at Ust-Poluy were the most numerous ones. In fact, practically all categories and types of artifacts known for the Ust-Poluy culture have been found there. Because of this, we have constructed the classification tables for objects from Ust-Poluy, and the data pertaining to finds at other sites are contained in the descriptions; the objects themselves are depicted in the plates illustrating complexes of finds by sites. When some category of finds is lacking at Ust-Poluy, or is poorly represented, the category is described with references to the appropriate tables where the materials from other sites are depicted.

IMPLEMENTS USED IN HUNTING AND FISHING

LAND-HUNTING IMPLEMENTS
(PLATES LV AND LVI)

Bone and antler arrowheads. These may be divided into a number of subgroups:

1. Hafted, of elongated-oval shape, subtriangular in cross section. They are made from fragments of the tubular bones of large animals, most often from the shinbones of the reindeer. They vary in size from 5.3 to 14.3 cm, the most common size being 10–12 cm.

2. Hafted, of elongated-oval shape and of rhombic and plano-rhombic cross section. They are made of reindeer antler, in the same sizes as those of the preceding group.

3. Hafted, of elongated-oval shape, triangular in cross section. They are made of reindeer antler, in sizes of 10 to 12 cm.

4. Hafted, with an elongated shank of round or rectangular cross section. They are made of reindeer antler and vary in size from 6 to 15 cm. Large specimens are rare.

5. Socketed heads with both open and closed sockets. They vary in size from 8.8 to 13.7 cm and are made of reindeer antler.

6. Blunt arrowheads with a round or faceted head. They occur both as socketed and hafted and are of different materials, often reindeer antler.

7. Multipronged (most often five-pronged) arrowheads, both hafted and socketed. They are of various materials, mostly reindeer antler.

8. Clawlike heads with an inserted transverse barb. The barb on the

surviving specimens is semilunar. These heads are made primarily of reindeer antler. One bronze arrowhead of this type was found at Ust-Poluy.

9. Harpoon points of reindeer antler. The tips are plano-rhombic in cross section, with two symmetrical barbs. Lengths are from 5.5 to 8 cm.

The following are represented by single specimens:

10. Trihedral point with open socket. They are made of reindeer antler or walrus tusk, in sizes of 7 to 8 cm.

11. Bullet-shaped arrowheads of reindeer antler.

12. Arrowhead of reindeer antler, elongated-triangular in shape, with a notch in the base.

The arrowheads which we have consolidated into groups 1, 2, 3, and 4 are well known from Ananino sites and also from more westerly sites belonging to the Dyakovo culture.[58] In general, it should be noted that these forms are very primitive and widely distributed. Blunt heads, the so-called bird arrowheads, are well known for the forest and circumpolar zone of Eurasia and North America, in the archaeological sites from Scandinavia to Alaska, and in the ethnographic materials of Siberia, thus including an enormous territory and a very long time span.[59]

DISTRIBUTION OF BONE ARROWHEADS BY SITES

Group	Ust-Poluy	Katra-Vozh	Nyaksimvol	Salekhard
1	272	5	54	
2	51	1	3	
3	19	1		
4	14		1	1
5				
6	22			
7	8	1		
8	10			
9	14			

Pointed small blades. These are of reindeer antler, quite abundant in the Ust-Poluy sites, perhaps associated with bows. They may be subdivided into two basic groups:

1. Pointed, plano-convex, having a groove in the upper, sharpened end on the flat side and a ridge on the convex side. In many specimens the upper end with the convex side is polished. In a number of cases there are traces of polishing on the inner surface as well, along the edge, in the place where the groove appears. When two such blades are put together, an opening is formed in the upper end. This opening could have been used for securing the bowstring. Evidently such blades encircled the wood [at the end] of the bow. On the outer, convex side often there is an incised or scratched-on ornament or owner's mark. These artifacts are made of reindeer antler.

2. Flat, pointed small blades with a flattened wedge base. They may be subdivided into several groups based on the manner in which the

distal end was prepared: with two notches at the point; with two notches and a perforation at the point; without notches but with a perforation at the point; without notches, but with two perforations. All are of reindeer antler.

One may find an analogy to the small blades of the second group in materials from Ananino sites. In particular, those without perforations were found at the Konetsgorskoye village site. They were identified by A. V. Zbruyeva as basting needles [*kochedyk*, in the original].[60] No close parallels to the plano-convex blades of the first group are known. The blades from the Sargatskoye burial mounds of Omsk *oblast* are remote analogues. Data on the distribution of blades of the first and second groups by sites of the Ust-Poluy culture are shown in Fig. 44.

PARTS OF BRIDLES USED WITH REINDEER DECOYS

These curved small plates of reindeer antler have sharp, clearly convex barbs on the outer side. The degree of curvature of the plates varies from slightly curved ones to those forming nearly right angles. They have four to eight barbs. They have been found only at Ust-Poluy, where just four specimens have been discovered. Apparently they have no analogues in archaeological materials. The closest ethnographic equivalents are the front (forehead) bridle pieces of the Chukchi reindeer bridle, but these are considerably larger and more bulky.[61]

FISHING EQUIPMENT
(PLATE LVI, ITEM 5; PLATE LXXI, ITEMS 25–27)

The very small number of finds of fishing implements at the investigated sites and the very large heaps of fish scales found at Ust-Poluy and Salekhard lead one to assume that mainly weir fishing was practiced. Only fish-spear prongs have been found. These are made of reindeer antler. Both main and side prongs have been found. Only two specimens of main prongs have been found, one with two barbs, the other with four and a unique, serrated haft. There are two modifications of side prongs of fish spears; those with one barb, and those with several barbs. They vary considerably in size, from 7.8 to 17 cm, the spears with more than one barb being larger than those with one.

DISTRIBUTION OF FINDS OF FISH-SPEAR PRONGS BY SITES

Group	Ust-Poluy	Nyaksimvol	Salekhard
Single-barbed	3	1	1
Multibarbed		6	

HUNTING EQUIPMENT
(PLATE LVII)

Harpoon heads. Only hafted ones have been found. The available specimens can be divided into the following categories according to number and position of the barbs:

1. Harpoon heads with two symmetrical barbs; they vary in size from 11.5 to 19 cm.
2. Harpoon heads with one barb; size, 11–12 cm.
3. Harpoon heads with one barb and a side blade; size, 15.5 cm.
4. Harpoon heads with two asymmetrical barbs; size, 13.2 cm.
5. Needle-shaped harpoon head; size, 10.5 cm.

All these harpoon heads are made of reindeer antler. Those in the first and second groups could have been employed in seal hunting; however, their possible sphere of application is very broad and need not have been limited to the hunting of sea animals.[62]

DISTRIBUTION OF HARPOON HEADS BY SITES

Type	Ust-Poluy	Nyaksimvol
1	3	2
2	1	2
3	1	
4	1	
5	1	

Sockets and joint rings. These secured the head to the shaft. There are flat and oval ones as well as elongated specimens, one fitting into the other. All are of reindeer antler. All come from Ust-Poluy.

Socket pieces. Always of reindeer antler, the socket pieces are of various sizes.

Ice creepers. Four specimens are known, three intact and one fragment. All are from Ust-Poluy: MAE-5331, no. 892, square 37, bone, with five pairs of symmetrical ridges [cleats], 11.6 cm long; MAE-5455, no. 1177, square 98, reindeer antler, three pairs of symmetrical ridges, length 7.1 cm; MAE-5455, no. 1413, square 100, bone, two pairs of symmetrical ridges, length 6.6 cm. The ethnographic Chukchi ice creepers, although they are reminiscent of the Ust-Poluy in shape, differ considerably from them in size. The creeper with five pairs of symmetrical ridges from the Abverdjar campsite, assignable to the Dorset culture,[63] is much closer to the Ust-Poluy one.

MEANS OF TRANSPORTATION
(Plate LVIII)

The greater part of the finds represent various parts of the dog harness.

Swivels. The most common form is the two-part swivel consisting of a plate with perforations and a shank passed through the central perforation. The upper end of the shank has a head, the lower end has perforations—most often two, sometimes one or three. The shaft length varies from 3.7 to 9.5 cm; the diameter varies within very wide limits, but most often it is 0.7–1.2 cm. All known specimens are of reindeer antler. The plates may be subdivided into groups according to shape:

1. Rectangular, quite rarely square, with five perforations, one in the middle and one in each of the corners. They vary in size from 4 × 3 to 8 × 7.5 cm. The square ones are small, 3.8 × 3.8 cm. The plates are 0.4–0.8 cm thick.

2. Round, also with five perforations; diameter 5.1 cm.

3. Trapezoidal and irregular rectangular, with four perforations— one in the middle, two in the corners, and one in the middle of the small end of the plate.

4. Oval, with one perforation in the middle; diameter 5.2 cm.

5. Oval, with three perforations; size 4.6 × 3.1 cm, thickness 1.7 cm.

All the plates are of reindeer antler. (For the distribution of this type of swivel, see Fig. 44.)

A few isolated swivel specimens were also found at Ust-Poluy: two are tubular, of reindeer antler, one of them being decorated with an incision forming a wavy pattern; another consists of a shank passed through a socket and is also of reindeer antler.

Buckles. These are fasteners of stick form with perforations in the middle—most often two, less often one. As far as we can judge by the ethnographic materials, such fasteners could have been used to secure individual harness parts, to attach the reins, et cetera. They are made of reindeer antler. Our finds contain buckles of various sizes. Along with the large specimens, 14–16 cm long, there are medium-sized ones, 8–10 cm long, and even very small ones, about 5 cm long.

Such buckle fasteners are widely known in both the archaeological and the ethnographic materials of Siberia.

Two-part swivels of the plate type are encountered in Eskimo archaeology,[64] but the best analogues are to be found in the ethnographic material. Swivels consisting of rectangular plates with five perforations and a shank are known for the dog harness of the Caribou Eskimos, who use them to fasten the traces to the main rein during stops.[65]

UTENSILS

Vessels. Many potsherds were found at Ust-Poluy. They belong to large vessels of the cauldron type, usually on a high, hollow, conical pedestal. Some had horizontally positioned handles. Only the upper part of the vessel was ornamented.[66]

Owing to the lack of field notes for the year 1936, we cannot present a full picture of the distribution of pottery by excavation area, the total number of sherds per area, et cetera. However, what we do know from the field notes of 1935 furnishes us with adequate material for analyses. These notes indicate that during the field season of 1935, during the excavations at Ust-Poluy, 6,613 potsherds were collected. Unfortunately, V. S. Adrianov did not deliver all the pottery discovered in the excavations to the museum, although he did note the number of sherds taken and the number left in each excavation square. For example, we know that of the potsherds found during the 1935 expedition, 1,845 were left on the spot, and in Excavation V, which contained more than 60 percent of all the pottery found in that year's work, 1,161 of the 4,051 sherds were not removed. Furthermore, Adrianov left most of the sherds in the squares with the greatest amount of pottery. For example, in square 62, where 419 sherds were found, 245 were left on the spot and only 174 were removed; the museum collection has just 162. The fact that the material was only partially collected, especially where there were large accumulations, lent a highly fragmentary character to the pottery collection, and probably this is the reason why only three vessels were reconstructed from the extensive Ust-Poluy material. This negligible number of whole vessels, coupled with the fact that the potsherds in the collection are usually small, dissociated, and not susceptible to forming a complete picture of the details of shape, led us to categorize the Ust-Poluy pottery chiefly on the basis of the ornamentation.

In the pottery collections from Ust-Poluy (from the excavations of 1935 and 1936), 3,280 ornamented sherds were analyzed. They were classified into three groups according to type of ornamentation: those decorated with impressions of a comb or linear stamp or a combination of such impressions with corded or pitted ornamentation, and also corded or pitted decorations above or a combination of the two (Fig. 30, B); those decorated with impressions of a figured stamp or combinations of impressions of a figured stamp and a cord or a comb (Fig. 30, A); those decorated with cannelures, impressions of fine-toothed combs, and small pits (Fig. 30, C).

The potsherds combined in B belong to quite large vessels, with mouth diameters of 20 to 30 cm; even larger vessels are known, with diameters as large as 48 cm. The ornament was applied in horizontal ribbons around the neck and never was applied lower than the rounding of the body of the vessel. The surface was sometimes smoothed, but never burnished. The paste contained grass and crushed micaceous slate.

The potsherds combined in A are distinguished only by their ornamentation.

The potsherds combined in C differ sharply from those described above. They belong to considerably smaller cuplike vessels with a rim diameter of 14–15 cm. The working of the surface differs greatly among the pieces, but they were always carefully smoothed or burnished.

The count showed that most of the sherds belonged to Group II (B)— more than 80 percent of all the pottery; Group III (A) comprised 15 percent, and Group I (C) only 4 percent.

The pottery from the other sites was processed similarly. We have summarized the results in the diagram showing the percentage relationships of the three groups for each of the sites. We consider the following results to be particularly significant:

All three of our pottery groups were found at points farthest apart, Ust-Poluy and Nyaksimvol. This gives us a sound basis for assuming that these groups were not local features.

Some sites have only two groups of pottery, and what is even more interesting, one of the sites (Makar-Visyng-Tur) has only one. This

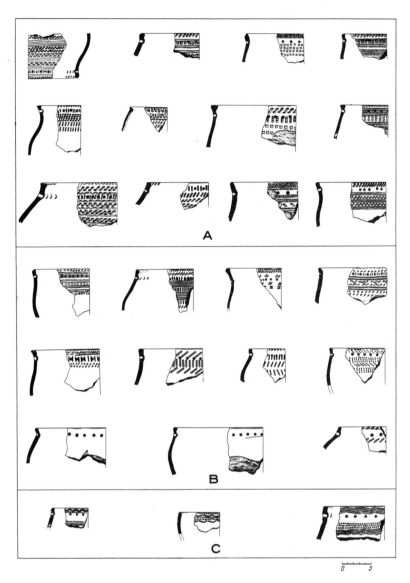

Fig. 30. Pottery from Ust-Poluy.
A–Group III; B–Group II; C–Group I.

strongly suggests that the groups are chronological. If this be true, the pottery may give us a basis for estimating the chronology of the sites.

Bone and antler spoons. These are subdivided into two basic groups: those with a deep scoop and those that are flat. The first group (Plate LIX) may be divided into several subgroups on the basis of the shape of the handle.

1. Deep spoons with a curved handle:

MAE 5331-2463, Ust-Poluy, from square 76. Made of mammoth tusk. The handle terminates in the sculptured representation of the head of a wild goose. At the upper end of the handle, immediately below the sculpture, there is a perforation. The handle is oval in cross section (Plate LIX, items 1, 2).

MAE 5455-1292, Ust-Poluy, from square 99. Made of mammoth tusk. The handle ends in the head of an aquatic bird (perhaps a goose). The handle is round in cross section (Plate LIX, item 4).

MAE 5455-802, Ust-Poluy, from square 99. Fragment of a curved handle decorated with the sculptured representation of an eagle. The handle is round in cross section; the material is mammoth tusk (Plate LIX, item 3).

Wooden ladles and spoons with handles shaped as sculptured bird heads are direct counterparts of these few spoons. Wooden ladles of this type were found in the Gorbunovo peat bog in the Urals and in the bog campsites of the Baltic coastal area and Finland.[67] The similarity is apparent not only in the specific details of shape and the subject matter, but in the very style of the represented bird, which is extremely laconic and meager in graphic techniques, but highly realistic as a whole. The specimens described above may serve as examples.

MAE 5331, Ust-Poluy, no square number. A spoon of walrus tusk with a high curved handle ending in the sculptured representation of a walrus head. On the arc of the handle, immediately below the sculpture, is a perforation. The handle is round in cross section and highly polished (Plate LIX, item 6).

MAE 5455-4176, Ust-Poluy, from square 87. A bone spoon with a curved handle ending in the sculptured head of an animal (Plate LIX, item 7).

MAE 5455-1293, Ust-Poluy, from square 99. A spoon of reindeer antler. In the upper end of the curved handle there are two perforations separated by a wide groove.

MAE 5455-4828, Ust-Poluy, surface collection. A spoon of reindeer antler with a curved handle and a perforation in the upper end of the handle. The handle is plano-oval in cross section.

2. Deep spoons with straight handles. Very rare. The few samples found include:

MAE 5331, Ust-Poluy, no square number. A spoon of reindeer antler with a slight hollow and a very short handle shaped into the sculptured head of some sort of animal with an open mouth and protruding tongue. There is a perforation at the base of the handle (Plate LIX, item 11).

MAE 5331-82, Ust-Poluy, from square 4. A spoon of reindeer antler with a very short handle shaped into a sculptured group depicting a duck sitting on the head of some animal, perhaps a hare (Plate LIX, item 5).

SM* inventory no. 1138, Nyaksimvol. Fragment of a spoon of reindeer antler with a very short handle formed into the sculptured representation of an animal (bear?) at rest.

MAE 5455-903, Ust-Poluy, from square 96. Spoon of reindeer antler with a slight hollow and a short straight handle ending in the sculptured representation of the head of an animal with large ears (Plate LIX, item 11). Its closest parallel is a spoon from eastern Finland pictured by Ailio

* [SM, Sverdlovsk Regional Museum. Translator, A.I.N.A.]

(Fig. 31). The Ust-Poluy and Finnish spoons are similar not only in shape but also in the style of the animal representation, although admittedly the animal on the spoon from Finland is depicted even more laconically and in a more generalized way than the one from Ust-Poluy. Ailio opined that the Finnish spoon belongs to the Neolithic and may be associated with an ancient sacrificial site.[68]

3. Deep spoons made from the sterna of waterfowl, often with a perforation in one end, probably for suspension. All known specimens are from Ust-Poluy (Plate LXIII, item 10).

The flat spoons may be divided into two main groups: those with a simple handle and those with incised or sculptured handles.

The first subgroup, in turn, may be separated into two modified types:

a. Flat spoon-spatulas with a straight handle having a perforation in the upper end (Plate LX). They are 8–16 cm long, with a bowl thickness of 0.1–0.3 cm, and were fabricated from various materials (bone, reindeer antler). They have been found at Ust-Poluy and Katra-Vozh.

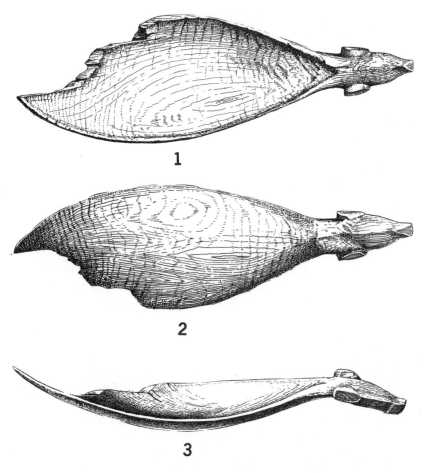

Fig. 31. Wooden spoon with zoomorphic handle, from Finland (after Ailio).
1–front; 2–back; 3–side view.

Spoons of similar shape have been found among Eskimo archaeological materials.[69]

b. Flat spoon-spatulas with a straight handle ending in a ring (Plate LX). All are of reindeer antler and are 7.5–14.3 cm long, with a bowl thickness of 0.15–0.2 cm. All were found at Ust-Poluy. Parallels to these spoons may also be found in Eskimo materials; particularly close analogues appear in the Ipiutak material.[70]

It is more convenient to study the spoons of the second subgroup by dividing them according to the subject of the carved and sculptured representations that decorate the handle. For example, there are the spoons decorated with images of reindeer or elk heads. All are of reindeer antler, 11.5–15.2 cm long, with a bowl thickness of 0.2–0.5 cm. The representation at the ends of the handles are generally bilateral. Eight specimens of this type are known (see Plate LXI):

MAE 5331-2308, Ust-Poluy, from square 73.

MAE 5331-1904, Ust-Poluy, from square 64. Immediately below the sculptured head [of the handle] there is a perforation (Plate LXI, items 10 and 11).

MAE 5455-4823, Ust-Poluy, surface material. There is an incised ornament on one side of the handle.

MAE 5331-2309, Ust-Poluy, from square 73. In the center of the spatula part, there is a sign in a cartouche, and on the same side the spoon is decorated with concentric lines that follow the contour of the spoon (Plate LXI, items 5, 6).

MAE 5331-4430, Ust-Poluy, from square 93. Fragment of handle (Plate LXI, item 4).

MAE 5331-1704, Ust-Poluy, from square 61. The entire spoon, including the handle, is ornamented on one side with incised zigzags that follow the contour of the spoon; there is a perforation at the base of the handle (Plate LXI, items 1–3).

MAE, no number. The handle is shaped like an elk's head. The image is unilateral, and it is not modeled on the hollowed side of the spoon. Only an eye is shown. There is a very small perforation at the base of the handle (Plate LXI, items 7–9).

MAE 5331-1558, Ust-Poluy, from square 58. A long flat handle decorated with a very crudely made representation of a reindeer's head.

The flat spoons decorated with representations of birds and compositions which include birds are all made of reindeer antler. They are 12.5–13.5 cm long; the bowl is 0.2–0.3 cm thick (Plate LXII):

MAE 5455-3995, Ust-Poluy, from square 78. A long straight handle decorated with the sculptured representation of a duck on the side of the spoon. There is a perforation in the upper end of the handle.

MAE 5331-1751, Ust-Poluy, from square 62. A straight flat handle decorated with a sculptured bird with outstretched wings. There is a perforation directly below the sculpture.

MAE 5455-4742, Ust-Poluy, from square 99. The handle ends in the carved bilateral representation of an eagle at rest. The handle is decorated on both sides with an incised ornament consisting of two rows of zigzag patterns.

MAE 5331, no number. The handle ends in a sculptured group, the bilateral representation of an eagle pecking the head of a reindeer.

MAE 5331-2184, Ust-Poluy, from square 70. A long flat handle ending in a composition that is but partially preserved and includes a bird. The handle is decorated with incised wavy lines.

In addition, there are several spoons decorated with diverse representations:

MAE 5455-3756, Ust-Poluy, from square 69. A flat spoon of reindeer antler with a straight handle with a sculptured composition including two animals, one of which stands on the head of the other. The mouths of both animals are open, their tongues protrude and meet. The sculpture is bilateral. On one side both the bowl and the handle are covered with carved ornamentation; only the middle part of the bowl lacks ornamentation. The spoon is 13.5 cm long and the bowl is 0.3 cm thick.

MAE 5455-4826, Ust-Poluy, surface material. Fragment of a flat antler spoon with a straight handle ending in a ring closed with the heads of two big-eared animals with opposing mouths. The mouths of the animals are open, the tongues protrude. The modeling is carefully done on one side only, the other showing only the ears, the open mouths, and the tongues. The eyes are not delineated. The inside of the bowl is decorated with incised lines.

MAE 5331-588, Ust-Poluy, found in trimming a pit. The handle of a spoon of reindeer antler ending in a sculptured representation of two elk (?) heads, back to back. The image is unilateral, with only the eyes depicted on the obverse side.

Tubular needle-cases. Only a few specimens of tubular needle-cases were found, all at Ust-Poluy (Plate LXIII, items 1–7). Despite the small number of finds, they may be divided into two groups:

1. Needle cases made of the tubular bones of birds. Two specimens are known. Both are sawed-off pieces of swan (or goose?) wing bones. Neither is ornamented. The needle cases are oval in cross section, this being determined by the natural shape of the bone.

2. Bone needle-cases, square in cross section:

MAE 5455-3360, Ust-Poluy, from square 134. Made of a metatarsal of an artiodactylous animal, most likely a roe deer. It is decorated on all sides with incised ornamentation.

MAE 5331-1187, Ust-Poluy, from square 47. Needle case made from a tubular bone. It is rectangular in cross section and is covered with decoration on three sides; two sides are decorated with an incised grid, the third with incised zigzags.

MAE 5455-1584, Ust-Poluy, from square 102. Made from the metatarsal of an artiodactylous animal. The middle part of the needle case is square in cross section, while the ends are round. It is decorated on two sides with an incised pattern.

Simple tubular needle-cases made from the [long] bones of waterfowl are very widely distributed. This had already been noted by Birket-Smith, who wrote that the "simple tubular needle-case should be included among a number of Paleo-Eskimo artifacts. It was found in the Ipiutak culture and has been described for the Dorset culture. It is a prototype from which the most advanced Eskimo types evolved. This view is confirmed by the unusually broad distribution of the type, which has been known in Europe since the Upper Paleolithic."[71]

Simple needle-cases made from the tubular bones of waterfowl occur widely in the ethnographic materials of Siberia. Needle cases of rectangular cross section are quite familiar to archaeologists. The bone needle-case from the Glyadenovo cemetery is very similar to those of Ust-Poloy in both shape and type of ornamentation.[72] One of the "tubes" from the Uyak campsite on Kodiak Island is also similar to that of Ust-Poluy.[73] In this case, one should note especially that this tube was decorated with an incised pattern widely employed at Ust-Poluy for ornamenting bone artifacts. Needle cases very similar to the ones from Ust-Poluy are known from the Oleniy ostrov (northern) burial ground. Needle cases of rectangular cross section are found far less frequently in the ethnographic materials than are needle cases of bird bones. Needle cases very similar to those of Ust-Poluy in both shape and ornamentation are known among the Lopars [Lapps].[74]

Needles. Only one specimen has been found. It comes from Ust-Poluy (MAE 5331-1864, Ust-Poluy, square 63). It is a thin bone needle with a round perforation in its upper end; length, 11.5 cm.

Socketed, scraperlike objects. These, which may have been used as back-scratchers, are of reindeer antler (Plate LXIII, items 11–15). They vary in size from 2.75 to 6.6 cm, and they always have a perforation or a socket for hafting. The edge is sometimes serrated. Ten specimens are known, all from Ust-Poluy. It is interesting that six of them are definitely associated with the sacrificial place. No counterparts of these objects are known to archaeology. Objects very similar in form but much larger have been found in the ethnographic materials collected among the Taymyr Samoyeds (Fig. 32). A socketed object of antler with a serrated edge hafted to a wooden handle is called a "kosa" by the Entsy, and a "khaza" or a "khaza-manre" by the Nentsy. We have the following information about the purpose of this object. According to the data taken from the informant I. I. Silkin (an Enets of the Bay clan, Vorontsovo hamlet in Ust-Yenisey *rayon*, Taymyr *okrug*), it has two purposes: for digging out arctic-fox holes in order to set traps in them, so that no scent or outlines of human hands are left, and for digging up roots known to the Entsy as *badue* and to the Nentsy as *vakuy*. Reindeer like to eat these roots, and formerly they were cooked and eaten by people as well.

According to another informant, P. A. Komarov (a Nenets of the Nenyang clan, Malaya Kheta settlement at the mouth of the Malaya Kheta River, 90 km downriver from Dudinka), there are smaller objects of this type with small teeth and a short handle that are used to comb fleas from the back.[75] Keeping in mind the miniature size of the Ust-Poluy socketed scraping tools, let us assume that they are comparable and were used for the same purpose, but were merely smaller. These data tend to confirm the opinion already expressed, that the Ust-Poluy objects were most likely used as back-scratchers. Perhaps an indirect confirmation of this is the fact that many of our finds are associated with the ritual site discovered at Ust-Poluy in squares 62 and 99. Also, let us recall that among some peoples, for example the Indians of the American Northwest, the shaman is not permitted to scratch his body with his hand, but must use a scratcher.[76]

Knives made from pieces of bone. Ninety-two specimens in all have been found, all at Ust-Poluy. They had a sharp working edge (Plate LXIII, items 16, 17). Most of them were made from scapulae and other bones of the seal, but some were made from scapulae of reindeer or wolves.[77]

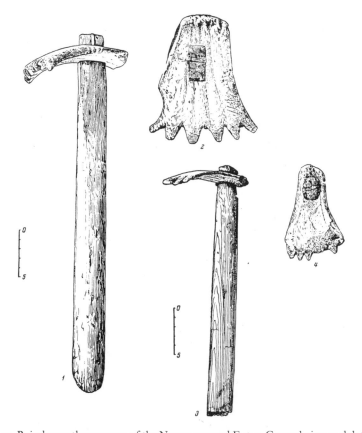

Fig. 32. Reindeer antler scrapers of the Nganasans and Entsy. General view and details.

There are several similar instruments of reindeer antler with a carefully sharpened edge. Such implements are widely used among Siberian peoples, particularly the Ob Ugrians. The Sosva Mansi use knives made from reindeer scapulae to clean fish.[78] Bone implements very similar to these knives have been found in archaeological sites in Alaska.[79]

Scraper-spatulas. These are flat, spatulalike implements usually made of reindeer antler and only rarely of other material (for example, whale rib). They can be divided into two groups on the basis of a single feature, the treatment of the working edge: those with a serrated edge and those with a smooth edge. In both groups, the scrapers vary greatly in length, from 9.75 to 21.1 cm, but those 13–15 cm long are the most common.

The shape varies in both groups, evolving toward a more clearly defined handle, which gradually changes from a broad and flat handle to a narrower and rounded one. The spatula itself also gradually assumes more distinct and rounder outlines. Sometimes the handle has one or several perforations. Very often the spatula has scratched-on or incised representations, most often geometric, but sometimes more complex and imaginative. In some cases they are enclosed in a cartouche. Figure 44 shows the distribution of the finds of this category of implements by archaeological site.

T-shaped scrapers. These implements are made of reindeer antler and have an asymmetric blade and flat handle. The overall length of the implement is 7–8 cm; the handle is 5–6 cm long. The working edge is thin, carefully sharpened. These scrapers were found only at Ust-Poluy (Plate LXIV, items 1–4).

Handles for iron knives. These occurred frequently in many of the sites. Their distribution is given in Fig. 44. They are made of reindeer antler and can be divided into three groups according to the width of the handle:

1. Broad, 2–3 cm wide and 8.6–12.35 cm long. As a rule they are oval in cross section, sometimes subtriangular. There is a perforation in the upper part—most often in the corner, sometimes in the middle. Usually such handles are undecorated; in some cases, however, they have ornamentation in the form of vertical bands or grooves covering the entire surface or broad horizontal grooves girdling the upper part of the handle. In one case, the handle is decorated with the sculptured representation of an eagle's head with its beak open.

2. Narrow, 1.2–1.55 cm wide and 6.7–10 cm long. The handle is oval in cross section, without ornamentation. In a number of cases there is one perforation, or several, in the upper corners.

3. Medium, 1.6–1.95 cm wide and 7.4–11.5 cm long. These are oval in cross section, less often triangular. In most cases they have one perforation, or several, in the upper corners. Often they are decorated with incised ornamentation, linear or crosshatched and arranged in pairs, simulating animal tracks. In this group there is one handle decorated with the sculptured representation of a dog in harness.

The tang of the iron knife was inserted into the handle. Several specimens were found with the iron remains of the knife in the handle, but these are so corroded that it is impossible to determine the shape of the blade and the method of sharpening. In most cases, however, the handle had been split open and the remnants of the knife removed from it.

The bone knife-handles just described differ from present-day ones (widely employed in the northern reaches of the Ob) both in diameter and by the presence of a groove or perforation in the upper end. This difference can be attributed to the shape of the sheath. The present Ob Ugrians have deep sheaths that are attached to the leg. Knives which have handles with perforations in the upper end are carried in shallow sheaths and the perforation is used to secure the knife. The Lapps use sheaths of this type with similar mountings.[80]

Snow-shovel blade edges. There are eight specimens of snow-shovel blade edges, all from Ust-Poluy; all are of the same shape and practically the same size. The length of the upper edge varies from 26 to 28.6 cm. They have a deep groove with a transverse partition in the middle and perforations for fastening (Plate LXV).

MAE 5331-1540, from square 57. A blade edge made of whalebone; it has three perforations below the groove, one in the middle and one in each corner.

MAE 5331-1167, a fragment of a blade of walrus ivory in surface-collected material from a cellar pit.

MAE 5331-1167, from square 46. Made of mammoth ivory; the single perforation is on the side, considerably below the groove.

MAE 5455-4029, from square 79. Made of mammoth ivory; the deep groove has a transverse partition in the middle, directly below which there is a perforation.

MAE 5331-1019, from square 40. Along the upper edge, in the middle part, are three perforations; this artifact is made of mammoth ivory.

MAE 5455-2914, from square 124. Broken in the middle section; blade of mammoth ivory.

MAE 5455-4243, from square 89. Fragment of blade made of mammoth ivory.

MAE 5455-3378, from square 134. Fragment of a blade made of mammoth ivory.

Snow shovels. Snow shovels were used in arctic and subarctic regions, mainly on the edges of the forest, and are known in the eastern part of subarctic America, on Kamchatka, and in Lapland. In Siberia, as Birket-Smith noted, they are found only sporadically. Snow shovels of various shapes are well known in Eskimo archaeology. Blades very similar to those of Ust-Poluy have been found in Alaska, for example in the Tigara burial ground.[81] Snow-shovel blade edges of the same type, very similar in shape to those of Ust-Poluy, are known in the Thule culture.[82] However, the closest counterparts are the snow shovels of the Caribou Eskimos, which duplicate the Ust-Poluy shovels both in shape and in the means of fastening the blade.[83]

Combs. These were found at a number of sites (Fig. 33). Their distribution is shown in Fig. 44. All specimens are carved from single pieces of antler or bone. They may be divided into two groups on the basis of shape: (1) high, with flat and broad teeth; (2) broad, with fine teeth that are rectangular in cross section. The overwhelming majority of the lower Ob combs belong to the first group:

MAE 5455-4977, Katra-Vozh, from square 9. Made of reindeer antler; three teeth. The teeth are flat, oval in cross section, and there is a circular perforation in the handle. The total height is 8.8 cm, length of the teeth 4.5 cm (Fig. 33, item 9). There is a fragment of a bone three-toothed comb from Salekhard which is greatly deteriorated.

MAE 5331-1703, Ust-Poluy, from square 61. Made of reindeer antler; five teeth. The middle tooth is two-thirds the length of the others (most likely it was broken off, then resharpened and polished); the handle is decorated with a complex openwork composition. Total height 10.3 cm, length of the teeth 4.5 cm (Fig. 33, item 8).

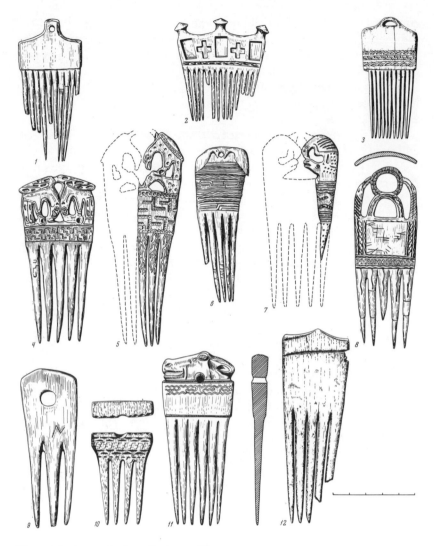

Fig. 33. Antler combs from the lower Ob.
  1 to 3–combs of the second group; 4 to 12–combs of the first group.

MAE 5331-2330, Ust-Poluy. Fragment of a five-tooth comb of reindeer antler. The handle is decorated with a composition containing the figure of an eagle pecking at the head of a reindeer (Fig. 33, item 5).

MAE 5331-2092, Ust-Poluy, from square 68. Fragment of a comb of the same type as the preceding. Only a portion of one tooth remains, and it, judging by the patina, was broken off in antiquity (Fig. 33, item 7).

MAE, no number (from the collection of V. S. Adrianov; this item has not been catalogued). A six-tooth comb, the handle of which has a sculptured representation of the head of an animal with its mouth open; in the middle of the handle, just below the sculpture, there is a perforation (Fig. 33, item 11).[84]

MAE 5455-4989, Katra-Vozh, from square 10. A five-toothed comb of reindeer antler, probably unfinished. Judging by its similarity to the preceding combs, the handle was to have been decorated with a representation of an animal's head. The height is 12.4 cm (Fig. 33, item 12).

MAE 5455-4821, Ust-Poluy, surface-collected material. A six-tooth comb of reindeer antler. The handle is decorated with the sculptured representation of two birds (Fig. 33, item 6).

MAE, no number (from Adrianov's collection; this item has not been catalogued). A five-tooth comb of reindeer antler. The handle is decorated with carved figures of two eagles whose heads and wings touch. Total height of the comb 10 cm, length of the teeth 6 cm (Fig. 33, item 4).

MAE, no number (from Adrianov's collection; not catalogued). According to available data, it was found on the right bank of the Poluy River between Angalskiy Cape [Cape Angal] and Salekhard. It is a four-tooth comb decorated with incised graphic ornamentation. There was a perforation in the handle (Fig. 33, item 10).[85]

There are two combs in the second group:

MAE 5331-2273, Ust-Poluy. A multitooth comb made of bone. Eleven teeth remain, one was broken off in antiquity; the face is decorated with a graphic geometric design; in the middle of the back there is a projection in which there is a semioval perforation. Height 7.4 cm (Fig. 33, item 3).[86]

MAE, no number (Adrianov's collection; not catalogued). A fourteen-tooth comb of reindeer antler. The teeth are fine, rectangular in cross section; the handle's edge is decorated with knobs, and on the handle there are large crosses in relief placed among rectangles (Fig. 33, item 2).

MAE 5455-754, Ust-Poluy, from square 92. Ten-tooth comb of reindeer antler. The teeth are long, rectangular in cross section; in the middle of the handle's edge there is a projection with a perforation. Height of the comb is 7.9 cm, length of the teeth, 5.3 cm (Fig. 33, item 1). This comb occupies an intermediate position between the first and second types, inasmuch as it belongs to group one in size but is similar to group two in that it is multitoothed and has fine teeth that are rectangular in cross section.

The comb from the Buy fortified hill site on the Vyatka River [in European Russia] reminds one of the combs of the lower Ob. Of this comb only the sculptured handle and the upper part of the teeth remain. The decorative sculpture on the handle, as A. V. Zbruyeva points out, is a highly stylized representation of a beast of prey, made in the manner typical of Ananino art.[87]

Our evidence of the distribution of simple combs in Siberia is highly fragmentary. I purposely omit the Tagar bone combs, which differ so much from the combs of the lower Ob in shape that I do not feel it would serve any purpose to include them here. A five-tooth comb made from a piece of elk antler was found in the hamlet of Obyul in the Chulym River basin. Another one-piece antler comb was in a Karasuk grave near the village of Kopeny in the upper Yenisey basin.[88] At present, we do not have any material from eastern Siberia. Several individual finds have been made in northeastern Asia, on the Okhotsk coast and in Kamchatka at Korf Bay (Zaliv Korfa).[89]

One-piece combs made of reindeer antler or bone are frequently found in the Eskimo archaeological sites and are an ancient element of Eskimo culture, representing one of the characteristic features of that culture in its various stages of development. Birket-Smith, in analyzing the material culture of the Caribou Eskimos, took into account all the known material, both ethnographic and archaeological, and determined the geographic distribution of simple combs. According to his data, combs carved from a single piece of wood, bone, or mammoth ivory are found among the Eskimos and the northwest Indians and occasionally are encountered in Siberia.

Although there are practically no combs in North American ethnographic materials, save those mentioned, they are well known and are frequently found in archaeological sites of the northeastern United States.[90] The North American archaeological material was classified by two outstanding specialists in Iroquoian archaeology, A. Parker and A. Skinner. They established that the bone or antler combs decorated with carving were used by all Iroquois, beginning "with prehistoric times and down to the Middle Colonial period." It is not known when they ceased to be used, but in any event it was long after the first contacts with Europeans. Both these authors consider the three-, four-, and five-tooth combs with large broad teeth and a straight smooth handle, sometimes with a perforation, to be early forms. Later, in the opinion of Parker and Skinner, combs of more advanced forms appeared—broad combs with a large number of teeth, sometimes as many as twenty. The handles of such combs were usually decorated with openwork carving, realistic representations of animals, birds, and people.[91] On the whole, this classification is valid today. However, we must note that a bone comb decorated with the sculptured representation of a bird, closely resembling the later Iroquois combs, was discovered by MacNeish in the Frontenac culture. If that find truly belongs to the stratum MacNeish claims for it, some specimens of archaeological combs with carved birds may belong to a much earlier time, if we consider the C^{14} dating of Frontenac.[92] The lower Ob combs which we have designated as the first group have their parallels in the North American archaeological combs which the investigators associate with the Iroquois. Despite the enormous territorial and chronological distances between the two, which should cause considerable differences in the shape and style of the representations, they have essential features in common. In addition to the common tendencies in shape, we note some concurrences in details. First, this applies to the motifs of the sculptured representations, the common motif being birds. It is interesting that in both the North American and the lower Ob combs, the birds are depicted in an identical pose—face to face. The most primitive of the lower Ob combs from Katra-Vozh, the three-tooth combs with flat, large teeth and a perforation in the simple smooth handle, are also completely analogous to those found among the North American Indians.[93] The combs which we have combined in the second group have some, although not particularly close, counterparts in the archaeological Eskimo combs, to which they show a similarity in graphic ornamentation and some details in the treatment of the handle. A multitooth comb with a projection in the middle of the handle also is comparable with some of the Eskimo combs.[94]

MAE 5331-1346, Ust-Poluy, square 51. Fragment of an epauletlike clasp. From the part that remains we estimate the diameter of the plate to have been about 10 cm. The outer edge is decorated with hemispheres, while the middle part contains representations of four bears with their heads turned toward the center. The very center of the plate evidently was smooth and somewhat convex. The clasp was made of an alloy with a high copper content.[95]

MAE 5455-4227, Ust-Poluy, square 89. A rectangular plate with representations of bears. It was cast from the same alloy as the previous item and its dimensions are 5.3 × 4.9 cm. It is fringed by cordlike decoration, and the central part of the plate is decorated with the same kind of cord pattern. The central part contains images of three heads of prostrate bears. On the reverse side there are four loops for fastening.[96]

MAE 5455-4810, Ust-Poluy, surface-collected material. A rectangular plate decorated with small mounds and a meanderlike pattern on its border. Cast; made of the same alloy as the preceding item, its dimensions are 6.2 × 4.9 cm. Like the preceding item, it has four loops for fastening.[97]

MAE 5455-2077, Ust-Poluy, square 113. A flat badge made of copper or bronze, about 4.7 cm in diameter. It is very thin, only about 0.05 cm. One side is decorated with four sketched concentric circles.

MAE 5455-4684, Ust-Poluy, square 99. A cast bronze badge, about 5 cm in diameter. One side is decorated with concentric circles, in part scratched on and in part made in the casting.

MAE 5331-1347, Ust-Poluy, square 51. A cast bronze badge about 3.5 cm in diameter and 0.75–1.0 mm thick. One side is decorated with concentric circles made in the casting.[98]

SM 1138, Nyaksimvol. A flat bronze badge, 5.3 cm in diameter. One side is decorated with two rows of concentric circles; a complex composition, including an anthropomorphic image, is scratched on the other side.

MAE 5455-4682, Ust-Poluy, square 99. A bronze badge 2.2 cm in diameter. It has a lug moulded to the reverse side and the image of a human face scratched on the front.[99]

MAE 5455-3560, Ust-Poluy, square 99. A bronze badge, 4.3 cm in diameter. There are two loops on the back; the images of anthropomorphic beings leaning against each other and a coiled animal are scratched on the face side.[100]

SM 1138, Nyaksimvol. A cast bronze brooch, about 7.5 cm in diameter. The center is convex, surrounded by a circular rounded ridge made in the casting, this ridge being separate from the center.

SM 1821, Nyaksimvol. A large cast bronze brooch. The face is decorated with sketched concentric circles. The very center of the brooch is convex, surrounded at a distance by a small ridge of the same relief.

SM 1027, Nyaksimvol. A cast bronze brooch. Like the preceding one, it has a convex center surrounded by a ridge. The central circle of the brooch runs through ten perforations fashioned in the form of rays. The back of the brooch has four symmetrically arranged loops for attachment.

MAE 5455-1281, Ust-Poluy, square 99. A bronze umbonate badge, decorated along the edge with flat circles separated from the convex center by a plaitlike ridge.[101]

MAE 5455-4811, Ust-Poluy, surface-collected material. A bronze umbonate badge. Decorated with three concentrically placed rows of cord with an eight-point rosette in the center. On the back, as in the preceding case, there is a loop for fastening.[102]

SM 1138, Nyaksimvol. A cast bronze badge, 4.6 cm in diameter. One side is smooth; the other has seven mammiform convexities in the middle part. The edge of the badge is serrated.

SM 1138, Nyaksimvol. Openwork bronze brooch. The image of some insect, probably a grasshopper, is inscribed in a circle. The inner part of the circle consists of a single line of beads* made in the casting. The back of the brooch is provided with two pairs of loops arranged symmetrically in the upper and lower part of the brooch.

MAE 5455-4315, 5331-379, 5455-3560, Ust-Poluy, squares 21, 138, 91. Small cast bronze badges with smoothly polished surfaces.[103]

SM 1138, Nyaksimvol. A cast rectangular bronze plate. On the outer surface there is an ornament consisting of two rows of depressed serrations. On the back there are two loops for fastening. This plate is an exact counterpart of one from the Ananino burial ground.[104] The ornamental plates from Ananino and Nyaksimvol are identical not only in shape and ornamentation, but in size (see Fig. 45, items 14, 15). Both are thick, and in this they differ substantially from the later plates found at the Pyanyy Bor [Pyanobor] burial grounds, where badges of the same shape were found, but thinner and larger ones.[105]

MAE 5455-4809, Ust-Poluy, surface-collected material. A bronze ring. The outside of the ring is oval and 4.25 cm long. It is decorated with a pattern in relief consisting of small circles with dots, a cord, and "little ducks."[106]

SM 1027, Nyaksimvol. A bronze ring (see Plate LXXI, item 10). Similar to the preceding item. It differs only in decorative pattern, which consists of a meander that fills the middle part of the outside of the ring, which in turn is fringed by a band of straight and wavy lines. Elements of this design are very common and were used to decorate bone artifacts at Ust-Poluy (Plate LXVIII).

SM 1138, Nyaksimvol. Silver facings of brooches. Two specimens are known:

1. A very thin facing 15.2 cm in diameter. The stamped relief ornamentation is arranged in three concentric zones: outer, middle, and

---

* [Literally, "peas" (*goroshiny*). Translator, A.I.N.A.]

inner. The outer zone consists of two bands, crenulate along the edge of the mounting and reticulate; the middle zone consists of a large ribbon zigzag pattern filled out with dots; the inner zone, in the form of a reticulate band, borders the center of the brooch, which is without ornament. The unornamented surface is gilded.

2. A similar thin facing 12.9 cm in diameter. Small tacks for fastening remain along the edge of the inner side. The facing is quite crumpled. A stamped design and gilding cover the middle of the mounting. In the center is a six-lobed rosette in relief; the lobes are delineated by double lines. It is surrounded by a ring of cording, around which is a fairly broad band filled with poorly defined ornamentation, most reminiscent of a running spiral, or wave, motif.

The ornamental motifs used in decorating the Nyaksimvol mountings are well known in archaeology. Also, they were widely used to decorate metal artifacts. The punctate fill-in is found regularly on the silver phalerae and brooches, on which the wave motif or the running spiral is very common. The rosette in several variants was one of the favorite ornamental elements of the gold and silver horse trimmings of the Sarmatians of the northern shores of the Black Sea.[107] It is interesting that these ornamental motifs were also used to decorate the wooden plaques of the horse trimmings. Good examples of this may be found in the materials of the first Tuekta and the second Pazyryk burial mounds.[108]

ARMAMENT

Plate armor. This is represented by a large number of different plates which may be classified on the basis of shape (see Plate LXVI):

1. Elongated rectangular plates. There are many specimens, whose distribution by sites is given in Fig. 44. All are made of reindeer antler. They differ in size as follows: length 8.45 to 11.9 cm, width 1.6 to 2.7 cm, thickness 0.2 to 0.8 cm. As a rule, the plates have two pairs of symmetrically arranged perforations—round, oval, or rectangular. Besides the unornamented ones, there are those decorated with an incised pattern, usually consisting of several horizontal bands filled with cross-hatching, zigzag, or other figures common to the ornamentation of bone artifacts from the lower Ob region.

Usually armor was made from such rectangular plates. They were joined by thongs pulled through the perforations. Many of these plates bear clear traces of these thongs in the form of a polishing where the thongs passed (Fig. 34).

2. Elongated curved plates of reindeer antler. Two are known, both from Ust-Poluy:

MAE 5455-3664, square 64. A large curved plate narrowing toward the ends; length, 26.7 cm; three pairs of oval perforations.

MAE 5455-3665, square 64. The same kind of plate, but smaller (17.7 cm). Perhaps the curved plate served as an armhole in the armor.

3. Breastplates. Two are known, both from Ust-Poluy (see Plate LXVII):

MAE 5331-378, square 21. Made of whalebone; 20.9 cm wide, 14.5 cm high in the middle part and 16 cm high along the sides, 0.6 cm thick. It is decorated with the representation of a warrior holding a sword in each hand.

MAE 5331-108, square 5. A blank for a breastplate. It is made from the broad part of an elk antler and is similar in shape to the preceding.

4. Plates which taper toward one end. Two are known, both from Ust-Poluy and both of reindeer antler. Each is 0.5 cm thick. Perhaps conical plates were used to construct helmets (Plate LXVI, items 7, 9).

5. Wrist guards. Four specimens are known, all from Ust-Poluy. They are reindeer antler. The best preserved specimen is 6.3 cm wide and 0.25 cm thick. Two have arrow-shaped engraved ornamentation on the outer side (Plate LXVI, item 1).

Fig. 34. Eskimo bone armor plate (from the collections of the MAE).

Armor plate is known in Ural and Siberian archaeology. Bone armor plates have been found in a number of Trans-Uralian and Irtysh River sites, in the burial mounds near Shadrinsk,[109] in the Kokonovka burial mounds near Omsk, and elsewhere.[110] Bronze armor plates were found among the materials from the burial mounds on Cape Chuvashskiy [Potchevash], near Tobolsk.[111] Armor made of bone or antler plates fastened in the same manner as those of Ust-Poluy appear in the ethnographic materials of the peoples of northeastern Asia and of the Eskimos. Armor plate is well known in the ethnographic materials of Asia and North America as well as in the materials of Europe of the Middle Ages. In the opinion of several authors, their source was somewhere in central or middle Asia.[112]

Bronze arrowheads. These fall into three categories:

1. Three-bladed arrowheads with an open socket. They are unusual because of their large size, being about 8 cm long, with a diameter of about 0.9 cm in the lower part of the socket. The points and edges of the blades were sharpened. In a number of cases there are small raised bands on the socket; sometimes the raised lines are situated between the blades. Six of the specimens of this type are from Ust-Poluy; one is from Nyaksimvol.[113]

2. Large, three-bladed arrowheads from the Sortynya fortified hill site (see Fig. 44).

3. A three-sided arrowhead, 4.5 cm long, with a closed socket. There is one specimen, from Zelenaya Gorka.[114]

Arrowheads of the first group were found in the Glyadenovo ossuary and at a number of sites in the forest zone of western Siberia.[115] The large, three-bladed arrowheads with closed sockets are widely represented in the antiquities of Narym *kray*, particularly among the artifacts collected at Mount Kulayka.[116] Three-sided arrowheads of the Zelenaya Gorka type are found chiefly beyond the limits of the forest zone of western Siberia. We know of them basically from the finds on the eastern slopes of the southern Urals, where they were especially popular among the Sarmatians of the 4th century B.C. Smirnov, in referring to the finds at the Chudaki fortified hill site on the Iset River, pointed out that later such arrowheads were known to the northern neighbors of the Sarmatians of the southern Urals.[117] It is interesting that among the finds at the ancient village site of Konetsgorskoye there were both large three-bladed and three-sided arrowheads with a closed socket that are very reminiscent of the bronze arrowhead from Zelenaya Gorka (see Fig. 45, item 5).[118]

Daggers. There are two specimens of bronze pommels for dagger hilts, both from Ust-Poluy, cast from bronze in the form of two facing volutes.[119]

Miniature bronze mace (Fig. 45, item 9). One specimen is known, from Ust-Poluy. The blade is flattened and narrow, sharpened on both sides, the butt is shaped like the head of some highly generalized animal, and the socket is decorated with the head of a bird of prey.

The closest counterparts to these are from western Siberia, the Urals, and the region of the Ananino culture.[120]

Art Objects

Art is represented by ornamentation, drawing, and plastic techniques (Plates LXVIII and LXIX).[121] The Ust-Poluy ornamentation has been analyzed in previous papers on the Ust-Poluy culture, so that in this presentation we shall dwell chiefly on plastic art. It is represented by two forms—bone carvings and figure casting.

In the finds from Ust-Poluy there are two types of carving in bone: flat representations made by primitive "smooth" carving with a shallow graving surface, and round sculpture, that is, more complex, three-dimensional carving that required a skilled master. Animals and birds were the subject matter of the representations. In addition to single figures, there are compositions most often containing an animal and a bird, sometimes two birds or two animals, or just their heads. Usually such carved images decorate everyday objects and utensils: spoon handles of iron knives, combs, belt buckles, et cetera.

Stylistically the Ust-Poluy small sculptured pieces may be divided into two groups, the first of which is characterized as follows:

MAE 5331-2463, Ust-Poluy, square 76. The head of a red-billed wild goose done in three-dimensional carving. The color features of the plumage are indicated by scarification. This round sculpture forms the end of the curved handle of a deep spoon made of mammoth ivory.

MAE 5331, Ust-Poluy, no number. The three-dimensional image of a walrus head. The characteristic vibrissae of the upper, fleshy lip are emphasized. This sculpture forms the end of the high-arched handle of a deep spoon made of walrus ivory (Fig. 35).

MAE 5331, Ust-Poluy, no number. The representation of an animal head with an open mouth and protruding tongue, done in three-dimensional carving. Round sculpture is represented by the very short figured handle of a shallow spoon carved from reindeer antler (Fig. 36).

MAE 5455-903, Ust-Poluy, square 96. A three-dimensional representation of an animal head with protruding ears. This round sculpture terminates a short handle of a shallow spoon carved from reindeer antler.

MAE 5331, Ust-Poluy, no number. Sculptured head of a bird of prey with open beak. The eye is shown realistically, and the lachrymal gland, which is highly developed in daylight birds of prey, is depicted. This sculpture decorates the handle of an iron knife made of antler (Fig. 37).

A characteristic feature of the technique used in these sculptures is the extreme laconism. The portrayals of birds and animals are very close to nature, and figurative devices are used sparingly. Usually there are two techniques of depiction: representation of a typical contour, and emphasis on a few but very specific details. This latter technique may be demonstrated especially clearly in the material cited. Such is the case of the walrus; the vibrissae of the upper lip are sharply defined, leaving no doubt as to the animal intended, despite the very laconic depiction of only one head. The representation of the head of waterfowl is very interesting in this respect: the features of the coloration of the plumage, emphasized by the engraving, are typical of the red-billed wild goose.

Three-dimensional sculpture has ancient traditions. The closest counterparts are found in the wooden and bone sculpture chiefly of the Bronze Age. A number of parallels may be drawn from the ancient objects of the Urals, the Baltic region, and Finland.[122] Stylistically, all belong to a cycle of well-known animal sculpture, which G. Gjessing combined in the concept "north Eurasian style." The depictive techniques characteristic of this mode were already used in ancient Ural carvings and were typical of them. This was noted by Eding in his description of carved representations of birds taken from the Gorbunovo peat bog.[123]

A large number of sculptured representations in both flat and three-dimensional carving are included in the second stylistic group, of which the following are characteristic:

MAE 5331-588, Ust-Poluy, found in trimming a pit. A flattish representation of two reindeer heads positioned back-to-back and done in smooth carving. The representation is complete on one side, truncated on the other, with only the eyes modeled. They are in relief, with an exaggerated, elongated, large lachrymal sac. The representation formed the end of a handle of a spoon-spatula (?) carved from reindeer antler (Fig. 38).

MAE 5331-2308, Ust-Poluy, square 73. A flat, carved representation of a reindeer head with mouth open. It terminates a short, straight handle of a spoon-spatula made of reindeer antler. The carving is bilateral, with both sides identical. The stylized lachrymal sac is depicted as a large droplike depression.

MAE 5331-1904, Ust-Poluy, square 64. The flat, bilateral representation of the head of a roe deer. This carving terminates the long, flat handle of a shallow spoon of reindeer antler (Fig. 39).

MAE, (Ust-Poluy?), no number. A low-relief carving of an elk head, complete on one side only, with just the eye modeled on the other. The eye is shown with a large droplike lachrymal sac. The sculpture forms the short handle of a flat spoon-spatula of reindeer antler (Fig. 40).

MAE 5331-1182, Ust-Poluy. A bulky representation of a reindeer head with open mouth and protruding tongue. Note the eye in relief, without the pupil, with an emphasized lachrymal sac carved in the form of a depression. This round sculpture, made of reindeer antler, forms the end of the handle of an iron knife (Fig. 41).

MAE, no number. Two eagles, with heads touching and wings spread, made in "flat" carving. The plumage is depicted with depressed, elongated ovals. The claws are stylized as rings. The representation is unilateral. It decorates the handle of a comb carved from reindeer antler (Fig. 42).

MAE 5331-2092, Ust-Poluy, square 68. A flat carving depicting a bird of prey on the head of a reindeer. It is part of a composition which decorated the handle of a comb carved from reindeer antler (Fig. 33, item 7).

MAE 5331, no [field] number. A composition done in low relief, representing a bird of prey pecking the head of a reindeer. This bilateral carving decorates the handle of a flat spoon-spatula made of reindeer antler. The image is realistic, although somewhat generalized. The

Figs. 35 to 39. Walrus head; head of an animal with open mouth; head of a bird of prey; "Janus" reindeer heads; roe deer head.

accurately depicted contour of the wing is emphasized by a row of raised rectangles arranged in parallel rows (Fig. 43).

These items not only retain the graphic techniques characteristic of the ancient Ural carvings, but they have something new in their manner of execution which allows us to classify them as a separate group. The ancient technique that makes them similar to the Ural sculptures is the characteristic contour, which can be detected easily if they are compared with representations of different species of deer. The typical external features of each type of animal are stressed: for the elk, the massive, long, hook-nosed head, the muzzle with its characteristic, strongly developed upper lip, and the skin-fold hanging from the chin and covered with long hairs; for the male roe deer, the slightly branching antlers covered with irregularly shaped protuberances, and so on. In addition to these techniques there is the tendency, quite foreign to the Ural sculpture, to show greater detail and to stylize these details. This may be observed in many of the specimens. For example, it is characteristic to exaggerate the lachrymal sac in depicting the eye. This is always

Figs. 40 to 43. Elk head; reindeer heads; eagles; bird of prey pecking the head of a reindeer.

emphasized; sometimes the sac is very large, and in most cases it is depicted as a drop-shaped depression. The closest parallels to the bone carvings of the second group may be found among the artifacts of west Siberian figure casting. Among these there are objects that are not only similar to those under description with respect to style but are identical in composition and subject.

A composition of this type shows a bird pecking the head of a reindeer.[124] Bronze pendant figures from south of Tobolsk and from the Severnaya Sosva are analogous not only in subject, but in the treatment of the details. They are so close to the carvings which decorate some of the Ust-Poluy combs that one may suggest that they are prototypes in carving of the later bronze castings of this composition. The actual composition found in both the carved and the cast images is known for a territory very remote from the northern Trans-Ural, in a culture belonging to an entirely different sphere. In the groups depicting a bird pecking the head of a reindeer we can see the somewhat reworked subject of animal battles, so familiar from the art of the so-called Scytho-Siberian animal style. The reduced variant of this scene, in which only the head of an animal is depicted instead of the entire tormented animal, is shown by Andersson in the Ordos bronze materials.[125] A wooden pommel with a representation of a deer head in the beak of a griffon, found in the second Pazyryk burial mound, is a variant of this same subject.[126] Although stylistically it is completely foreign to the Ust-Poluy specimens, I cite it here, because of its close analogy in subject and treatment. Thus, the carvings of the second group are sculptures which, with regard to subject, can be traced to another cultural sphere located far to the south, beyond the forest zone. We have already mentioned that the distinctive feature of some of the representations we have examined is the striving toward stylization of the details, particularly the eyes. Realistic treatment is characteristic of the ancient Ural sculpture: the eye is depicted either as open with a pupil or closed without a pupil, but it is always shown realistically, and in a number of cases, the lachrymal gland is also shown. Emphasis of the lachrymal sac is characteristic of the second group of Ust-Poluy sculptures, and the exaggeration of the lachrymal sac is one of the specific features. Similar emphasis of the lachrymal gland appears in the Achaemenidian representations of animals in the round.[127] The question arises whether or not this tendency toward stylization in the manner of depicting the eye should be considered an influence of ancient Iranian art. Although the distance from the regions of Achaemenidian art is great, I consider such an influence to be possible. The stylization of bird claws in Ust-Poluy carvings, where they are shown as two rings, is completely foreign to ancient Uralian sculpture. Examples of such treatment of bird claws are to be sought rather in the art of the steppe zone.

Bronze casting of figures has been described in a section of V. N. Chernetsov's special work,[128] which contains a detailed description and characterization. Therefore, we shall limit ourselves here merely to a brief enumeration of figure castings (Plate LXIX, items 3–7, 11–14):

MAE 5331-526, Ust-Poluy, square 23. The representation of an owl cast from bronze. Length 5.2 cm; flat work except for the beak. On the breast there is a mask, depicted as three points.

MAE 5455-3538, Ust-Poluy, square 138. An owl cast from bronze. Length, 3.5 cm; somewhat more schematic than the preceding one.

MAE 5455-1743, Ust-Poluy, square 104. The small bronze figure of a bird of prey with outstretched wings. Length, 3.5 cm. The bird is depicted in flight, with the claws drawn up.

MAE 5455-3538, Ust-Poluy, square 138. A cast-bronze composition, consisting of a three-headed bird of prey poised over three animals resembling otters.

MAE 5455-4806, Ust-Poluy, surface-collected material. A cast-bronze composition consisting of a bird of prey poised over a bear. There is a mask on the breast of the bird, and there are three highly schematic human figures on the tail of the bird and three on the body of the bear.

MAE 5455, (Ust-Poluy?), no [field] number. A low-relief representation of a bird cast from bronze.

MAE 5331, (Ust-Poluy?), no [field] number. A cast-bronze, hollow human figure holding a vessel in its hands.

MAE 5331-483, Ust-Poluy, square 17a. A cast-bronze representation of a fantastic creature with a human mask on its chest.

MAE 5455-4807, Ust-Poluy, surface-collected material. The cast figure of an anthropomorphic being with a disproportionately large head and small extremities. The figure was given an animal head. The details of the extremities are shown on the side obverse to the face.

MAE 5455-3823, Ust-Poluy, square 72. An anthropomorphic figure like the preceding one, with the same disproportionately large head and depiction of the extremities on the obverse side.

SM 1821, Nyaksimvol. An anthropomorphic figure with a disproportionately large head. Very similar to the preceding.

The bas-relief moldings of anthropomorphic and zoomorphic beings carved from clayey shale—all of which were found at Ust-Poluy—are described in detail and characterized in Chernetsov's work.[129] Here we shall limit ourselves to a brief enumeration of them.

MAE 5455-4798/12, Ust-Poluy, square 99:

1. A composition containing the figure of a man with an animal in his arms, surrounded by animal faces.

2. Schematic representation of three human figures standing in a row.

3. Three pillarlike human figures in the same pose.

4. Three human figures whose faces, unlike those preceding, are carefully modeled; they have the characteristic, large heads.

5. Schematic representation of seven human figures standing in a row.

6. Schematic representation of a bird with outstretched wings; two beavers are depicted on the opposite molding.

7. Two animals standing on their hind legs with backs touching.

MAE 5455-4839/19, Ust-Poluy, surface-collected material. Representation of a man standing; the face is carefully modeled.

Conclusions

In summarizing the results, we have compiled information which includes objects of specific shape that were found repeatedly at the sites, in addition to the cauldronlike vessels on hollow pedestals (see Fig. 44). These objects include everyday items and weapons as well as elements of clothing and artifacts associated with ideological concepts. We should like to point out the special bronze anthropomorphic large-headed representations, birdlike and zoomorphic bronze castings made in a specific style, bone, one-piece combs, bone and reindeer antler spoons with handles decorated with carvings and round sculpture, highly uniform and characteristic bone knife handles that infer a specific shape of the sheath, and distinctive scraper-spatulas. Fig. 44 shows that the Ust-Poluy type of pottery is accompanied by a specific complex of bone and metal artifacts. This affords the possibility of combining the studied sites into a single archaeological culture, which has been called the Ust-Poluy culture in the preliminary publications.

The data which makes it possible to synchronize the Ust-Poluy sites with sites of other cultures on adjacent territories are also indicated in Fig. 44. The finds of bronze arrowheads are highly significant for this synchronization. Almost all types of bronze socketed arrowheads and their bone counterparts found in the various sites of Ust-Poluy culture—at Ust-Poluy, Nyaksimvol, Zelenaya Gorka, and Sortynya—are also found in the material of one of the Ananino sites, Konetsgorskoye village (see Fig. 45). In the Ananino sites, we find counterparts of other objects from Ust-Poluy and Nyaksimvol: bronze plates for sewing onto clothing, which plates have a highly distinctive ornamentation consisting of two bands of vertical serrations (Nyaksimvol—Ananino burial ground; Fig. 45, items 14, 15); a bronze belt buckle in the form of two griffons (Ust-Poluy—Ufa burial ground; Fig. 45, items 12, 13); and maces (Ust-Poluy—finds in the Kama region; Fig. 45, items 9–11). These latter counterparts were noted repeatedly by investigators in both the Ob and Kama regions.[130] The finds of these objects in various sites of the Ust-Poluy culture permit a synchronization with the Ananino and, accepting Zbruyeva's chronology, the specification of the time of the Ust-Poluy culture as the second half of the 1st millennium B.C., probably between the 5th and the 3rd centuries B.C. The two silver brooch facings (Fig. 45;

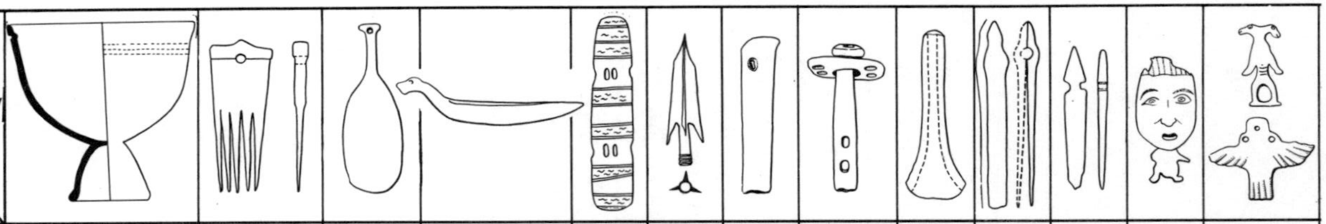

SITES \ ARTIFACTS CHARACTERISTIC OF THE UST-POLUY CULTURE	(bird figure)	(head figure)	(dagger)					(arrow)	(tube)	(knife)	(spoon)	(comb)	(vessel)
Ust-Poluy	$\frac{8}{11}$	$\frac{2}{4}$	$\frac{43}{49}$	$\frac{53}{54}$	$\frac{106}{109}$	$\frac{93}{98}$	$\frac{181}{191}$	$\frac{6}{8}$	$\frac{37}{46}$	$\frac{7}{8}$	$\frac{29}{30}$	$\frac{6}{13}$	+
Salekhard			$\frac{1}{49}$				$\frac{2}{195}$				$\frac{1}{30}$	$\frac{1}{13}$	+
Katra-Vozh	$\frac{1}{11}$		$\frac{1}{49}$	$\frac{1}{54}$		$\frac{5}{98}$	$\frac{3}{195}$		$\frac{1}{46}$		$\frac{1}{30}$	$\frac{2}{13}$	+
Pel-Vozh									$\frac{1}{46}$				+
Makar-Visyng-Tur		$\frac{1}{4}$											+
Sorovoy Mys	$\frac{1}{11}$							$\frac{1}{8}$					+
Sortynya								$\frac{1}{8}$					+
Nyaksimvol	$\frac{1}{11}$	$\frac{1}{4}$	$\frac{4}{49}$	$\frac{1}{54}$	$\frac{3}{109}$		$\frac{9}{195}$		$\frac{7}{46}$	$\frac{1}{8}$			+

Fig. 44. A compilation of objects characteristic of the Ust-Poluy culture. The denominator in the fractions indicates the number of finds in the lower Ob region, while the numerator indicates the number of finds at the given site. The plus sign indicates the presence of Ust-Poluyan vessels on hollow pedestals.

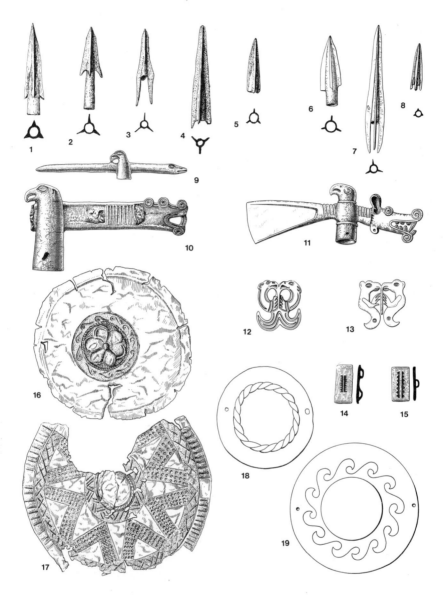

Fig. 45. Composite presentation of objects from various sites of the Ust-Poluy culture and similar objects from adjacent territories.

1 to 4—arrowheads from Ust-Poluy; 5—arrowhead from Zelenaya Gorka site; 6 to 8—arrowheads from the Konetsgorskoye village site (after Zbruyeva); 9—mace from Ust-Poluy; 10—bimetallic poleaxe from the lower Ob region; 11—poleaxe from the Kama region (after Zbruyeva); 12—belt buckle from Ust-Poluy; 13—belt buckle from the Ufa burial ground (after Zbruyeva); 14—ornamental plate from the Nyaksimvol fortified hill site; 15—ornamental plate from the Ananino burial ground; 16, 17—brooch facings from the Nyaksimvol fortified hill site; 18—metal-framed round plate from the Pazyryk burial mound (after Rudenko); 19—metal-framed round plate from the Tuekta burial mound (after Rudenko). Materials: 1—walrus ivory; 2 to 9, 11 to 15—bronze; 10—bronze and iron; 16, 17—silver; 18, 19—wood.

items 16, 17) found at the Nyaksimvol fortified hill site do not contradict this dating. I am of the opinion that it is scarcely proper to compare these brooch facings with the cast silver phalerae; rather they should be compared with the metal-framed round wooden plates, used as horse trimmings, of the kind found in the first Tuekta and the second Pazyryk burial mounds (Fig. 45, items 18, 19).[131] The similarity of the ornamentation on the wooden plates in these burial mounds to the brooch facings from Nyaksimvol makes them comparable and confirms the date established on the basis of analogues to objects from the Ananino sites.

Previous papers on this subject have established that two components played an important role in the formation of the Ust-Poluy culture, namely, the local element, evidently associated with the cultures of the boreal zone, and the Ugrian element which came from the middle Irtysh region.[132] Judging from the archaeological data, the local component was basically of Ural origin and its appearance in the North was tied to the extensive resettlement of Ural tribes during the Neolithic and Bronze ages. In this connection it is appropriate to mention the discovery in Finland of a number of objects made of Uralian pine, including sled runners; also we may cite Gjessing's opinion that the ancient proto-Lappish art of Scandinavia has Uralian roots.[133]

The carriers of the Ust-Poluy culture were fishermen and hunters who were familiar with the use of dogs as draft animals. They had a complex economy based on fishing, hunting of land animals, and hunting of sea mammals. These occupations were not equally important in the various areas of distribution of this culture. In the southern regions fishing and hunting prevailed, while in the northern regions the dominant role was played by reindeer hunting and the hunting of sea mammals, with some fishing. In its type of economy, the Ust-Poluy culture is similar to the cultures of the coastal-continental type, of the so-called prewhaling stage of the Paleo-Eskimo culture, represented by such sites as Ipiutak. The settlements of the Ust-Poluyans were situated on river capes and high floodplain terraces; in a number of cases they were fortified by a ditch and bank (Ust-Poluy, Nyaksimvol). It is also possible that the fortified settlements were refuges used by the population of a particular territory in the event of military danger or some other kind of extraordinary event. This may be the reason why these fortified sites had sacrificial places. Despite the fragmentary nature and incompleteness of our knowledge of the Ust-Poluy culture, even now we know that the Ust-Poluyans were familiar with several types of dwellings. Evidently, in addition to the semisubterranean dwellings found at the Salekhard settlement, surface dwellings were used in the more southerly regions. We project this, although in a highly conjectural manner, on the basis of the study of Makar-Visyng-Tur. Possibly a type of temporary [surface] winter dwelling was used also in the north; otherwise it would be difficult to explain the numerous finds of snow-shovel blade edges at Ust-Poluy.

The material culture of the Ust-Poluyans included a number of objects with parallels over very extensive territories, both in the ethnographic material and the archaeological material of northern Eurasia and North

America. Historically, the materials can be divided into several categories:

1. Primitive objects distributed over a very extensive territory. These include most of the bone arrowheads, the hafted harpoon heads, and the simple unornamented needle-cases made of bird bones. It may be assumed that these objects are a result of convergence.

2. Objects found in the boreal zone: reindeer-antler devices for leashing dogs, and bone knives for cleaning fish.[134] The similarity of these objects may also be explained by convergence due to similar forms of economy that existed under similar geographic conditions.

3. Objects widely distributed in the boreal zone, but having a number of specific features that become apparent in the details. These include the snow-shovel blades, the ice creepers, and the dog-harness swivels. The similarity of details leads us to entertain the possibility of ties in the individual cases. Cultural elements that were not due to geographic conditions but which yielded similar forms nonetheless may play an important role in explaining the nature of these possible contacts. Such factors are the knife handles and corresponding shapes of the sheaths, the combs, and some types of spoons.

The abundance of close parallels in specific forms cannot explain them on the basis of convergence alone. However, it is also difficult to assume that diffusion played an important role. In this matter, we can agree fully with Larsen that in cases of a very low density of population, diffusion could scarcely have any great significance.[135] We must seek another explanation and propose that there may have been movements of large or small groups of people, and that these movements must have taken place in the relatively recent past, inasmuch as the combination of boreal cultures with dog breeding was not present anywhere earlier than the second half of the 1st millennium B.C. The earliest known site of a culture of this type with dog breeding is Ust-Poluy. In this connection, it is interesting to note that the dog skulls from Ipiutak belong to dogs of Siberian origin.[136]

It may be assumed that the presence of dog breeding for draft animals afforded the hunting tribes of the arctic belt of Siberia an opportunity to expand their range of nomadic migrations considerably. This brought about more frequent contacts between the tribes of the boreal zone, and perhaps the movement of individual groups over very great distances.

Notes and References

ABBREVIATIONS

ESA	Eurasia septentrionalis antigua (Helsinki)
FUF	Finnisch-Ugrische Forschungen
GAIMK	Gosudarstvennoy Akademii istorii materialnoy kultury
IAK	Izvestiya Arkheologicheskoy komissii
IOAIE	Izvestiya Obshchestva arkheologii, istorii i etnografii pri Kazanskom universitete
IRGO	Izvestiya Russkogo Geograficheskogo obshchestva
IZSORGO	Izvestiya Zapadno-Sibirskogo otdela Russkogo geograficheskogo obshchestva
KSIIMK	Kratkiye soobshcheniya o dokladakh i polevykh issledovaniyakh Instituta istorii materialnoy kultury Akademii Nauk SSSR
MAR	Materialy po arkheologii Rossii
MAVGR	Materialy po arkheologii vostochnykh guberniy Rossii
MIA	Materialy i issledovaniya po arkheologii SSSR
OAK	Otchet Arkheologicheskoy komissii
RGO	Russkoye geograficheskoye obshchestvo
SA	Sovetskaya arkheologiya
SE	Sovetskaya etnografiya
SMAE	Sbornik Muzeya antropologii i etnografii
SMYA	Suomen Muinais muistoyhdistyksen aikakauskirja
TGIM	Trudy Gosudarstvennogo istoricheskogo muzeya
TIE	Trudy instituta etnografii
TKIChP	Trudy komissii po izucheniyu chetvertichnogo perioda Akademii Nauk SSSR
VDI	Vestnik drevney istorii
ZRAO	Zapiski Russkogo arkheologicheskogo obshchestva
ZSORGO	Zapiski Sibirskogo otdela Russkogo geograficheskogo obshchestva
ZUOLE	Zapiski Uralskogo obshchestva lyubiteley yestestvoznaniya
ZZSORGO	Zapiski Zapadno-Sibirskogo otdela Russkogo geograficheskogo obshchestva

PART I

1. T. J. Arne, *Barsoff Gorodok* (The fortified hill site Barsov), Stockholm, 1935.

2. S. G. Boch, Stoyanki v basseyne Severnoy Sosvy i Kondy (Sites in the basins of the Severnaya Sosva and Konda rivers), *TKIChP*, no. V, Leningrad, 1937.

3. V. P. Levasheva, Predvaritelnye soobshcheniya ob arkheologicheskikh issledovaniyakh Zapadnosibirskogo muzeya za 1926–1927 gg. (Preliminary reports on the archaeological investigations of the West Siberian Museum in 1926–1927), *Izvestiya Gosudarstvenogo zapadnosibirskogo muzeya*, no. 1, Omsk, 1928.

4. G. N. Prokofyev, Etnogoniya narodov Ob-Yeniseyskogo basseyna (Ethnogeny of the peoples of the Ob-Yenisey basin), *SE*, no. 3, 1940, pp. 67–76.

5. The Man-ya River is a left tributary of the upper Severnaya Sosva River.

6. A. P. Okladnikov indicates that a trunnion axe was found at the Neolithic site Tikhoye Pleso (on the Lena River) in the horizon below the layer with objects belonging to the Kitoy period. Okladnikov distinguishes two types of trunnion axes—the Angara and the Baykal. The Angara axes were made by a flaking technique, from flinty slate. They are long (about 30 cm), triangular in cross section, and have a narrow working end. The Baykal axes were made from crystalline rock by point flaking; they are shorter and have a rounded butt.

7. V. M. Florinskiy, *Pervobytnye slavyane po pamyatnikam ikh doistoricheskoy zhizni* (The indigenous Slavs, according to remains of their prehistoric life), Tomsk, 1894, vol. 2, p. 144, fig. 3, items 26, 27.

8. F. A. Uvarov, *Arkheologiya Rossii* (The archaeology of Russia), vol. 2, no. 135, p. 10, fig. 6.

9. Florinskiy, *Pervobytnye slavyane . . .* , p. 145, fig. 4, items 29, 30.

10. Ibid., p. 144, fig. 3, item 28; p. 145, fig. 4, item 32.

11. Boch, Stoyanki v basseyne . . . , p. 150.

12. Ibid.

13. Ibid.

14. J. Ailio, Fragen der russischen Steinzeit (Problems of the Russian Stone Age), *SMYA*, vol. 29, Helsinki, 1922.

15. D. N. Eding, Gorbunovskiy torfyanik (The Gorbunovo peat bog), *Materialy po izucheniyu Tagilskogo okruga*, no. 3, Tagil, 1929; idem, Reznaya skulptura Urala (The carved sculpture of the Urals), *TGIM*, no. 10, Moscow, 1940.

16. A. V. Shmidt, Stoyanka u stantsii Levshino (The campsite at Levshino station), *SA*, no. 5, 1937.

17. O. N. Bader, Novye raskopki bliz Tagila v 1944 g. (New excavations near Tagil in 1944), *KSIIMK*, no. 16, 1947, pp. 139–47; idem, Novyy tip neoliticheskogo poseleniya na Urale (New type of Neolithic settlement in the Urals), *SE*, no. 2, 1949, pp. 144–50.

18. Shmidt, Stoyanka u stantsii Levshino, p. 27, fig. 12.

19. Eding, Reznaya skulptura Urala, p. 25.

20. O. N. Bader, Neoliticheskaya stoyanka Borovoye Ozero I na r. Chusovoy (The Neolithic campsite Borovoye Ozero I on the Chusovaya River), *MIA*, no. 22, 1951, pp. 14–32; report of O. N. Bader for 1947–48 presented at the

OPI IMMK (arkhiv IIMK)—Section of Field Research of the Institute of the History of Material Culture (Archives of the Institute).

21. Shmidt, Stoyanka u stantsii Levshino, p. 26.

22. Bader, Novyy tip neoliticheskogo poseleniya na Urale, p. 146.

23. A. Ya. Bryusov, Uralskaya arkheologicheskaya ekspeditsiya (The Ural archaeological expedition), *KSIIMK*, no. 37, 1951, p. 74.

24. G. A. Chernov, Arkheologicheskiye nakhodki na reke Shchuchey (Archaeological finds on the Shchuchya River), *KSIIMK*, no. 40, 1951, fig. 26, items, 1–9.

25. Bader, Novye raskopki bliz Tagila . . . , fig. 50, items 3, 4.

26. Ya. V. Stankevich, Neoliticheskaya stoyanka u "Gremyachego ruchya" (The Neolithic campsite at Gremyachiy Ruchey [Roaring Creek]), *SA*, no. 5, 1937, p. 234, fig. 2, item 2.

27. N. A. Prokoshev, Kamskaya ekspeditsiya 1935 g. (The Kama expedition of 1935), *SA*, no. 1, 1937, p. 258.

28. Shmidt, Stoyanka u stantsii Levshino, p. 20, fig. 8, item 4.

29. Stankevich, Neoliticheskaya stoyanka u "Gremyachego ruchya," p. 234; ibid., p. 259, fig. 3, item 4.

30. Ailio, in Fragen der russischen Steinzeit, classifies the finds from Petkash as "thin-butted" axes and dates them to the 2nd and 3rd periods of Montelius's system, which, in absolute chronology, corresponds approximately to the second half of the 3rd millennium B.C.

31. I. Ya. Slovtsov, O nakhodkakh predmetov kamennovo veka bliz Tyumeni (Finds of Stone Age objects near Tyumen), *ZZSORGO*, Book 7, no. 1, 1887.

32. P. A. Dmitriyev, Lipchinskaya neometallicheskaya stoyanka (The Lipchinskaya New Metal Age campsite), *Trudy Sektsii arkheologii RANION* [*Rossiyskaya assotsiatsiya nauchno-issledovatelskikh institutov obshchestvennykh nauk*], no. 2, Moscow, 1928, p. 67.

33. Ibid.

34. O. N. Bader, Stoyanki Nizhneadishchevskaya i Borovoye Ozero I na r. Chusovoy (The Nizhneye Adishchevo and Borovoye Ozero I campsites on the Chusovaya River), *MIA*, no. 22, 1951, p. 10.

35. A. P. Okladnikov, Neolit i bronzovyy vek Pribaykalya (The Neolithic and Bronze Age of the Cis-Baykal), *MIA*, no. 18, 1950, pp. 158, 164.

36. A. Ya. Bryusov, *Ocherki po istorii plemen yevropeyskoy chasti SSSR v neoliticheskuyu epokhu* (Essays on the history of tribes in the European part of the U.S.S.R. during the Neolithic period), Moscow, 1952, pp. 150–53.

37. V. M. Raushenbakh, Keramika shigirskoy kultury (Pottery of the Shigir culture), *KSIIMK*, no. 43, 1952, p. 57, fig. 18; Bryusov, *Ocherki po istorii plemen* . . . , p. 36.

38. Bader, Stoyanki Nizhneadishchevskaya . . . , p. 20.

39. Bryusov, *Ocherki po istorii plemen* . . . , pp. 160–62.

40. S. P. Tolstov, Drevnosti Verkhnego Khorezma (Antiquities of Upper Chorasmia), *VDI*, no. 1, 1941, p. 158.

41. See Plate III, item 1, and Plate IV, item 4 of this article; S. P. Tolstov, *Drevniy Khorezm* (Ancient Chorasmia), Moscow, 1948, fig. 13.

42. A. V. Zbruyeva, Drevniye kulturnye svyazi Sredney Azii i Priuralya (Ancient cultural ties between Central Asia and the Cis-Ural region), *VDI*, no. 3, 1946, p. 185.

43. Tolstov, *Drevniy Khorezm*, p. 64; idem, *Po sledam drevnekorezmiyskoy*

tsivilizatsii (Traces of the ancient Chorasmian civilization), Moscow, 1948, p. 71.

44. Tolstov, *Drevniy Khorezm*, Plates 14, 15.

45. Bryusov, Uralskaya arkheologicheskaya ekspeditsiya, p. 74.

46. Tolstov, *Drevniy Khorezm*, p. 349.

47. V. N. Chernetsov, Rezultaty arkheologicheskoy razvedki v Omskoy oblasti (Results of an archaeological survey in Omsk *oblast*), KSIIMK, no. 17, 1947, pp. 79–91. In this paper, I erroneously assigned the Yekaterininskoye campsite to the Late Bronze Age, because of a knife in the collections of the Omsk Museum listed as "from the Yekaterininskoye campsite" (*KSIIMK*, no. 17, 1947, fig. 34, item 10). On account of this knife, I felt I had to assign the late date to the site, despite the archaic aspect of the pottery. Now I have discovered that this bronze knife was listed in error, owing to the inaccuracy of the data supplied by the person who found it. It bears no relation to Yekaterininskoye.

48. Dmitriyev, Lipchinskaya neometallicheskaya stoyanka; idem, Vtoraya Andreyevskaya stoyanka (The Andreyevskaya II campsite), *TGIM*, no. 8, Moscow, 1938. On the dating of these sites, *vide infra*.

49. P. L. Dravert, K mineralogii kaynozoyskikh otlozhenii Ob-Irtyshskogo basseyna (The mineralogy of the Cenozoic deposits of the Ob-Irtysh basin), *IZSORGO 1925–1926 gg.*, vol. 5, Omsk, 1926, p. 134.

50. Dmitriyev, Lipchinskaya neometallicheskaya stoyanka, pp. 61–70.

51. Ibid., Plate 5, figs. 1, 2; Bader, Novye raskopki bliz Tagila . . . , fig. 50, items 9, 10, 12.

52. Dmitriyev, Lipchinskaya neometallicheskaya stoyanka, Plate 5, fig. 3.

53. Bryusov, Uralskaya arkheologicheskaya ekspeditsiya, p. 75.

54. M. N. Komarova, Pogrebeniya Okuneva ulusa (The Okunevo *ulus* burials), *SA*, no. 9, 1947, p. 54; fig. 6—the Yarki burial ground near Bateni.

55. Shmidt, Stoyanka u stantsii Levshino, p. 26.

56. Dmitriyev, Vtoraya Andreyevskaya stoyanka, p. 108.

57. Ibid., p. 98.

58. Ibid.

59. Ibid., Plate 1; fig. 4, item 5.

60. Ibid., Plate III; fig. 5, item 10.

61. Ibid., Plate II; figs. 32, 33.

62. Ibid., Plate III; figs. 14, 23.

63. Raushenbakh, Keramika shigirskoy kultury, pp. 55–68.

64. Bryusov, Uralskaya arkheologicheskaya ekspeditsiya, p. 74; Bader, Novyy tip neoliticheskogo poseleniya . . . , p. 146.

65. Bryusov, *Ocherki po istorii plemen* . . . , p. 157.

66. Komarova, Pogrebeniya Okuneva ulusa.

67. M. N. Komarova, Tomskiy mogilnik; pamyatnik istoriy drevnikh plemen lesnoy polosy Zapadnoy Sibiri (The Tomsk burial ground; remains of the ancient tribes inhabiting the forest belt of western Siberia), *MIA*, no. 24, 1952, pp. 7–50.

68. Ibid., p. 13, fig. 5.

69. Ibid., p. 13.

70. Chernetsov, Rezultaty arkheologicheskoy razvedki v Omskoy oblasti, pp. 82–86.

71. Komarova, Tomskiy mogilnik, p. 28. In addition to the twelve burials cited, Komarova notes indications of the existence of "Neolithic" burials on

Malyy Cape, i.e., of the type of Bolshoy Cape (e.g., the vessel in plot 88 and the stone implements below the level of the 11th burial).

72. The "near" is rather arbitrary, inasmuch as Samarovo is 500 km from Tobolsk.

73. Chernetsov, Rezultaty arkheologicheskoy razvedki v Omskoy oblasti, fig. 34, items 8, 9.

74. W. Moszyńska, Zhilishche ust-poluyskoy kultury i stoyanka epokhi bronzy v Salekharde (A dwelling of the Ust-Poluy culture and a Bronze Age campsite at Salekhard), *MIA*, no. 35, 1953, Plate IV, item 9.

75. Ibid., Plate II, item 14.

76. Ibid., Plate IV, item 9; Plate V, items 9, 14.

77. Eding, Reznaya skulptura Urala, p. 96.

78. The honeycomb ornamentation, according to K. V. Salnikov, is similar to the ornamentation of the Early Bronze Age pottery from Kysyk-Kul. Analogies may also be found at the Lipchinskaya and Andreyevskaya II campsites.

79. O. A. Krivtsova-Grakova, Alekseyevskoye poseleniye i mogilnik (The Alekseyevka settlement and burial ground), *TGIM*, no. 17, Moscow, 1949, fig. 53, item 1.

80. V. N. Chernetsov, Opyt tipologii zapadnosibirskikh keltov (Experimental typology of West-Siberian celts), *KSIIMK*, no. 16, 1947, pp. 65–78. (At present we are more certain of an earlier dating of celts of the Ivanovskaya type. The dating should be ca. 1100–900 B.C. Author, August 1968.)

81. Director of the Tobolsk Museum, died 1952.

82. A. P. Okladnikov, *Istoriya Yakutii* (History of Yakutia), vol. 1, Yakutsk, 1950, p. 166, table 21, fig. 1. It should be noted that Okladnikov erroneously stated that the Andreyevskaya sword was found in Shadrinsk *okrug*.

83. Tobolsk Museum, catalog of the Historical Section, No. 64; No. 4458 in the accessions book.

84. Ibid., No. 69; No. 6515 in the accessions book.

85. Chernetsov, Opyt tipologii zapadnosibirskikh keltov, fig. 22.

86. *OAK* (Report of the Archaeological Commission) for 1907, p. 121, figs. 127, 128; M. P. Gryaznov, Drevnyaya bronza Minusinskikh stepey (Ancient Bronzes of the Minusinsk steppes), *Sbornik Gosudarstvennogo Ermitazha*, 1947, Plate 2; fig. 2.

87. Gryaznov, Drevnyaya bronza . . . , p. 247.

88. Ibid., Plate 2; fig. 8.

89. Ibid., Plate 3.

90. A. Shtukenberg, *Materialy dlya izucheniya mednogo (bronzovogo) veka vostochnoy polosy Yevropeyskoy Rossi* (Materials for the study of the Copper [Bronze] Age in the eastern part of European Russia), Kazan, 1901.

91. Chernetsov, Opyt tipologii zapadnosibirskikh keltov, p. 68.

92. A. O. Heikel, *Antiquités de la Sibérie occidentale*, Helsingfors, 1894.

93. P. A. Dmitriyev, Shigirskaya kultura na vostochnom sklone Urala (The Shigir culture on the eastern slope of the Urals), *MIA*, no. 21, 1951, p. 41; p. 45, fig. 1, items 18, 19.

94. Okladnikov, Neolit i bronzovyy vek Pribaykalya, p. 160, fig. 15.

95. Tolstov, *Drevniy Khorezm*, Plate 11.

96. For example, at the campsites at Khulyum-sunt and Andreyevskoye Lake, and at Gorbunovo in the Urals (see Eding, Reznaya skulptura Urala, fig. 15).

97. A. P. Okladnikov, Arkheologicheskiye dannye o drevneyshey istorii Pribaykalya (Archaeological data on the earliest history of the Cis-Baykal region), *VDI*, no. 1, 1938, p. 248, fig. 4.

98. A. P. Okladnikov, K izucheniyu neolita Vostochnogo Priuralya i Zapadnoy Sibiri—tezisy (Notes on the study of the Neolithic period in the eastern Cis-Ural region and western Siberia—theses), *Doklady nauchnykh konferentsiy Molotovskogo gos. universiteta*, nos. 1–4, Molotov, 1948.

99. Bader, Stoyanki Nizhneadishchevskaya . . . , p. 22, fig. 10.

100. Bader, Novye raskopki bliz Tagila. . . .

101. A. A. Formozov, Kelteminarskaya kultura v Zapadnom Kazakhstane (The Kelteminar culture in western Kazakhstan), *KSIIMK*, no. 39, 1949, pp. 49–58; idem, Arkheologicheskiye pamyatniki v rayone Orska (Archaeological remains in Orsk *rayon*), *KSIIMK*, no. 36, 1951, pp. 115–21; idem, K voprosu o proiskhozhdenii andronovskoy kultury (On the problem of the origin of the Andronovo culture), *KSIIMK*, no. 39, 1951, pp. 3–18.

102. Formozov, K voprosu o proiskhozhdenii . . . , p. 10.

103. Ibid., p. 13.

104. Chernetsov, Rezultaty arkheologicheskoy razvedki v Omskoy oblasti, p. 81. The Omsk campsite is situated on the left bank of the Irtysh, opposite the city of Omsk. Although the campsite has been known for thirty years, it has not yet been investigated, but most of it has already been disturbed, and in a few years it will disappear altogether. I surveyed it in 1945 and again in 1948 and 1949. From my firsthand acquaintance with it, I expressed the opinion that it was not older than Andronovo. I based this opinion on the find of a potsherd with meandering Andronovo ornamentation beneath one of the undisturbed hearths. However, now I must point out that this opinion, which is correct with respect to that particular hearth, must not be extended to the campsite as a whole. The hearths in the depressions between the dunes or sandy ridges of the lower end of the ancient island undoubtedly are not of the same age. Some of them, as the one in which the potsherd was found, had a thin hearth layer, while others had a very thick one. Artifacts of later periods were not found in the lower horizons of these hearths. Therefore, it would be more correct to regard the Omsk campsite as a site of very long duration, originating at least at the very beginning of the Metal Age. This would explain the thickness of the culture-bearing layer of the campsite, which in places is more than a meter thick, and the exceptional abundance of material included in it, among them stone objects.

105. While I do not wish to go into the problem of the origin of the Andronovo culture here, I feel I must express my complete disagreement with the concepts proposed by A. A. Formozov in his paper "K voprosu o proiskhozhdenii andronovskoy kultury" (On the problem of the origin of the Andronovo culture), published in no. 39 of *KSIIMK* in 1951. In attempting to bring different points of view on the origin of the Andronovo culture into agreement, the author expresses the opinion that "in the Eneolithic, in the territory of diffusion of the Andronovo culture, there was not just one Afanasevo culture and not a single 'Turgay' culture covering all of Kazakhstan, but a number of cultures. We may say that the Afanasevo culture did not go far into Kazakhstan, where three groups of Eneolithic campsites can be noted: Semipalatinsk, southern Ural, and Cis-Aral (Kelteminar). Further assembly of materials from eastern Kazakhstan and Central Asia probably will allow us to specify the boundaries of several additional pre-Andronovo cultures. . . . In the process,

we shall not deny a genetic connection between the Andronovo and Afanasevo cultures, but see in the Afanasevo only one of the sources of the Andronovo culture."

Formozov asks, "Why did a number of local cultures combine in a unified culture over a large territory during the Andronovo epoch?" He finds the answer in the attainment of the appropriate stage of economic development by the tribes, the carriers of these local cultures, namely, stockbreeding, agriculture, and metallurgy. "The universal diffusion of stock-breeding and agriculture removed the need for specialization (i.e., local differences. Author). The uniform way of life brought with it a uniformity in the types of dwellings and, in this connection, in the types of vessels; it created a community of agricultural ideology and a subsequent uniformity in the magical ornamentation of the vessels."

Formozov sees the origin of the Andronovo culture in the amalgamation of various cultures, based on the development of agriculture, stockbreeding, and metallurgy. In the relations between the individual tribes, there took place "not simply a transfer of things, but probably a movement of groups of the population, the forcing out of some tribes by others, mixing. . . . The extensive interrelations of cultures in this large territory and, undoubtedly, peoples of different physical types brought about a combination not only of a single material culture, but of a new physical type. The main development on which this mixing of peoples was based were, let me repeat, metallurgy, stockbreeding, and agriculture in the steppe and forested steppe zones of northern Asia. Therefore, the 'Neolithic tribes' of the forests of the eastern Cis-Ural and the Cis-Baykal, who continued to practice hunting and fishing, and the agriculturalists of the piedmont Anau culture, did not participate in the founding of the Andronovo community" (p. 17).

Viewing the Andronovo culture as the result of the diffusion of various cultures when they reached a certain stage of economic development, Formozov naturally raised the question, "Why did not the Andronovo sphere include the steppes north of the Black Sea, as it, too, had stock-breeding, agriculture, and metallurgy at the beginning of the 2nd millennium B.C.?" (p. 18). He finds the answer very simple. Beyond the limits of the Andronovo "cultural region" lay a region of other contacts, which was responsible for the differences in the "cattle-breeding-agricultural Timber-Frame culture that was similar in appearance to the Andronovo." In operating with completely abstract cultures, Foromozov did not even raise the question of how legitimate it would be to pass judgments on the origin of the Andronovo culture without touching on, even lightly, the problems of the ethnic affinity of its carriers.

106. Chernetsov, Rezultaty arkheologicheskoy razvedki v Omskoy oblasti, p. 90. In this paper, I mistakenly called the campsite a fortified hill site. It should be noted that the earthen rampart and ditch belong to a present-day cemetery. The custom of surrounding a cemetery with a rampart and ditch and not a fence is widespread in Omsk *oblast*.

107. Ye. [Elizabet] M. Bers, Arkheologicheskaya karta g. Sverdlovska i ego okrestnostey (Archaeological map of Sverdlovsk and its environs), *MIA*, no. 21, 1951, p. 194, fig. 3, items 7, 8.

108. M. P. Gryaznov, Kostyanoye orudiye paleoliticheskogo vremeni iz Zapadnoy Sibiri (Paleolithic bone implement from western Siberia), *KSIIMK*, no. 31, 1950, pp. 165–67.

109. N. F. Kashchenko, O nakhozhdenii ostatkov mamonta okolo Tomska

(Find of the remains of a mammoth near Tomsk), *Izvestiya Akad. Nauk*, vol. 5, no. 1, 1896.

110. O. N. Bader, K istorii pervobytnogo obshchestva na Tagilskom Urale (On the history of the primitive society in the Tagil Urals), *Doklady nauchnykh konferentsii Molotovskogo gos. universiteta*, no. 5/6, Molotov, 1951, p. 33; idem, Arkheologicheskiye issledovaniya na Urale v 1946 g. (Archaeological investigations in the Urals in 1946), *KSIIMK*, no. 20, 1948, pp. 78–81.

111. Bader, Stoyanki Nizhneadishchevskaya. . . .

112. Bryusov, *Ocherki po istorii plemen.* . . .

113. According to the data of Yu. Kreynovich, B. O. Dolgikh, et al.

114. A. V. Shmidt, Drevniy mogilnik na Kolskom zalive (Ancient burial ground on Kola Gulf), in *Kolskiy sbornik*, Leningrad, 1930, pp. 160 ff.; V. N. Chernetsov, Drevnyaya primorskaya kultura na poluostrove Yamal (An Ancient littoral culture of the Yamal Peninsula), *SE*, no. 4/5, 1935, pp. 109–33.

115. G. F. Debets, *Paleoantropologiya SSSR* (Paleoanthropology of the U.S.S.R.), Moscow, 1947.

116. V. N. Chernetsov, Ornament lentochnogo tipa u obskikh ugrov (Ribbon type of ornamentation among the Ob Ugarians), *SE*, no. 1, 1948, p. 151.

117. N. N. Cheboksarov and T. A. Trofimova, Antropologicheskoye izucheniye mansi (Anthropological investigation of the Mansi), *KSIIMK*, no. 9, 1941, pp. 34–36.

118. V. N. Chernetsov, Fratrialnoye ustroystvo obsko-yugorskogo obshchestva (The phratrial organization of the Ob-Ugarian society), *SE*, no. 2, 1939, pp. 20–40; see particularly p. 23.

119. It would be improbable to project that such a settlement was not exogamous, since this would require the assumption that the two phratries existed within its limits, which the above data on the dissemination of the clans would contradict. Even now, when the clan structure is breaking up, one may observe a tendency toward avoiding marriages within a settlement, even among the representatives of the different clans surviving in it. In earlier forms of exogamy, the main condition for its existence and development had to be complete exclusion of marriages within a group of people living in one place.

120. Chernetsov, Opyt tipologii zapadnosibirskikh keltov, p. 68.

121. Ibid., p. 66.

122. *Otchet Ob-Irtyshskoy ekspeditsii 1948 g.* (Report on the 1948 Ob-Irtysh expedition), MS, Archives of IIMK.

123. In S. G. Boch's sketch, on p. 151 [of his report, Stoyanki v basseyne . . .], where the fortified hill site is described, he points out, "The campsite described by us was noted by V. Chernetsov as the fortified hill site Sortynya II." An error crept into Boch's work here. It should be "the campsite Sortynya I." Owing to this error, Boch, in describing the pottery of Sortynya I (p. 152), points out that Chernetsov discovered in it vessels with hollow bases. In fact, the pedestaled vessels were discovered at Sortynya II, which is o.5 km from Sortynya I.

124. In the material collected from the surface at the foot of the scarp, there is a small number of potsherds that are identical to the vessel from the lower layer of Sortynya II, i.e., that classified as Bronze Age. It was not found in the layer. Probably the layer containing it was thin and completely destroyed when the fortified hill site was built.

125. Chernetsov, Drevnyaya primorskaya kultura na poluostrove Yamal, p. 110.

126. Ibid., Plate 1, fig. 2.

127. Ibid., Plate 1, fig. 3.

128. V. N. Chernetsov, Zelenaya Gorka bliz Salekharda (Zelenaya Gorka near Salekhard), *KSIIMK*, no. 25, 1949, pp. 67–74.

129. For technical reasons, drawings of the Zelenaya Gorka pottery were not included in the article referred to in note 128, but they are represented in the present work (see Plate XVIII).

130. W. Moszyńska, Keramika ust-poluyskoy kultury (Pottery of the Ust-Poluy culture), *MIA*, no. 35, 1953, pp. 107–20.

131. Eding, Gorbunovskiy torfyanik, pp. 16–17, table 7; fig. 22, items 30–36.

132. According to A. V. Zbruyeva in Drevniye kulturnye. . . .

133. See, for example, fig. 6, item 16, in M. P. Gryaznov, Pamyatniki mayemirskogo etapa epokhi rannikh kochevnikov na Altaye (Remains of the Mayemir stage of the early nomadic epoch in the Altay), *KSIIMK*, no. 18, 1947, pp. 9–17.

134. Gryaznov, Pamyatniki mayemirskogo etapa . . . , fig. 6, item 18.

135. Moszyńska, Zhilishche ust-poluyskoy kultury. . . .

136. V. N. Chernetsov, Izobrazitelnoye iskusstvo Priobya. Okhotnichi zatesy (The figurative arts of the Cis-Ob region. Hunters' marks), MS.

137. Chernetsov, 'Ornament lentochnogo tipa u obskikh ugrov.

138. Gryaznov, Pamyatniki mayemirskogo etapa . . . , p. 16, fig. 6, item 18.

139. Eding, Gorbunovskiy torfyanik, Plate 7.

PART II

1. P. S. Pallas, *Puteshestviye po raznym provintsiyam Rossiyskogo gosudarstva* (Journey through the various provinces of the Russian state), vol. 4, St. Petersburg, 1788, pt. 3.

2. V. Volegov, Zverinyy i rybnyy promysl na Rostesskom Urale (The hunting and fishing industry in the Rostesskiy Urals), *Okhota*, January, 1860, p. 18.

3. V. N. Chernetsov, K istorii rodovogo stroya u obskikh ugrov (History of the clan structure among the Ob Ugrians), *SE*, nos. 6–7, 1947, pp. 159–83.

4. J. Budenz, *Magyar-Ugor Összensonlitó Szóntár* (Hungarian-Ugrian comparative dictionary), Budapest, 1873–81.

5. F. Belyavskiy, *Poyezdka k Ledovitomu moryu* (Journey to the Arctic Ocean), Moscow, 1833, p. 120.

6. V. N. Chernetsov, Bronza ust-poluyskogo vremeni (The bronzes of the Ust-Poluy period), *MIA*, no. 35, 1953, pp. 121–78.

7. A. A. Dunin-Gorkavich, *Tobolskiy sever* (The Tobolsk North), vol. 3, Tobolsk, 1911, p. 101, fig. 26, item 12.

8. Ibid., item 6; O. Finsch and A. Brehm, *Puteshestviye v Zapadnyuyu Sibir d-ra O. Finsha i A. Brema* (The journey to Western Siberia of Doctor O. Finsch and A. Brehm), Moscow, 1882; Pallas, *Puteshestviye po raznym provintsiyam . . .*, p. 119.

9. A. A. Spitsyn, Priuralskiy kray (The Ural district), *MAVGR*, I, Moscow,

1893, Plates II and III; F. D. Nefedov, Otchet ob arkheologicheskikh issle-doraniyakh v Prikame proizredennykh letom 1893 goda (An account of archaeological investigations carried out during the summer of 1893), *MAVGR*, III, Moscow, 1899, Plate 13, figs. 1, 2, 3; V. A. Zbruyeva, Konets-gorskoye selishche (The unfortified townsite of Konetsgorskoye), *MIA*, no. 30, 1952.

10. Similar bone points are known in the Abramovskiy barrow on the Om River, dating to the Late Bronze Age, and in one of the Ust-Tartas barrows, dating to a late stage of the Sarmatian period.

11. S. K. Patkanov, *Tip ostyatskogo bogatyra po ostyatskim bylinam i georicheskim skazaniyam* (The nature of the Ostyak warrior according to the Ostyak lays and heroic tales), St. Petersburg, 1891, p. 29.

12. A. F. Middendorf, *Puteshestviye na sever i vostok Sibiri* (Journey to the North and East of Siberia), St. Petersburg, 1878, pt. 2, sec. 5.

13. V. G. Bogoraz, Ocherk materialnogo byta olennykh Chukoch (Sketch of the material culture of the Reindeer Chukchi), *SMAE*, vol. 2, St. Petersburg, 1901, Plate XV, item 5.

14. L. I. Shrenk [Schrenk], *Ob inorodtsakh Amurskogo kraya* (On the natives of Amur *kray*), vol. 2, St. Petersburg, 1899, p. 177; A. M. Zolotarev and M. G. Levin, K voprosu o drevnosti proiskhozhdeniya olenevodstva (On the question of the early origin of reindeer-herding), *Problemy proiskhozhdeniya evolyutsii i porodoobrazovaniya domashnikh zhivotnykh*, vol. 1, 1940, p. 179.

15. Anonymous, Zverinaya promyshlennost Udskogo kraya i sopredelnykh k nemy mest (The hunting industry in Uda *kray* and places adjoining it), *ZSORGO*, Book 2, 1857, p. 8. (Cited by Zolotarev and Levin, q.v.)

16. Middendorf, *Puteshestviye na sever i vostok Sibiri*, p. 366. In mentioning the past century [that is, the 18th], Middendorf has in mind the journey of Sarychev.

17. P. S. Pallas, *Neue nördische Beyträge zur physikalischen und geographischen Erd- und Völkerbeschreibung, Naturgeschichte und Oekonomie*, St. Petersburg und Leipzig, 1781–96, vol. 1, p. 244. (Cited by Middendorf, q.v.)

18. Belyavskiy, *Poyezdka k Ledovitomu moryu*, pp. 76–77.

19. A. V. Shmidt, Drevniy mogilnik na Kolskom poluostrove (An ancient graveyard on the Kola Peninsula), *Kolskiy sbornik*, Leningrad, 1930, Plate 2, fig. 3.

20. Dunin-Gorkavich, *Tobolskiy sever*, fig. 26, item 13.

21. Eyriye [Eyriés], *Zhivopisnoye puteshestviye po Azii* (A picturesque journey through Asia), Moscow, 1839, pp. 83–84. [Translation from the French by E. Korosh.]

22. A. B., Opyt issledovaniya o drevney yugre (Attempt at a study of the ancient Ugrians), *Vestnik RGO*, no. 14, 1855, p. 171.

23. V. Zuyev, *Materialy po etnografii Sibiri 18 v. (1771–1772). Opisaniye zhivushchikh Sibirskoy gubernii v Berezovskom uyezde inovercheskikh narodov, ostyakov i samoyedtsev, studentom Vasilyem Zuyevym* (Materials on the ethnography of Siberia in the 18th century, 1771–1772. Description of the pagan peoples living in Berezov *uyezd*, Siberian *guberniya*, Ostyaks and Samoyeds, assembled by the student Vasiliy Zuyev), published by the AN SSSR, Moscow, 1947, pp. 79–80.

24. Ibid., p. 90, footnote 70.

25. V. N. Chernetsov, Drevnyaya primorskaya kultura na poluostrove Yamal (An ancient littoral culture of the Yamal Peninsula), *SE*, no. 4/5, 1935.

26. M. G. Levin, O proiskhozhdenii upryazhnogo sobakovodstva (On the origin of harness dog-breeding), *SE*, no. 4, 1946, p. 90.

27. K. Birket-Smith, *Report of the Fifth Thule Expedition*, vol. 5, *The Caribou Eskimos: Material and social life, and their cultural position*, Copenhagen, 1929, p. 181, fig. 54a.

28. V. S. Adrianov's field notes of the 1935 Ust-Poluy excavations. The field notes are in the Museum of Physical Anthropology and Ethnography [in Leningrad].

29. S. K. Patkanov, *Die Irtysch-Ostjaken und ihre Volkspoesie*, St. Petersburg, 1900. The heroic tale of the two sons and husband of a Taparsk woman, p. 30.

30. Chernetsov, Drevnyaya primorskaya kultura. . . .

31. Personal communication, B. O. Dolgikh.

32. U. T. Sirelius, *Die Handarbeiten der Ostjaken und Vogulen*, Helsingfors, 1903, p. 14, fig. 13.

33. Ibid., p. 15, fig. 16.

34. A. Heikel, *Antiquités de la Sibérie occidentale*, Helsingfors, 1894, Plate VII, fig. 11.

35. Shmidt, Drevniy mogilnik . . . , Plate 4, figs. 2 and 3.

36. N. N. Novokreshchennykh, Glyadenovskoye kostishche na r. Kame Permskoy gub. (The Glyadenovo ossuary on the Kama River in Perm *guberniya*), *Trudy Permskoy gubernskoy uchenoy arkhivnoy komissii*, vol. 11, pt. 2, 1914, Plate 14, item 23.

37. Tobolsk Guberniya Museum, *Izdeliya ostyakov Tobolskoy guberniy* (Handiwork of the Ostyaks of Tobolsk *guberniya*), Tobolsk, 1911, pp. 46–47.

38. Budenz, *Magyar-Ugor Összensonlitó Szóntár*, p. 531.

39. V. I. Podgorbunskiy, Zametki po izucheniyu goncharstva yakutov (Notes on the study of Yakut pottery), *Sibirskaya zhivaya starina*, no. 7, Irkutsk, 1928, pp. 129–30, Plate 1, fig. 1.

40. Chernetsov, Bronza ust-poluyskogo vremeni.

41. Sirelius, *Die Handarbeiten der Ostjaken und Vogulen*, p. 14, fig. 15.

42. Lacking an adequate number of blades, we cannot tell whether there was a difference between the knives of men and women. The present-day ones are distinguished only by the form of the blade.

43. The tale was narrated by Volodya Yadne (age 25) and recorded in 1946.

44. N. L. Gondatti, *Sledy yazychestva u inorodtsev Severo-Zapadnoy Sibiri* (Traces of paganism among the natives of northwestern Siberia), Moscow, 1888, p. 42.

45. L. I. Varaksina, Kostenosnyye gorodishcha Kamsko-Vyatskogo kraya (The ossuaries of the fortified hill sites of the Kama-Vyatka area), *IOAIE*, vol. 34, nos. 3–4, Kazan, 1929, p. 95, Plate IV, fig. 6.

46. V. A. Gorodtsov, Podcheremskiy klad (The Podcherem cache), *SA*, no. 2, 1936.

47. At present, the Mansi use very large wooden pestles for crushing bird cherries.

48. V. S. Adrianov, Raskopki u Sale-Kharda v 1935 g. (Excavations at Sale-Khard in 1935), *SA*, no. 1, 1936, p. 278.

49. A. A. Popov, *Nganasany* (The Nganasans), Izdanniya Instituta ethnografii AN SSSR, Moscow-Leningrad, 1948; Birket-Smith, *The Caribou Eskimos*, p. 225, fig. 86a.

50. Personal communication, V. N. Chernetsov. He also reported that the Bakhtiarov clan, now living on the Lozva River, derives from the Vishera,

whence it came to the Lozva only during the 19th century. The Kurikov clan lives on the Pelym.

51. A. A. Spitsyn, Arkheologicheskiye razyskaniya o drevneyskikh obitatelyakh Vyatskoy gub. (An archaeological search for the ancient inhabitants of Vyatka *guberniya*), *MAVGR*, 1, 1893, pp. 43, 53–54, Plate II, fig. 6.

52. *OAK*, 1913–15.

53. T. Mathiassen, *Report of the Fifth Thule Expedition*, vol. 4, *Archaeology of the Central Eskimos*, pt. 2, *Thule culture and its position within the Eskimo culture*, Copenhagen, 1927, p. 115.

54. Chernetsov, Bronza ust-poluyskogo vremeni.

55. V. N. Chernetsov, Ust-poluyskoye vremya v Priobye (The Ust-Poluy period in the Ob region), *MIA*, no. 35, 1953, p. 223, fig. 2.

56. Heikel, *Antiquités de la Sibérie occidentale*, Plate III, figs. 2, 4, 5, 7–11; Novokreshchennykh, Glyadenovskoye kostishche . . . , Plate 2, fig. 22.

57. Chernetsov, Bronza ust-poluyskogo vremeni; A. M. Kastren [Castrén], Etnograficheskiye zamechaniya i nablyudeniya Kastrena o loparyakh, karelakh, samoyedakh i ostyakakh, izvlechennye iz yego putevykh vospominaniy 1838–1844 gg. (Castrén's ethnographic comments and observations on the Lapps, Karelians, Samoyeds, and Ostyaks, taken from his travel recollections of 1838–1844), *Etnograficheskiy sbornik* [published by Rossiyskoye geograficheskoye obshchestvo], no. 4, 1858.

58. The excavations of V. P. Levasheva in 1927.

59. *ZUOLE*, no. 7, 1883, p. 75; *MAR*, no. 37, 1918, p. 62.

60. V. N. Chernetsov and W. Moszyńska, Gorodishche Bolshoy log (The fortified hill site of Bolshoy Log), *KSIIMK*, no. 37, 1951.

61. For example, at the campsite of Tiutey-sale on the west coast of the Yamal Peninsula [see Chernetsov, Drevnyaya primorskaya kultura. . . . Editor, A.I.N.A.]

62. Shrenk [Schrenk], *Ob inorodtsakh Amurskogo kraya*.

63. Birket-Smith, *The Caribou Eskimos*, pt. 1, descriptive part.

64. *Istoricheskiy arkhiv*, vol. 3, 1940, p. 93.

65. Zolotarev and Levin, K voprosu o drevnosti . . . ; K. Donner, Über das Alter der ostjakischen und wogulischen Renntierzucht, *FUF*, vol. 18, Helsinki, 1927.

66. Such, at least, was the pit house excavated by us on [Cape] Salekhard.

67. Zuyev, *Materialy po etnografii Sibiri* . . . , p. 29.

68. V. N. Chernetsov, Opyt tipologii zapadnosibirskikh keltov (Experimental typology of West-Siberian celts), *KSIIMK*, no. 16, 1947.

69. P. S. Pallas, *Puteshestviye po raznym provintsiyam Rossiyskogo gosudarstva* (Journey through the various provinces of the Russian state), vol. 1, St. Petersburg, 1788, pp. 56–57.

70. V. N. Chernetsov, Ocherk etnogeneza obskikh yugrov (Sketch of the ethnogenesis of the Ob Ugrians), *KSIIMK*, no. 9, 1941, pp. 18–28.

71. Chernetsov, Bronza ust-poluyskogo vremeni, pp. 121–78.

72. G. N. Prokofyev, Tezisy doklada na temu "Etnogenez narodnostey Ob-Yeniseyskogo basseyna (nentsev, nganasanov, selkupov, khantov i mansi)" —Abstracts of reports on the theme "Ethnogenesis of the peoples of the Ob-Yenisey Basin (the Nentsy, Nganasans, Selkups, Khanty and Mansi)," *SE*, no. 3, Sbornik Statey, 1940, pp. 67–76.

73. Chernetsov, Drevnyaya primorskaya kultura. . . .

PART III

1. Typical Ust-Poluy sites were found and partly excavated during recent years by Valentina Viktorova at the mouth of the Lozva and on the upper Tavda.

2. A. A. Spitsyn, Shamanskiye izobrazheniya (Shamanistic representations), *ZRAO*, vol. 8, 1906, p. 135, fig. 424.

3. V. I. Kanivets, *Kaninskaya peshchera* (Kaninskaya cave), Moscow, 1964, pp. 84–92; fig. 21, item 2; fig. 29, item 1; fig. 30; fig. 31.

4. I. M. Myagkov, Drevnosti Narymskogo kraya (Antiquities of Narym *kray*), *Trudy Tomskogo krayevogo muzeya*, vol. 2, Tomsk, 1929.

5. Sbornik *Basandayka* (Collection of papers entitled *Basandayka*), Tomsk, 1947, Plate X, fig. 6.

6. Ibid., Plate XI, fig. 12.

7. Ibid., Plate XII, figs. 1–3; Plate XVII, fig. 6; Plate XVIII, fig. 6; Plate XIX, figs. 2, 3.

8. The materials from the fortified hill site have not been published; the information was obtained from M. P. Gryaznov, to whom I extend my sincere thanks.

9. V. N. Chernetsov and W. Moszyńska, Gorodishche Bolshoy log (The Bolshoy Log fortified hill site), *KSIIMK*, no. 37 1951, pp. 78–87.

10. Discovered by A. Artsybasov, a pupil at Public School No. 15.

11. Spitsyn, Shamanskiye izobrazheniya, fig. 453.

12. The bone inventory was analyzed by V. I. Tsalkin.

13. V. N. Chernetsov, Bronza ust-poluyskogo vremeni (Bronzes of the Ust-Poluy period), *MIA*, no. 35, 1953, pp. 174–78.

14. V. N. Chernetsov, Opyt tipologii zapadnosibirskikh keltov (Experimental typology of West-Siberian celts), *KSIIMK*, no. 16, Moscow, 1947, p. 75.

15. W. Moszyńska, Keramika ust-poluyskoy kultury (Pottery of the Ust-Poluy culture), *MIA*, no. 35, 1953, p. 118.

16. A. V. Zbruyeva, Istoriya naseleniya Prikamya v ananinskuyu epokhu (History of the population on the Kama in the Ananino period), *MIA*, no. 30, 1952.

17. Chernetsov, Opyt tipologii . . . , p. 75.

18. M. I. Rostovtsev, Kurgannye nakhodki Orenburgskoy oblasti epoki rannego i pozdnego ellinizme (Burial-mound finds of the Early and Late Hellenistic epochs in Orenburg *oblast*), *MAR*, no. 37, Petersburg, 1918, Plate IV, fig. 10.

19. M. P. Gryaznov, Drevnyaya bronza Minusinskikh stepey (Ancient bronzes of the Minusinsk steppes), *Sbornik Gosudarstvennogo Ermitazha*, Leningrad, 1947, pp. 154, 164.

20. K. F. Smirnov, Vooruzheniye Savromatov (Armament of the Sarmatians), *MIA*, no. 101, Moscow, 1961, p. 106, Plate V.

21. K. F. Smirnov, Vooruzheniye Savromatov, Plates V and VII.

22. Myagkov, Drevnosti Narymskogo kraya, pp. 77–78.

23. Ibid., pp. 64 and 78.

24. Zbruyeva, Istoriya naseleniya Prikamya. . . .

25. Chernetsov, Bronza ust-poluyskogo vremeni, pp. 121–78.

26. Myagkov, Drevnosti Narymskogo kraya, p. 58.

27. Chernetsov, Bronza ust-poluyskogo vremeni.

28. S. S. Chernikov, *Drevnyaya metallurgiya i gornoye delo zapadnogo Altaya* (Ancient metallurgy and mining in the western Altay), Alma-Ata, 1949.

29. S. V. Kiselev, Drevnyaya istoriya Yuzhnoy Sibiri (The early history of southern Siberia), *MIA*, no. 9, 1949, pp. 142–44.

30. The word *š'oχriŋ* is the possessive form of the word *š'oχri*, a narrow knife.

31. Presently in the Omsk Museum.

32. *Kratkoye opisaniye o narode ostyatskom, sochinennoye Grigoriyem Novitskim v 1715 g.* (Brief description of the Ostyak people, written by Grigoriy Novitskiy in 1715), Sankt Peterburg, L. Maykov [published], 1884, pp. 82–84.

33. Now in the Tyumen Museum.

34. Now in the Tobolsk Museum, card catalog No. 10859.

35. W. Moszyńska, Kamennaya skulptura Priobya (Stone sculpture on the Ob), *KSIIMK*, no. 43, 1952; W. Moszyńska, On some anthropomorphic images from West Siberia, in *Popular beliefs and folklore tradition in Siberia*, translation revised by Stephen P. Dunn, edited by V. Diószegi, Budapest, 1968, fig. 5 (a, b, c, d).

36. A. Heikel, *Antiquitiés de la Sibérie occidentale*, Helsingfors, 1894, table III, fig. 2.

37. A two-faced staff (warder) from Krutinka *rayon*, Omsk *oblast*.

38. T. A. Trofimova, Antropologicheskiy sostav drevneyshego naseleniya Prikamya i Priuralya (The physical anthropological composition of the earliest people of the Kama and Ural regions), *MIA*, no. 22, 1951, pp. 97–109.

39. L. Yermolayev, Ishimskiy klad (The Ishim cache), in *Opisaniye kollektsiy Krasnoyarskogo muzeya* (Description of the collections of the Krasnoyarsk Museum), Krasnoyarsk, 1914, Plate 8, figs. 3–6.

40. V. N. Chernetsov, Ocherk etnogeneza obskikh yugrov (Outline of the ethnogenesis of the Ob Ugrians), *KSIIMK*, no. 9, 1941, pp. 18–28.

41. Only a formalistic approach to the materials could explain M. P. Gryaznov's view that the "silver goblets of the Turkic period" were the prototype of Ust-Poluy pottery (*KSIIMK*, no. 48, 1952, p. 10, figs. 32–36). However, in contrast to the Scythian type of cauldron, goblets of this type have never been found by anyone in the archaeological remains of the lower Ob. The Turkic foliage ornament that is characteristic of these goblets is entirely foreign to the ornamentation of the Ust-Poluy period, for which cord ornamentation is typical.

42. P. A. Dmitriyev, Zhertvennye kamni Zauralya (Sacrificial stones of the Trans-Ural region), *KSIIMK*, no. 19, 1948, pp. 12–21.

43. Kiselev, Drevnyaya istoriya Yuzhnoy Sibiri, pp. 142–44.

44. G. N. Prokofyev, Etnogoniya narodov Ob-Yeniseyskogo basseyna (Ethnogeny of the peoples of the Ob-Yenisey Basin), *SE*, no. 3, 1940, pp. 67–76.

45. G. N. Prokofyev, Tezisy doklada 29 maya 1940 g. (Notes on the lecture delivered 29 May 1940), in *Materialy Komissii po etnogenezu* (Materials of the Commission on Ethnogenesis), Otdeleniye istoricheskokh nauk i filologii Akademii Nauk SSSR (Division of History and Philology, Academy of Sciences of the U.S.S.R.).

46. G. A. Chernov, Stoyanka drevnego cheloveka v servernoy chasti Bolshezemelskoy tundry (Campsite of ancient man in the northern part of the Bolshezemelskaya tundra), *KSIIMK*, no. 36, 1951, pp. 96–114; idem, Arkheo-

logicheskiye nakhodki na reke Shchuchey (Archaeological finds on the Shchuchya River), *KSIIMK*, no. 40, 1951, pp. 96–104.

47. Chernov, Stoyanka drevnego cheloveka. . . .

48. This latter problem will be treated more specifically later.

49. S. Patkanov [Patkanoff], Über das Volk der Sabiren (On the people of the Sabir), *Keleti Szemle*, vol. 1, no. 4, Budapest, 1900, pp. 258–77.

50. K. Grot, *Madyary i Moraviya s poloviny IV do X v.* (Hungarians and Moravia from the middle of the 4th to the 10th centuries), Sankt Peterburg, 1881, p. 217.

51. Patkanov [Patkanoff], Über das Volk der Sabiren.

52. B. Munkácsi, A magyar lovasélet ösisége (The antiquity of Hungarian horse breeding), *Népélet*, Budapest, 1931.

53. B. Munkácsi, Verschiedenheiten der arischen Lehwörter der fin.-mag. Sprachen (Differences in the Aryan loan words in the Finno-Ugric languages), *Keleti Szemle*, vol. 4, no. 3, 1903, pp. 374–84; idem, Alanische Sprachdenkmäler im ungarischen Wortschatze (Alan linguistic monuments in the Hungarian vocabulary), *Keleti Szemle*, vol. 5, no. 3, 1904, pp. 304–29.

54. A. G. Schrenk, *Reise nach dem Nord-Osten des Europäischen Russlands*, Dorpat, 1848, p. 430.

55. The word *sirti*, more exactly *siirtya* (A. Schrenk, *siirté*), or (Nenets) *s'i^{h}irt'a'*, should be regarded as consisting of two separate components, the first of which, *s'i^{h}ir*, is merely a revocalization of the aforementioned ethnonym *s'iBir*. In the second component, *-t'a'*, the final guttural occlusive replaces the *y* which had occurred there, in agreement with the regular change observed in the Nenets language, as, for example, *n'enec'a'* < *n'enec'an* (**n'ene-t'an*), the autonym of the Nenets people, *n'an-~n'a'* ("mouth"), etc. (Prokofyev). The initial form of this name can, therefore, be reconstructed as *s'iBir-t'an*, where *-t'an*, as was established by G. Prokofyev, is the general autonym of the aboriginal arctic tribes, in all probability with the meaning "people," like the Ket *d'eŋ*, and the Yukagir *t'in*, which has entered into a whole series of northern Samoyedic autonyms, as *ńene-c'an* (Nentsy, *ŋanasan* (the Taymyr Samoyeds), *ene-c'en* (Entsy—the Yenisey Samoyeds), etc.

PART IV

1. T. J. Arne, *Barsoff Gorodok* (The fortified hill site Barsov), Stockholm, 1935, p. 81.

2. M. V. Talitskiy, Verkhneye Prikamye v X–XIV vv. (The upper Kama region in the 10th–14th centuries A.D.), *MIA*, no. 22, 1951, p. 75.

3. A. P. Smirnov, Ocherki drevney i srednevekovoy istorii narodov Srednevo Povolzhya i Prikamya (Notes on the ancient and medieval histories of peoples living along the Middle Volga and Kama basins), *MIA*, no. 28, 1952, p. 195.

4. V. N. Chernetsov, *Vogulskiye skazki* (Vogul tales), Leningrad, 1935.

5. V. N. Chernetsov, Zelenaya Gorka bliz Salekharda (Zelenaya Gorka near Salekhard), *KSIIMK*, no. 25, 1949, pp. 67–74.

6. U. T. Sirelius, Über die primitiven Wohnungen der finnischen und obugrischen Völker, *FUF*, vol. 6, Helsinki, 1906.

7. Plates XXXVII and XXXVIII illustrate pottery from Us-Tolt, of the

Karym and Orontur periods, treated in the appropriate sections of this work (see pp. 173 and 197).

8. S. G. Boch, Stoyanki v basseyne Severnoy Sosvy i Kondy (Sites in the basins of the Severnaya Sosva and Konda rivers), *TKIChP*, no. V, Leningrad, 1937, p. 156.

9. Located about 1,000 km by river from Karym [63°55′ N; 65°03′ E].

10. W. Moszyńska, Keramika ust-poluyskoy kultury (Pottery of the Ust-Poluy culture), *MIA*, no. 35, 1953, pp. 113, 114; Plate V.

11. V. A. Gorodtsov, Podcheremskiy klad (The Podcherem cache), *SA*, no. 2, 1937, Plate I, fig. 3.

12. I. Ya. Slovtsov, O nakhodkakh predmetov kamennovo veka bliz Tyumeni v 1883 godu (Finds of Stone Age objects near Tyumen in 1883), *ZZSORGO*, Book 7, no. 1, 1887.

13. MAE, collection no. 5455-4840.

14. For example, see S. I. Rudenko, *Graficheskoye iskusstvo ostyakov i vogulov* (Graphic arts of the Ostyaks and Voguls), *Materialy po etnographii Russkogo muzeya*, vol 4, no. II, Leningrad, 1929, Plate VII, figs. 1–4; Plate IX, fig. 1.

15. Ibid., fig. 13.

16. Gorodtsov, Podcheremskiy klad, figs. 32–34.

17. Talitskiy, Verkhneye Prikamye . . . , fig. 32, item 1.

18. Gorodtsov, Podcheremskiy klad, p. 116 and fig. 10.

19. Privately owned.

20. O. N. Bader, Arkheologicheskiye pamyatniki Tagilskovo kraya (Archaeological remains in the Tagil district), *Uchenye zapiski Permskogo Universiteta*, vol. 8, no. 2, 1953, p. 323.

21. D. P. Shorin, O drevnostyakh v okressnostyakh Tagilskovo zavoda. Rukopis (Antiquities in the vicinity of the Tagil factory), MS, *Arkhiv IA*, in Leningrad.

22. V. I. Moshinskaya (W. Moszyńska), Gorodishche i kurgany Potchevash (The fortified hill sites and burial mounds at Potchevash), *MIA*, no. 35, 1953, p. 207, Plate IX (second drawing from left in second row from top).

23. Moszyńska, Keramika ust-poluyskoy kultury, p. 109, Plate II and fig. 9.

24. V. N. Chernetsov, Ornament lentochnogo tipa u obskikh ugrov (Ribbon type of decoration among the Ob River Ugrians), *SE*, no. 1, 1948, p. 147; Plate I; Plate IV, figs. 6, 7, 12, 13.

25. Ibid., Plate VI, figs. 14, 15; V. I. Moshinskaya (W. Moszyńska), Materialnaya kultura i khozyaystvo Ust-Poluya (The material culture and economy at Ust-Poluy), *MIA*, no. 35, 1953, p. 105, Plate XVII, fig. 3.

26. Chernetsov, Ornament lentochnogo tipa . . . , Plate VI, fig. 13.

27. Ibid., fig. 7; S. A. Teploukhov, Opyt klassifikatsii drevnikh metallurgicheskikh kultur Minusinskogo kraya (An experimental classification of the ancient metallurgical cultures of Minusinsk *kray*), *Materialy po etnografii*, vol. 3, Leningrad, 1927, p. 82; Plate VIII, fig. 22.

28. Smirnov, Ocherki drevney . . . , p. 118, Plate XXIV, fig. 5.

29. M. Khudyakov, Drevnosti Kamy po raskopkam A. A. Spitsyna v 1898 g. (The antiquities of the Kama from the excavations of A. A. Spitsyn in 1898), *Materialy GAIMK*, no. 2, Leningrad, 1933; the Zuyeva cemetery, burial no. 157, p. 13, Plate IV, fig. 6; F. D. Nefedov, Kotlovskiy mogilnik (The Kotlov cemetery), *MAVGR*, vol. III, 1899, Plate XIII, fig. 22.

30. Smirnov, Ocherki drevney . . . , p. 118.

31. *MAR*, no. 26, Sanktpeterburg, 1902, Plate VIII, fig. 6.

32. Ibid., Plate VI, fig. 13.

33. Smirnov, Ocherki drevney . . . , p. 99.

34. Gorodtsov, Podcheremskiy klad, p. 131.

35. Smirnov, Ocherki drevney . . . , pp. 97–99.

36. Gorodtsov, Podcheremskiy klad, fig. 27.

37. A. Spitsyn, Veshchi s inkrustatsiyey iz Kerchenskikh katakomb, 1904 g. (Inlaid work from the Kerch catacombs, 1904), *IAK*, no. 17, Sanktpeterburg, 1905, p. 115.

38. Ibid., p. 119, fig. 30.

39. Gorodtsov, Podcheremskiy klad, fig. 6.

40. Spitsyn, Veshchi s inkrustatsiyey . . . , figs. 1, 6, 20.

41. Gorodtsov, Podcheremskiy klad, figs. 28, 29.

42. *OAK* for 1895, Sanktpeterburg, p. 66, fig. 163.

43. *OAK* for 1892, Sanktpeterburg, p. 93, fig. 55.

44. Gorodtsov, Podcheremskiy klad, p. 141.

45. V. N. Chernetsov, K voprosu o proniknovenii vostochnoyo serebra v Priobe (The penetration of eastern silver [objects] into the Ob region), *TIE*, novaya seriya, vol. 1, 1947, pp. 114, 115.

46. B. Munkácsi, Vogul Népköltésy Gyüjtemény, vol. 1, Budapest, 1892–1902, p. 184.

47. V. I. Moshinskaya (W. Moszyńska) and V. N. Chernetsov, Gorodishche Andryushin Gorodok (The fortified hill site of Andryushin Gorodok), *KSIIMK*, no. 51, 1951, p. 96. The date for Andryushin Gorodok which I insisted upon in my joint report with W. Moszyńska must now be changed to a somewhat later one, and the culture represented by the site must be more sharply separated from the Potchevash culture.

48. *Problemy GAIMK*, 1933, nos. 9–10, p. 22.

49. Moshinskaya (Moszyńska), Gorodishche i kurgany Potchevash, Plate XVII. The pot in fig. 8 is incorrectly represented by the artist. Actually the neck of the pot is straighter and higher, the body is more rounded, and the shoulders are more sharply defined.

50. This term was proposed by P. A. Dmitriyev, who discerns considerable resemblance between the Trans-Ural and the Ananino materials. The term must be accepted only conditionally, until the Trans-Ural is more fully studied; in any case, the term is not well chosen, because the Trans-Ural culture appears to be an independent one rather than a variant of the Ananino.

51. R. E. Kols, Atlas nizhnego techeniya reki Taz (Atlas of the lower course of the Taz River), *RGO*, Leningrad, 1930, leaf 1; idem, Reka Taz: Opisaniye i poyasneniya k atlasu RGO (The Taz River: Description and explanation to the atlas of the RGO), Leningrad, 1930, p. 16.

52. Gorodtsov, Podcheremskiy klad, p. 138.

53. Ibid., Plate III, fig. 1.

54. Ibid., pp. 137 and 138, Plate III, figs. 4, 5.

55. Ibid., p. 139.

56. A. A. Spitsyn, Drevnosti Kamskoy Chudi (Antiquities of the Kama Chuds), *MAR*, no. 26, Sanktpeterburg, 1902, p. 23.

57. A. V. Shmidt, K voprosu o proiskhozhdenii permskovo zverinovo stilya (On the origins of the Perm animal style), *SMAE*, vol. 6, Leningrad, 1927, p. 138.

58. Ibid., p. 139.

59. Ibid., p. 141.

60. Gorodtsov, Podcheremskiy klad, p. 128.

61. Ibid.

62. Smirnov, Ocherki drevney . . . , pp. 97–102.

63. Ibid., p. 81.

64. A. A. Spitsyn, Shamanskiye izobrazheniya (Shamanistic representations), *ZRAO*, Otdeleniye russkoy i slavyanskoy arkheologii, vol. 8, no. 1, 1906, pp. 29–145.

65. Smirnov, Ocherki drevney . . . , p. 187, figs. 3, 4.

66. Shmidt, K voprosu o proiskhozhdenii . . . , p. 131.

67. Ibid., p. 153.

68. A. A. Spitsyn, Shamanizm v otnoshenii k russkoy arkheologii (Shamanism in reference to Russian archaeology), *ZRAO*, novaya seriya, vol. 11, nos. 1 and 2, 1899.

69. A. V. Shmidt, Einige Motive der prähistorischen Kunst Transuraliens, *Artibus Asiae*, no. 1, 1930–32, pp. 6–18; on the subject of flat casting, see V. Chernetsov, Drevnyaya istoriya nizhnego Priobya (Ancient history of the lower Ob), *MIA*, no. 35, 1953, pp. 177, 178.

70. *MIA*, no. 35, 1953.

71. Arne, *Barsoff Gorodok*.

72. *MIA*, no. 35, 1953, p. 137, figs. 10, 13, 14; p. 147, fig. 5; p. 168, and others.

73. Moshinskaya (Moszyńska), Gorodishche i kurgany Potchevash, p. 217.

74. Shmidt, K voprosu o proiskhozhdenii . . . , p. 132, Plate 1, figs. 1–8.

75. *MIA*, no. 28, 1952, Plate XX, fig. 14

76. Arne, *Barsoff Gorodok*, p. 105, fig. 25.

77. Ibid., fig. 51.

78. Spitsyn, Shamanskiye izobrazheniya, fig. 8.

79. Ibid., fig. 4.

80. G. A. Chernov, *Arkheologicheskiye nakhodki na r. Shchuchya* (Archaeological finds on the River Shchuchya), *KSIIMK*, no. 40, p. 98, fig. 26, item 10.

81. MAE, collection no. 1457. This constitutes Zhuravskiy's collections from the sites Moy-Yarey in the Bolshezemelskaya tundra.

82. I have seen such small knives among the Nentsy (Samoyeds) on the Yamal Peninsula at the time of the Bear Feast. One may not eat bear meat without using a knife. Obviously the knife, like metal in general, has a magic power to avert evil. (This applies even to the dogs; if the Nentsy give leftover bear meat to a dog, he is tethered with a metal chain.) Sometimes when metal knives were lacking they made wooden imitations of them.

83. Arne, *Barsoff Gorodok*.

84. Tobolsk Museum, $\frac{902\text{-}6}{\text{n-}12}$, inv. no. 6821.

85. Arne, *Barsoff Gorodok*, p. 95.

86. Ibid., pp. 95, 96.

87. Ibid., fig. 59.

88. Ibid., figs. 88a, 91, 93, 102, 104, and others.

89. For example, on the vessels from burials nos. 3, 5, and 32 (ibid., figs. 18, 22, 88, 102, 104, and others).

90. Arne, *Barsoff Gorodok*, p. 14.

91. *MAR*, no. 26, Sanktpeterburg, 1902, Plate XI, fig. 5; Smirnov, Ocherki drevney . . . , Plate XLI, fig. 7.

92. Spitsyn, Shamanskiye izobrazheniya, illustrations nos. 336, 357, 358,

366. The artifacts from the Lenk-Ponk cemetery, which are kept in the State Hermitage and which are sketched in Spitsyn's work, could not be shown here, unfortunately, as the Section of Indigenous Archaeology in the Hermitage did not fill our order and send the necessary photographs.

93. Smirnov, Ocherki drevney . . . , Plate XLI, fig. 6.

94. Spitsyn, Shamanskiye izobrazheniya, illustration no. 358.

95. *ZRAO*, vol. 11, n.s., nos. 1 and 2, 1899.

96. *OAK* for 1910, p. 230, fig. 282.

97. J. R. Aspelin, *Antiquités du nord finno-ougrien*, fig. 574 (cited by Arne in *Barsoff Gorodok*). If we presume that the article to which Arne refers is the same as that cited by Spitsyn in his Shamanskiye izobrazheniya, illustration no. 370, then it should not be called a bracelet, but a rectangular plaque with a representation of a bear.

98. Arne, *Barsoff Gorodok*, pp. 60, 74.

99. Ibid., figs. 145, 150, 156.

100. Ibid., fig. 86; *MAVGR*, III, p. 118, fig. 67.

101. Arne, *Barsoff Gorodok*, fig. 57.

102. Album *OAK* for 1892–98, Sanktpeterburg, fig. 2081.

103. V. N. Chernetsov, Bronza ust-poluyskogo vremeni (Bronzes of the Ust-Poluy period), *MIA*, no. 35, 1953, p. 128, Plate III, fig. 2.

104. A. P. Smirnov, Novyy sarmatskiy mogilnik v Voronezhkoy oblasti (The new Sarmatian cemetery in Voronezh oblast), *VDI*, no. 3–4, 1940, pp. 364–66; V. V. Shkorpil, Zametki o relefe na pamyatnike s nadpisyu Yevpatoriya (Remarks on the relief sculpture of a monument with an inscription of Eupatorius), *IAK*, no. 37, p. 32, fig. 8.

105. Gorodtsov, Podcheremskiy klad, p. 117, fig. 17.

106. Album *OAK* for 1892–98, fig. 1811.

107. Ibid., fig. 283.

108. Arne, *Barsoff Gorodok*, fig. 86; *MAVGR*, III, p. 118.

109. Arne, *Barsoff Gorodok*, fig. 57.

110. Ibid., fig. 145 and possibly 150.

111. Ibid.

112. *MAR*, no. 26, Sanktpeterburg, 1902, Plate III, fig. 8.

113. Smirnov, Novyy sarmatskiy mogilnik . . . , p. 101; *MAR*, no. 26, Sanktpeterburg, 1902, Plate XXXVIII, fig. 7.

114. V. A. Oborin, Rozhdestvenskoye gorodishche i mogilnik (The Rozhdestvenskiy fortified hill site and cemetery), *Uchenye zapiski Permskogo Universiteta*, vol. 9, no. 3, 1953, Plate V, fig. 5, p. 177.

115. Arne, *Barsoff Gorodok*, p. 120, fig. 153.

116. *MAR*, no. 26, Sanktpeterburg, 1902, Plate III, fig. 2.

117. Ye. M. Bers, Nikito-Ivdelskiye stoyanki (The Nikito-Ivdel sites), Permskyy Gosudarstrenyy Universitet, *Doklady nauchnykh konferentsiy*, nos. 1–4, 1948, p. 52.

118. Ibid.

119. Arne, *Barsoff Gorodok*, p. 127, fig. 160.

120. Chernetsov, Bronza ust-poluyskogo vremeni, p. 131, Plate IV, fig. 8.

121. Tobolskiy musey, no. 4076, "Vyselok Vata Lokosovskoy upravy" ("The hamlet Vata in the Lokosovskaya *uprava*").

122. Bers, Nikito-Ivdelskiye stoyanki, fig. 4, item 1.

123. Ibid., fig. 4, item 4.

124. Arne, *Barsoff Gorodok*, p. 97.

125. Smirnov, Novyy sarmatskiy mogilnik . . . , Plate XLI, fig. 4.

126. *MAR*, no. 26, Sanktpeterburg, 1902, Plate VI, fig. 21.

127. Arne, *Barsoff Gorodok* (for a comparison of burials nos. 67 and 23, see p. 78; for burial no. 1, see pp. 79, 80; burial no. 48 is dated by the knife, which cannot belong to a period earlier than the 10th century A.D.).

128. V. P. Levasheva, Orudiya obrabotki zemli v russkoy derevne X–XIII vv. n.e. (Agricultural tools in a Russian village of the 10th–13th centuries A.D.), MS. I hereby express my gratitude to the author for her kind permission to use the information contained in her manuscript.

129. *OAK* for 1913–15, Petrograd, 1918, pp. 175, 176.

130. Ibid., p. 177.

131. Arne, *Barsoff Gorodok*, p. 51.

132. Ibid., p. 57.

133. N. A. Prokoshev, Pogrebeniye na r. Chusovoy (A burial on the Chusovaya River), *SA*, no. 3, 1937, p. 132.

134. B. N. Gorodkov, Poyezdka na Salym (A journey to the Salym River), *Yezhegodnik Tobolskogo gubernskogo muzeya*, vol. 21, 1911, p. 53; Tobolsk, 1913.

135. *MAR*, no. 26, Sanktpeterburg, 1902, Plate III, fig. 5.

136. Oborin, Rozhdestvenskoye gorodishche i mogilnik, p. 173, Plate IV, fig. 7.

137. Arne, *Barsoff Gorodok*, fig. 42, p. 80.

138. Prokoshev, Pogrebeniye na r. Chusovoy, figs. 3, 4.

139. F. D. Nefedov, Kostromskiye kurgany (The Kostroma *kurgans*), *MAVGR*, vol. III, Moscow, 1899, Plate V.

140. N. N. Gurina, Doklad na Obedinennoy konferentsii po arkheologii, etnografii i antropologii Pribaltiki v 1955 (Report to the Joint Congress of the archaeology, ethnography and physical anthropology of the Baltic region in 1955), *Tezisy dokladov sektsii arkheologii*, Moscow, 1955, p. 10.

141. Chernetsov, Zelenaya Gorka bliz Salekharda, pp. 67–74.

142. The bone materials were identified by V. I. Tsalkin.

143. Smirnov, Novyy sarmatskiy mogilnik . . . , p. 132.

144. *Palma*: in Siberia a heavy, one-edged blade attached to a shaft. It is used in hunting.

145. The collection from the Isker fortified hill site, no. 1161, in the Tobolsk Museum; *Yezhegodnik Tobolskogo gubernskogo muzeya*, vol. 25, Tobolsk, 1915, Plate IV, fig. 5.

146. V. M. Florinskiy, *Pervobytnye slavyane po pamyatnikam ikh doistoricheskoy zhizni* (The aboriginal Slavs judged by the remains of their prehistoric life), vol. 2, Tomsk, 1894.

147. Arne, *Barsoff Gorodok*, fig. 134 and p. 78.

148. A. Popov, Orudiya okhoty u narodov Sibiri v XIX i pervoy chertverti XX stoletiya (Hunting equipment among the Siberian peoples in the 19th and the first quarter of the 20th centuries), MS.

149. P. de la Martiner, Puteshestviye v severnye strany, 1653 g. (A journey to northern countries in 1653). Translation of the first edition (Paris, 1671) and notes by V. Semenkovich, *Zapiski Moskovskogo arkheologicheskogo instituta*, vol. 15, pp. 50, 93.

150. Ibid., p. 53.

151. Ibid., p. 93.

152. Quoted after A. Nordensheld [Nordenskjöld], *Vokrug Yevropy* (Around Europe), Sanktpeterburg, 1881, p. 94.

153. De la Martiner, Puteshestviye v severnye strany . . . , p. 91.

154. M. Alekseyev, *Sibir v izvestiyakh zapadno-yevropeyskikh puteshestvennikov i pisateley* (Siberia in the accounts of West European travellers and writers), vol. 1, Irkutsk, 1939, p. 180.

155. Franz Belyavskiy, *Poyezdka k Ledovitomu moryu* (A journey to the Arctic Ocean), Moscow, 1833, p. 258.

156. V. N. Chernetsov, Ust-poluyskoye vremya v Priobye (The Ust-Poluy period in the Ob region), *MIA*, no. 35, 1953, p. 241. [For a translation, see pp. 113–37 of this work. Editor, A.I.N.A.]

157. V. N. Chernetsov, Drevnyaya primorskaya kultura na poluostrove Yamal (An ancient littoral culture of the Yamal Peninsula), *SE*, no. 4/5, 1935, p. 131.

158. Ibid., p. 124; see also *MIA*, no. 35, 1953, p. 241.

159. M. P. Gryaznov, Raskopki Altayskoy ekspeditsii na Blizhnikh Yelbanakh (Excavations of the Altay expedition at Blizhniye Elbany), *KSIIMK*, no. 26, 1949, p. 116. Gryaznov's dating of the Fominskaya culture to the 7th–8th centuries A.D., and more so, the ascribing of this date to the Ust-Poluy (*KSIIMK*, no. 48, 1952, pp. 97–100) seem to be a misunderstanding based on a series of erroneous conclusions (for example, the ascribing of the Pyanobor figurine of an eagle from Ples village to the Lomovatovo culture) and the arbitrary omission of certain artifacts (the epaulettelike fastenings, the bird figurines, pendants in the form of cicadas from the Fominskaya burial, celts, picks, three-edged bronze arrowheads from Ust-Poluy, the representation of Artemis from the Istyak cache, etc.), which directly contradict the date suggested by the author.

160. Chernetsov, Zelenaya Gorka bliz Salekharda, p. 72.

161. Gorodkov, Poyezdka na Salym, p. 52.

162. L. Shults, Kratkoye soobshcheniye ob ekskursii na reku Salym, Surgutskogo uyezda (A brief report on the excursion to the Salym River in Surgut *uyezd*), *Yezhegodnik Tobolskogo gubernskogo muzeya*, vol. 21, 1911, p. 10; Tobolsk, 1913.

163. Alexander Castrén, *Nordische Reise und Vorscheugen*, Band IV (Ethnologische Vorlesungen), St. Petersburg, 1857, p. 113.

164. Moshinskaya (Moszyńska), Materialnaya kultura . . . , Plate XV, item 1, p. 99. [In the translation (pp. 75–111) it is Plate XXXII, item 1.]

165. Smirnov, Ocherki drevney . . . , p. 216.

PART V

1. W. G. Bogoraz, Elements of the culture of the circumpolar zone, *American Anthropologist*, vol. 31, 1929, pp. 579–601 (N.B. p. 595).

2. W. Thalbitzer, Parallels within the culture of arctic peoples, *Annales do XX congresso internacional de Americanistas*, Rio de Janeiro, 1924.

3. F. Boas, Migrations of Asiatic races and cultures to North America, *Scientific Monthly*, vol. 28, 1929, pp. 5, 110–17.

4. G. Hatt, Moccasins and their relations to arctic footwear, *Memoirs of the American Anthropological Association*, vol. 3, no. 3, 1916; idem, North American and Eurasian culture connections, *Proceedings of the 5th Pacific Science Congress, Victoria and Vancouver, Canada, 1933*, vol. 4, Toronto, 1934.

5. K. Birket-Smith, *Report of the Fifth Thule Expedition*, vol. 5, *The Caribou Eskimos: Material and social life, and their cultural position*, Copenhagen, 1929.

6. Ibid.

7. K. Birket-Smith, *The Chugach Eskimos*, Copenhagen, 1953, p. 230.

8. A. M. Zolotarev, The ancient culture of North Asia, *American Anthropologist*, vol. 40, no. 1, 1938, pp. 14, 22.

9. Gutorm Gjessing, Circumpolar stone age, *Acta Arctica*, fasc. II, Copenhagen, 1944.

10. Ibid., pp. 5–6.

11. Ibid., pp. 9–10, 31–32, 64.

12. Much earlier ones have been found in the South Russian steppes, in *Yamnaya* [Pit] culture sites, with which Gjessing's Arctic "coastal culture" can in no way be associated.

13. Gjessing, Circumpolar stone age, pp. 57–59.

14. Ibid., p. 70.

15. H. Larsen and F. Rainey, Ipiutak and the arctic whale hunting culture, *Anthropological papers of the American Museum of Natural History*, vol. 42, New York, 1948.

16. Ibid., p. 161.

17. V. N. Chernetsov, Drevnyaya istoriya nizhnego Priobya (The early history of the Cis-Ob region), *MIA*, no. 35, 1953, pp. 7–71 [translated into English; see pp. 1–74 of this work]; idem, Bronza ust-poluyskogo vremeni (Bronzes of the Ust-Poluy period), *MIA*, no. 35, 1953, pp. 121–78; idem, Ust-poluyskoye vremya v Priobye (The Ust-Poluy period in the Ob region), *MIA*, no. 35, 1953 [translated into English; see pp. 115–37 of this work].

18. V. N. Chernetsov, Ocherk etnogeneza obskikh yugrov (Outline of the ethnogenesis of the Ob Ugrians), *KSIIMK*, no. 9, 1941, pp. 18–28; idem, Osnovnye etapy istorii Priobya s drevneyshikh vremen do X v. (Principal stages of the history of the Ob region from antiquity to the 10th century), *KSIIMK*, no. 13, 1946; idem, Bronza ust-poluyskogo vremeni; idem, Ust-poluyskoye vremya v Priobye.

19. Chernetsov, Bronza ust-poluyskogo vremeni; idem, Ust-poluyskoye vremya v Priobye.

20. M. P. Gryaznov, Nekotorye itogi trekhletikh arkheologicheskikh rabot na Verkhney Obi (Some results of three years of archaeological work on the upper Ob), *KSIIMK*, no. 48, 1952, pp. 93–102 (N.B. p. 97).

21. L. R. Kyzlasov, *Tashtykskaya epokha* (The Tashtyk period), Moscow, 1960, p. 173.

22. M. P. Gryaznov, Istoriya drevnikh plemen Verkhney Obi (History of the ancient tribes of the upper Ob), *MIA*, no. 48, 1956, p. 137.

23. Ibid., p. 139.

24. *MAVGR*, no. 1, 1893, Plate 3. [Publication of the Moskovskoye arkheologicheskoye obshchestvo; see list of abbreviations.]

25. D. B. Shimkin, Western Siberian archaeology (an interpretive summary), in *Men and cultures*, selected papers of the 5th International Congress of Anthropology, Philadelphia, 1960.

26. C. S. Chard, The western roots of Eskimo culture, *Separata del II tomo des actas del XXXIII Congreso Internacional de Americanistas*, San José, Costa Rica, 20–27 July, 1958; Shimkin, Western Siberian archaeology.

27. V. S. Adrianov, Raskopki u Salekharda v 1936 g. (Excavations at Salekhard in 1936), *SA*, no. 1, 1936; A. M. Tallgren, Problems concerning the

Central-Russian gorodishche civilization, *ESA*, vol. 10, 1936, pp. 170–85; Chernetsov, Ocherk etnogeneza obskikh yugrov; Chernetsov, Osnovnye etapy istorii Priobya . . . ; Chernetsov, Drevnyaya istoriya nizhnego Priobya; Chernetsov, Ust-poluyskoye vremya v Priobye; V. I. Moshinskaya [Moszyń-ska], Materialnaya kultura i khozyaystvo Ust-Poluya (Material culture and economy of Ust-Poluy), *MIA*, no. 35, 1953; Moshinskaya [Moszyńska], Keramika ust-poluyskoy kultury (Pottery of the Ust-Poluy culture), *MIA*, no. 35, 1953, pp. 107–20; I. A. Talitskaya, Materialy k arkheologicheskoy karte Nizhnego i Srednego Priobya (Materials for an archaeological map of the lower and middle Ob region), *MIA*, no. 35, 1953.

28. Chernetsov, Bronza ust-poluyskogo vremeni, p. 146; idem, Ust-poluy-skoye vremya v Priobye, p. 228.

29. A. Kannisto, *Materialen zur Mythologie der Wogulen*, Helsinki, 1958, p. 267.

30. Ibid., p. 268

31. F. Belyavskiy, *Poyezdka k Ledovitomu moryu* (Journey to the Arctic Ocean), Moscow, 1833, pp. 92–93.

32. Kannisto, *Materialen zur Mythologie der Wogulen*; V. N. Chernetsov, Zhertvoprinosheniye u vogul (Sacrifices among the Voguls), *Etnografissle-dovatel*, no. 1, Leningrad, 1927.

33. A. Shchekatov, *Slovar geograficheskiy Rossiyskago gosudarstva, sobrannyy Afanasiyem Shchekatovym*, Chast chetvertaya, otdeleniye I (Geographic diction-ary of the Russian state, compiled by Afanasiy Shchekatov, Part Four, Section One), Moscow, 1805, p. 963.

34. Kannisto, *Materialen zur Mythologie der Wogulen*, pp. 257–58.

35. P. S. Bogoslovskiy, Istoriya pravitelstvennogo obsledovaniya v XVIII v. Permskogo kraya v etnograficheskom otnoshenii (History of 18th century ethnographic investigation of the Perm district by the government), *IOAIE*, vol. 34, nos. 3–4, 1929, p. 41.

36. V. Pavlovskiy, *Voguly* (The Voguls), Kazan, 1907.

37. O. Finsch and A. E. Brehm, *Reise nach West-Sibirien im Jahre 1876*, Berlin, 1879 [pages cited in this paper are from the Russian translation, *Puteshestviye v Zapadnuyu Sibir*, Moscow, 1882], p. 487.

38. Yu. I. Kushelevskiy, *Severnyy polyus i zemlya Yalmal: Putevye zapiski*, St. Petersburg, 1868. This work has not received the attention it should from ethnographers, who do not regard it seriously, mainly because of its unfortu-nate title (The North Pole and the Yalmal land: Notes of a traveler). One may assume that this inexperienced and naive author truly reported all the ethno-graphic information which he collected during his long sojourn in the Obian north. In cases where his data have checked, they have proved to be worthy of attention. His power of observation is confirmed by, inter alia, his discussion of the impossibility of distinguishing ethnographically (despite his attempts to do so) between the Obdorsk Ostyaks and Samoyeds. This is quite natural, as we now know, because the "Obdorsk Samoyeds" were Samoyedized Os-tyaks (clans Salyander, Poronguy, et al.).

39. From notes recorded in 1938 by V. N. Chernetsov on the basis of an account of N. Bakhtyarov (Lozva River, Anchukh-Paul).

40. A. M. Kastren [Castrén], Etnograficheskiye zamechaniya i nablyudeniya Kastrena o loparyakh, karelakh, samoyedakh i ostyakakh, izvlechennye iz yego putevykh vospominaniy 1838–1844 gg. (Castrén's ethnographic com-ments and observations on the Lapps, Karelians, Samoyeds, and Ostyaks,

taken from his travel recollections, 1838–1844), *Etnograficheskiy sbornik* [published by Rossiyskoye geograficheskoye obshchestvo], no. 4, 1858, p. 308.

41. Ibid., pp. 309–10.

42. Finsch and Brehm, *Puteshestviye v Zapadnuyu Sibir*, p. 486.

43. Kastren [Castrén], Etnograficheskiye zamechaniya . . . , p. 310.

44. Finsch and Brehm, *Puteshestviye v Zapadnuyu Sibir*, p. 486.

45. Kushelevskiy, *Severnyy polyus i zemlya Yalmal*, p. 54.

46. Shchekatov, *Slovar geograficheskiy* . . . , pp. 962–63.

47. V. I. Moshinskaya [W. Moszyńska], Zhilishche ust-poluyskoy kultury i stoyanka epokhi bronzy v Salekharde (A dwelling of the Ust-Poluy culture and a Bronze Age campsite at Salekhard), *MIA*, no. 35, 1953, pp. 179–88; Talitskaya, Materialy k arkheologicheskoy karte. . . .

48. Moshinskaya [Moszyńska], Zhilishche ust-poluyskoy kultury. . . .

49. Chernetsov, Bronza ust-poluyskogo vremeni; idem, Ust-poluyskoye vremya v Priobye; Moshinskaya [Moszyńska], Keramika ust-poluyskoy kultury.

50. V. N. Chernetsov, Zelenaya Gorka bliz Salekharda (The Zelenaya Gorka site near Salekhard), *KSIIMK*, no. 25, 1949, pp. 67–74; Chernetsov, Drevnyaya istoriya nizhnego Priobya; Talitskaya, Materialy k arkheologicheskoy karte. . . .

51. Moshinskaya [Moszyńska], Keramika ust-poluyskoy kultury.

52. S. G. Boch, Stoyanki v basseyne Severnoy Sosvy i Kondy (Campsites in the Severnaya Sosva and Konda basin), *TKIChP*, vol. 5, 1937; Chernetsov, Bronza ust-poluyskogo vremeni, Moshinskaya [Moszyńska], Keramika ust poluyskoy kultury; Talitskaya, Materialy k arkheologicheskoy karte. . . .

53. Boch, Stoyanki v basseyne . . . ; V. N. Chernetsov, Komandirovka v Berezovskiy rayon Ostyako-Vogulskogo okruga, 1935 g. (Mission to the Berezov *rayon* of the Ostyak-Vogul *okrug*, 1935), *SA*, no. 3, 1937; Chernetsov, Bronza ust-poluyskogo vremeni; Moshinskaya [Moszyńska], Keramika ust-poluyskoy kultury; Talitskaya, Materialy k arkheologicheskoy karte. . . .

54. Chernetsov, Komandirovka v Berezovskiy rayon . . . ; idem, Bronza ust-poluyskogo vremeni; Moshinskaya [Moszyńska], Keramika ust-poluyskoy kultury; Talitskaya, Materialy k arkheologicheskoy karte. . . .

55. Chernetsov, Bronza ust-poluyskogo vremeni; Moshinskaya [Moszyńska], Keramika ust-poluyskoy kultury; Talitskaya, Materialy k arkheologicheskoy karte. . . .

56. Talitskaya, Materialy k arkheologicheskoy karte. . . .

57. Ibid.

58. *MAVGR*, no. 1, 1893, Plates 2 and 3; L. I. Varaksina, Kostenosnye gorodishcha Kamsko-Vyatskogo kraya (Fortified hill sites containing bones, Kama-Vyatka *kray*), *IOAIE*, vol. 34, nos. 3–4, 1929, Plate I; A. V. Zbruyeva, Istoriya naseleniya Prikamya v ananinskuyu epokhu (History of the Kama basin people in the Ananino period), *MIA*, no. 30, 1952, Plate 10.

59. Zbruyeva, Istoriya naseleniya Prikamya . . . , Plate 41, item 14; J. G. D. Clark, *Prehistoric Europe: The economic basis*, London, 1952, p. 36; Larsen and Rainey, Ipiutak and the arctic whale hunting culture, Plate 1, items 20, 21.

60. Zbruyeva, Istoriya naseleniya Prikamya . . . , Plate 46, item 6.

61. *Fondy Otdela Sibiri MAE* (Collections of the Siberian Division of the Museum of Anthropology and Ethnography).

62. R. F. Heizer, *Archaeology of the Uyak site, Kodiak Island, Alaska*, Berkeley, California, 1956, pp. 57–58.

63. G. Rowley, The Dorset culture of the eastern Arctic, *American Anthropologist*, vol. 42, 1940, pp. 490–99; fig. 1d.

64. J. L. Giddings, *The Arctic woodland culture of the Kobuk River*, Philadelphia, 1952, Plate 10, item 7.

65. Birket-Smith, *Caribou Eskimos*, vol. 1, fig. 54, p. 181.

66. For a detailed description of the Ust-Poluy pottery by sites, see Moshinskaya [Moszyńska], Keramika ust-poluyskoy kultury. Here we have limited ourselves to a general description employing those data which were not included in the aforenamed paper. The classification and the periodization proposed in that paper hold fully here. The additions and changes in the present paper are based on our reprocessing of the pottery collection.

67. D. N. Eding, Novye nakhodki na Gorbunovskom torfyanike (New finds in the Gorbunovo peat bog), *MIA*, no. 1, 1940, Plate 2 (item 1), Plate 4 (item 2); C. A. Nordman, *Die steinzeitlichen Tierskulpturen Finnlands*, Ipek, 1936–37; A. M. Tallgren, Some north Eurasian sculptures, *ESA*, vol. 12, 1938.

68. J. Ailio, Zwei Tierskulpturen, *SMYA*, vol. 26, 1912.

69. Giddings, *Arctic woodland culture*, Plate 41, item 38.

70. Larsen and Rainey, Ipiutak and the arctic whale hunting culture, Plate 23, item 5.

71. Birket-Smith, *Chugach Eskimos*, p. 188.

72. N. N. Novokreshchennykh, Glyadenovskoye kostishche na reke Kame Permskoy gubernii (The Glyadenovo cemetery on the Kama River, Perm *guberniya*), *Trudy Permskoy gubernskoy uchenoy arkhivnoy kmoissii*, vol. 11, pt. 2, 1914, Plate 14, item 23.

73. Heizer, *Archaeology of the Uyak site*, p. 77, fig. 50.

74. A. V. Shmidt, Drevniy mogilnik na Kolskom zalive (Ancient burial ground on Koa Gulf), *Kolskiy sbornik*, Leningrad, 1930, Plate 4, items 2 and 3.

75. Materials collected in the field by the Taymyr team of the northern expedition of the Ethnography Institute, Academy of Sciences of the U.S.S.R., 1962.

76. E. Gunther, *Northwest Coast Indian art: An exhibit at the Seattle World's Fair, Fine Arts Pavilion, April 21–October 21, 1962*, Seattle, 1962, p. 85.

77. The osseous materials were identified by V. E. Garrut, Associate of the Zoological Institute, Academy of Sciences of the U.S.S.R.

78. From information collected in the field by V. N. Chernetsov.

79. Heizer, *Archaeology of the Uyak site*, pp. 71–72, Plate 70, item c.

80. E. Manker, *Lapparnas heliga ställen* (Sacred places of the Lapps), Uppsala, 1957.

81. Larsen and Rainey, Ipiutak and the arctic whale hunting culture, p. 176, Plate 89, item 26.

82. T. Mathiassen, *Report of the Fifth Thule Expedition*, vol. 4, *Archaeology of the Central Eskimos*, pt. 1, *Descriptive part*, Copenhagen, 1927, p. 48, Plate 16, item 6.

83. Birket-Smith, *Caribou Eskimos*, p. 82, fig. 13.

84. Now lost. Only a photograph and a tracing of it remain. These constitute front and side views, from which the description was derived.

85. Lost. Only tracings remain, on one of which the place where the object was found was noted.

86. Lost. Only the description and a sketch remain.

87. Zbruyeva, Istoriya naseleniya Prikamya . . . , pp. 291–92.

88. The material from these excavations had not been published as of July

1968. I wish to thank N. L. Chlenova and L. P. Zyablin for acquainting me with it.

89. R. S. Vasilyevskiy, Drevnyaya koryakskaya kultura po raskopkam na Okhotskom poberezhye (The ancient Koryak culture as based on excavations on the coast of the Sea of Okhotsk), *Voprosy Sibiri i Dalnego Vostoka*, 1961, pp. 321–28. I. S. Vdovin and N. N. Dikov have told me of finds of bone combs on Kamchatka. One specimen was decorated with a graphic ornament, another with the sculptured representation of an animal.

90. Birket-Smith, *Caribou Eskimos*; K. Birket-Smith, The composite comb in North America, *Ethnos*, vol. 2, no. 2, 1937.

91. A. Skinner, Notes on Iroquois archaeology, *Indian Notes and Monographs*, vol. 18, New York, 1921, pp. 77–80; A. C. Parker, The origin of the Iroquois as suggested by their archaeology, *American Anthropologist*, vol. 18, 1916.

92. R. MacNeish, The archaeology of the northeastern United States, in J. B. Griffin, ed., *Archaeology of the Eastern United States*, Chicago, 1952, p. 47; W. Ritchie, Northeastern cross-ties with the Arctic, *Arctic Institute of North America, Technical Paper no. 11*, 1962.

93. Skinner, Notes on Iroquois archaeology.

94. Mathiassen, *Archaeology of the Central Eskimos*, p. 115, fig. 6.

95. For a detailed description, the composition of the alloy, and the characteristics of the object see Chernetsov, Bronza ust-poluyskogo vremeni, pp. 127–30.

96. For detailed characteristics and analogues, ibid., pp. 130–34.

97. Ibid., p. 134 contains a detailed description of this item.

98. Ibid., p. 135, for details of the Ust-Poluy ornamental plates.

99. Ibid., p. 136.

100. Ibid.

101. Ibid., p. 134, for a detailed description and analogues.

102. Ibid., p. 135, for additional details.

103. Ibid., pp. 135–36.

104. MAE 1093; Zbruyeva, Istoriya naseleniya Prikamya . . . , Plate 17, item 2.

105. V. I. Kanivets, *Kaninskaya peshchera* (The Kaninskaya cave), Moscow, 1964; V. F. Gening, Uzlovye problemy izucheniya pyanoborskoy kultury (Basic problems in the study of the Pyanobor [Pyanyy Bor] culture), *Voprosy arkheologii Urala*, no. 4, Sverdlovsk, 1962.

106. Chernetsov, Bronza ust-poluyskogo vremeni, p. 135.

107. K. F. Smirnov, *Severskiy kurgan* (The Severskiy burial mound), Moscow, 1953.

108. S. I. Rudenko, *Kultura naseleniya Tsentralnogo Altaya v skifskoye vremya* (The culture of the population of the central Altay region in Scythian times), Moscow, 1960, pp. 124–25, fig. 75; idem, *Kultura naseleniya gornogo Altaya v skifskoye vremya* (The culture of the population of the High Altay in Scythian times), Moscow, 1953, p. 183, Plate 42.

109. A. N. Zyryanov, Kurgany i gorodishcha v Shadrinskom uyezde Permskoy oblasti i nakhodki v nikh (The burial mounds and fortified hill sites of Shadrinsk *uyezd* of Perm *oblast* and the finds in them), *ZUOLE*, vol. 7, no. 3, Yekaterinburg, 1881.

110. *MAR*, no. 37, Petrograd, 1918, p. 62; G. B. Zdanovich, Nakhodki iz kurgana na reke Kurtamysh (Finds in the burial mound on the Kurtamysh River), *Voprosy arkheologii Urala*, no. 6, Sverdlovsk, 1964, pp. 86–93, Plates

1–4; unpublished materials of V. P. Levasheva's excavations of 1927 are preserved in the Omsk Regional Museum (Kokonovka burial mounds).

111. A. Heikel, *Antiquités de la Sibérie occidentale*, Helsingfors, 1894, Plate 3, items 4, 5, 7–11.

112. B. J. N. Thordeman, The Asiatic splint armour in Europe, *Acta Archaeologica*, vol. 4, fasc. 1, Copenhagen, 1933, pp. 117–50; V. V. Antropova, Voprosy voyennoy organizatsii i voyennogo dela u narodov kraynego severovostoka Azii (Military organization and military affairs of the peoples of the far northeastern part of Asia), *Sibirskiy etnograficheskiy sbornik*, pt. 2, being *TIE*, novaya seria, vol. 35, 1957.

113. Bronze arrowheads from Ust-Poluy, as well as the casting mould for such arrowheads, are described in detail by Chernetsov, Bronza ust-poluyskogo vremeni, pp. 124–26.

114. Ibid., p. 148, for more details.

115. A. A. Spitsyn, Glyadenovskoye kostishche (The Glyadenovo ossuary), *ZRAO*, vol. 12, 1901, Plate 12; Chernetsov, Bronza ust-poluyskogo vremeni, p. 127.

116. I. M. Myagkov, Drevnosti Narymskogo kraya (Antiquities of Narym kray), *Trudy Tomskogo krayevogo muzeya*, vol. 2, 1929; Chernetsov, Bronza ust-poluyskogo vremeni, p. 127.

117. K. F. Smirnov, Vooruzheniye Savromatov (Armament of the Sarmatians), *MIA*, no. 101, 1961, p. 58.

118. Zbruyeva, Istoriya naseleniya Prikamya . . . , p. 238.

119. For a more detailed description, see Chernetsov, Bronza ust-poluyskogo vremeni, p. 124.

120. Ibid., pp. 122–24 for more details.

121. See Moshinskaya [Moszyńska], Materialnaya kultura i khozyaystvo Ust-Poluya, for a description and classification of Ust-Poluy ornaments.

122. Eding, Novye nakhodki na Gorbunovskom torfyanike; M. Gimbutas, *The prehistory of eastern Europe*, pt. 1, Cambridge, England, 1956, Plate 43; Nordman, *Die steinzeitlichen Tierskulpturen Finnlands*.

123. Eding, Novye nakhodki na Gorbunovskom torfyanike.

124. V. N. Chernetsov, Nizhneye Priobye v I tys. n.e. (The Lower Cis-Ob in the 1st millennium A.D.), *MIA*, no. 58, 1957, Plate 18, item 8.

125. J. G. Andersson, Hunting magic in the animal style, *Bulletin of the Museum of Far Eastern Antiquity*, vol. 4, Stockholm, 1932, p. 293.

126. Rudenko, *Kultura naseleniya gornogo Altaya* . . . , Plate 33.

127. C. K. Wilkinson, Art of the ancient Near East: The first millennium B.C., *Bulletin of the Metropolitan Museum of Art*, April, 1960, figs. 29, 31, 33; A. Godard, *L'art de L'Iran*, Paris, 1962, Plate 73.

128. Chernetsov, Bronza ust-poluyskogo vremeni, pp. 137–46.

129. Ibid.

130. Zbruyeva, Istoriya naseleniya Prikamya . . . , pp. 178–81; Chernetsov, Ust-poluyskoye vremya v Priobye, p. 150.

131. Rudenko, *Kultura naseleniya Tsentralnogo Altaya* . . . , pp. 124–25, fig. 75; idem, *Kultura naseleniya gornogo Altaya* . . . , p. 183, Plate 42.

132. Chernetsov, Ocherk etnogeneza obskikh yugrov; idem, Ust-Poluyskoye vremya v Priobye, p. 235 ff.

133. Ailio, Zwci Tierskulpturen, p. 277; U. Sirelius, Ueber die Art und Zeit der Zähmung des Renntiers, *Journal de la Société Finno-Ougriennes*, vol. 33, Helsinki, 1916–20, p. 17; Gjessing, Circumpolar stone age, pp. 61–62.

134. Moshinskaya [Moszyńska], Materialnaya kultura i khozyaystvo Ust-Poluya, Plate 6, item 1, and Plate 11, items 1, 11, 12.

135. H. Larsen, Archaeology in the Arctic, *American Antiquity*, vol. 27, no. 1, 1961, p. 13.

136. Larsen and Rainey, Ipiutak and the arctic whale hunting culture, pp. 255–59.

List of Place Names of Major Importance

AKSENOVA FINDS. First millennium A.D. Aksenova is a village in Tyumen *oblast* (formerly Tara *okrug*, Tobolsk *guberniya*) on the upper reaches of the Malenkiy Ik River, a left tributary to the Ishim. Map II (90); 57°00′ N, 70°00′ E.* Near the village, finds were made of silver and bronze bracelets, hollow figures of animals, and other objects. Stored in Tobolsk Museum; nos. 4580, 4581. [Ref.: W. Moszyńska, 1949.]

ALAFEYSKOYE (ISKER, KUCHUMOVO) FORTIFIED HILL SITE. Bronze Age, Potchevash culture, and the 15th century A.D. Alafeyskoye Mountain is 16 km southeast of Tobolsk in Tyumen *oblast* on the Sibirka River, a right tributary to the Irtysh. Map II (39); 58°00′ N, 68°00′ E. The site is situated on Alafeyskoye Mountain near the junction of the Sibirka and the Irtysh. It is enclosed with a triple rampart and trench. The ruins were repeatedly excavated, but so far not systematically. There have been many fortuitous finds. The bulk of the objects from Isker are in the Tobolsk Museum, as are the field notes of M. S. Znamenskiy, containing also maps of Isker, the former metropolis of Yermak, its surroundings, and also sketches of numerous finds uncovered at different times during the excavations. [Ref.: I. Ya. Slovtsov, 1887, no. 147; N. L. Skalozubov, 1902, p. 23; V. N. Radlov, 1894, p. 117; V. N. Pignatti, 1914; V. P. Levasheva, 1928, p. 91; idem, 1950, p. 341 ff.; A. Heikel, Otchet o sostoyanii kollektsiy Tobolskogo gubernskogo muzeya, 1894; idem, 1893, p. XXII; idem, 1894, pp. XXV–XXVI; *OAK* for 1913–15, pp. 230–46; *Tobolskaya Pravda* (newspaper), 1940.]

ANDREYEVSKOYE CEMETERY. Found on the north bank of Andreyevskoye Lake (see Andreyevskoye *kurgans*), 2 km from the Andreyevskiye native village (*yurty*), near the fishing huts. Map II (64); 57°00′ N, 65°30′ E. [Ref.: I. Ya. Slovtsov, 1887, no. 137.]

ANDREYEVSKOYE (ZHILYE) FORTIFIED HILL SITE. First millennium B.C. On the north shore of Andreyevskoye Lake (see Andreyevskoye burial mounds) at a distance of 0.5 km from Andryushin Gorodok (q.v.); is similar to

---

* The geographical coordinates here and throughout this list do not refer to an exact location, but to an area. For example, the coordinates 66°20′ N, 66°30′ E indicate an area bordered by 20′ from the south to the north (that is, between 60°20′ and 66°40′ N lat.) and 30′ from the west to the east (that is, between 66°30′ and 67°00′ E long.) in which the site is located.

Andryushin Gorodok, although probably slightly older. Map II (69); 57°00′ N, 65°30′ E. [Ref.: I. Ya. Slovtsov, 1884; V. N. Chernetsov, 1951.]

ANDREYEVSKOYE I, II, III, FORTIFIED HILL SITES. On the south and west shores of Andreyevskoye Lake (see Andreyevskoye *kurgans*). Described by I. Ya. Slovtsov. Map II (66 and 67). [Ref.: I. Ya. Slovtsov, 1887, nos. 123–25; idem, 1884.]

ANDREYEVSKOYE KURGANS (BURIAL MOUNDS). Near Tyumen, a city in Tyumen *oblast* near Andreyevskoye Lake on the right bank of the Tura River. Map II (63); 57°00′ N, 65°30′ E. On the road from Andreyevskiye *yurty* (native village), on the northern bank of Andreyevskoye Lake, toward Duvan Channel on the left of the road are located five small burial mounds. [Ref.: I. Ya. Slovtsov, 1887, nos. 129–33.]

ANDREYEVSKOYE OZERO (LAKE). Broad stretches of this lake carry the names Pervoye Pleso (lake), Vtoroye Pleso, Pesyanka, Batarlyga, and Zhulkino. They are separated by narrows (*pereyma*). The lake, located at 58°50′ N, 67°00′ E, is the source of the Alymka River, which is a left tributary to the Irtysh.

ANDREYEVSKOYE SITES. Neolithic and Bronze Ages. Around Andreyevskoye Lake (q.v.), a series of sites dating to different periods, beginning with the Early Neolithic and including different stages of the Bronze Age. Map II (65, 71, and 72); 57°00′ N, 65°30′ E. [Ref.: I. Ya. Slovtsov, 1884; P. A. Dmitriyev, 1938, pp. 93–110; idem, 1951, p. 13 ff.; idem, 1951, p. 71; K. V. Salnikov, 1951, p. 47; V. N. Chernetsov, 1953, pp. 25, 37.]

ANDRYUSHIN GORODOK FORTIFIED HILL SITE. Ca. 1000 B.C. Situated on the north shore of Andreyevskoye Lake (q.v.). The first preliminary survey work was done under the guidance of I. Ya. Slovtsov. In 1951 the West Siberian expedition of I.I.M.K. carried out excavations of the site. Map II (68); 57°00′ N, 65°30′ E. [Ref.: I. Ya. Slovtsov, 1887, no. 126; idem, 1884; V. N. Chernetsov, 1951.]

ARKHIYEREYSKAYA ZAIMKA BURIAL MOUNDS. Arkhiyereyskaya Zaimka is a site 10–12 km north of Tomsk in Tomsk *rayon* and *oblast* at the mouth of the Bolshoy Kirgizka River, a right tributary to the Tom, which in turn is a right tributary to the Ob. Map II (32); 56°20′ N, 84°30′ E. In 1886 S. K. Kuznetsov opened a group of burial mounds. The cemetery is dated by T'ang Chinese coins and the principal parts assigned to the 8th century A.D. Individual objects belong to a significantly earlier time. [Ref.: *OAK* for 1896, p. 94 ff.]

BARSOVA GORA (MOUNTAIN). Between eleven and twelve kilometers west of the town of Surgut, and 2 km from the new village of Belyy Yar (see Barsov Gorodok). Approximately 61°00′ N, 73°00′ E.

BARSOV GORODOK CEMETERY. From the 8th to the 12th centuries A.D. Situated in the same locality as the Barsov Gorodok fortified hill site (q.v.). Excavated by Martin in 1885. The collection is in the Stockholm Museum. For a detailed account see the works of T. J. Arne, 1935.

BARSOV GORODOK FORTIFIED HILL SITES. Near Surgut, a town in the Khanty-Mansi National *okrug*, Tyumen *oblast*, on the right bank of the Ob. Map II (26); 61°00′ N, 73°00′ E. A steep bank, "Barsov Hill," is situated on the bank of the Utonlaya Channel, 11–12 km west of the town of Surgut. An investigation by the Swedish archaeologist Martin in 1885 revealed that the ruins extended for a distance of 4.5 km. In 1895 N. Pavlov made a schematic plan of the ruins, which is now in the library of the Tobolsk Museum. For a description of the monuments see the works of T. J. Arne. [Ref.: I. Ya. Slovtsov, 1887, no. 185; T. J. Arne, 1935.]

BASARGUL. A village in Tyumen *oblast*. Map II (55); 57°00' N, 70°30' E.

BELOGORYE (UNA-PAY) FORTIFIED HILL SITE. Belogorye is a village in the Khanty-Mansi National *okrug*, Tyumen *oblast* (formerly Tobolsk *guberniya*). Una-Pay is on the Ob, across from Belogorye. Map II (23); 61°00' N, 68°30' E. In Tobolsk Museum are a series of finds (beads, buttons, arrows, metal figures of animals, human bones, and others) from the burial mound at Una-Pay (Catalogue of Acquisitions of Tobolsk Museum, no. 1505). N. L. Skalozubov points out the rich archaeological remains in the environs of Belogorye native village. [Ref.: N. L. Skalozubov, 1902, p. 27; W. Moszyńska, 1949.]

BEREZOV FORTIFIED HILL SITE. Berezov is a town in the Khanty-Mansi National *okrug*, Tyumen *oblast*, on the left bank of the Severnaya Sosva River. Map I (12); 63°40' N, 65°00' E. Two kilometers south of Berezov are remains of a fortified hill site. [Ref.: I. Ya. Slovtsov, 1887, no. 81.]

BEREZOV RAYON FINDS. First millennium B.C. In the Khanty-Mansi National *okrug*, Tyumen *oblast*, on the Ob and Severnaya Sosva Rivers (the exact locations are not known; generally 36°30' N, 64°30' E). Map I (14). [Ref.: A. V. Shmidt, 1935, p. 211; V. N. Chernetsov, 1941, p. 23; idem, 1947, p. 113.]

BEZYMYANNOYE I, FORTIFIED HILL SITE. Near Tara in Omsk *oblast*, on Bezymyannoyy stream, a right tributary to the Irtysh. Map II (43); 56°40' N, 74°00' E. On the left bank of the stream along the floodplain of its upper reaches, on a high cape, V. N. Chernetsov discovered a fortified hill site. It consisted of inner, middle, and outer cities surrounded by ramparts and trenches. Chernetsov made small exploratory excavations and assigned it to the beginning of the 2nd millennium A.D. [Ref.: V. N. Chernetsov, 1947, pp. 86–88.]

BEZMYANNOYE II, FORTIFIED HILL SITE. Close to Bezymyannoye I (q.v.), on the right side of the stream. It is not very large, the finds are not extensive, and its date is unclear. Map II (44). [Ref.: V. N. Chernetsov, 1947, p. 88.]

BEZYMYANNOYE III, FORTIFIED HILL SITE. On the right bank of the Bezymyannoyy, 0.5 km from Bezymyannoye II (q.v.). It is in the form of a rectangle with its northeastern corner cut off. A characteristic feature that presents itself is the square projecting rampart that is similar to that of Bezymyannoye I and allows for assignment of both sites to the same period. The site was surveyed in 1945 by V. N. Chernetsov. The excavation was not carried through. Map II (45). [Ref.: V. N. Chernetsov, 1947, pp. 88–89.]

BOGANDINSKOYE FORTIFIED HILL SITE. First millennium A.D. Bogandinskoye is a small village in Tyumen *oblast*, 30 km from Tyumen on the right bank of the Pyshma River, a right tributary to the Tura. Map II (70); 56°40' N, 65°30' E. [Ref.: I. Ya. Slovtsov, 1887, no. 241; V. N. Chernetsov, 1951.]

BOLSHAYA RECHKA VILLAGE, BURIAL MOUND, AND SETTLEMENT. Fominskaya culture.

BOLSHOY LOG (BIG RAVINE) FORTIFIED HILL SITE. Bronze Age. First millennium B.C. to first millennium A.D. Located 6 km from Omsk, on the right bank of the Om River, 10 km from its mouth. Map II (93); 55°00' N, 73°30' E. The site was investigated in 1949 by V. N. Chernetsov and W. Moszyńska. The excavations indicated that the site had been in existence over a long period of time. Its lower horizon appears to be Late Bronze Age; the upper, 12th–14th centuries A.D. [Ref.: V. N. Chernetsov and W. Moszyńska, 1951, pp. 78–88.]

BOROVOYE OZERO I. A site located at approximately 53°10′ N, 70°20′ E.

BUY FORTIFIED HILL SITE. On the Vyatka River in European Russia. Approximately at 58°20′ N, 50°50′ E, in Kirov *oblast*.

CAPE KHAEN-SALE. A pit house settlement on the Yamal River situated at 73°00′ N, on the shore of the Malygin Strait, 1.5 km east of the cape.

CAPE KOZLOV BURIAL MOUND AND CEMETERY. At Andreyevskoye Lake, on a raised bank at the foot of Cape Kozlov opposite Bolshoy Ostrov. Discovered in 1950.

CAPE MORZHOVOY (TIUTEY-SALE). At Tiutey River on the Yamal Peninsula in the Nenets National *okrug*. The river empties into the Kara Sea. The coordinates are 71°00′ N, 68°00′ E.

CAPE SHAYTAN FINDS. First millennium A.D. Twelve kilometers from Berezov in Khanty-Mansi National *okrug*, Tyumen *oblast*, on the left bank of the Severnaya Sosva River; 63°40′ N, 64°30′ E. According to V. N. Chernetsov this was a sacred place, and possibly a settlement or fortified hill site, about the 10th century A.D. [Ref.: V. N. Chernetsov, 1948.]

CAPE SKURATOV. At 72°58′ N, 69°25′ E, in Tyumen *oblast*.

CHES-TYY-YAG SITE. Neolithic. Saranpaul is a village in the Khanty-Mansi National *okrug*, Tyumen *oblast*, on the Lyapin (Sygva) River, a left tributary to the Severnaya Sosva. Map I (18); 64°00′ N, 60°30′ E. In 1935 V. N. Chernetsov investigated and partially excavated the site. [Ref.: V. N. Chernetsov, 1937, p. 254.]

CHUSOVAYA RIVER. A tributary to the Kama, which it joins near Perm; 58°05′ N, 56°20′ E.

EVI-VOZH FORTIFIED HILL SITE. Located on a small cape formed by the junction of a rivulet with the Ob River, a short distance downstream from Kushevat, on the right bank of the Ob; 65°05′ N, 65°28′ E.

GILEVKA KURGANS (BURIAL MOUNDS). Gilevka is a village in Tyumen *oblast* (formerly Tobolsk *guberniya*) on the right bank of the Tobol. Map II (56); 56°20′ N, 66° 00′ E. In the vicinity of the village, which is 15–20 km south of the city of Yalutorovsk, within an area of 22–23 km², I. Ya. Slovtsov investigated 23 *kurgans*, 7 on the right side of the road and 16 on the left. The *kurgans* are situated at some distance from each other and some are surrounded by trenches. [Ref.: I. Ya. Slovtsov, 1887, nos. 662–84.]

GOLAYA SOPKA FORTIFIED HILL SITE AND CEMETERY. Near the mouth of the Ishim River, 7–8 km down the Irtysh from the settlement of Ust-Ishim at the village of Novo-Nikolsk (q.v.), on a hillock.

GORBUNOVO PEAT BOG. Gorbunovo is a village near Nizhniy Tagil, Sverdlovsk *oblast*. The Tagil River is a right tributary to the Tura. Map II (78); 57° 40′ N, 59°30′ E. During excavation work in Gorbunovo peat bog, in 1908, an underwater log bridge was uncovered; it was constructed of timbers 9–13 cm in thickness. The length of the bridge had not been ascertained, but it was reported by the workers to exceed 42.5 m. The Gorbunovo peat bog formerly contained a small lake, which was drained at the start of the work.

The upper layer was made up entirely of peat. Under it was a layer of buried wood, and still lower peat again. Under the last layer the bridge was found. At one end of the bridge was a small house with a gabled roof. Inside it were found clay pots and stone tools. In 1926 systematic excavations were initiated, principally under the supervision of D. N. Eding. [Ref.: *IAK*, 1909, p. 86; D. N. Eding, 1929; idem, 1937*a*, pp. 133–46; idem, 1937*b*; idem, 1940*a*, 1940*b*, pp. 41–57; idem, 1941, pp. 130–31; S. V. Kiselev, 1942, p. 44; K. V. Salnikov, 1949, p. 22.]

GORBUNOVO SITES: "PERVAYA BEREGOVAYA" AND "U STRELKI." Not far from Gorbunovo underwater bridge (see Gorbunovo peat bog). Early sites, pertaining to different periods, beginning with the Late Neolithic and Early Bronze Ages. Map II (79); 57°40' N, 59°30' E. [Ref.: D. N. Eding, 1940, p. 8; S. V. Kiselev, 1942, p. 45; V. M. Raushenbakh, 1952, p. 56.]

GOROKHOVO (CHUDAKI) FORTIFIED HILL SITE. From the 3rd to the 1st centuries B.C. Gorokhovo is a village in Yurgamish *rayon*, Kurgan *oblast*, on the left bank of the Yurgamish River, a left tributary to the Tobol. Map II (58); 55°00' N, 64°30' E. The fortified hill site is located 2.5 km from the village. Known locally as Chudaki or Gorodok. [Ref.: A. A. Spitsyn, 1903; I. A. Kastanye, 1910, p. 26; V. V. Golmsten, 1938, p. 247; K. V. Salnikov, 1940, pp. 69–71; idem, 1947, pp. 221–38; idem, 1949, p. 71.]

GREMYACHIY RUCHEY FINDS. Neolithic site in north central Urals.

ISET LAKE, SITES, SETTLEMENTS, CEMETERIES, SACRIFICIAL PLACES, ET CETERA. Northwest of Sverdlovsk, Sverdlovsk *oblast*, near Iset Lake and the head-waters of the Iset River. Map II (89); between 56°40' and 57°00' N, 60°00' E. On the shores and the islands of Iset Lake are a large number of sites and other archaeological remains. Ye. M. Bers indicates in her work 15 sites, 1 fortified hill site, 2 settlements, 2 cemeteries (Koptyaki 1–20), 3 sacrificial places, inscriptions, and a series of fortuitous finds. [Ref.: Ye. M. Bers, 1951, nos. 101–28.]

ISHIMKA CACHE, SACRIFICIAL PLACE. Ishimka is a village in Achinsk *rayon*, Krasnoyarsk *kray*, on the left bank of the Chulym River. Map II (31); 56°00' N, 90°00' E. [Ref.: L. Yermolayev, 1914.]

ISTYAK CACHE. Second and first centuries B.C. Istyak is a native village of Tobolsk *okrug*, Tyumen *oblast* (formerly Tobolsk *guberniya*), on the right bank of the Vagay River, a left tributary to the Irtysh. Map II (40); 57°00' N, 69°00' E. [Ref.: V. N. Chernetsov, 1947, p. 114; N. A. Lytkin, 1890, p. 13; I. M. Myagkov, 1927, pp. 68–69; idem, 1929, p. 76; *OAK* for 1894, pp. 45, 169.]

IVDEL FINDS. Ivdel is a village in Sverdlovsk *oblast* (formerly Verkhotursk *ulus*, Perm *guberniya*) on the Ivdel River, a right tributary to the Lozva. Map II (60); 60°40' N, 60°00' E. In 1887, while on an expedition to the Urals, D. N. Anuchin, F. A. Uvarov, and others obtained different objects on the hill of Ivdel. "Three small idols 'Chud representations' were found at the summit of the hill. They were copper representations of men, and on either side of the head was a reindeer or something else." [Ref.: D. N. Anuchin, Dnevnik ekpeditsii 1887 goda na Ural (Diary of the 1887 expedition to the Urals), Archives of the Museum of Physical Anthropology in Moscow, 1887*a*.]

IVDEL I AND II, FORTIFIED HILL SITES. Upstream from Ivdel in Sverdlovsk *oblast* (formerly Verkhotursk *ulus*, Perm *guberniya*) on the Ivdel River, a right tributary to the Lozva. Map II (61 and 62); 60°40′ N, 60°00′ E. In the diary of D. N. Anuchin are the following notes: "Gondatti received information that 20–40 versts from Ivdel were two fortified hill sites. Apparently, one of them was examined. . . . The area of it was overrun by forest, surrounded by a rampart and ditch. No finds were made. Legend has it that the *Chud* once lived here, according to others—Yermak." [Ref.: D. N. Anuchin, Dnevnik ekpeditsii 1887 . . . , 1887*a*; idem, 1887*b*.]

KAMA RIVER. A major left-bank tributary to the middle Volga, joining the latter just south of Kazan.

KANINSKAYA CAVE. Near the source of the Tura. Named after Kanin Nos, a promontory on the upper Pechora, some 47 km north of the mouth of the Unya River.

KARGALY FINDS. Near the village of Kargaly in Tyumen *oblast* on the Ishim River. Map II (92); 57°00′ N, 70°30′ E. [Ref.: *OAK* for 1898, pp. 81, 189; *OAK* for 1907, pp. 121, 139.]

KARYM FORTIFIED HILL SITE. Karym is a village in the Khanty-Mansi National *okrug*, Tyumen *oblast*, on the right bank of the Karym-ya (Kharom-ya) River, a left tributary to the Yukonda, which is in turn a left tributary to the Konda. Map II (53); 60°00′ N, 66°30′ E. [Ref.: S. G. Boch, 1937, no. 29.]

KATRA-VOZH SETTLEMENT. Tyumen *oblast*, Yamal-Nenets National *okrug*. A settlement on the left bank of the Ob at the mouth of the Sob, 50 km from Salekhard; 66°20′ N, 66°05′ E.

KHAEBIDYA-PEADERA (SAMOYEDIC FOR "SACRED WOOD") SITE. In the Bol-shezemelskaya tundra near the coast of the Barents Sea.

KHALMER-SEDE FINDS. In the Taz delta; 67°28′ N, 78°40′ E.

KHARA-PATKA SITE. Bronze Age; 1st millennium B.C. Near Kushevat (q.v.); a many-layered site investigated in 1925 by D. N. Redrikov. Map I (8); 65°00′ N, 65°00′ E. [Ref.: V. N. Chernetsov, 1953, p. 65.]

KHAR-SOYM (KHORSEM-PAUL) CEMETERY. Eighteenth to nineteenth centuries A.D. On the right bank of Khar-Soym Channel, 1.5 km downstream from Salekhard. A Khanty cemetery. Map I (6); 66°20′ N, 66°30′ E. [Ref.: V. N. Chernetsov, 1946.]

KHAR-SOYM NOMADIC CAMP. Third to second centuries B.C. A thin cultural layer belonging to a temporary camp was discovered 1.5 km downstream from Salekhard (q.v.), on both banks of the Khar-Soym, which discharges into the Shaytanka River, a right tributary to the Poluy. Map I (5). [Ref.: V. N. Chernetsov, 1946; A. P. Smirnov, 1948, p. 113.]

KHULYUM-SUNT (KHULYUM-SUNT-PAUL) SITE. Neolithic. Khulyum-sunt is a village in Khanty-Mansi National *okrug*, Tyumen *oblast*, at the mouth of the Khulyum River, a right tributary to the Severnaya Sosva. Map I (20); 62°40′ N, 61°30′ E. [Ref.: V. N. Chernetsov, 1941, p. 19.]

KINTUSOVO CEMETERY. A cemetery situated next to Kintusovo fortified hill site (q.v.), which was investigated in 1911 by an expedition of the Tobolsk Museum. Map II (25); 60°00′ N, 71°00′ E. [Ref.: B. N. Gorodkov, 1913, pp. 1–100; L. R. Shults, 1913, pp. 8–11.]

KINTUSOVO (AR-JAX-VAS) FORTIFIED HILL SITE. Kintusovo is a settlement in Khanty-Mansi National *okrug*, Tyumen *oblast* (formerly Tobolsk *guberniya*), on the upper reaches of the Salym River, a left tributary to the Ob. Map II

(24); 60°00′ N, 71°00′ E. The fortified hill site is located on the east bank of Lake Kintusovo and attributed to the Ust-Poluy culture. It was investigated by Yanko, and again in 1911 by an expedition of the Tobolsk Museum. The finds are in the Tobolsk Museum. [Ref.: B. N. Gorodkov, 1913, pp. 1–100; L. R. Shults, 1913, pp. 8–11; W. Moszyńska, 1949.]

KOKONOVKA BURIAL MOUND. Kokonovka is a village in Omsk *oblast* on the right bank of the Irtysh River. Map II (51); 55°00′ N, 73°00′ E. In 1927 V. P. Levasheva excavated a burial mound near the village to verify the character of the interments dug up by amateurs. These excavations proved to be synchronous. [Ref.: V. P. Levasheva, 1928, p. 129; P. A. Dmitriyev, 1929, p. 187.]

KOZLOVA PEREYMA ("KOZLOV'S NARROWS"). Near Kozlova (town), west by southwest of Novosibirsk, at 54°55′ N, 81°55′ E.

KRASNOGORSKOYE (ZMEYEVO) FORTIFIED HILL SITE. Near the village Krasnogorskoye, in Tyumen *oblast* (formerly Tobolsk *guberniya*), on the right bank of the Iset River. Map II (84); 56°20′ N, 65°30′ E. Also see Lizunovo. [Ref.: I. Ya. Slovtsov, 1887, no. 241.]

KRASNOOZERKA KURGANS (BURIAL MOUNDS). Krasnoozerka is a village opposite the town of Tara in Omsk *oblast*. Krasnoye Ozero [Lake] is on the right bank of the Irtysh. Map II (42); 56°40′ N, 74°00′ E. [Ref.: V. N. Chernetsov, 1947, pp. 89–91.]

KUNOVAT GORODOK (TOWN). Kunovat is a village in the Yamal-Nenets National *okrug*, Tyumen *oblast* (formerly Kunovat *volost*, Berezov *ulus*, Tobolsk *guberniya*), at the mouth of the Kunovat River, a right tributary to the Ob. Map I (9); 64°40′ N, 65°30′ E. [Ref.: I. Ya. Slovtsov, 1887, no. 180.]

KUSHEVAT FORTIFIED HILL SITE. Kushevat is a small village in the Yamal-Nenets National *okrug*, Tyumen *oblast* (formerly Kunovat *volost*, Berezov *ulus*, Tobolsk *guberniya*), located on the right bank of the Ob River. Map I (22); 65°00′ N, 65°00′ E. Near the village is a fortified hill site situated on a many-layered site. [Ref.: V. N. Chernetsov, 1949, p. 70.]

KUZNETSOVAYA (MENSHIKOVAYA) BURIAL GROUND. Between the villages of Kuznetsovaya and Menshikovaya, Kurgan *oblast* (formerly Tobolsk *guberniya*), along the upper Suer River, a right tributary to the Tobol. Map II (57); 55°20′ N, 66°30′ E. [Ref.: I. Ya. Slovtsov, 1887, no. 349.]

LAKE KUNCHUR. Located between the Tura and the Iska rivers about 60 km from Tyumen (57°09′ N, 65°26′ E), at approximately 57°10′ N, 66° 30′ E.

LAKSEYA. Sacrificial caves on the right bank of the Ivdel River, 1 km from the mouth of the Lakseya; approximately 60°40′ N, 60′10′ E.

LENK-PONK. A small water-washed burial mound on the banks of the Ob, between the village of Skripunova and the Apriny *yurty* about 60 *versts* from the large village of Samarovo; approximately 61°05′ N, 68°30′ E.

LIPCHINSKOYE. Bronze Age site near the large village of the same name in Sverdlovsk *oblast* at the mouth of the Lipka River, a right tributary to the Tura. Map II (76); 57°20′ N, 64°30′ E. The site was discovered in 1924 by P. A. Rossomakhin. In 1925 it was excavated by P. A. Dmitriyev, who described the site, excavations, and finds. [Ref.: P. A. Dmitriyev, 1928, pp. 61–68; idem, 1929, pp. 198–99; idem, 1951, p. 13; *Obzor deyatelnosti sektsii arkheologii*, 1928, p. 93; K. V. Salnikov, 1951, p. 97.]

LIZUNOVO FORTIFIED HILL SITE. Located 100 *sazhens* (213 m) from the Zmeyevo fortified hill site near Krasnogorskoye (q.v.). It is surrounded by an oval embankment behind a trench 2 *arshines* (1.5 m) in depth. Map II (85). [Ref.: I. Ya. Slovtsov, 1887, no. 241.]

LOMBVOZH (TĀN WĀRUP-ĒKWA FORTIFIED HILL SITE). Lombvozh is a village in Khanty-Mansi National *okrug*, Tyumen *oblast*, on the Lyapin (Sygva) River, a left tributary to the Severnaya Sosva. Map I (17); 63°40′ N, 61°00′ E. Near the village of Lombvozh is the fortified hill site Tān wārup-ēkwa. It was surveyed in 1935 by V. N. Chernetsov. The excavated material consisted mostly of pottery. [Ref.: V. N. Chernetsov, 1937, p. 254.]

LOZVA CACHE. At 59°36′ N, 62°20′ E; in Sverdlovsk *oblast*.

LUGOVSKAYA KNOLL. Lugovskaya is a village in Narym *kray*, Tomsk *oblast* (formerly Parabelskaya *volost*, Tomsk *guberniya*), on the Ket River, a right tributary to the Ob. Map II (30); 58°40′ N, 81°30′ E. [Ref.: A. F. Plotnikov, 1901, p. 238.]

LYULI-KAR SITE. First millennium A.D. Verkhniye (Upper) Lyulikary is a settlement in Khanty-Mansi National *okrug*, Tyumen *oblast*, on the right bank of the Severnaya Sosva. Map I (15); 63°00′ N, 64°30′ E. [Ref.: V. N. Chernetsov, 1948; S. G. Boch, 1937, no. 11.]

MALAYA KHETA SETTLEMENT. At the mouth of the Malaya Kheta River, 90 km downstream from Dudinka; 69°34′ N, 84°32′ E.

MAN-YA RIVER. A short tributary to the Khulga River (at approximately 64°15′ N, 60°30′ E), which in turn enters the upper reaches of the Severnaya Sosva.

MEDVED-KAMEN. Located near Nizhniy Tagil in Sverdlovsk *oblast* on the Tagil River, a right tributary to the Tura. Map II (82); 57°40′ N, 59°30′ E. In 1946 extensive excavations were made in a small cave in the cliff of Medved-Kamen above the Tagil River, where in 1945 O. N. Bader discovered fragments of 4th millennium B.C. fauna. The cave is 12 km northwest of Nizhniy Tagil and 37 m above the river. Early fauna was deposited in a yellow, oozy, argillaceous clay atop the rock floor of the cave. An upper layer contained remains of hearths and poorly preserved iron objects. [Ref.: O. N. Bader, 1948, p. 79 ff.]

MOLCHANOVA FORTIFIED HILL SITE. First millennium A.D. Molchanova is a village in Tyumen *oblast* (formerly Tobolsk *guberniya*) on the left bank of the Tura. Map II (75); 57°00′ N, 65°00′ E. [Ref.: I. Ya. Slovtsov, 1887, no. 91.]

MURLINSK FINDS. First millennium B.C. In the vicinity of the Murlinsk native village (see Murlinsk northern burial mounds) an iron sword, Sarmatian in appearance, was found; also articles of cast bronze, and bronze arrows. The objects are in the Tara Regional Museum. Map II (49). [Ref.: W. Moszyńska, 1949.]

MURLINSK NORTHERN BURIAL MOUNDS. The Murlinsk native village, Omsk *oblast* (formerly Tara *okrug*, Tobolsk *guberniya*), on the Murlinsk River, a right tributary to the Irtysh. Map II (47); 56°40′ N, 74°30′ E. On the northern side of the Murlinsk native village, in the region of Aytkulov, is a group of 15 burial mounds investigated in 1867 by Ye. I. Malakhov, a Tara merchant, who mapped the burial mounds and sent the map to Moscow University. [Ref.: I. Ya. Slovtsov, 1887, nos. 893–907.]

MURLINSK SOUTHERN BURIAL MOUNDS. There are ten burial mounds located 1 km south of the Murlinsk native village (see Murlinsk northern burial mounds), excavated in 1867 by Ye. I. Malakhov. The objects were forwarded to Moscow University. Map II (48). [Ref.: I. Ya. Slovtsov, 1887, nos. 883–92.]

NARVA KURGAN. At 55°25′ N, 93°39′ E, in Drasnoyarsk *kray*.

NIZHNE-TURINSKIY SITE. Near Nizhne-Turinskiy *zavod* (factory). Located in Sverdlovsk *oblast* (formerly Verkhotursk *ulus*, Perm *guberniya*), on the upper Tura. Map II (83); 58°20′ N, 59°30′ E. [Ref.: O. N. Bader, 1948, p. 79.]

NIZHNEYE ADISHCHEVO CAMPSITE. At the mouth of the Chusovaya River, a tributary to the Kama; 58°10′ N, 56°50′ E.

NIZYAMY II, FORTIFIED HILL SITE. Tyumen *oblast*, Khanty-Mansi National *okrug*. On the right bank of the Ob, near Nizyamy native village, on a small cape at the mouth of the Nisan-Iogan River. Map I (11); 62°32′ N, 65°52′ E.

NOVO-NIKOLSK. A settlement on the Irtysh River, north of Ust-Ishim; 57°40′ N, 71°15′ E.

NYAKSIMVOL FORTIFIED HILL SITE. A village in Khanty-Mansi National *okrug*, Tyumen *oblast*, at the mouth of the Nyaysa, a right tributary to the Sosva, in its upper reaches. Map I (21); 62°20′ N, 60°30′ E. [Ref.: W. Moszyńska, 1949.]

OBYUL HAMLET. In the basin of the Chulym River in Krasnoyarsk *kray*; 55°34′ N, 88°45′ E.

OKUNEVO SITE (ULUS). Orautur is a small village in Khanty-Mansi National *okrug*, Tyumen *oblast*, on the left bank of the Okunevo River, a tributary to the Zatumannaya-Konda (i.e., the upper reaches of the Konda River); 60°40′ N, 63°30′ E. [Ref.: S. G. Boch, 1937, no. 19.]

OLENIY OSTROV (NORTHERN) BURIAL GROUND. At 67°06′ N, 32°24′ E, in Murmansk *oblast*.

OLONETS GUBERNIYA FINDS. Near Orontur II fortified hill site on the shore of Lake Orontur (Orautur), at 60°59′ N, 63°40′ E, a copper representation of a lion was found. A drawing of it is in S. G. Boch, 1937, p. 160, fig. 2.

PALKINO SITES, CEMETERIES, FORTIFIED HILL SITE, AND ISOLATED FINDS. Palkino is a village in Sverdlovsk *oblast* (formerly Verkh-Iset *volost*, Yekaterinburg *ulus*, Perm *guberniya*) at the mouth of the Reshet River, a right tributary to the Iset. Map II (88); 56°40′ N, 60°00′ E. Near the village were three sites, three cemeteries, a fortified hill site, cliff drawings, and other finds. Among the many accounts and literary contributions, see Ye. M. Bers, 1951, nos. 135, 140–47, and V. M. Raushenbakh, 1952, p. 56.

PEL-VOZH. In Tyumen *oblast*, Yamal-Nenets National *okrug*; 66°12′ N, 66°40′ E.

PEREYMINSKIY (PEREYMA) CEMETERY. On a terrace above the floodplain, opposite a second narrows about 2 km from the cemetery at Cape Kozlov. Approximately 57°00′ N, 65°30′ E.

PETKASH (PETKASPAUL). A Neolithic site. Petkash is a village in the Khanty-Mansi National *okrug*, Tyumen *oblast*, on the right bank of the Severnaya Sosva. Map I (16); 63°20′ N, 62°30′ E. [Ref.: W. Moszyńska, 1949.]

POINT VIII. A campsite less than 100 m from Andreyevskoye I (q.v.), where Neolithic pottery was found. Approximately 57°00′ N, 65°30′ E.

POLUDENKA I AND II. Neolithic and Bronze Age sites. Near Nizhniy Tagil, Sverdlovsk *oblast*. The Poludenka River is a left tributary of the Tura. Map II (80); 57°40′ N, 59°30′ E. Twelve kilometers west of Nizhniy Tagil on the right bank of the Poludenka River in 1944, O. N. Bader discovered and partially excavated a site. The excavations continued in 1945 and 1946. Not far from it, on the left bank of the river, a similar site was discovered in 1946. [Ref.: O. N. Bader, 1947, pp. 139–47; idem, 1948, p. 80; idem, 1949; A. P. Smirnov, 1948, p. 111; V. M. Raushenbakh, 1952, p. 56.]

POLUDENKA (CHUDSKIYE BUGRY) KURGANS (BURIAL MOUNDS). A few of the more recent burial mounds are located at the site Poludenka I (q.v.) at a place known as Chudskiye Bugry to the native population; Map II (81). First excavations were made in 1845, second in 1924. [Ref.: O. N. Bader, 1947, pp. 139–44.]

POTCHEVASH (CAPE CHUVASHSKIY) FORTIFIED HILL SITE. Potchevash culture. On the eastern outskirts of Tobolsk (58°12′ N, 68°15′ E), in the locality called Cape Chuvashskiy, or Potchevash, on the right bank of the Irtysh River. The site was investigated in detail by W. Moszyńska in 1951. [Ref.: I. Ya. Slovtsov, 1887, p. 194; M. S. Znamenskiy, 1891; idem, 1901; A. A. Spitsyn, 1893, p. 46; idem, 1906, p. 226; A. Heikel, Otchet o sostoyanii kollektsiy Tobolskogo gubernskogo muzeya, 1894, p. XXV; idem, 1894, pp. 1–49; I. M. Myagkov, 1927, p. 69; P. A. Dmitriyev, 1929, p. 188; V. N. Chernetsov, 1947, p. 114; W. Moszyńska, 1953, p. 189.]

PYASYADAY [PYASEDAY] RIVER FINDS. On the north shore of the Yamal Peninsula, between the Tiutey-Yaha and the Pyasyaday-Yaha rivers at approximately 71°30′ N, 68°00′ E.

RUDYANSKOYE (GLYADENY) FINDS. Rudyanskoye is a village in Sverdlovsk *oblast* (formerly Znamensk *volost*, Kamyshlovsk *ulus*, Perm *guberniya*), at the mouth of the Reft River, a left tributary to the Pyshma, which is in turn a right tributary to the Tura. Map II (73); 56°40′ N, 61°30′ E. [Ref.: Ye. M. Bers, 1951, no. 205.]

RUS-KHAR-SOYM. In Tyumen *oblast*, Khanty-Mansi National *okrug*, on the right bank of the Ob, upstream from the Nizyamskiye *yurts* at the mouth of the rivulet Rus-Khar-Soym; 60°33′ N, 65°42′ E.

SALEKHARD I, CEMETERY. Eighteenth and nineteenth centuries A.D. In 1946, V. N. Chernetsov investigated a Khanty cemetery on the right bank of the Poluy River in Salekhard (66°32′ N, 66°35′ E). The cemetery was partially disturbed. [Ref.: V. N. Chernetsov, 1946; A. P. Smirnov, 1948, p. 113.]

SALEKHARD II (YELOVYY CAPE), CEMETERY. Eighteenth and nineteenth centuries A.D. A Khanty cemetery on Yelovyy Mys (Cape) near Salekhard (q.v.), investigated in 1946 by V. N. Chernetsov. [Ref.: A. P. Smirnov, 1948, p. 113.]

SALEKHARD SITE. Bronze Age. V. N. Chernetsov and W. Moszyńska in 1946 discovered and investigated this Bronze Age site near Salekhard Landing; 66°32′ N, 66°35′ E (see Zelenaya Gorka). [Ref.: A. P. Smirnov, 1948, p. 113; W. Moszyńska, 1953, p. 188.]

SALEKHARD (SHAYTANKA) SITE. Near Salekhard on the left bank of the Shaytanka River, a right tributary to the Poluy. Map I (7); 66°20′ N, 66°30′ E. [Ref.: V. N. Chernetsov, 1946.]

SALEKHARD VILLAGE. Near Salekhard Landing; 66°32′ N, 66°35′ E. A settlement with pit dwellings belonging to the Ust-Poluy culture. [Ref.: W. Moszyńska, 1953, p. 180.]

SALTOVO CEMETERY. Saltovo is a village in Volgograd *oblast* at approximately 50°38′ N, 46°39′ E.

SAMAROVO FINDS AND FORTIFIED HILL SITE. Bronze Age; Ust-Poluy culture
and others. Near the city of Khanty-Mansiysk in the Kanty-Mansi National
okrug, Tyumen *oblast* (formerly Samarovo village, Tobolsk *guberniya*), at the
mouth of the Irtysh River. Map II (35); 60°40′ N, 69°00′ E. In the 1850s a
metal mirror with an Arabic inscription of the Abbasid caliphate was found
here (10th or 11th centuries A.D.). The exact location of the find is unknown.
It was obtained from the Khanty of Samarovo. A stone adze and earthenware of the Ust-Poluy type were subsequent, fortuitous finds in the vicinity
of Samarovo. In the Omsk Museum there is an iron spearhead from the
Samarovo fortified hill site. [Ref.: Savelev, 1852, pp. 122–64; *ZhMNP*,
1855, p. 269; V. P. Levasheva, 1950, pp. 341–50.]

SARANPAUL II (MAN-NYASLAN-TUR), FORTIFIED HILL SITE. Saranpaul is a village
in Khanty-Mansi National *okrug*, Tyumen *oblast*, on the Lyapin (Sygva)
River, a left tributary to the Severnaya Sosva. Map I (19); 69°00′ N, 60°30′ E.
[Ref.: V. N. Chernetsov, 1937, p. 254.]

SARGATSKOYE BURIAL MOUNDS. Sargatskoye is a village in Omsk *oblast* on the
left bank of the Irtysh River. Map II (50); 55°20′ N, 73°00′ E. [Ref.: V. P.
Levasheva, 1928*b*, p. 159; idem, 1948, pp. 86–88; P. A. Dmitriyev, 1929,
p. 188.]

SAUSKANSKIYE (KHANSKOYE) CEMETERY. Across the river from Sauskanskiye
yurty (native village) in Tobolsk *okrug*, Tyumen *oblast* (formerly Tobolsk
guberniya), on the right bank of the Irtysh River. Map II (38); 58°00′ N,
68°00′ E. [Ref.: I. Ya. Slovtsov, 1887, no. 148.]

SEREBRYANKA FINDS. Serebryanka is a village in Tyumen *oblast* (formerly
Kargalinsk *volost* of Tara *okrug* in Tobolsk *guberniya*), on the left bank of the
Ishim River. Map II (90); 57°00′ N, 70°30′ E. [Ref.: *OAK* for 1897, pp. 76,
186.]

SHADRINSK FORTIFIED HILL SITE. West of Shadrinsk (see Shadrinsk *kurgans*),
on the left bank of the Iset River; 56°00′ N, 63°30′ E. In an historical
exposition of I. Ya. Slovtsov, it was shown that in 1662 when Vichegod
emigrants were settling at Shadrinsk, the embankments and trenches were
still in evidence. In 1912 surveys of the site were made by Yu. P. Argentov-
skiy, a student at St. Petersburg University. [Ref.: *ZhMVnD*, 1855; *ZhMNP*,
1855, p. 91; *OAK* for 1912, pp. 98, 105; K. V. Salnikov, 1949, p. 68.]

SHADRINSK KURGANS (BURIAL MOUNDS). Shadrinsk is a city in Kurgan *oblast* on
the left bank of the Iset River. Map II (86); 56°00′ N, 63°30′ E. V. Ya.
Tolmachev notes three groups of burial mounds in the vicinity of the city.
[Ref.: A. A. Spitsyn, 1906, p. 221.]

SHAYTAN [DEVIL'S] CAVES. Near Ivdel, 60°40′N, 60°25′ E (see Ivdel finds). In
the diary of D. N. Anuchin, according to N. L. Gondatti, the following is
entered: "In the two so-called Shaytan caves at Ivdel are vestiges of sacrificial gifts; burnt bones of horses, cows and a few skulls of bears. The
majority were not large and there were no noticeable remnants of any
antiquities." [Ref.: D. N. Anuchin, 1887.]

SHCHUCHYA RIVER CAMPSITE. Neolithic. The site is on the middle Shchuchya, a
left tributary to the Ob that joins it about 80 km downstream from Salekhard
at approximately 67°20′ N, 68°30′ E. The site is located north of the polar
circle and was discovered in 1950 by G. A. Chernov.

SHIGIR PEAT BOG SITE, VILLAGE, FORTIFIED HILL SITE, INTERMENTS, AND

INDIVIDUAL FINDS. Between the cities of Nevyansk, Kirovograd, and Verkh-Neyvinskiy on the upper Neyva River (Tura basin). Map II (77); 57°20′ N, 60°00′ E. In a peat bog on the southern cape of Lake Shigir the first finds of a primitive culture were made in 1880. M. V. Malakhov made the investigations in the same year. Five culture-yielding layers were determined. In the vicinity of the peat bog the following were discovered: 4 sites, 2 villages, 1 fortified hill site, 1 interment, and 31 locations of individual objects. [Ref.: M. V. Malakhov, 1882, pp. 11–13; D. I. Lobanov, 1897; *OAK* for 1941, pp. 88, 106; *OAK* for 1906, pp. 133, 149; *IAK*, 1907, pp. 21–22; *OAK* for 1913–15, pp. 173–74; D. N. Eding, 1937, p. 135; K. V. Salnikov, 1949, pp. 22–23; Ye. M. Bers, 1951, nos. 4–44; V. M. Raushenbakh, 1952, p. 56.]

SOROVOY MYS (CAPE) SETTLEMENT. Ust-Poluy culture and others. Berezov is a city in the Khanty-Mansi National *okrug*, Tyumen *oblast*, on the left bank of the Severnaya Sosva River. Map I (13); 63°55′ N, 65°03′ E. [Ref.: S. G. Boch, 1937, no. 14; V. N. Chernetsov, 1948.]

SORTYNYA I, FORTIFIED HILL SITE. Located on the left, precipitous bank of the Severnaya Sosva River, approximately 1 km upstream from the village of Sortynya [Sartyn-ya]; 63°22′ N, 62°45′ E.

SORTYNYA II, FORTIFIED HILL SITE AND CAMPSITE. Discovered in 1931, investigated in detail in 1935. Situated on the left, precipitous bank of the Severnaya Sosva River, 2 km upstream from the village of Sortynya [Sartyn-ya]; 63°22′ N, 62°45′ E. The upper layers of the site belong to a fortified hill site of the Ust-Poluy period.

SORTYNYA III. Three kilometers upstream from the village of Sortynya [Sartyn-ya] (63°22′ N, 62°45′ E) on the left bank of the Severnaya Sosva River.

SURGUT FINDS. Surgut, a town in the Khanty-Mansi National *okrug*, Tyumen *oblast*, on the right bank of the Ob. Map II (28); 61°00′, 73°00′ E. [Ref.: W. Moszyńska, 1949.]

SUZGE-TURA. A hill on which are located Suzgun I and II (q.v.). Also a fortified hill site which chronologically followed Suzgun I; approximately 58°00′ N, 68°00′ E.

SUZGUN I (ALEMASOVSKAYA), FORTIFIED HILL SITE. Thirteenth to fourteenth centuries A.D. Alemasovskaya is a village in Tobolsk *okrug*, Tyumen *oblast*, on the right bank of the Irtysh. Map II (37); 58°00′ N, 68°00′ E. An Ostyak (Khanty) fortified hill site. [Ref.: I. Ya. Slovtsov, 1887, no. 170; V. N. Chernetsov, 1948.]

SUZGUN II (ALEMASOVSKAYA), SACRIFICIAL PLACE. See Suzgun I. In 1948 an expedition under the leadership of V. N. Chernetsov excavated the sacrificial place (Suzgun II), near the village of Alemasovskaya. [Ref.: V. N. Chernetsov, 1948.]

TĀN WĀRUP-ĒKWA. See Lombvozh.

TAZ RIVER. On the Yamal Peninsula. Flows into Tazovskaya Guba (Taz Gulf) at 67°15′ N, 80°45′ E.

TIUTEY-SALE PIT HOUSES. On the west coast of the Yamal Peninsula at the junction of the Ser-Yaha and the Tiutey-Yaha rivers near the point where the latter empties into the Kara Sea; approximately 71°30′ N, 67°30′ E.

TOKAREVA FINDS. Tokareva is a village in Sverdlovsk *oblast* (formerly Perm *guberniya*) on the right bank of the Sysert River, a right tributary to the Iset. Map II (87); 56°20′ N, 60°30′ E. [Ref.: Ye. M. Bers, 1951, no. 297.]

TOMSK CEMETERY. Neolithic; Bronze Age; 1st millennium B.C.–1st millennium A.D. In Tomsk *oblast*, on the right bank of the Tom River, a right tributary to the Ob. Map II (33); 56°20′ N, 84°30′ E. On the outskirts of Tomsk is a high cape with a deep ravine on its southern and northern slopes. A survey in 1887 by A. V. Adrianov revealed that the ravine contained human bones, bronze and stone objects, and sherds. Excavations on the cape disclosed a rich cemetery, which was investigated by A. V. Adrianov and S. K. Kuznetsov in 1887 and 1889. M. N. Komarova analyzed the materials as belonging to four different periods of the ancient history of the tribes on the Tom River: the Neolithic and the Bronze Ages, the Bolsherechenskaya culture (7th–6th centuries B.C.), and the 1st millennium A.D. [Ref.: *OAK* for 1882–88, pp. CLXXVII–CLXXVIII; *OAK* for 1889, pp. 83, 112; A. V. Adrianov, 1892, pp. 99–111; S. K. Kuznetsov, 1890, pp. 123; M. B. Shatilov, 1927, pp. 5, 26; G. V. Trukhin, 1947, pp. 188–89; S. V. Kiselev, 1949; M. N. Komarova, 1951, pp. 5–50.]

TOMSK (LAGERNOYE) FORTIFIED HILL SITE. Near Tomsk cemetery (q.v.), aligned with the southern cape, was a fortified hill site now almost completely washed away by the river. Only a double trench and a low fortification remain visible. Map II (34); 56°20′ N, 84°30′ E. [Ref.: *OAK* for 1889, p. 84; G. V. Trukhin, 1947, p. 188; V. N. Chernetsov, 1947, p. 73.]

TOROPKOVA (LENK-PONK) CEMETERY. Toropkova is a settlement in the Khanty-Mansi National *okrug*, Tyumen *oblast* (formerly Tobolsk *guberniya*), at the mouth of the Salym River, a left tributary to the Ob; 61°00′ N, 70°30′ E. [Ref.: S. K. Patkanov, 1891; L. R. Shults, 1913, p. 16.]

TUEKTA BURIAL MOUNDS. In Altayskiy *kray*; 50°50′ N, 85°53′ E.

TYUKOVA. A village 15 km from Tobolsk (58°12′ N, 68°16′ E) on the Rogalikha River.

TYUKOVA KURGAN (BURIAL MOUND). Tyukova is a village in Tobolsk *okrug*, Tyumen *oblast* (formerly Berkulsk *volost*, Tobolsk *guberniya*), on the Irtysh River. Map II (36); 58°20′ N, 68°00′ E. [Ref.: W. Moszyńska, 1949.]

TYUMEN KURGANS (BURIAL MOUNDS). Tyumen is in Tyumen *oblast*, on the right bank of the Tura River. Map II (74); 57°00′ N, 65°00′ E. At the distance of 1.5 km downstream from Tyumen, on the Tura River, are three burial mounds. I. I. Lepekhin mentions these as being "intentionally high." Now the mounds are almost levelled. They were partially excavated in 1892 by I. Ya. Slovtsov and in 1893 by A. Geykel. [Ref.: I. I. Lepekhin, 1821, Part IV, p. 3; I. Ya. Slovtsov, 1887, nos. 93–95; P. A. Dmitriyev, 1929, p. 187.]

UNA-PAY. See Belogorye.

UST-KURENGA FINDS. Neolithic. Ust-Kurenga is a large village in Omsk *oblast* (formerly Tara *okrug* of Tobolsk *guberniya*), in the upper course of the Shish River, a right tributary to the Irtysh. Map II (41); 57°20′ N, 75°30′ E. [Ref.: V. N. Chernetsov, 1948.]

US-TOLT FORTIFIED HILL SITE. Situated near the village of Karym (Kharom-Pavyl), 60°12′ N, 66°40′ E, on the middle reaches of the Yukonda River, a left bank tributary of the Konda.

UST-POLUY FORTIFIED HILL SITE. Situated on the high, right bank of the Poluy River, 3.5 km downstream from Salekhard (see Zelenaya Gorka). Map I (4);

66°20′ N, 66°30′ E. [Ref.: V. S. Adrianov, 1935 and 1936, p. 278; V. N. Chernetsov, 1941, p. 23; idem, 1946, p. 155; idem, 1947, p. 113; idem, 1947, p. 73; A. P. Smirnov, 1948, p. 113; S. V. Kiselev, 1942, p. 48; W. Moszyńska, 1953, p. 72; idem, 1953, p. 107.]

VAKH RIVER. A right tributary to the Ob; approximately 61°00′ N, 77°30′ E.

VARVARINKA (AKTSYBAR-KALA) FORTIFIED HILL SITE. Varvarinka *yurts*, Tyumen *oblast* (formerly Tobolsk *guberniya*), on the Varvarinka River, a right tributary to the Tobol. Map II (54); 57°20′ N, 67°00′ E. [Ref.: I. Ya. Slovtsov, 1887, no. 140; A. Heikel, 1894.]

VASYUGAN FINDS. In Narym *kray*, Tomsk *oblast* (formerly Vasyugan *volost*, Tomsk *guberniya*), on the Vasyugan River, a left tributary to the Ob. Map II (29); 59°00′ N, 79°00′ E. [Ref.: I. M. Myagkov, 1929, pp. 57, 64.]

VAYGACH ISLAND. At 70°00′ N, 59°30′ E, in Arkhangelsk *oblast*.

VORONTSOVO HAMLET. In Ust-Yenisey *rayon*, Taymyr *okrug*, at 71°44′ N, 83°33′ E.

VOYNOVA-GILEVA. A village near which a burial mound is located. Between Tyumen (57°09′ N, 65°26′ E) and Andreyevskoye Lake (58°54′ N, 66°54′ E).

VOZH-PAY (NIZYAMY I) FORTIFIED HILL SITE. The Nizyamskiye *yurts* are in the Khanty-Mansi National *okrug*, Tyumen *oblast*, on the right bank of the Ob. Map I (10); 62°20′ N, 65°30′ E. The site, investigated in 1948 by V. N. Chernetsov, is situated at the mouth of the Nisan-Iogan River, a right tributary to the Ob. [Ref.: V. N. Chernetsov, 1948.] (See Nizyamy II.)

VOZNESENSKOYE BURIAL MOUNDS. S. M. Chugunov surveyed a group of 30 burial mounds. They were situated between the villages of Voznesenskoye and Spasskoye (see Voznesenskoye fortified hill site). [Ref.: S. M. Chugunov, 1897, pp. 139–40; *Arkheologicheskiye pamyatniki Baraby*, 1934, no. 16.]

VOZNESENSKOYE FORTIFIED HILL SITE. Opposite the village of Voznesenskoye in Novosibirsk *oblast* (formerly Kainsk *okrug*, Tomsk *guberniya*), on the left bank of the Om. Map II (94); 55°20′ N, 76°00′ E. [Ref.: S. M. Chugunov, 1897, pp. 139–40; V. P. Levasheva, 1928, pp. 87–97; idem, 1950, pp. 341–50; F. V. Melekhin, 1928, p. 140; *Arkheologicheskiye pamyatniki Baraby*, 1934, no. 16; S. V. Kiselev, 1938, p. 242; V. N. Chernetsov, 1947, p. 79.]

YAMAL PENINSULA CAMPSITE. On the coast of the Kara Sea at 71°21′ N, 67°35′ E, 2 km to the southwest of the point of the cape, where the high and steep bank gives way to the gentle dunes. One of the northernmost Early Iron Age sites (see Tiutey-sale).

YAR-SALE. Nenets National *okrug*, Tyumen *oblast*, on the southwest shore of the Ob Gulf; 66°51′ N, 70°48′ E.

YA-VAY PENINSULA SITE. Approximately 72°30′ N, 75°15′ E, near entrance to Ob Gulf (Obskaya Guba).

YEKATERININSKOYE SITE. Neolithic. Yekaterininskoye is a village in Tara *rayon*, Omsk *oblast* (formerly Tara *okrug*, Tobolsk *guberniya*), at the mouth of the Abrosimovka River, a right tributary to the Irtysh. Map II (46); 56°40′ N, 74°30′ E. The first floodplain (in most places not preserved), stretches along the right bank of the Irtysh for a distance of nearly 250 m downstream from the mouth of the Abrosimovka River. At its distal end, under a thin soil layer there is a stratum, nearly 30 cm thick, of dark-colored sand mixed with charcoal, containing earthenware and a small quantity of animal bones and stone artifacts. V. N. Chernetsov investigated the site in 1945 and was of the opinion that it was Late Neolithic. A large part of the site was apparently washed away, and a study of the remaining area met with great difficulty because of buildings located along the bank. [Ref.: V. N. Chernetsov, 1947, pp. 82–84.]

YURGENSON (OMSK) FINDS. In the city of Omsk, on the grounds of the former Yurgenson factory, bronze objects including a bit, belt decorations (facings), and a sharp-butted axe were found. Map II (52); 54°40′ N, 73°00′ E. [Ref.: W. Moszyńska, 1949.]

ZELENAYA GORKA BURIAL MOUND (?). Map I (3); 66°20′ N, 66°30′ E. [Ref.: A. P. Smirnov, 1948, p. 113; V. N. Chernetsov, 1949, pp. 67–74.]

ZELENAYA GORKA SETTLEMENT. With the excavations of the site of Zelenaya Gorka (q.v.) a settlement with semisubterranean dwellings was uncovered. Map I (2). [Ref.: A. P. Smirnov, 1948, p. 113; V. N. Chernetsov, 1949, p. 70.]

ZELENAYA GORKA SITE. Near Salekhard, a city in Yamal-Nenets National *okrug*, Tyumen *oblast*, on the right bank of the Poluy River, a right tributary to the Ob. Map I (1); 66°20′ N, 66°30′ E. At Cape Zelenaya Gorka on the right bank of the Poluy River, 5 km downstream from Salekhard, during an archaeological reconnaissance of the Mangazeya expedition of 1946 under the guidance of V. N. Chernetsov, an intensively reddish-colored layer belonging to the Early Iron Age was uncovered. [Ref.: A. P. Smirnov, 1948, p. 113; V. N. Chernetsov, 1949, p. 70.]

ZOBACHEVKA FINDS. At 58°33′ N, 55°58′ E, in Perm *oblast*.

ZUYEVA FORTIFIED HILL SITE. Zuyeva is a village in Sverdlovsk *oblast* (formerly Tobolsk *guberniya*), on the left bank of the Tavda. Map II (59); 59°00′ N, 63°00′ E. [Ref.: I. Ya. Slovtsov, 1887; idem, 1892, p. 73; V. M. Florinskiy, 1894, p. 231.]

Index

Adrianov, V. S., 3, 77, 90, 100, 106, 261, 270, 284

Adzes: Ches-tyy-yag, 10, Pl. II; Khorsem-paul, 19, Pl. V; Khulyum-sunt, 16–17, Pl. V; Krasnogorskoye, 42, Pl. XIV; Nyaksimvol, 18, Pl. V; Petkash (Petkas-paul), 18; Samarovo, 41–42, Pl. XIII; Sortynya, 14, Pl. IV; Sortynya II, 44, Pl. XV; Trans-Ural and Ob regions compared, 7–8, Pl. I; Ust-Kurenga, 31, Pl. XI; various sites compared, 21–22

Agriculture, Ugrian, 241

Ailio, J., 299, 328 n. 14, 329 n. 30, 353 n. 133

Alekseyev, M., 347 n. 154

Andersson, J. G., 318

Andreyev, H., xx

Andreyevskaya I site: lamellar blades, 25–26; located, 22; pottery described and compared, 26–28, Pl. VIII; Slovtsov's excavation and finds described, 22–24, Pl. VII

Andreyevskaya II campsite: finds described, 37–39; located, 37; pottery ornamentation compared, 39–41; transitional between Neolithic and Metal Ages, 35

Andreyevskoye Lake sites: located, 22; Slovtsov's dating disputed, 22

Andronovo period, pottery compared, 38, 40, 46–47

Andryushin fortified hill site, related to Andreyevskaya I, 22

Armament, various sites, summarized, 311–13, Fig. 34

Arne, T. J., 2, 142, 193, 207, 212, 214, 218, 219, 231, 344 nn. 76, 87, 88, 89, 90, 345 nn. 99, 100, 124, 346 nn. 127, 147

Arrowheads: Andreyevskaya I, 23, Pl. VII; Ches-tyy-yag, 10, Pl. II; Kintu-sovo stage, 229, 233, 236; Lipchin-skaya, 36–37; Nyaksimvol, 18, Pls. II, LXXI; Petkas-paul, 18–19, Pl. V;

Sortynya II, 44, Pl. XV; Tiutey-sale, 68, 206; Ust-Poluy, 80–82, Pls. XX, LV; various sites, 291–92, 313

Art: Ust-Poluy, 108–10 *passim*, Pl. LXVIII; various sites, summarized, 314–19, Figs. 35–43, Pl. LXIX

Aspelin, J. R., 345 n. 97

Awls, Ust-Poluy, 92, Pl. XXVI

Back scratchers, Ust-Poluy, Pl. LXIII

Bader, O. N., 7, 20, 24, 39, 56, 59, 117, 167, 329 nn. 25, 38

Barrow, Stephen, 242

Barsov Gorodok site: excavated, 141; pottery described and compared, 207–208 *passim*

Beads, as grave goods, 177

Belyavskiy, F., 80, 85, 242, 281, 336 n. 18

Bers, E. M., xix, 217, 219, 333 n. 107

Birket-Smith, K., 89, 251, 253, 308, 338 n. 63, 351 nn. 65, 71, 83

Blades: antler, pointed, 292, 293; slate, Ches-tyy-yag, 10

Blades, lamellar: Andreyevskaya I, 23, 25–26, Pl. VII; Ust-Kurenga, 31–32

Boas, F., 251, 252

Boborykino culture, dated, xxiii

Boch, S. G., 3, 8, 19, 158, 159, 197, 286, 334 n. 123

Bogoraz, V. G., 251, 336 n. 13

Bogoslovskiy, P. S., 282

Bolshoy Log site, located, described, 119

Bones, animal: Khaen-sale, 235; Pere-minskiy cemetery, 177; Tiutey-sale, 68, 203; Ust-Poluy, 275

Bonework: Kintusovo stage, 227; Ust-Poluy, general, 124

Borovoye Ozero I site: pottery compared with other Uralian and western Siberian sites, 20; stonework compared, 24

Bortvin, N. I., 223–24

Index

Nyaksimvol campsite: contents described, 287–89, Pl. LXXI; located, 18

Oborin, V. A., 345 n. 114, 346 n. 136
Ob region, extent defined, 1
Okladnikov, A. P., 22, 49, 56, 236, 329 n. 35, 331 n. 94
Okunevo culture, Yenisey valley, xxi
Ornamentation, pottery: Ust-Poluy, general, 108–10, Pl. XXXIV; various Eneolithic and Bronze Age sites compared, 44–49, Pl. XV; Zelenaya Gurka, 68–69
Ornaments, various sites, summarized, 309–11
Orontur Lake sites, located and contents described, 197
Orontur stage, described, 197, 221

Palashenkov, A. F., 3, 4, 159, 201, 286, 287
Pallas, P. S., 87, 107–108, 335 n. 1
Papay, K., 134
Patkanov, S. I., 209
Patkanov, S. K., 4–5, 82, 90, 134, 135
Pavlov, N., 207
Pavlovskiy, V., 349 n. 36
Pel-Vozh site, contents described, 284
Pendants, bronze: Kintusovo stage, 225–26, Pl. LII; Orontur Lake and other localities, 198 ff., Pls. XLVIII, XLIX
Pestles, stone, Ust-Poluy, 99, Pl. XXVIII
Petkash (Petkas-Paul) site, described, 18
Physical types, Ust-Poluy, 129–30
Pignatti, V. N., 2, 49, 92, 148, 193, 238
Pit houses: Andreyevskaya II, 37–38; as indicators of social change, 70; Ches-tyy-yag, 9–10; Khaen-sale, 234–35; Salekhard, 106; Sortynya campsite, 14; Sortynya I hillsite, 66; Tiutey-sale, 202–203; Us-Tolt, 150; Ust-Poluy, 106; Zelenaya Gurka, 233
Plakhov, A. P., 4
Plaques, bronze: Cape Shaytan and other localities, 198 ff., Pl. XLV; Kintusovo stage, 226, Pl. LII
Platelets, armor: Ust-Poluy, 102, Pls. XX, LXVI; various sites, summarized, 311–13, Fig. 34
Podgorbunskiy, V. I., 94
Point VIII: lamellar blades, 26–27; located and described, 24–25; pottery described and compared, 26–27, 28, Pl. VIII; stonework compared, 24
Poleaxes, Ust-Poluy, 128
Poludenka I site: pottery compared, 20; pottery ornamentation compared, 39–41; stone implements compared, 21; trunnion adzes compared, 7

Poludenka II site, pottery ornamentation compared, 39
Popov, A. A., 241, 337 n. 49
Potchevash culture, compared with Ust-Poluy, 115–17, 136, 137
Pottery: Andreyevskaya I site, compared, 26–27, Pl. VIII; Andreyevskaya II, 38; Barsov Gorodok, 207–208; Cape Kozlov, 175–77; Ches-tyy-yag, 10–13, Pls. II, III; conservatism of form, 142; Ivanovskiy Convent, 65; Khulyumsunt, 20, Pl. VI; Kintusovo stage, 223–25, 227–28; Lipchinskaya, described and compared, 35–36, Pl. XII; ornamentation (pit) compared, 39–41; Orontur Lake, 197; Orontur type from other sites, 201–205 *passim*, Pls. XLVI, XLVII; Pereyminskiy cemetery, 181–82, 188–89, Fig. 15, Pl. XLIII; Petkash, 19, Pl. VI; Salekhard I, 42–43; Sarmatian, 73; site comparisons made, 20–21; Sortynya, 14–15, 19 ff., Pls. III, IV; Sortynya I hillsite, 66; Sortynya II, 44, Pl. XV; Tiutey-sale, 68; Us-Tolt, 151–58, Pls. XXXV–XXXVIII; Ust-Poluy, general, 124; various sites, summarized, 295–97, Fig. 30; Yekaterininskoye, compared, 28–31, Pls. IX, X; Zelenaya Gurka, 68–69
Prokofyev, G. N., 5, 60, 110, 132, 133
Prokoshev, N. A., 329 n. 27, 346 n. 138
Property marks, Ust-Poluy, 106–107, Pl. XXXIII

Radiocarbon dating, Neolithic sites, xx, 37
Rainey, F., 254, 255, 351 nn. 70, 81, 354 n. 136
Rassadovich, A. I., xix, xxiii
Raushenbakh, V. M., xix, 27, 39
Redrikov, D. N., 3, 42, 206, 284, 286
Reguli, A., 134
Religious concepts, Ust-Poluy, 130
Ritchie, W., 352 n. 92
Rogalev, F. S., 287
Rossomakhin, P. A., 4, 35, 37, 49
Rostovtsev, M. I., 339 n. 18
Rowley, G., 351 n. 63
Rudenko, S. I., 342 n. 14, 352 n. 108, 353 nn. 126, 131
Rus-Khar-Soym site, contents described, 289

Sacrifice: animal, Mansi, 220, Ob Ugrians, 282; dog, Ust-Poluy, 90; human, 282; type of locality, 281–82
Šafařik, J., 135